D1246841

AMERICAN-EAST EUROPEAN TRADE

Controversy, Progress, Prospects

By

Phillip D. Grub and Karel Holbik

Published by

THE NATIONAL PRESS, INC.
128 C STREET NORTHEAST
WASHINGTON, D. C. 20002

Library of Congress Catalog Card Number: 68-8698

Manufactured in the United States of America
by
McGregor & Werner, Inc.
Washington, D. C.

Preface

The potential markets for United States goods and services in Eastern Europe are sizable and United States firms have not kept pace with this spectacular growth. Western European countries are making rapid strides to gain inroads into these new and rapidly expanding markets. Unless positive action is taken soon, many of these newly opened channels will be lost insofar as American business is concerned.

Congressman Gerald R. Ford of Michigan, the House Minority Floor Leader has stated: "There is no more important policy issue before the Congress than the question of East-West trade. The consideration so far given to this matter leaves us unsatisfied. There has been no comprehensive study of the problems involved. There are too many unknowns."

Senator Warren G. Magnuson of Washington, Chairman of the Interstate and Foreign Commerce Committee stated in a speech before the San Francisco World Trade Association: "We in government have not fulfilled our obligation either to inform the American businessman of the desirability of increased trade with East European countries in non-strategic goods or to eliminate those impediments to East-West trade which remain as a vestige of outmoded and discarded foreign policy." He continued: "Government and business are trading partners in the drive to expand American exports. The interests of government and business are mutual–not conflicting. If government acts as a roadblock to foreign commerce, then it is failing in its primary obligation. And the governments of most trading nations have taken a leading and aggressive role in promoting the export trade of their citizens. Though your Government has begun to play its rightful role in export promotion, we have not yet matched the efforts of our competitors."

International trade is a mechanism through which channels of communication can be opened. Trade across national boundaries stimulates the exchange of ideas, technology and products. As such, this flow of goods and information can be an effective instrument of "bridge building," in diminishing the existing communication gap and promoting better understanding between East and West.

Some Americans see East West trade as a means to increase East-European affluence which would detract from the Soviet's revolutionary objectives. Others, however think that East-West trade is and can only be a one way bridge which would provide no economic gains for the United States. They also argue that not all goods and equipment (at least not the best) can be purchased by the East in Western countries other than the U. S. because the most up-to-date and sophisticated equipment is only available here.

United States foreign trade, while but a small percentage of total gross national product, has an importance far beyond what the figures might indicate. This importance is especially pronounced in the area of trade with Eastern Europe, for such trade becomes inexorably and directly tied with the overall pursuit of American national interest.

Where once this trade was insignificant and tightly restricted, the political thaw in East-West relations generally, the growing liberalism and polycentrism in Soviet bloc relations, and the recent attempts at modernizing and rationalizing their economies–all have pushed the issue of East-West trade to the forefront.

Why is this true? A major problem exists in trying to reconcile foreign trade with foreign policy–the two often do not mesh. Further, a negative attitude has placed a stigma on East-West trade, influencing American corporations not to seek expansion of their operations in Eastern Europe.

The realities of world industrial production have changed significantly since the United States instituted the present export controls which have been a basis for United States-East European trade policy. Fifteen years ago the United States was the sole world's supplier of most industrial and advanced technological equipment; today numerous countries compete effectively with the United States in the world market for capital goods. Our allies, including England, West Germany, France and Japan, all have trade policies that encourage market penetration in East Europe in what we consider to be strategic goods.

Only by covering the entire broad spectrum of approaches to East-West trade can a composite picture be constructed which will be helpful to businessmen, students, and scholars alike. Such a composite view of a complex and timely issue is offered in this book, which contains a compilation of views, opinions, and analyses of this growing issue by experts throughout the field.

There are two categories of approaches to East-West trade represented in the selected articles. The first category can best be termed the political considerations of East-West trade. The existence of the Soviet bloc as a military threat to the United States does not preclude economic intercourse, but it does mean that such relations with a powerful group of nations of different social and world views must be based on sound political considerations.

By opening channels of trade and communication, one encourages liberalization of restrictions and differences of opinion. Economic inroads may be used as a lever to obtain political gains. Because there is a growing acceptance of the compatibility of East-West trade with United States national interests, there is also a growing need to understand the basic economic realities of doing business with the communist countries. It is a discussion of these economic realities that comprises the second category of articles.

These approaches are by no means mutually exclusive; indeed, in few areas is there as much complement as in East-West trade. The result is a broad and comprehensive total view of the field, which is essential to an understanding of any of its many dynamic aspects.

The editors wish to express their appreciation to the persons who contributed papers for the book as well as to the publishers who gave permission to publish significant articles from their publications. A special word of thanks is extended to our research assistants Norman A. Brown, Jonathan Parker, and Stephen Ricciardi as well as our typists, Sue Fagin, Deborah Johnston, and Joyce Troutman.

Table of Contents

Page

Chapter 1
AMERICAN-EAST EUROPEAN TRADE IN TRANSITION: OFFICIAL POLICY AND VIEWS

Chapter 2
EAST-WEST TRADE IN CONTEMPORARY POLITICAL ENVIRONMENT

Chapter 3
EAST-WEST TRADE IN WESTERN EXPERIENCE

Chapter 4
EAST-WEST TRADE AND AMERICAN BUSINESS

Chapter 5
THE FUTURE OF EAST-WEST TRADE

Chapter 1

AMERICAN-EAST EUROPEAN TRADE IN TRANSITION: OFFICIAL POLICY AND VIEWS

East-West Trade Relations Act of 1966

Secretary of State Dean Rusk's 1966 letter of transmittal to the U. S. Congress, in which authority was sought for the President to negotiate commercial agreements and to increase U. S. trade in peaceful goods with the Soviet Union and other East European nations, follows in its entirety. This bill was introduced in both Houses of Congress (H.R. 151212 and S. 3363), but has not become a law.

May 11, 1966

Dear Mr. Speaker: At the direction of the President, I am sending to the Congress proposed legislation to provide the President with the authority necessary to negotiate commercial agreements with the Soviet Union and other nations of Eastern Europe to widen our trade in peaceful goods, when such agreements will serve the interests of the United States.

This authority is needed so that we may grasp opportunities that are opening up to us in our relations with the Soviet Union and the countries of Eastern Europe. It is needed, at a time when we are opposing Communist aggression in Viet-Nam, in order to carry forward the balanced strategy for peace which, under four Presidents, our country has been pursuing toward the Communist nations. It is needed to play our part with the NATO nations in reducing tensions and establishing normal and lasting peaceful relations between the West and East in Europe.

New Opportunities

It is the normal and traditional practice of the United States to encourage peaceful trade with other countries—even those with which we have serious differences. Yet for nearly two decades, we have put major restrictions on our trade with the Soviet Union and Eastern Europe. We applied these restrictions only when the Soviet Union extended control over its Eastern European neighbors and embarked on a course of aggressive expansionism. They properly signified our moral protest against the subjugation of half a continent and gave our protest practical economic effect. Now, however, the hopes that guided our policy have begun to be realized.

In recent years, there have been substantial changes among the Communist nations, within themselves, and in their relations to the nations of Western Europe. Windows in Eastern Europe are being gradually opened to the winds of change. Most of the countries of Eastern Europe have shown signs of increasing independence in guiding their own economic and political courses. They have shown greater concern for the needs of their citizens as consumers. A growing trade in peaceful goods has sprung up between Eastern Europe and the Western world. The Soviet Union itself has recognized this need for more responsive action in its own country as well as in Eastern Europe.

This process of change is continuing. It presents growing opportunities for the United States and for the cause of freedom. But we are not now able to take full advantage of these opportunities. Our trade policies which once served our national interest no longer do so adequately.

What then is needed?

The weakness of our position is the outdated, inflexible requirement of law that we impose discriminatory tariffs on the import of goods from Communist countries. All imports from the Soviet Union and Eastern Europe, excepting Poland and Yugloslavia, are subject to the original rates of duty in the United

States Tariff Act of 1930. The President has no authority to negotiate with any of these countries for the advantages that we can gain from offering them the more favorable rates that have been negotiated under reciprocal trade agreements over the last thirty years and that now apply to imports from all other nations with whom we trade. We alone of all the major Free World countries have so tied our hands.

The inability of the President to negotiate on this matter sharply reduces his power to use the great economic power of our trade as a bargaining instrument.

In the light of this situation, the President said in his 1965 State of the Union Message:

> In Eastern Europe restless nations are slowly beginning to assert their identity. Your government, assisted by leaders in labor and business, is exploring ways to increase peaceful trade with these countries and with the Soviet Union. I will report our conclusions to the Congress.

Accordingly, to supplement the studies being made in Government, on February 16, 1965, the President appointed a Special Committee on U.S. Trade Relations with Eastern European Countries and the Soviet Union under the Chairmanship of Mr. J. Irwin Miller. Each member was a widely respected and experienced leader from business, labor or the academic world.

The Special Committee made its report to the President on April 29, 1965. That report provides a searching and balanced analysis of this complex and important subject. It deserves careful study by all citizens and members of the Congress interested in this subject and in this proposed legislation.

The Special Committee concluded that to accomplish our purposes in Eastern Europe we must be able to use our trade policies flexibly and purposefully. The Committee recommended, specifically, that the President should be given discretionary authority to negotiate commercial agreements with individual Communist countries when he determines any such agreement to be in the national interest and to grant them in such agreements the tariff treatment we apply to all our other trading partners.

The Administration agrees with this recommendation of the Special Committee and this is the principal authority asked in the proposed legislation.

Benefits of the Legislation

We must consider the potential benefits and liabilities that may flow from enacting or failing to enact the proposed legislation.

There is abundant evidence that without the authority this legislation would provide, we are losing and will continue to lose significant opportunities to influence the course of events in Eastern Europe. By denying ourselves the ability to enter into meaningful commercial agreements with these nations, we deprive ourselves of the economic benefits that will come to us from increasing trade. More important, we deprive ourselves of a bargaining tool of considerable strength and utility. We unnecessarily limit our influence in Eastern Europe relative to the influence of other nations engaged in or opening wider trade there.

The enactment of the proposed legislation would not weaken or injure the position of the United States in any way. The legislation does not in itself make any grant or concession of any kind to the Soviet Union or any Eastern European country. It would not weaken our legislation, our policy or our controls on exports of strategic goods to Communist countries. Its sole effect would be to give the President added strength to negotiate with these Communist countries to obtain concessions and benefits that will serve the national interest of our country in return for granting the same tariff arrangements already available to other countries.

The benefits of the legislation could be numerous and valuable.

First, improving our trade relations with these countries would be profitable in itself. As their national economies turn more and more toward consumer needs and desires, they will become more attractive markets for our exports. We lead the world in the efficient production of goods which enrich the quality of everyday life. We can expect that new and increasing export opportunities will open up for American industry, American agriculture and American labor. While this trade potential may be modest for the foreseeable future in relation to total United States exports, it could, nevertheless, be significant over the years and of particular importance to American agriculture and to certain American industries.

Although any agreement with any individual nation will necessarily and properly open the way for increased sales of that nation's products to Americans who want to buy them, we have no reason to fear such trade. American industry is the most competitive in the world and thrives on the stimulus of competition.

Second, authority to relax tariff restrictions will give the President the ability to negotiate more effectively for any of several objectives important to the United States. These might include, for example, provisions for the settlement of commercial disputes, the facilitation of travel by United States citizens, the protection of United States copyrights, patents and other industrial property rights, assurances to prevent trade practices injurious to United States labor and industry, settlement of financial claims and lend-lease obligations, more satisfactory arrangements in cultural and information programs—and others of our economic, political and cultural objectives. These possibilities are of course only illustrative and it is improbable that all of them could be dealt with in a single agreement. We will need to test each negotiation for the gains to be made in it.

The Congress may be confident that no agreement will be made under this authority except in return for benefits of equal importance to the United States. Moreover, each agreement will include a provision for suspension or termination upon reasonable notice, so that the President may—and the Congress may be certain he would—suspend or end the obligations of the United States if he determined the other party were not carrying out its commitments.

Third, the most important benefits from any such agreements would develop more slowly. We cannot expect trade alone to change the basic nature of the Communist system in any Eastern European country nor to settle fundamental differences between us. We can, however, expect that the many close relationships normally growing out of trade will provide opportunities for influencing the development of their societies toward more internal freedom and peaceful relations with the free world.

A healthy growth of trade will help to reduce the present dependence of these Eastern European countries on each other and the Soviet Union. They will be encouraged to rebuild the friendly ties they have historically had with the West. Independent action will become more attractive and more feasible. The conclusion of an agreement with any of these countries will be an inducement to others to seek the same benefits.

The very nature of trade, the necessity to follow established rules of behavior, the increased contact with the West, the increasing use of Western goods, the growing appreciation of their quality and of the efficient methods of their manufacture, the growing understanding of the skills, opportunities and earnings of free labor in the United States and other Western nations, the greater exposure to the miracles of American agriculture—all these things could encourage increasing liberalization of the internal economies of the Eastern European nations.

The Soviet Union and other nations of Eastern Europe are increasingly conscious of their stake in stability and in improving peaceful relations with the outside world. Progress toward normal trade relations will increase that stake.

Under the terms of the proposed legislation, each agreement would be only one step in the process of reducing tensions. Agreements would not be of indefinite duration but would be subject to periodic review and to renewal at regular intervals. Each review could become a new opportunity for a useful dialogue with a Communist country. Each renewal could be adapted to encourage the further peaceful evolution of that individual country and the improvement of our relations with it.

There is wide and growing understanding throughout the country that improved conditions for peaceful trade with the Soviet Union and the countries of Eastern Europe would be in the national interest and should be a proper subject of negotiation with those countries. Many business, industrial and agricultural leaders and other expert witnesses who testified in the extensive hearings held on this subject by the Senate Foreign Relations Committee and the House Foreign Affairs Committee concluded that the United States could benefit from the possibility of wider peaceful trade with the Eastern European countries under proper safeguards. So too have a number of leading private organizations that have studied the problem.

To fulfill his Constitutional responsibilities for the conduct of our foreign policy in this complex era, the President must have available to him every appropriate bargaining tool. Nowhere is this need more critical than in our relations with the Communist countries. Granting this flexible authority to the President would not be a concession to the Communist world. Rather, it would give him a valuable instrument of foreign policy to be used where and when it will advance the interests of the United States.

Conducting a Balanced Strategy

In addition to the gains already stated which the proposed legislation can help to realize, it can be an important element in our balanced strategy for peace.

We are reaffirming in Viet-Nam—as we have on many earlier battlefields—our determination to aid free and independent nations to defend themselves from destruction by Communist aggression or subversion. But determined resistance to such force is only a part of our strategy to maintain a peaceful world.

It has equally been our purpose to demonstrate to the Communist countries that their best interests lie in seeking the well-being of their peoples through peaceful relations with the nations of the free world. We want the Soviet Union and the nations of Eastern Europe to understand that we will go step by step with them as far as they are willing to go in exploring every path toward enduring peace. We require only that our willingness and our actions be genuinely matched by theirs.

We are confident that this policy is sound even when we are fighting against Communist weapons in Viet-Nam. Indeed, it is when we are resisting force with force that it is most important to hold open every possible avenue to peace. We need to make unmistakably clear to all the Communist nations of Eastern Europe that their best interests lie in economic development and peaceful trade, not in support of futile attempts to gain advantage through the use of force.

The Legislation

The proposed legislation contains five principal provisions.

The first states the purpose of the Act, particularly to use peaceful trade and related contacts with Communist countries to advance the long-range interests of the United States.

The second authorizes the President to enter into a commercial agreement with a Communist country when he determines it will promote the purposes of the Act, will be in the national interest and will result in benefits to the United States equivalent to those provided by the agreement to the other party.

The third states some of the benefits we may hope to gain in such agreements.

The fourth limits each agreement to an initial period of three years, renewable for three-year periods. It requires that each agreement provide for regular consultations on its operations and on relevant aspects of United States relations with the other country. It also requires that each agreement be subject to suspension or termination at any time on reasonable notice.

The fifth is the central provision recommended by the responsible groups studying this matter: the President would have authority to proclaim most-favored-nation treatment for the goods of Communist nations with which a commercial agreement is made under the Act. Such MFN treatment would continue only so long as the agreement is in effect.

The President would have the authority to suspend or terminate any proclamation made pursuant to this Act. The President should do so whenever he determines that the other party to the agreement is no longer fulfilling its obligations under the agreement, or that suspension or termination is in the national interest.

As part of his negotiating power with respect to a commercial agreement with the Soviet Union, the President would have authority to terminate the existing provisions of law excluding certain furs of Soviet origin.

The authority of the Act would not extend to Communist China, North Korea, North Viet-Nam, Cuba or the Soviet Zone of Germany.

The bill expressly provides that it does not modify or amend the Export Control Act or the Battle Act which together control the export of military articles and strategic goods and technology which would adversely affect the national security and welfare of the United States.

The bill does not change in any way existing laws and regulations prohibiting aid and limiting credit to Communist countries.

All agreements will be promptly transmitted to both Houses of Congress.

Conclusion

In 1958 President Eisenhower made it clear that "the United States favors the expansion of peaceful trade with the Soviet Union" and spoke of the importance of trade as a means of strengthening the possibilities for independent actions by the countries of Eastern Europe.

President Kennedy in his first State of the Union Message declared his determination that "we must never forget our hopes for the ultimate freedom and welfare of the people of Eastern Europe."

In December, 1964, President Johnson expressed our wish "to build new bridges to Eastern Europe—bridges of ideas, education, culture, trade, technical cooperation and mutual understanding for world peace and prosperity." In May of this year, the President again referred to the way in which "the intimate engagement of peaceful trade, over a period of time, can influence Eastern European societies to develop along paths that are favorable to world peace."

The authority asked in this legislation will help attain these goals.

In Greece, Berlin, Korea, Cuba, and now, Viet-Nam we have tried to convince the Communist countries that the road of aggression and subversion has a dead end. This legislation will help us provide that positive counterpart to that lesson. It will give the President a vital instrument of negotiation to maintain essential balance in our relations with the Soviet Union and with the Communist countries of Eastern Europe and to respond to their growing desire and opportunity for wider contacts with the West. It will thereby serve our own interests and the cause of peace and stability.

Sincerely yours,

Dean Rusk

Recent Congressional Developments in Trading With Eastern Europe

Edwin J. Feulner, Jr.

Congressional action and reaction since 1966 is explored in the following article by the associate editor of Intercollegiate Review. *Significant pieces of legislation to come before the Congress on East-West trade are discussed, along with interesting insights into Congressional opinion on these measures.*

The concept familiarly known as "building bridges to the East" moved from the realm of rhetoric to the arena of practical politics with the publication of the "Report to the President of the Special Committee on U. S. Trade Relations with East European Countries and the Soviet Union" on April 29, 1965. This report of the Presidential Committee, frequently referred to as the Miller Committee for its chairman, J. Irwin Miller, Chairman of the Board of the Cummins Engine Company, was hailed within the Administration as providing a set of policy guidelines for what was termed the "safe" expansion of American trade with the Communist nations.

The Committee has been assigned a specific task, within a precise framework: "to explore all aspects of expanding peaceful trade in support of the President's policy of widening constructive relations with the countries of Eastern Europe and the Soviet Union."[1]

Working within this frame of reference, the Committee heard from various witnesses, examined a number of briefing papers, and issued a final report which was interpreted as support for the Administration's position on trading with the Communists.

The Miller Committee report included a number of *caveats* which greatly circumscribed its call for expanded trade. The main concession recommended was the granting of most-favored-nation status (MFN) on a selected, individual basis to the countries of Eastern Europe. Such a concession would enable the country so favored to export more of its goods to the United States under lower tariff rates. As a result it would be possible for the particular Eastern European country to sell more of its goods in the United States thereby earning dollars which could be used for the purchase of American goods. Most-favored-nation status had already been granted to Yugloslavia and Poland, and the results of their prior concessions, in the eyes of the Administration, justified the belief that the selective granting of MFN to the other Eastern European countries would provide us with "useful opportunities to influence attitudes in these countries in directions favorable to our national interest."[2]

The Miller Committee recommended that trade in stretegic goods which could "significantly enhance Communist military capabilities"[3] should not be decontrolled. The determination of what precisely is "strategic" would henceforth be determined by the Department of Defense, rather than the present committee, headed by the Department of Commerce.

No "across the board" concessions should be granted and we should demand commercial concessions from the countries of Eastern Europe before easing up on our trade restrictions. These concessions might, for example, take the form of patent protection, anti-dumping agreements entered into by the Communists, and understandings on a wide range of other issues in non-economic categories such as cultural and informational questions.

Credits would be limited to a five year maximum, a limit which is generally agreed to by all of the Western nations which adhere to the Berne Agreement. Another conclusion which the Committee reached was that trade with the Communists should not be subsidized nor should it receive artificial encouragement.

Furthermore, while the Committee recommended giving the President the discretionary power to grant MFN status to the countries of Eastern Europe, the Committee also recommended that this, and other commercial "tools," be used as a two-edged sword, which means that the possibility for revoking most-favored-nation status for various political reasons must be preserved as a real option.

Thus, the Miller Committee report provided the Administration with a framework which it could use as a basis for its previously announced policy of "building bridges."

---

*An earlier version of this article appeared as the introductory chapter of *Trading With The Communists*, by Samuel F. Clabaugh and Edwin J. Feulner, Jr. Permission to include material from *Trading With The Communists* is gratefully acknowledged.

[1] "Report to the President of the Special Committee on U. S. Trade Relations with East European Countries and the Soviet Union," U. S. Department of State (Washington, D. C.: Government Printing Office, 1965), p. 1.

[2] *Ibid.*, p. 32.

[3] *Ibid.*, p. 18.

Shortly thereafter the Committee for Economic Development, a private organization of leading U. S. businessmen, issued a report. It was released in conjunction with French, German, Italian and Japanese groups, and covered trading with the Communists. The basic policy recommendations of the CED report were similar to those of the Miller Committee. The Miller and CED recommendations, however, were limited to Eastern Europe and the Soviet Union, while the foreign associates of the CED recommended that Communist China be included in the easing of these restrictions. The U. S. Committee for Economic Development did not concur in the China recommendation of the other groups.

A novel feature of the CED report was the recommendation that a new Committee on East-West Trade be formed as a part of the Organization of Economic Cooperation and Development. This committee would coordinate policy and practices among the Western countries in a consultative and advisory role.

Using these governmental and private reports as a foundation, the Administration decided to push its program of bridge-building to the Communist countries of Eastern Europe. On May 17, 1966, Senator Warren Magnuson (D-Wash.), Chairman of the Senate Commerce Committee, introduced for himself and for Senator Jacob Javits (R-N.Y.) and Senator Mike Mansfield (D.-Mont.), the Majority Leader, the "East-West Trade Relations Act of 1966" (S. 3363). This bill was referred to the Senate Finance Committee. A companion bill (H.R. 151212) was introduced by former Congressman Eugene Keogh (D-N.Y.) and was referred to the Committee on Ways and Means of the House of Representatives.

The main thrust of the Magnuson legislative proposal was to give the President the discretionary authority which the Miller Committee report recommended he should have. The letter of transmittal to the President of the Senate and to the Speaker of the House came from the Secretary of State. In it, Mr. Rusk called for the early enactment of the Administration's bill.

Congressional reaction to the legislation was not very positive. With a Congressional election in the offing, and with public opinion opposed to trade with Communists while we are fighting Communists in Vietnam, there was no immediate activity in the form of hearings or Congressional pressure for enacting the legislation.

On October 7, 1966, the President made a surprise appearance before the National Association of Editorial Writers in New York City and announced a series of steps which the Administration was instituting to strengthen U. S. relations with Eastern Europe. They include the following:

(1) early Senate action on the Soviet-U.S. Consular Agreement;

(2) the enactment of a commercial air agreement with the Soviet Union;

(3) granting the Export-Import Bank permission to guarantee commercial credits to Poland, Hungary, Bulgaria and Czechoslovakia;

(4) the exchange of cloud photographs taken by weather satellites;

(5) the signing of a new cultural agreement with the Soviets.

Several specific provisions were made for the easing of trade barriers with the Communists:

(1) "We intend to press for legislative authority to negotiate trade agreements which could extend most-favored-nation tariff treatment to European Communist states;

(2) "We will reduce export controls on East-West trade with respect to hundreds of non-strategic items;

(3) "The Export-Import Bank is prepared to finance American exports for the Soviet-Italian FIAT Auto plant."

The reaction to the President's speech in the Soviet Union was very hostile. Radio Moscow boasted of continued Soviet assistance to North Vietnam to defeat "the American imperialist aggressors." Then, on October 15th, a week after the President's speech, Communist party leader Brezhnev rejected the President's proposals for "bridge building" out of hand.

The week after the President's speech, Mrs. Edna Kelly (D-N.Y.), Chairman of the Subcommittee on Europe of the House Committee on Foreign Affairs, called a day of hearings to delve into the President's intentions. Four witnesses testified before the Subcommittee and they all expressed their agreement with the President's policy.

Robert McNeill, Deputy Assistant Secretary of Commerce for Trade Policy, defended the Administration's action in removing 400 items from the Export Control List. Mr. McNeill pointed out that the lists are constantly undergoing review by the relevant groups in the Departments of Commerce, Defense and State, and that these items were only on our export lists, not on the COCOM embargo list which is agreed to by the nations of Western Europe, the United States and Japan. Thus the Administration decided to avoid the question of what is "strategic" by removing these 400 items from the strategic list and summarily making them "non-strategic" goods, not requiring a validated license.

While no report was issued by the Kelly Subcommittee, the general tenor of the questioning was not very receptive to the administration proposals.

At the opening of the 90th Congress, the President again called for an expansion of East-West relations saying in his State of the Union Message that "Our objective is not to continue the cold war, but to end it." The President specifically reiterated his earlier pleas that an East-West Trade Act be enacted by the Congress.

Despite the President's plea, the first session of the Democratic-controlled 90th Congress adjourned without a bill even being introduced. In June 1967 Senator Magnuson, joined by Senator Thurston B. Morton (R-Ky.), announced that the Senate Commerce Committee would hold a series of hearings on the experiences of American businessmen engaged in trade with the countries of Eastern Europe. These hearings were scheduled to begin on June 28, 1967. On June 6th Senator Magnuson was compelled to issue a statement postponing the hearings because of the increasing Soviet involvement in the Middle East crisis and their provocative statements against Israel. The Commerce Committee chairman further states that "the speed with which they (the hearings) will be rescheduled.... will depend to a great extent on the policy adopted by the Soviet leadership."

About the same time, the Republican leadership of the Congress expressed interest in the issue of trading with the Communists. On May 11, 1967, Congressmen Charles E. Goodell (R-N.Y.), Chairman of the Planning and Research Committee, and Melvin R. Laird (R-Wisc.) Chairman of the House Republican Conference, announced the formation of a "Republican Task Force on East-West Trade to investigate thoroughly all aspects of the question of East-West Trade." This Task Force was to be composed of eleven Republican members of the House of Representatives, chaired by Congressman Delbert L. Latta (R-Ohio). On May 25, 1967, the Republican leadership of the Congress, Senator Everett Dirksen (R-Ill.) and Congressman Gerald Ford (R-Mich.), announced their opposition to any expansion of East-West trade as long as the Soviets continued to supply the major portion of outside assistance to North Vietnam.

Another expression of interest in the issue came from the former Governor of Connecticut, John Davis Lodge, brother of the former U. S. Ambassador to South Vietnam. Governor Lodge announced the formation of a group called the "Committee to End Aid to the Soviet Enemy (C.E.A.S.E.)" which quickly gained a list of Congressional supporters.[4]

One of the most hotly debated transactions ever entered into with the Communists was the decision of the President to permit Export-Import Bank financing of about $50 million worth of precision machine tools for the $500 million FIAT automobile plant to be constructed on the Volga River in the Soviet Union. This loan would actually be to an Italian firm, the *Instituto Mobiliare Italiano*, which is financing the purchase of the machine tools to the FIAT corporation for eventual use in the Soviet Union. A Congressional delegation, consisting of four members of the House Banking and Currency Committee, visited Eastern Europe and the Soviet Union in late 1966 to investigate this proposal. Following their return, they issued a report unanimously favoring the transaction, and U. S. participation in it.

The Subcommittee favored the transaction primarily on the basis that it is wise to encourage the Soviets to use their resources on consumer goods rather than on military hardware. They argued further that with the passage of time the automobiles constructed in this factory will demand an increase in Soviet road construction, gas station and garage facilities, and other related activities. On the other hand, opponents of the transaction point out that the automobiles from this plant will be available only to the managerial elite and bureaucrats of the Communist Party and not to the average Soviet worker. Furthermore opponents contend that automobile plants are readily converted into plants for military vehicles and equipment, as the United States and the Soviet Union did with various facilities in World War II.

The Export-Import Bank was brought before the full House Banking and Currency Committee for an extension of its charter and an expansion of its lending authority. Following prolonged questioning by several members of the Committee, particularly Representative Paul A. Fino (R-N.Y.), the request of the Export-Import Bank was reported favorably out of Committee by the close vote of 17-14. The closeness of the vote was attributed to the question of the Export-Import Bank involvement in the FIAT financing.

On the Senate Floor, after prolonged debate over the FIAT transaction, and on the financing of arms sales to underdeveloped countries by the Export-Import Bank, two amendments were added to the bill. The first of these amendments, introduced by Harry F. Byrd (D-Va.), would prohibit the Export-Import Bank from financing any trade with any government which is at war with the United States or with nations which aided such belligerents. Thus, the Byrd Amendment would block financial loans and guarantees to all of the Communist nations except Yugoslavia.

The second amendment to pass on the floor of the Senate was an amendment sponsored by Senator Karl Mundt (R-S.D.), specifically prohibiting the Export-Import Bank from financing any part of an automobile plant in the Soviet Union, or in a third country for transshipment to the Soviet Union. The amendment was specific and without qualification and dooms

---

[4]A position paper containing views of C.E.A.S.E. toward East-West Trade appears in the International Finance Subcommittee Hearings of the Senate Banking and Currency Committee, July 24, 1968.

Export-Import Bank participation in the FIAT transaction.

The Mundt Amendment was more specific and limiting than the amendment adopted in the Senate Banking Committee. The Committee proposal, co-authored by Senators John G. Tower (R-Texas) and Bourke B. Hickenlooper (R-Iowa), would have required a favorable Presidential determination in the case of each transaction with the Communist countries involving the use of Export-Import Bank credit facilities.

Following the Senate action on the Export-Import Bank Bill, the House of Representatives passed a rider to the Foreign Assistance Act of 1967, sponsored by Congressman Paul Findley (R-Ill.), which removed most-favored-nation status from those countries which are supporting the North Vietnamese war effort. This amendment was specifically aimed at Poland, which supplies war materiel to the North Vietnamese. Congressman Findley's argument, as expressed on the floor of the House on several occasions, was that a flexible East-West trade policy has to mean that the Administration is willing to withdraw concessions when the demand arises, as well as to grant them on other occasions. This argument was also used by Representative Findley when he advocated the granting of most-favored-nation status to Czechoslovakia in early 1968. Findley viewed the internal changes in Czechoslovakia as indicating a liberalizing trend which should be encouraged. His position was opposed by the Administration, which preferred to give the President discretionary authority to grant most-favored-nation status to any Communist nation upon his own determination.

Another House amendment to the Foreign Assistance Act of 1967 was submitted by Representative H. R. Gross (R-Iowa). This amendment prohibited American purchase of any military equipment or supplies from any country whose ships are trading with North Vietnam. The admitted goal of this amendment was to stop American purchase of British equipment while British flag vessels–owned and operated by Chinese Communists resident in Hong Kong–trade with North Vietnam. Both of these amendments were defeated in conference, before the President signed the bill into law.

Another incident occurred during the summer of 1967 which raised considerable debate on the question of East-West trade in the halls of the Congress. Senator Karl Mundt questioned the granting of an export license to Poland for a "Worden-type Gravity Meter" valued at $102,000, by the Department of Commerce Office of Export Control. Senator Mundt informed his colleagues that the meter was highly sensitive and could be used for determining guided missile trajectories. The response of the Director of the Office of Export Control, Rauer Meyer, was that the license had not yet been granted, that a comparable meter was available from the Soviets and from other Western countries, and that the Communists' military needs were for gravity meters usable at sea, while this Worden meter was usable only on land. Several members of the Senate joined Mundt in his criticism of this transaction. Then the newly formed House Republican Task Force on East-West Trade issued a press release and a letter to the Secretary of Commerce signed by all eleven Task Force members, calling on the Secretary to issue a complete report to the Congress before taking any further action on this transaction.

Finally the Department announced that the applicant "was terminating his interest in the transaction and asked that the license be cancelled." This was done, and the meter was never shipped.

An ironic sequel to this transaction was that the Department of Commerce had authorized the shipment of two similar Worden Gravity meters to Rumania several years earlier. This fact was discovered after the battle over the meter to Poland had taken place.

The Senate side of the Congress maintained a high level of interest in East-West Trade as the 90th Congress progressed. Senator Karl Mundt introduced an amendment to the President's income surtax proposal which would have placed a separate additional tax levy on those firms who were engaged in trading with the Communist nations. The amendment was defeated on the floor of the Senate, but it did express the mood of many members of Congress. It also brought on a counter-move by the Senate forces who supported an increase in trade with the Communist nations.

These members of the Senate introduced a resolution which would express the sense of the Senate as favoring an expansion of trade, and as opposing the restriction which had been previously voted on the Export-Import Bank. The hearings opened under the Chairmanship of Senator Walter Mondale (D-Minn.) before the International Finance Subcommittee of the Senate Banking and Currency Committee. Mondale was joined by twelve colleagues–nine Democrats and three Republicans in introducing his "Sense of the Senate" resolution. The hearings continued for several months, but lead-off witness, Senator Strom Thurmond (R-S.C.) indicated the majority position of the Congress in the election year 1968, when he strongly attacked any proposal which would expand trade with the Communists at this time.

Fair Trade Until Free Trade

Senator Vance Hartke

Many members of Congress have issued policy statements to reflect their views on the subject of East-West trade. The following statement was released for general distribution in 1967 by Senator Hartke.

International free trade fosters the movement of goods from the most efficient producers to their markets. In theory, all the world's goods should properly allocate themselves. However, as this is not the case what we are really talking about is not free trade, but fair trade.

The U.S. must maintain certain safeguards. These safeguards are what the Congress had in mind in granting authority for the Kennedy Round of negotiations in Geneva. I certainly do not support protectionist policy for its own sake but feel we should retain certain safeguards until such time as our international trading partners reciprocate. We most certainly should receive as much as we give in concessions of tariffs, non-tariff barriers, American Selling Price and anti-dumping codes. The time has come, I feel, when we would quit looking at our international trade policies as an instrument of our aid programs. The countries we trade with most enjoy a high degree of economic health and we should enter into agreements that recognize them as trading partners and not charity cases.

There are certain areas that cause us all concern. As steel is our No. 1 domestic industry, I speak here specifically of it. I feel that an international conference on steel should be called in the near future. The continued increase in total international over capacity in steel production will have even more harmful effects than presently obtained. I further feel that in this area we must have effective safeguards to prevent further dumping of subsidized steel in this country. I know that the present capital expansion and modernization of our producing facilities will occasion an international sales campaign. This will show our partners that we can and do produce the best steel in the world and deliver it at competitive prices. My deep concern in this problem has prompted me to request a steel imports study which was released in late May, 1967.

Increasing our share in the international agriculture market is another area of particular concern to me. Soybean and feed grain sales have increased rapidly in past years. However, an increase in our dollar sales in meats and other agricultural produce is needed. I look forward to increased sales abroad as a means of helping provide the farmer with a more adequate return for his investments in time and money. At the same time, our agricultural exports play an important role in reducing our balance of payments deficits. It is imperative that our trade negotiators bear this in mind.

All developed countries should accept their responsibilities to cooperate in helping developing nations help themselves. Here is an area that requires the closest planning and international cooperation. As the world looks forward to a huge increase in population, the present agriculture producing capacity of those countries most in need of food is cause for deep and imperative concern for us all. To better help those in need the developed countries must put their own international trade and monetary houses in order.

The proposition of increased trade with Eastern Bloc nations is of course, of grave concern to us all. I should hope, when the time comes, that there will be a sensible exchange in all civilized areas of international intercommunication. When you have many connections with a certain country or area, it is less likely there will be violence based on misunderstanding or miscalculation.

I feel that if all countries concerned realize that it will be to their own eventual best interest to give in all areas as much as they would like to receive, there can be important and needed increases in free trade. Free trade, judiciously arrived at, can insure international and domestic economic progress, fostering a world climate where peace is maintained and commerce flourishes.

A Senator Looks at East-West Trade

Senator Warren G. Magnuson

The Interstate and Foreign Commerce Committee of the Senate plays a major role in the development of official trade policy. In the following address by the chairman of this committee, delivered before the World Affairs Council in Tacoma, Washington, Senator Magnuson projects the need for a progressive trade policy in keeping with national interests and objectives.

For at least ten years now, the Communist countries of Eastern Europe have been undergoing a revolutionary reversal of their relationship to the industrialized, capitalist West. Stalin was determined to weld the Communist Bloc into a self-contained economic and political whole, totally independent economically, as well as politically, from the West. Trade was tolerated only to meet emergency needs, or to supply prototype plant and equipment to be copied and reproduced. The Bloc was gripped in a state of economic isolation which the economists call "autarky."

Stalin died. The West prospered beyond our brightest hopes and expectations, while the Communist East bogged down in the rigidities and waste of Communist dogmas. As the political grip of Moscow on the satellite capitals relaxed perceptively, the national self-interest of each of the Eastern European countries began to assert itself—even within the local Communist Party superstructures which the Russians had placed in power.

Gradually at first, then with a quickened pace, the countries of Eastern Europe turned to their traditional trading partners in the West—not to exploit one-shot deals—but to reinstate the mutually beneficial long term partnerships on which Europe thrived before the erection of the Iron Curtain.

To rebuild economies shattered by the war and shuttered by the inefficiencies of Communist planning, these countries looked to England, France, Italy, and ironically, West Germany to supply the sinews of modern industrial economies.

But from the beginning the shopping lists carried by the Communist buyers from the East were endless, while their pocketbooks were almost always bare.

With few exceptions, the products produced in Eastern Europe were shoddy, untailored to Western standards. Not only was the quality inferior but the Cold War isolation of the East had left its manufacturing and trading enterprises grossly ignorant of product tastes and trading methods of the West.

The Communist Party "Apparachik" who was placed in charge of a shoe factory because of his political reliability may have been a deadly guerilla fighter in the revolution, but he met his factory's quota of a hundred thousand pairs of shoes by producing 200,000 left shoes! And few were the Party faithful who could strike a hard bargain over a negotiations table with Western businessmen.

Bankers hardly fit the stereotype of the victorious proletariat, but how do you finance exports and imports without a modern banking system? And if you are hostile to visitors, buyers and money-laden tourists will shun you for friendlier climates.

So if you are a Communist state in Eastern Europe faced with an unquenchable thirst for products and know-how from the West, some inevitable and very interesting things begin to happen to you.

First, you become less concerned with Party loyalty and more concerned with ability in your choice of enterprise managers—specifically, the ability to turn a profit, a word which slowly creeps back into your vocabulary. You look for able, young, university graduates with ambition and, with surprising frequency, you even rehabilitate pre-war merchants who have been barely existing on the fringes of your Communist state.

And then you turn increasingly to greater market incentives for firms and workers. Profit rather than quantity becomes the key to production. Labor and management are rewarded with bonuses not far exceeding arbitrary quotas of inferior widgets which no one will buy, but for producing quality widgets sold at a profit.

Gradually, your closely controlled economy and society begins to loosen up. All of your export executives must learn English, because English is now the dominant international language of traders. Also, the Chamber of Commerce subscribes to *Time* magazine and the *London Economist*.

Travel to the West becomes a necessity, and the conscientious commercial representative in London or New York can't shut himself up in the self-contained cell of his embassy or legation. He has to get out and mix and sell. And then he gets corrupted by Western influences, begins to dress well, wants a car—an American car. One young fellow who led a Communist Trade Delegation to Egypt told us that as soon as he landed in Cairo he headed for the latest James Bond movie—despite the official view of his government that James Bond is the prototype of the reactionary imperialist. He envies the open political views of his Western counterparts. Soon he begins to try his hand at a political joke or two on his own government.

"Why don't Hungarian workers go on strike," one Hungarian asked us. The answer, "Because nobody would know the difference."

"Why doesn't Switzerland have a Communist government? Because it is too small to afford it."

The Communist trader begins to think of himself more as a trader and less as a Communist. We asked a director of the Foreign Trade Bank for one of the Eastern European countries how he would characterize his work. "I would like to think of myself as a merchant banker, just like the English merchant bankers."

"I would like to forget that I am working for the government" the head of one trading company told us and another, who had been the director of an exporting enterprise for nearly twenty years, watching it expand and grow, proudly referred to it as "my company."

Competition creeps in. Two or three trading companies compete over who can do the best job buying and selling heavy machinery. A state manufacturing enterprise with vague jurisdictional lines and a hustling managing director decides it can build and operate chicken processing plants more efficiently than the outfit that is doing the job now—and does.

How do these Eastern traders feel about America? "As a businessman," he will tell you, he has the greatest admiration for American goods, technology production techniques, and our ability to deliver on time. The way to say know-how in Rumanian is "know-how."

He likes Americans—he likes to deal with them. He respects and trusts the American business ethic. If he had enough dollars, he would buy everything from the Americans.

And he likes Americans personally, as he gets to know them. The Agricultural Minister of one of the Eastern countries has come to the United States several times to purchase plants and equipment and has developed close friendship with the Americans with whom he deals. One told me that he had brought the Minister to his home in the Mid-West for a weekend of relaxation and, on Sunday morning, asked his guest if he would join the family at church. The Minister replied that he would like to go, if it were a small church, where no one would see him.

How does he feel about Vietnam? He wishes it would go away. Does he have a missionary zeal to spread Communism throughout the world? Not likely. Aggressive expansion of Communism threatens peaceful relations with the West; a threat to peaceful relations with the West is a threat to his job.

In short, we have a stake in the new breed of Communist traders because they have a stake in us.

Suppose the secret police in his country threaten to arrest a tourist who tries to talk politics with a citizen. The trader protests, "Leave the tourist alone, we need hard currency."

He wants to buy a corn flake or potato chip factory from an American firm. He is hoping that the United States Office of Export Control will grant an export license. Does he want his government to announce that it is shortly sending volunteers to Vietnam? He does not want to rock the boat and lose the contract.

But the manager of a state trading company has his problems. He promises the combine that manages all food processing that the Americans will deliver a corn flake factory faster and better than anyone else. The Foreign Trade Bank allocates precious, hard-earned currency for the factory and the contract is negotiated and signed. But the Young Americans for Freedom decide to picket the firm that is selling the plant (one Rumanian official said he knew it was the "Young Democrats" that were the root of the trouble). The American firm now gets cold feet and cancels the contract, at the last minute.

The Food combines' Five Year Plan for producing corn flakes is shot and the plant manager blames his Trade Ministry for getting involved with the no-good Americans.

And do you know who is happy with this result? The Young Americans for Freedom are happy with the result and the Communist Secret Police are happy with the result. Communist hard liners rub their hands and say "See, we told you so. To trade with the Americans is to buy trouble. Capitalists are no____ good."

"You kept us from sending volunteers to Vietnam, you kept our shipments of supplies limited, you muzzled our military men and our diplomats, all because of this ridiculous notion of coexisting with the West. It is time to forget this nonsense and get on with our wars of liberation."

The position and moderating influence of the traders declines.

This is where our own East-West Trade Policy comes in, and it might be useful for us at this point to briefly review that policy.

Generally speaking, our relations with the Communist world in the last two or three decades have had both defensive and affirmative aspects.

Defensively during the course of the last twenty years, the United States has had to confront Communist military aggression, and subversion in many parts of the world. This we have done, this we will continue to do so long as necessary. We believe in and we abide by the principle that no power has the right to impose its ideas or its system on others through the use of arms.

Greece was threatened by Communist subversion in the immediate post war years; we did not hesitate to come to the aid of Greece. We did not hesitate to send our young men and commit our resources to the Korean War to insure that peace and stability would prevail in the North Pacific. Because we did not hesitate, Communist China as well as Stalin's Russia learned painfully and at considerable cost that the United States is unflinching when faced with the threat of force.

In Europe we have made it clear to friends and foes alike that we stand by our commitments. We have been tested twice in Berlin, and today the citizen of Berlin does not fear for his future. When the Soviet leadership concluded that we could not be stared down in a nuclear confrontation through the planting of missiles in Cuba, we stood firm. Circumspection prevailed.

And so, fitfully and painfully, a measure of restraint has come to characterize American-Soviet relations. Make no mistake of it, this restraint exists primarily because we have permitted the Soviets no illusions about our willingness and determination to meet force with force.

By standing firm, as we are, we are also strengthening the hand of those Communists, such as the traders of whom we have spoken, who seek to discourage international adventures which threaten the life line of trade.

While these defensive aspects of our policy have been designed to dampen the appetites of the radical Communists, the affirmative aspects have been designed to extend a firm hand to the moderates who shun aggression. We helped Yugloslavia with its efforts to maintain independence from the Soviet Union, and we have helped Yugoslavia to move away from doctrinaire Communism to a freer economic and political system.

President Eisenhower supplied surplus grains to Poland partly in response to that country's maintenance of a free enterprise agricultural system.

Now we are attempting to strengthen the hand of the Eastern traders. Proposing to Congress the East-West Trade Relations Act, which I have had the honor to sponsor in the Senate, President Johnson has demonstrated to the East his good faith in seeking to abolish the discriminatory tariff rates imposed during the ice age of the Cold War.

Step by step we are attempting to build those bridges of confidence which must become thoroughfares if peace is ever to return to this planet which we share, like it or not, with the Communists.

We have now agreed with the Soviet Union to a treaty on the peaceful uses of outer space. We have concluded a civil air agreement providing direct air service between New York and Moscow. I, myself, have been deeply involved in the recent conclusion of a just and reasonable Fisheries Agreement. The result has been an agreement far more favorable than we earlier thought possible. The Soviet negotiators accepted logical recommendations without trying to interject cold war objections.

We have renewed the US-USSR Exchange Agreement for another two years. We now have before us in the Senate for ratification the US-Soviet Consular Convention which would constitute an unprecedented breakthrough, furnishing protection to substantial progress toward an agreement to prevent the spread of nuclear weapons.

The President has authorized the Export-Import Bank to guarantee commercial credits to Poland, Hungary, Bulgaria, and Czechoslovakia, as well as Rumania. Export controls have been amended to permit the sale, under simplified licensing procedures to Eastern Europe, of several hundred non-strategic items. Our Legations in Budapest and Sofia and the Hungarian and Bulgarian Legations in Washington have been raised to the status of embassies.

We have just concluded a new two-year agreement with Rumania on Cultural, Scientific and Educational Exchanges. And the National Academy of Sciences has concluded agreements with several of its European counterparts for specific scientific exchanges.

Are these efforts really worthwhile? And are they really in our interest? Wouldn't we rather have the Rumanians making corn flakes than increasing jet fuel production?

But does all this answer the basic painful question, "Why should we trade with the Communists when they are supplying the weapons that kill our boys in Vietnam?" Fortunately, the answer cannot be as simple as the question, but there is an answer.

First and foremost trade in strategic goods is banned, both by agreement with our Western allies and by our own laws, and no one proposes to lift that ban. Second, nothing that we do on our trade policy will deny the North Vietnamese access to any military equipment. The Communist world is self-sufficient in military production and has been for many years.

Ironically, the Russians are supplying us with scarce magnesium, vital to US aircraft production and therefore to the Vietnam war effort.

On the other hand, our Intelligence sources tell us that the bulk of the enemy equipment in Vietnam is Chinese in origin with Soviet supplies constituting a "relatively minor component." According to Deputy Under Secretary of State Kohler, "The big Soviet military aid has gone to North Vietnam in the form of anti-aircraft guns, and missiles and radar and fighter planes, items the Soviets describe as defensive."

There seems, in fact, to have been some element of restraint here, perhaps referred by Moscow as paralleling our own limited purposes in Vietnam.

Clearly the growing and continuing need for trade with the West *does* act as a restraining influence on the Communists. If we remove that trade potential, then the Communists will have nothing to lose by pulling out all the stops.

As Senator Henry Jackson observed in an incisive and compelling speech, which he made to the Senate last week:

> "We need to learn the art of doing two things at once: to work with the Soviet Union where we can and to keep up our strength as a basis for working with them and for encouraging them to view us with a healthy respect. This is not easy to do, for it is an old tendency of ours to see things in black and white terms, but it is the task we face.
>
> In general, we should be ready to do business with Moscow wherever our interests and theirs truly converge. There may therefore be advantages to each side in an expansion of the peaceful contacts growing out of trade and tourism and other exchanges."

There is perhaps no field as fertile for the Monday morning quarterback as foreign policy. We could easily lose count of the foreign policy decision of the last two decades which have failed to bear the test of time and reflection.

The Marshall Plan, in its main force and objectives, must surely rank as a singlular American triumph in foreign diplomacy as well as in international compassion, but we may have erred in coldly excluding the Soviet Union and the satellites from the Plan. Of course, we had justification enough arising from Stalin's aggressive behavior. But the decision to further isolate the Soviet Bloc may well have strengthened and confirmed the worst suspicions of the Russians and provoked them to veer more sharply along the road to the Cold War and the Iron Curtain.

I make these observations not to unearth old chestnuts or to pick the bones of past policies which may have appeared wise and just at the time, but only to dramatize the constantly shifting nature of foreign affairs, the hazards of viewing both friendly and hostile relations as permanent fixtures.

Change, rapid fomenting change, characterizes not only our society, but all societies. Our challenge is to recognize, if possible to anticipate, change and to be alert to respond to change.

East-West Trade: "A Realistic Approach"

Proceedings and debates on the floors of the House and Senate provide interesting dialogue when any controversial issue is brought before these distinguished bodies. The following transcript, taken from the Congressional Record, *includes remarks by Senators Dominick, Lausche, Hansen and Mundt on the subject of East-West trade.*

Mr. DOMINICK. Mr. President, administration pressures on Congress for trade expansion with the Communist-controlled countries of Eastern Europe, including the Soviet Union, multiply day by day. It is indeed ironic and disheartening to hear many of our own industrialists parrot these suggestions at the very time when our men in Vietnam are being killed by Soviet weapons; when the Israelites are forced to fight for their existence against five nations, all armed by the Soviets–and the President may speak of the so-called "Spirit of Glassboro" but what is far more significant at the moment, at least, to the peace and security of the Middle East is the spirit reflected by the Soviet's rearming of the United Arab Republic; and while the Soviet replacement of weapons is taking place, the United States is figuratively sticking its fingers in its ears. In view of the recent Soviet shipments of arms to the Arab countries, the United States must take steps to see to it that the Soviets should not again upset the critical military balance of power in the Middle East–and Cuban terrorists mount their attacks on Latin American governments with weapons and training financed by the Soviet Union.

It is only fair to ask, Mr. President, whether this country has gone so far down the road of moral decay in search of the almighty dollar that we are willing to help build the economies of nations which are fighting us in every hemisphere.

In his state of the Union message of 1965, President Johnson requested vigorous expansion of trade with the Eastern European nations, and reiterated his wish again in 1967. We are metaphorically urged to build bridges to the East to enable the traffic of technological, nuclear, and economic knowledge to flow more smoothly than it has in past years. The result of expanded trade, so says this administration, will be to relax tensions and foster a closer understanding between the Eastern and Western worlds.

Mr. President, these are goals that I am sure are desired by everyone in this Chamber, but are they realistic? Is trade for trade's sake the road to peace? In this case, is trade for trade's sake with Communist-controlled corporations in any way beneficial to our interests?

Following his state of the Union message in 1965, President Johnson created a Special Committee on U.S. Trade Relations with East European Countries and the Soviet Union. The Special Committee submitted a report to the President on April 29, 1965, and with only one dissenting voice agreed cautiously that increased trade between the East and the West would not be harmful provided strategic goods were kept out of Communist hands, but this report clearly conceded that the Soviet Union had little to offer in the way of exports and that trade would be most advantageous if kept at a minimum. The report also stressed that the United States should use expanded trade as a lever to obtain concessions and a satisfactory settlement of lend-lease agreements. Needless to say, there has been little comment on this latter point by the proponents of expanded trade.

In a statement of personal reservation in this report, one member–and I certainly want to congratulate him–Mr. Nathanial Goldfinger, director of research for the AFL-CIO and trustee for the Joint Council on Ecomonic Education, spoke out clearly. After stating that he was not opposed to trade per se, he said:

> Trade relations with the Soviet Union and its European satellites should be viewed as a tool to our Nation's foreign policy. Therefore, the Report should have placed greater emphasis on the political aspects of this issue.
>
> There is also inadequate caution in the report about the risk of exporting American technology–particularly advanced technology–to those countries. In centrally planned totalitarian states, military and economic factors are closely related. There is no reason to believe that the export of the American machinery and equipment to those countries will necessarily rebound to the benefit of their people.
>
> Moreover, in our readiness to engage in bilateral trade negotiations with individual countries of the Soviet Bloc, *we should have no illusions about the ability of trade, in itself, to alter Communist attitudes and policies. Neither is trade, as such, a sure force for peace, as indicated by the two World Wars between trading nations.* [Emphasis added]

Mr. Goldfinger's reservations are well taken and in my opinion reflect an awareness of the realities we must face; his statement is the most succinct and accurate description that I have heard of the philosophy that should be reflected in our trade policies, and I endorse it wholeheartedly.

It is important for us to remember that we are not talking about trade with our allies in Western Europe or with Latin American countries which form with us a hemispheric alliance. We are talking about countries whose training and actions are based upon a commitment to weaken and eventually destroy the economic and political principles that we believe in. It is the goal

Reprinted from the Congressional Record, Vol. 113, No. 113, (July 21, 1968)

of the Soviet Union and her satellites to destroy these principles wherever they exist in the world and to replace them with the Communist ideology. In the past, their attempts to achieve this goal in such places as Laos, Indonesia, Berlin, Cuba, and, most recently, in the Middle East, have led to direct and dangerous threats to world peace.

Mr. President, during the years of the cold war, our nation has paid an enormous price in blood and dollars to block and contain Soviet attempts to extend her influence into the free world. The total dollar figure, including economic aid, foreign military aid, and direct military aid that is traceable to the struggle against communism, is $574 billion—over one-half trillion dollars. The war in Vietnam alone will cost American taxpayers over $24 billion this year and a toll in American lives that no sum of money will ever replace. Yet, 85 percent of the military and economic materials that go to the North Vietnamese are being supplied by the same countries to whom we are now urged to grant extensive trade privileges.

Some of our economists and business representatives say trade with the Communist countries must be considered as a solely economic problem. They believe we must consider the need of U.S. business to compete in a world market where our European allies are already trading at the rate of around $6 billion a year. They see expansion of trade as an important economic span for building bridges to the East. They list other economic benefits to be accrued from expanded trade relations as: the possible arrangement for the protection of patents; the settlement of commercial disputes; the establishment of facilities and activities for the promotion of trade and tourism; the granting of the most-favored-nation status to certain countries for trade purposes; nondiscriminatory treatment for American products; the arrangement for the settlement of American financial and property claims against the Communist nations concerned.

This is all well and good, but it is unrealistic for us to form trade policies on a primarily economic basis when the Soviet Union bases its policies on both economic and political considerations. I cannot see how we can play a game of trade with our political hand tied behind our back and deal our cards with only our economic hand. We need both hands to play the game effectively. In the face of the cold war and Communist actions throughout the world, political considerations must not be overlooked or taken lightly.

To get some idea of the scope of the implications of trade with Communist nations, let us look first at what we have learned as a result of our past experiences in trading with the East.

In 1962, a Judiciary Subcommittee which was studying the effect of U.S. trade policies on the U.S.S.R. and other Soviet bloc countries came to the conclusion that—

> Over a period of many years, the free world has been making a direct contribution to the Communist military and industrial strength by sales of vital materials and technology to the Soviet Bloc. * * * The bloc countries have been able, partly as a result of this procurement, to export their own machinery and technology to other countries—always with political strings attached.

Furthermore, the committee predicted that—

> Unless the United States and our allies [were] willing to institute more realistic curbs on bloc procurement, this buildup [would] continue, despite the critical confrontation of East and West taking place in many areas of the world, such as Cuba, Berlin, and Vietnam.

This prediction was made 6 years ago, but it is just as valid today as it was then. Let us now look for a moment to see how realistic our trade restrictions have been in the last 6 years and to consider the results of our policies.

In 1963, the Commerce Department granted a seemingly harmless request by Russia to buy $9.5 million worth of highly automated mining machinery to mine potash—a chemical used in the manufacture of fertilizers. This was followed 3 years later by the licensing of technical data that enabled a U.S. firm to build six fertilizer plants in Soviet Russia. These plants would have a combined productive capacity of 4,830 tons of fertilizer a day. Shortly thereafter, Secretary of Agriculture, Orville L. Freeman, returning from a visit to South Vietnam, reported:

> There is a strong demand for fertilizer chemicals and improved seeds [in South Viet Nam.] Fertilizer is as important as bullets.

This was the situation in the south, but the need for such chemicals is known to be even more acute in North Vietnam. We are now made bitterly aware, from Tass broadcasts in Moscow, that volume shipments of fertilizer are among the supplies that are regularly shipped to North Vietnam by the U.S.S.R.

On July 8, 1965, an export license was issued to the Soviet Union authorizing the shipment of chemical pulpwood valued at $3,375,000. Chemical pulpwood is used to manufacture rayon tire cord which, in turn, is used in the production of both automobile and truck tires. Trucks, of course, are one of the most important vehicles used to transport supplies to Communist Vietnamese troops fighting against our people in South Vietnam.

Five days later, a U.S. firm was authorized to ship $2,436,800 worth of grinding machines that are used in the grinding of cam shafts and crank shafts for the motors of automobiles and light trucks.

Mr. President, we are told by Secretary McNamara and the President that North Vietnam is supplying and equipping the Communists in the south. We also know that the Soviet Union is supplying 85 percent of all equipment and material for North Vietnam, which is then being redistributed through the south.

Mr. President, American pilots have risked their lives, and are today risking their lives daily, to destroy supply routes to Hanoi, yet supplies still flow to that city. Are the trucks that carry these supplies outfitted with parts that we helped to produce? Do they travel on tires that we helped to manufacture? Are they loaded with fertilizer that was produced in factories which we sold to the Soviets?

To further illustrate the complex implications of our trade agreements with the Communist bloc, I would like to quote the three paragraphs from a statement made by Representative Lipscomb in the September 2, 1965, *Congressional Record*. Mr. Lipscomb was a member of the Select Committee on Export Control during the 87th Congress and has consistently probed into the extraordinary results of U.S. trade policies. On this date he made the following statement to the House:

> Several months ago the Department of Commerce also issued a license to authorize selling to the U.S.S.R. of technical data for the production of what was listed by the Department merely as chemical products. It turned out that the technical data licensed for export was for the production of various items used to produce polystyrene. In response to my request for information on the end use, I was informed not what the polystyrene would be used for, but merely what some of its applications are such as in the manufacture of refrigerators, air conditioners, containers of many sorts, packaging for dishes, records, electronic coils, and others.
>
> What the Department of Commerce did not say, however, is that polystyrene has a large variety of direct military and industrial uses. It is used, for example, as a binder in explosives. According to the Air Force it is used to insulate the exterior walls of large buildings. Polystyrene is used by the Army as an adapter for attachment of fuses to demolition blocks. The Nazis used it as an ignitor for the V-2 rockets and for nonmagnetic mines during World War II.
>
> Polystyrene capacitors are used in the Minuteman program. Containers made out of this type of material have been found by our Armed Forces to be capable of safely holding comparatively large loads of explosive materials. Polystyrene is used in the manufacture of certain land mines which are fired by remote control. Polystyrene foam has been found to be an economical and lightweight material to replace wooden and steel containers to hold submarine smoke and illumination signals and marine location markers. These are only some of the many uses of this highly versatile and useful product.

One of the incredible aspects of this statement is the fact that, although polystyrene is one of the end products that may be produced from the technical data which we sold to the U.S.S.R., this data was considered nonstrategic by the Department of Commerce.

Fertilizer plants and pulpwood and gearmaking machinery were also labeled nonstrategic; yet we have just seen the potential impact that shipments of these commodities could have upon our efforts to block the Communists in Vietnam.

Let us take a look at some of the other so-called nonstrategic items that have been licensed for export to Communist countries. According to the Communist Control List that was published by the Department of Commerce on October 12, 1966, the following are "nonstrategic" goods which are licensed for shipment from us to the Soviet Union: Airborne communications equipment, generators for electronic equipment used to control aircraft, communications equipment, airborne navigation equipment, and electronic computer and parts.

Licensed for shipment to Czechoslovakia: Nuclear radiation detection and measuring instruments, electrical measuring and testing instruments, pyrotechnical rocket engines, and transmitter radio beacons and parts.

For Poland the licenses include: Electrical steel sheets, electrolytic tining and coil preparation line, components and tubes for electrical equipment, metalworking and cutting machine and parts, and radio communication receiver and parts.

The authorized shipments to East Germany include: Boring and drilling machines, data processing systems, and rotary combustion engines.

To Yugoslavia we are licensed to export copper scrap, semiconductors, aircraft parts, and communication cable. Hungary can import scientific and professional instrument parts, electronic navigational aids, airborne communication equipment and parts, and airborne navigational equipment and parts. Rumania is cleared to receive industrial instruments and parts, signal generators, hot aluminum sheet mills, and aluminum coldstrip mills. And, finally, Bulgaria's list includes industrial equipment and parts, electrical and electronic equipment and parts, and airborne radar–transponders–equipment.

Even more astonishing than this are the 400 allegedly nonstrategic commodities that the President has recently OK'd for export to the Kremlin. This is our President saying, "OK, you can ship these to Moscow." What does this list include?

Rifle-cleaning compounds, propeller blades, propellers, machine-made paper for dynamite, gun wadding, shell stock, parachute cloth, tarpaulins, tents, and several other items of very direct and obvious military application. Also, crude rubber, railways cross ties, iron ore mass, aluminum, manganese, lead, zinc, chromium, tin, scrap, metal, coke, liquefied petroleum gas, pig iron, carbon steel bars and rods, iron or steel rails, railway material, and various other things with obvious potential in connection with military industry.

We have licensed airborne communications equipment to Soviet Russia, and Soviet Mig fighters are in combat against our Air Force in Vietnam. They shot down three of them yesterday over Vietnam. Are these enemy fighters equipped with our own communications instruments? What about generators for electronic equipment used to control aircraft? What about ship stabilization equipment? Are Soviet ships using

U.S. equipment on their long journey to deliver war goods to the Haiphong Harbor in North Vietnam?

Unfortunately, in the past 6 years we do not seem to have heeded very well the cautious words which I mentioned earlier—words urging us to institute realistic curbs on Soviet and Eastern European procurement of Western goods.

A big step forward in this direction would be made if we would only recognize that when shipping to Communist nations there is no such thing as a nonstrategic commodity.

Goods that may seem of negligible importance to us are actually in desperate demand in the Soviet and Eastern European countries because their spending programs have been weighted heavily toward items of a direct military nature. Consequently, it has become necessary for them to import goods that they need but have not been able to develop because emphasis has been placed elsewhere. If these goods were not obtainable from us or other free world nations, it would become necessary for Soviet planners to divert money from military production in order to manufacture these nonmilitary goods which are now given a low-priority status.

We know, for instance, that agricultural yields in the Soviet Union during the past few years have been far off the mark set by the planners in the Kremlin. The index of agricultural production was lower in 1959 and 1960 than it was in 1958; and by 1961, the situation was so serious that in January of that year Premier Khrushchev announced a new era of high priority for agriculture. Yet, in 1961, agriculture investment increased only about 6 percent as compared with increases of 45 percent in 1954 and 38 percent in 1955. The situation had not improved very much by December 1963, when the Soviet Premier declared that Russia had suffered a "hard winter and severe drought" and that Soviet planning would have to concentrate on "setting up a mightly chemical industry so that in the next 7 years, it would be possible to increase sharply the production of mineral fertilizer."

Notice that Mr. Khrushchev wanted to concentrate on "setting up"—not developing—these plants. Soviet planners do not plan to divert money from military spending to develop their own chemical plants. They would rather import the technology needed to build them, and bypass the time-consuming and costly process of development. So what do we do? We label this information "nonstrategic" and send it to them with our blessings.

We must understand that every commodity we send to the Soviet Union is strategic because it contributes to her economic wealth and to her ability to maintain a policy of placing high priority on the production of military commodities.

I want to make it clear at this point that I am not suggesting that we suspend trade with Eastern European nations. Rather, I am simply suggesting that, in future trade with the Soviet bloc, we should exercise policies that are designed to insure that we receive as much as they do. This will mean that we must be far more demanding in terms of political concessions and less anxious to close a deal just because the price is right.

The clearest declaration of the intent behind the Soviet desire for increased Western trade was made by former Premier Khrushchev and published in Pravda—they always publish these statements, and let us know about it, but we never read them—on December 9, 1963. Speaking in reference to the effort to build up the Soviet chemical industry through machinery and plant imports, he affirmed that the purchase of such equipment from capitalist countries would provide the U.S.S.R. with "the opportunity of quicker fulfillment of its program—without wasting time on drawing up the plans and mastering the production of new types of equipment."

Thus, Mr. President, we can see that Soviets desire trade with the West either to strengthen weak areas of their own economy or to obtain technology and machinery that they lack and do not want to develop on their own. Success in these objectives means that Kremlin leaders can continue in full strength their policies of stirring unrest and revolution in the underdeveloped and emerging nations of the world. It also means that she can continue to support similar activities by her satellite states, such as Cuba, which as I pointed out in an earlier speech, now has 43 guerrilla training camps turning out more than 10,000 guerrillas a year just 90 miles from our shores.

As for the hope that increased trade with the Soviets would bring a change of production priorities that would emphasize consumer goods rather than defense materials, we have nothing to make us believe that this, in fact, will be the result, and we must not allow our hopes to cloud our view of the facts.

Mr. LAUSCHE. Mr. President, will the Senator yield for a question?

Mr. DOMINICK. I am happy to yield to the Senator from Ohio.

Mr. LAUSCHE. Is my understanding correct that the Senator from Colorado is attempting to develop the fact that the purchases made by Russia have been directed primarily to the acquisition of prototype processing machinery and the technical know-how of the United States, thus sparing itself the great cost and the delay of developing and doing the necessary research on processing machinery such as that it buys from us?

Mr. DOMINICK. That is certainly one of the great areas of effort that they have been exerting. They have been trying to avoid the need, as the Sentor has so well stated, of developing this series of plants, equipment, technology—the list could go on and on. They simply import it from us, we thereby strengthen their economy, and they cut us up in North Vietnam, Cuba, Berlin, and elsewhere, the result is that we strengthen their economy so that they in turn can produce more war materials.

Mr. LAUSCHE. One further question. Will the Senator from Colorado explain his views as to whether or not the developments that have taken place, as evidenced by the statements of Russia and its conduct in South Vietnam and other places, show that a lessening of tensions has occurred since the time it was proposed that we should liberalize our trade?

The argument was made, "If we liberalize, there will be a lessening of tensions, there will be greater contact between Russia and the United States, and the result will be that we will not be faced by the provocative efforts of Russia in creating trouble and attempting to undermine the very existence of our country."

Mr. DOMINICK. My good friend, the distinguished Senator from Ohio [Mr. Lausche], has put his finger on the key argument in the propaganda which the proponents of liberalized trade put out. As the Senator and I both know, that argument is wholly fallacious. There has been no attempt at any detente whatsoever. The Soviets today are rearming the Arab nations for future attacks on Israel; and as of today, they are still shipping new equipment into North Vietnam to kill our own people, who continue to be killed day after day by Soviet weapons. The attack on Da Nang the other day—and I happen to have been there in May—was made by Russian rockets. These happened to be 122-millimeter, but they have also been furnished 140-millimeter rockets, so as to be able to fire them from farther away.

All one has to do is look at the support furnished to Castro's government in Cuba by the Soviet Union. They are building up Communist governments and increasing the pressures on democratic governments all over the free world, at the same time that they are saying, "Give us your equipment and build up our economy." It makes no sense whatsoever.

Mr. LAUSCHE. Will the Senator yield further?

Mr. DOMINICK. I am happy to yield.

Mr. LAUSCHE. I have in my hand a book entitled "East-West Trade and United States Policy," written by Mose L. Harvey. In this book, the author summarizes the arguments that have been made by those who propose that we sell to and buy from Russia. Here is how he summarizes the arguments made in favor of liberalization:

> Conditions have altered drastically since the restrictive system was established; it is now beyond Western capacity to affect substantially communist (Soviet) military strength or economic development; in any event, Western Europe and Japan freely trade in goods other than items of direct military importance, and the communists can procure virtually anything they need from those sources; the only effect of continued U.S. restrictions is, therefore, to deny American business a fair share of a lucrative market; further, the expansion of U.S. trade with the European communists would serve useful ends in that it would open the way for increased contacts, make for a relaxation of tensions and lay foundations for better political relations, reduce the dependence of communist states on each other, encourage greater communist concentration on the export industries, reduce communist self-sufficiency, help U.S. business and labor and ease the U.S. balance of payments problem.

The most emphasized aspect of his summary of what the proponents of liberalized trade claim was that it would help to improve relations with Russia.

For some 4 years now there has been a liberalization of trade; and I again ask the Senator from Colorado, what are the evidences of a purpose on the part of the Russians to collaborate with us in achieving peace around the world and living in peaceful coexistence?

Mr. DOMINICK. There is absolutely not one iota of evidence to support that conclusion. Not only that, but the Secretary of Defense, Mr. McNamara, with whom I disagree on an enormous number of points, has said flatly and emphatically that there has been no change in the attitude of the Soviet Union and their intent to control the world. President Johnson has said that there has been no change in the objectives of the Soviet Union.

Mr. LAUSCHE. When Hitler and Mussolini began to develop their great strength, and when Japan developed its military power, is it not a fact that many of our people began to protest the sale of what were supposed to be nonstrategic materials to the Fascist countries fearing the dangers to our country in consequence of what materials we were selling to our enemies. Is it not also a fact that in World War II our men were giving of their lives and their bodies because of ammunition that had been made through the trade in which our country was engaging with Japan, Germany, and Italy?

Mr. DOMINICK. The Senator is entirely correct. One would think that, having made that mistake once, we would not do it again. But we are doing it today, and our people are being killed every day in South Vietnam by material and equipment that has been provided through the Soviet Union.

Mr. LAUSCHE. We are now indulging in the same evil practices of selling material to the Communist countries that we indulged in prior to World War II when we sold scrap iron, which was a nonstrategic material, to Japan.

Mr. DOMINICK. The Senator is entirely correct.

Mr. LAUSCHE. The Senator has identified the many things that we are selling which are labeled as nonstrategic, but which can quickly be converted into strategic materials.

Mr. DOMINICK. The Senator is correct.

The Senator from South Dakota [Mr. Mundt] made a very impressive speech last week on the same point concerning the need for us to become realistic insofar as trade policies are concerned.

It is our purpose to try to obtain a position by which we can try to persuade this administration to take a realistic policy concerning this situation and not merely go on wishfully thinking that if we get a couple of bucks for what we are selling, we will be better off and the Soviets will be nice boys. There has been no indication that this will be the case.

Mr. LAUSCHE. Mr. President, I compliment the Senator from Colorado for the very constructive presentation he is making to the Senate on the subject of East-West trade.

Mr. DOMINICK. I thank the Senator.

Mr. HANSEN. Mr. President, will the Senator yield?

Mr. DOMINICK. I yield.

Mr. HANSEN. Mr. President, I call attention to the April 24 speech of Leonid Brezhnev which the Committee on Government Operations had reprinted, as "The Soviet View of NATO." This was the subject of comment by Bernard Gwertzman and Crosby S. Noyes of the Washington Star.

Mr. Noyes highlighted the admission of Communist Party Boss Brezhnev that the periods of "slackened international tension" are those in which the Communist movement in Europe has had its ripest picking.

As the top Communist in Russia sees it, and this relates directly to East-West trade and the easing of tensions envisioned therefrom, the lesson of the past war years is plain:

> It teaches in particular that the cold war and the confrontation of military blocs, the atmosphere of military threat, seriously hamper the activity of revolutionary democratic (i.e. Communist) forces . . .
>
> And conversely, the past few years have shown clearly that in conditions of slackened international tension, the pointer of the political barometer moves left . . . the increase and the influence of West European Communist parties is most directly correlated with a reduction in tension which has taken place in Europe.

I think this bears out precisely the point that the distinguished Senator from Colorado is attempting to make today on the floor, that any way we want to look at it, the Soviet Union and communism has gained through these exchanges. When tensions have been relaxed, they have made their greatest gains.

Is that the conclusion of the Senator?

Mr. DOMINICK. The Senator is correct. I appreciate the reference of the distinguished Senator from Wyoming to Brezhnev's speech.

Some time ago when we were dealing with the right of the World Bank, I believe it was, to guarantee credit for wheat shipments made to Russia, Professor Nutter, of the University of Virginia, appeared before our committee.

Professor Nutter put it in a nutshell, to coin a pun, when he said that there was the general impression that a fat Communist is better than a lean Communist, and that consequently, if we fatten them up, they will be happier people. However, the history of the Soviet Union in particular indicates that each and every time their economy is fat, that is the time when we face our worst troubles around the world.

Consequently, the idea that by trade we will make them more amenable is wrong. It will simply increase their potential and willingness to create problems.

Mr. LAUSCHE. Mr. President, is it not a fact that when we sold wheat to Russia and the wheat was in the process of being delivered, it was established that Russia had transferred a part of that wheat to Cuba and to Egypt in order to fulfill its obligations to those two nations that are hostile to us, when, without the sale of our wheat, Russia could not have done so?

Mr. DOMINICK. I am delighted that the Senator from Ohio has brought up that point. It is absolutely correct.

This is one more indication of our trying to commit some kind of suicide.

Mr. President, the proposal to cooperate with the Fiat Co. of Italy to help finance and equip the Soviet-Fiat automobile factory is a good example of high hopes taking precedence over facts. Last October the administration announced that the United States is prepared to finance through our Export-Import Bank the export of nearly $50 million worth of high-quality, precision machine tools to equip this factory. Forbes magazine estimated on October 1, 1966, that—

> Three-quarters of the machinery that Fiat installs for the Russians will come from the U.S. either directly or indirectly through European subsidiaries and licensees of American firms. It will really be the United States that puts the Russians on wheels.

The idea here is to sponsor and encourage an "automobile boom" similar to the one that has caused so much change in our country. It is hoped that "putting the Russians on wheels" will result in the biggest alteration of the Russian society since 1917. But, in fact, we have no reason to expect that the automobiles produced in this factory would be available to the average Russian citizen. On the contrary, on March 1 of this year a report from the Central Intelligence Agency to the House Subcommittee on International Trade stated that the Soviets intend to produce cars for the Communist leaders, not the people. The report states:

> Essentially, the new Soviet program is designed to produce automobiles for the bureaucratic and managerial elite, not for the average citizen.

The CIA estimates that 23 percent of all Soviet passenger automobiles produced in 1967—a total of

54,000—will be exported to satellite states or to states that are nearly dominated by Russian influence. Is it not amazing that a total of 54,000 automobiles is all they produced? Furthermore, according to the CIA estimates, this figure will increase to 250,000 by 1974; and 1974, incidentally, is the year when the proposed Fiat plant is scheduled to be in full production.

Finally, the report states that—

> Within the next decade at least, the Soviet leadership not only has no plans to mass produce automobiles in imitation of the West, but would strenuously resist internal pressure to do so.

So it would seem that those who have visions of massive traffic jams in Moscow and Russian citizens clamoring to "put a tiger in their tank" will have to wait a long time to see these dreams fulfilled.

The Soviet citizen will continue to be denied an automobile until Soviet leaders decree they may have one, and Soviet Premier Kosygin's speech to a meeting of the State Planning Committee on March 19, 1965, outlined his thoughts pretty clearly. He said:

> Everything has been done to deprive even the leaders of big enterprises and organizations the right to use passenger cars. Let the people ride only in busses.

So, in this particular instance, we are asked to supply automobiles that would be used as incentives for the bureaucratic elite to increase their production of high priority defense and military materials. We are supplying automobiles that would be exported to satellite countries and used as propaganda to demonstrate the strength and versatility of the Soviet economy. Furthermore, as aptly pointed out in Senator Mundt's recent dramatic speech on the same subject, automobile plants are easily and readily convertible into war plants.

Mr. President, just so that I am not misunderstood, I would like to state again for the Record that I am not totally opposed to the expansion of trade with the East. I am not unaware that such expansion might offer some substantial benefits to the United States. But I am concerned that any expansion be based on intelligent, realistic policies—policies that reflect what we have learned from experience in dealing with Eastern European nations, and not just a policy in search of the quick buck.

Our experience should have taught us that substantial volume of trade with Communist countries will do little to ameliorate the enmity between the East and the West. The best example of this is the period of the 4 years of the lend-lease plan when the United States shipped $10 billion worth of goods to the Soviet Union. The effect on our relations with the Soviets was negligible; and what did we receive in return? Nothing. The Library of Congress has reported the following on Communist indebtedness to the United States:

> The question of the Soviet indebtedness to the United States on the World War II lend-lease credits is still open. The highest Soviet offer for the settlement of the unconsumed civilian-use commodities account has been $300 million, while the lowest United States asking figure has been $800 million.
>
> In addition, the Soviets have not as yet settled the question of 133 U.S. merchant ships and miscellaneous navy and army watercraft since the days of World War II.

Mr. President, there is evidence that some of these ships—our ships—are being used by the Soviets to transport goods to the Communist North Vietnamese troops. And yet, the Library of Congress goes on to say that—

> The Soviets have repeatedly demanded that negotiation aiming at the settling of these [lend-lease] financial questions involve also questions of trade concessions and financial credit.

Here is an excellent example of Soviet reactions to extensive trade with the West. They have hedged on their financial obligations, demanding further concessions from us, while at the same time using our ships to supply the North Vietnamese to whom they have pledged extensive military and economic support.

In order to be effective and in order for the United States to receive the maximum benefit from trade with the East, our policies must demand political agreements as well as economic ones. In the past, our practiced policies have not stressed this, but our stated policies have come much closer. If we would enforce our stated objectives, the rest of the world would have greater respect for our position, and we would make more certain progress. These objectives, as stated by the Department of State, are:

First, to prevent the Communists from extending their influence and domain; second, to achieve agreements and understandings which reduce the danger of a devastating war; and third, to encourage evolution within the Communist world toward national independence, peaceful cooperation, and open societies.

Those are direct quotes from the Department of State.

In short, there is a political quid pro quo built into our trade objectives. Unfortunately, we have not enforced this; but there is no reason to call the objectives invalid and then open the floodgates of East-West trade, ignoring political concessions.

Mr. HANSEN. Mr. President, will the Senator yield?

Mr. DOMINICK. I yield.

Mr. HANSEN. I am most impressed with the speech that is being delivered by the distinguished junior Senator from Colorado. It seems to me that inherent throughout the theme of his speech are some underlying observations and conclusions that should shake us all.

I am one of those who believe that Russia and China are conducting a war by proxy.

The U.S.S.R. is buying world war at cut-rate prices, with only the most indirect threat to Russia, herself. They supply the hardware while the battered and unfortunate guerrillas furnish the bodies. When the dust is settled, there may be fewer guerrillas left, but those still alive will constitute another satellite regime to live under the benevolent hand of Russian centralized planning and to form, eventually, another economic cow to be milked by Russia.

It is also well to keep in mind the words of Hungarian Gen. L. Czinege, who boasted, "The weapons protecting Hanoi on that front had been designed and manufactured in Hungary."

I call attention to the fact that Russia is using martial law to control her people. The Russian Government has never learned how to manage its society, except under conditions of siege, real or simulated. This has made the matter of population control quite simple. All the state had to do is to enforce martial law within its borders, maintain total rule by decree, and everything else falls into line. Without the war psychosis, there would be no rationale in the minds of the Russian people for submitting to the dictatorial tenets of an only slightly modified police state.

I believe the Senator from Colorado has made a perfect case here this morning for us to take a second hard look at the trade policies that this Government—the administration and the State Department—is urging we build up. The Senator has made an excellent case with respect to the hot war and the cold war.

In talking about a hot war, there is ample evidence, as the Senator has so brilliantly pointed out this morning, that American servicemen are dying this minute in Vietnam, killed by weapons which are the direct result of the various forms of trade that we have fostered and encouraged with Communist satellite countries.

We talk about the cold war tensions, and it has been amply demonstrated that in time of relaxed tension—as it is referred to by those who argue for expanded East-West trade—communism has marked up some of its greatest advances.

I compliment the Senator from Colorado for his very incisive and most persuasive comments.

Mr. DOMINICK. I sincerely express my appreciation to the distinguished Senator from Wyoming. I am delighted with his response and with his analysis of this problem, which fits so closely with mine.

In closing, I simply wish to report some of the things that I believe we might ask for in terms of expansion of trade with the East—the political concessions I have talked about earlier.

In future trade negotiations with the Soviet bloc, the United States should act on the assumption that all goods are strategic; and, even more important, demands could and should be included for such concessions as—and I use these only as examples:

Payment or partial payment of lend-lease obligations.

Liberalization of travel restrictions within the U.S.S.R., so that American citizens can travel around that country the way most Soviet citizens can travel around this country.

Initial steps designed to increase the circulation of western literature and publications behind the Iron Curtain. This might include freedom of access by newspapermen and true reporting out of Communist countries, whether it be the Soviet Union, Czechoslovakia, Poland, or whatever.

Increasing access through the Berlin Wall.

Assistance in obtaining peace negotiations with North Vietnam, instead of using all our force to tie us up there while our people get murdered.

Curtailment of aid to Castro's Cuba while it exports aggression. With respect to this item, I point out that the President recently reported that after Glassboro—I cannot believe this—Mr. Kosygin went to Cuba to talk to Castro, to talk firmly with him about the fact that he should not export any more terrorism through Latin and South America.

Mr. President, I cannot understand it. I cannot understand how he could make such a statement, but he did, and it was made publicly. The fact is that Kosygin went there to encourage Castro to increase pressure in Latin America and South America. I shall make a speech with regard to that matter next week. Incidentally, next month they are going to have a new meeting of the Tri-Continental Congress, which plans the overthrow in Latin America and South America.

Mr. MUNDT. Mr. President, will the Senator yield?

Mr. DOMINICK. I shall be happy to yield in just a moment.

Mr. President, we might ask for freedom of free world news coverage, or any number of other considerations which bear on the tensions which surround our relationship with the Eastern European states and the Soviet Union.

Perhaps, Mr. President, in the face of such demands, the Soviets and some of the Eastern European states will decide they are no longer interested in building bridges with the West; but without these concessions, the cost for constructing these bridges will be ours and the toll booth will be on our side.

Let us reaffirm that this generation of leaders is unwilling to exchange freedom for a mess of potage.

Mr. MUNDT. Mr. President, I am very much afraid that the "mess of potage" which the distinguished Senator from Colorado mentioned as the only dividend we get from East-West trade at the present time is seriously stained with the blood of American soldiers.

Mr. DOMINICK. There is no doubt about it.

Mr. MUNDT. There is indeed no question about it. This war is being prolonged in Vietnam and our American casualties are being escalated by stepped-up exports by Russia to the Communists in Hanoi of increasingly sophisticated weapons which certainly are adding to the growing lists of dead and wounded among our American forces.

Mr. President, primarily I wish to congratuate the Senator from Colorado on a masterful presentation. I wish that his address could be read by every American. It deals with a completely unprecedented situation in American history. Never before in the history of this Republic have we had a President, acting as Commander in Chief in time of war, encouraging the exporters and war-time profiteers of this country to step up their shipments of supplies to the enemy, because when supplies are shipped to Russia, which are used as substitutes for other items to go to Hanoi, it is certainly trading with the enemy.

• • •

Mr. President, I wish (the first two) two paragraphs of the address of the distinguished Senator from Colorado could be pasted in the board room of every American exporting firm. I wish they could be pasted on the front door of every international bank in America. I wish they could be included in the textbooks, and especially all the books on economics, which are in use in our high schools, private schools, colleges, and universities.

• • •

Mr. DOMINICK. Mr. President, I wish to express appreciation for the warm and cordial reception my speech received from the distinguished Senator from South Dakota. It is encouraging to me that we have such allies in this matter, and I hope that we will be able to create sufficient interest in the American people so that the feelings of the American people will come through to the administration. I do not believe that is happening now. All we hear are statements with regard to the quick buck.

Mr. ALLOTT. Mr. President, I wish to congratulate my colleague on the speech he has just given in connection with East-West trade. His speech was fair and objective. He has raised many questions in his speech, but I think there is one thing that he has done today in his speech which will be of more lasting significance than any of the individual points raised. He has laid out a clear case for going slow, and causing America to look at the realities of East-West trade, and not just look at the fast buck.

Senate Joint Resolution 169--Introduction of Joint Resolution Relating to East-West Trade

Senator Walter S. Mondale

An advocate of a more liberal trade policy towards U. S. trade with Eastern Europe is Senator Mondale of Minnesota. In the following speech made in the Senate, he discusses the adverse impact which present policies have on American business, as well as his views toward most-favored-nation treatment for Eastern Europe, the problems of credit and finance in expanding East-West trade, and the impact of economic warfare.

Mr. President, I introduce today, for myself and Mr. Clark, Mr. Hartke, Mr. Inouye, Mr. Javits, Mr. Kennedy of Massachusetts, Mr. Kennedy of New York, Mr. McGovern, Mr. Morton, Mr. Moss, Mr. Pell, Mr. Percy, and Mr. Young of Ohio, a joint resolution on East-West trade. It is intended to indicate that the Senate favors East-West trade in peaceful goods. Trade relationships do not develop when they are plagued with uncertainties and with financing and licensing restrictions.

Mr. President, nearly 2 years ago President Johnson, in recognition of the vast possibilities for peaceful ties to be found in the development of trade between East and West, said:

> Our task is to achieve a reconciliation with the East, a shift from the narrow concept of co-existence to the broader vision of peaceful engagement. And I pledge you today that Americans now stand ready to do their part... We seek healthy economic and cultural relations with the Communist states.

His words increase in timeliness with the recent turn of events in Eastern Europe. Changes in Rumania, Czechoslovakia, and Poland indicate efforts at greater independence within Eastern Europe and better relationships with the West. A central premise of economic reform in these countries is the necessity sooner or later of large Western credits and a sharp increase in trade with the West.

Yet today the American environment for increased East-West trade is far from reliable. In response to the President's leadership, the executive branch of the Government has encouraged American business interest in Eastern Europe; Congress, meanwhile, has done its part to destroy the kind of confidence business and private investors must have to develop a market. This subtle psychological barrier arising from an uncertain Government policy is the worst barrier of all to American participation in East-West trade.

The harshest restrictions coming from Congress have ended Export-Import Bank assistance for exports to Communist countries. Beginning with the Foreign Assistance Appropriation Act of 1964, all foreign aid legislation has included a provision prohibiting the Export-Import Bank from guaranteeing export credits to any Communist country unless the President determines it to be in the national interest to do so. He determined they were.

But the President's discretion ended in February with final passage of the bill to extend the lending authority of the Export-Import Bank. A provision was added to the bill forbidding the use of Eximbank credit to finance sales of American goods to any country whose government trades with nations with which the United States is engaged in armed conflict–North Vietnam. Congress in effect denied credit guarantees to American companies for their exports to the nations of Eastern Europe. The amendment included exports to be used in Communist countries such as the American machinery for the Fiat plant in the Soviet Union.

Another amendment attached to the excise tax bill and intended to limit East-West trade even further narrowly met defeat on the Senate floor in late March. It would have set up an insuperable barrier to such trade by imposing upon any American businessman who engages in export trade with any Communist country supplying material to North Vietnam a tax equal to 20 percent of the total taxable income of the taxpayer for that year.

The presumptions behind the amendments are that the nations of Eastern Europe supply major assistance to North Vietnam and that the nations of Eastern Europe, without nonstrategic foodstuffs and goods from the United States, would have no other sources of supply.

Both presumptions are wrong. Our exports to Eastern Europe are primarily agricultural commodities. In turn, the Eastern European countries trade only to a limited extent with North Vietnam. Their aid tends to be a pro forma commitment, designed to diminish the embarrassment in the Communist world, and not a fundamental or material commitment to North Vietnam.

When Congress prevents American businessmen from supplying certain peaceful commodities to consumers in Eastern Europe, other nations are only too willing to fill the breach. By our actions, either the Eastern Europeans are thrown back into the arms of the Soviets, or the French and other Western Europeans take over all of the growing, consumer-oriented markets of Eastern Europe.

Mr. President, we must prevent efforts in Congress attempting to block the expansion of economic relationships between Eastern Europe and the United States. With this in mind, we intend to begin hearings in the International Finance Subcommittee of the Banking and Currency Committee on problems of East-West trade. As you know, the subcommittee has responsibility for the Eximbank and the export control regulations.

We hope the hearings will provide legislative suggestions for increasing trade in peaceful goods and a hearing record of use in educating Congress and our people about the difficulties our policies are creating for our businessmen, for our diplomatic efforts abroad, and for those Eastern European leaders who are struggling to establish their independence.

I believe that our policy should be aimed at encouraging independence and bringing the United States and the nations of Eastern Europe into a better relationship through increased trade.

I base my views on a 3-week study tour of Europe which I made for the Subcommittee on International Finance in January. I talked with government officials, businessmen, journalists, and our diplomats in Western and Eastern Europe—in Brussels, London, Paris, Geneva, Vienna, Bucharest, Moscow, Prague, and Warsaw—identifying some of the problems and possibilities of expanded trade with Eastern European nations and Russia.

Let me relate a few of the things I learned.

Western Europeans are astonished by the repressive attitude Congress has taken toward trade with Eastern Europe. But they are frank to admit that they benefit from the absence of our competition. The volume of East-West trade in 1966 exceeded $10 billion, and other Western countries accounted for 96 percent of it. In the market experiencing the most rapid growth in world trade, the United States trails behind Sweden and Austria, accounts for less than one-half the volume of Italy and of France, less than one-third the volume of Japan and of Britain, and less than one-sixth the volume of West Germany.

The main effect of our export control policies and restrictions on export credits is the loss of a great deal of business to Western European competitors. Trade with Communist countries is subject to Government control and limitation in the form of quota and licensing restrictions. The Export Control Act of 1949 authorizes the President to prohibit the exportation of commodities which would prove detrimental to the security of the United States. Although the number of items on the export control list was reduced several years ago, American export licensing is still more stringent than COCOM's—the instrument of our allies for assessing the strategic nature of exports. By maintaining uniform export control policies, the United States fails to take account of changes within Eastern Europe. For example, the Czechs are 80 to 100 percent dependent on the Soviet Union for oil and iron ore. We do not prevent them from obtaining oil and iron ore, we only determine the source.

Although Eastern Europeans complain that U.S. export control legislation is an important inhibiting factor in our trade, it is probably more the uncertainty and delay in receiving licenses than the actual restrictions which make this a significant factor in trade relations. While the American businessman is waiting for approval of his proposed contract, his West German counterpart supplies the goods.

Since 1964 the Export-Import Bank has been prohibited from lending its own funds for the financing of American exports to any Communist country and since February, as I mentioned earlier, the Bank has been prohibited from guaranteeing or insuring loans extended by private lenders to finance American exports to Communist countries. Before the Eximbank credits to Communist countries were cut off, Russia and Eastern European countries had to prove their credit worthiness to a greater extent than was required of other nations.

These precautions are needless and counterproductive. There has never been default on any Western transaction with any Eastern European nation. The denial of Export-Import credits prohibits any trade which is not paid for on the spot. Goods and industries normally are bought on terms as long as 8 years and more. Especially for a country such as Romania engaged in making great investments, cash deals are impossible.

Romania's dramatic increase of trade with the Western nations, her rapid pace of industrialization, and her corresponding economic independence within the Eastern bloc has been made possible by the willingness of Western trading nations to extend substantial medium- and long-term credits supported by Government guarantees or insurance. The American hold-back in extending longer credit terms arises from the cold war conviction that the extension of longer credit terms represents an indirect extension of aid to our adversaries.

On the other hand Eastern countries have felt free to extend credit for the sale of hydroelectric or industrial equipment in the West, and the countries of Western Europe and Japan have extended credits in the 10- to 12-year range for sales to the East. In addition the British and Italians guarantee transactions at much lower rates than the Eximbank can.

Export-Import guarantees are vital if American suppliers are to compete in Eastern European markets. The lack of such a guarantee will be a serious barrier to American participation in East-West trade—and as long as this barrier remains in effect, we can expect to see American exports lose ground in their current 4 percent of the market.

I must add that American corporations are trading a great deal more with Eastern Europe and Russia than official figures show. This trade, which may run as high as $300 or $400 million a year, is carried on through American subsidiaries in Western Europe. These subsidiaries are eager to expand their trade with the Eastern European nations, and Eastern Europeans are eager to purchase goods of the quality developed with American know-how. Ironically, the balance-of-payments measures which limit American investment in Europe mean that a large increase in the American share of the Eastern European market will not be forthcoming through the mechanism of American subsidiaries.

Eastern Europeans, despite their inclination to favor American quality, are reluctant now to look to the United States for trade. They have learned that they simply cannot depend upon American trade. An Eastern European trade minister may be taking his life in his hands—certainly his job—by committing himself to a trade deal. When we back off, he pays the price. A high official in the Polish Foreign Ministry told me that there is great uncertainty there about U.S. trade policy; he cited the constant threat of the removal of most-favored-nation treatment for Poland along with Yugoslavia, Poland receives the benefits of lower tariffs under most-favored-nation arrangements with the United States—changes in Public Law 480, and the recent restrictions on the Export-Import Bank.

With the exceptions of Yugoslavia and Poland, Eastern European nations pay the prohibitively high Smoot-Hawley rates for their products. The lack of most-favored-nation treatment, a routine concession to most nations of the world, is a serious barrier to U.S. participation in East-West trade. A high Romanian trade official told me that lack of most-favored-nation treatment by the United States means that Romanian exports are directed to Western Europe, thereby limiting the potential for import of goods from the United States.

The most-favored-nation clause has been gradually extended to most of the Eastern countries by a very large number of Western countries. Refusal to apply it may be regarded as an exception except in the case of the United States. The President submitted an East-West trade relations bill of 1966 to give the Executive authority to negotiate trade agreements extending most-favored-nation treatment to European Communist states; Congress should enact such legislation.

Perhaps the most formidable opposition any American business wishing to trade with Eastern Europe faces is the threat of attacks or an actual campaign by certain groups which fear any contacts at all with Eastern Europe. Despite the State Department's efforts to reassure American businessmen, the groups inject themselves into the operation of our foreign policy through intimidation of individual companies.

Unfortunately, the campaign launched by Young Americans for Freedom against the Firestone Rubber Co.'s proposed synthetic rubber plant, a plant approved by our Office of Export Control—and Firestone's consequent withdrawal of its plans—left Romania with little faith in arrangements with American companies. At a time when Romania is attempting to assert her independence, this lack of faith becomes critical.

The apprehensions about East-West trade center on our participation in the economic advancement of a rival economic system. The presumption is that Eastern European countries cannot achieve economic success without us. The Soviet Union's achievements in space and the growing volume of trade on the part of Western Europeans with Eastern Europe show the weaknesses of that theory.

There is little support in either Western or Eastern Europe, among Government officials, economic and political experts, American diplomatic officers, and American and European businessmen for the fears commonly expressed in the United States that trade with Eastern Europe strengthens communism. Indeed, quite the opposite is felt to be the case—that America's restrictive policies force Eastern European nations to depend on Russia, and therefore strengthen Moscow's failing attempt to keep her former satellites dependent on her.

The time has come when we must deal head-on with the recurring myth of the efficacy of economic warfare. This is no longer a matter of question—hard evidence indicates that economic warfare measures are ineffective even under ideal "laboratory conditions."

In fact, economic warfare may have exactly the opposite effect from that we intend. By withholding trade, we encourage a nation to develop its own resources. Rigid export restrictions result in a denial forcing the creation of new industrial capacity to produce the item denied.

On the other hand, freely encouraged trade creates a certain dependency. Western Europeans today are chafing at the "technological gap" which grew from European overdependence upon U.S. industry and technology.

Internally, Western trade can have a profound effect on the nature of life in Russia and in Eastern Europe. An Italian official pointed out to me the implications of the Fiat contract with the Russians: they will need repairs, gasoline, highways, and insurance, all factors in social change.

As Communist economic policy devolves, producers may become more responsive to market demands. If Eastern European countries are to participate in greater trade with the United States, they will have to pay for their imports with increased exports since credit is difficult to obtain. To export, their products must be competitive with the highly sophisticated Western products and they must develop sales techniques which will meet Western consumer demands.

The United States can assist in a variety of ways. One is by the above-mentioned loosening of restrictions on Export-Import Bank credit. Another is by helping these nations find markets in the United States or elsewhere in the world. In many respects the Eastern European nations are more comparable to the developing nations of the world than to the Western European nations and the United States. A dialog to help the Eastern Europeans find markets is engaged in everywhere except the United States.

Eastern Europe is at an economic crossroads. It is not at all certain that they must move toward Western-type relationships. In chaos and with little encouragement from us they could go back to the older practices.

Changes are coming faster than we can keep track of them in Eastern Europe. A power struggle appears underway in Poland. With a change of government in Czechoslovakia have come astounding liberalizations in the areas of free speech and press. Romania's continued participation in the activities of the Soviet bloc's military and economic alliances is in question. And last week the Soviet Government announced ratification of a consular convention with the United States.

At the moment many of these changes are rebounding to favor the West. The Soviets canceled a quarterly delivery of wheat to Czechoslovakia; the Czechs turned to Canada for wheat to replace the Soviet imports. Instead of wheat shipments, the Russians offered the Czechoslovaks a $400 million loan in hard currency to be paid back with goods which Moscow buys from the West. The Czechs intend to use the loan to buy construction equipment and licenses for the chemical industry in the West, to expand warehouse and transport facilities, and to build hotels for Western tourists.

And while we are watching the current events in Eastern Europe, we must not forget that trade opportunities there provide a chance to add exports which assist a favorable balance of payments. In March, for the first time in 5 years, the United States had a trade deficit—our exports were outstripped by our imports. Now is not the time when we can afford to overlook the fastest growing market in the world—Eastern Europe.

We need to examine the relevancy of our trade policies—their relevancy to the events in Eastern Europe, to our payments problems, and to the competitive position of American business. It is time to dispel the public misconceptions saddling American participation in East-West trade with unnecessary and unproductive restrictions. Most important of all we must indicate that the Senate believes increased East-West trade in peaceful goods to be in the best interests of the United States. Only then will we overcome the subtle psychological barrier to such trade arising from an uncertain Government policy.

Winds of change are blowing across Eastern Europe, but the breezes rarely enter Congress. We must respond to these changes. If we do not, the nations of Eastern Europe and of the West will correctly decide that we have shunned an opportunity to alter the economic dependency with the Communist bloc. History will make the same judgment.

I ask unanimous consent that the joint resolution be printed in the Record.

The PRESIDING OFFICER. The joint resolution will be received and appropriately referred; and without objection, the joint resolution will be printed in the Record.

The joint resolution (S.J. Res. 169) relating to East-West trade, introduced by Mr. Mondale (for himself and other Senators), was received, read twice by its title, referred to the Committee on Banking and Currency, and ordered to be printed in the Record, as follows:

S.J. Res. 169

Whereas current export credit and other restrictions on United States trade in peaceful goods with Eastern Europe impede the response of the United States to changes within the Communist world; and

Whereas the changes in Eastern Europe are vital to the maintenance of United States objectives in building a peaceful, democratic world; and

Whereas an increase in United States exports to Eastern Europe will assist in meeting the United States balance of payments problems; and

Whereas public misconceptions plague efforts to expand East-West trade; Therefore be it

Resolved by the Senate and House of Representatives of the United States of America in Congress assembled, That it is the sense of the Congress that the Export Control Act regulations and the Export-Import Bank financing restrictions should be examined and modified to promote the best interests of the United States by permitting an increase in trade in peaceful goods between the United States and the nations of Eastern Europe.

Statement on U.S. Policy Toward East-West Trade

The United States Council of the International Chamber of Commerce issued the following statement on U.S. policy toward East-West trade on April 21, 1967, and transmitted it to President Lyndon B. Johnson.

The U.S. Council believes, for the reasons set forth in the next six paragraphs, that the United States should pursue a more flexible policy than in the past towards trade with Eastern Europe. To this end, the U.S. Council supports enactment of the proposed East-West Trade Relations Act and offers a further series of recommendations in the balance of this statement for measures it would urge the U.S. Government to take over a period of time should the climate for a regularization of trade between East and West continue to improve.

The recent NATO meetings decisively reflected the changes in East-West relations which have taken place in the last twenty years. After a generation of concentration on the defense of the West against the East, including commercial and economic policies oriented to that objective, the emphasis at this session and in the summary communique issued at its conclusion was almost exclusively on commercial policies in keeping with the developing detente between East and West. The noticeable improvement in relations among Western nations and those of Eastern Europe certainly has at least some of its origins in the growing coincidence of the long-run interests of the United States and Russia in peaceful conditions in the world at large. To the extent that this coincidence is recognized by both parties, there is reason to hope that recent guarded progress toward normalization of commercial contacts will prove durable.

The gradual relaxation of cold-war tensions has already brought about a substantial increase in trade flows between Eastern European countries and those of the rest of the world. Both industrialized and developing countries have participated in this growth. However, in comparison with other industrialized nations, U.S. trade with the Eastern European nations has remained very small. During 1965, for example, Western Europe and Japan exported $3.8 billion in goods to the Eastern European countries, excluding Yugoslavia, and imported almost $4.5 billion for them. U.S. figures for this same period were only $139 million in exports and $138 million in imports. As *The Economist* put it: "The communist countries remain the one market where America virtually leaves the field clear to Western Europe and Japan." The same article points out that Comecon (a limited Eastern European effort to mirror Common Market economic collaboration) includes within its perimeter over 330 million people—almost 60 million more than the countries of the EEC and the EFTA combined.

The U.S. Council does not believe that controls over strategic materials can at present be relaxed, but it does believe that the argument against trading with the USSR and other Eastern European countries on the grounds that such trade might contribute to their economic power is of limited validity. Trade by definition does not take place unless benefits accrue to both parties. If one nation refuses to participate, insofar as the second party can find another trading partner, the loss is entirely sustained by the country refusing to do business. This is the situation into which the United States has drifted. While other countries of the world are increasingly enjoying the benefits of expanded two-way trade with the Eastern European countries, our policies to a great extent deny these markets to our exporters and deny to our consumers those products in which the Eastern European countries are becoming competitive.

As other industrialized countries expand their markets within the Eastern countries, there is a natural tendency for the exporter's technology and standards to be accepted and adhered to in the importing nation. The longer that U.S. exporters refrain from participating in the markets of Eastern Europe the more firmly established in those markets will be the standards and technology of our competitors in other Western industrialized countries—and the more difficult will it be for American companies to enter these markets in the future.

From the U.S. view, the most fundamental gain of all may well be the imprint inevitably made by successful and growing daily commercial operations, carrying as they do a continuous effective argument for the freer contractual trading policies which they inculcate.

Accordingly, the U.S. Council believes that the time has come for the United States to do what it can to make possible a regularization of trade and payments with the Eastern European countries. New opportunities are in fact arising for the U.S. to negotiate with the countries of Eastern Europe for modification on their part of policies which have rigidly reinforced the differences between our economic systems. We should be ready to take advantage of these opportunities.

Specifically, as noted above, the U.S. Council supports enactment of the East-West Trade Relations Act of 1966. Eastern European nations have more and more been pursuing individual national policies over recent years. They no longer constitute a monolithic bloc. The United States should be in a position to forge new relationships with these countries individually. New economic policies are being adopted by Russia and the other Eastern European countries designed to make their production more responsive to market considerations and their prices more reflective of costs. These policies, if successfully implemented, should gradually result in the production of more goods marketable in the United States and Western markets generally. The President should be empowered to grant most-favored-nation status to Eastern nations, enabling their goods to be imported into the U.S. at the same tariff rates as those of other countries of the world. Since tariffs at present have little meaning in the controlled economies of Eastern Europe, other concessions should be sought in exchange, such as market access for U.S. products, the protection of industrial property rights, the right to more direct contact between U.S. businessmen and the ultimate consumer/supplier, and satisfactory arbitral arrangements for the settlement of commercial disputes.

The extension of most-favored-nation treatment to Eastern European countries should enable the U.S. consumer to benefit from competitive imports from the Eastern European countries, and, at the same time, enable those countries to earn the foreign exchange with which to purchase U.S. goods. United States suppliers should be able to participate to the fullest extent consistent with our national security in the markets of Eastern Europe. To permit this participation there should be further removals of non-strategic items from the Export Control List, as in the case of 400 items recently removed. Items which are freely available elsewhere in the world should not require individual export licenses in the United States.

The U.S. Council would not like to see a so-called credit race develop among Western suppliers to Eastern Europe. It recognizes, however, that recently credits of longer than five years duration have been granted in other industrialized countries. It does not believe that U.S. industry should be precluded from bidding on an equal basis with its competitors in other nations. It is recognized that a shortage of hard currencies in many ways places the countries of Eastern Europe in a position similar to that of many less developed countries, and that if sales of heavy equipment are to take place longer-term credits, more realistically representative of periods of amortization, may be essential. Bearing in mind that such exports are beneficial to the United States, the U.S. Council accordingly urges that U.S. suppliers be enabled to match the terms offered by their competitors. To this end, the credit guarantee policies of the Export-Import Bank should be similarly normalized to permit credits to be extended to buyers in Eastern European countries which are competitive with those of other Western suppliers, and the full use of these facilities should be encouraged. In principle, we believe that Eastern European governments should equally extend adequate credit to Western buyers, and would recommend that the Administration attempt to include provisions for reciprocal credit in trade agreements negotiated with individual countries.

The recent trend toward internationalization of production has not left Eastern Europe untouched. In the past few years a number of agreements have been concluded under which individual Western firms have undertaken to participate in the actual production of the USSR and other countries of Eastern Europe. American firms, which are prime initiators and leaders in the field of overseas production, should be able to participate in the opportunities which the large and growing markets of Eastern Europe present. U.S. government policy should support private efforts to respond to these markets. Where the underlying transaction warrants, credit terms should be as favorable as for other areas; similarly, the program of government guarantees against political risks ought in principle to include these markets. More systematic payment arrangements than now exist would be desirable, if not essential, to the growth of producing arrangements. To assist in the determination of credit-worthiness, and thus to expand the use of credits in business transactions, countries of Eastern Europe should be encouraged to publish financial data similar to that published by Western countries—and by Yugoslavia—covering gold and foreign exchange reserves, total foreign indebtedness, and repayment schedules.

Many, if not most, of the problems encountered in attempting to increase peaceful commerce between East and West stem from the lack of participation of the Eastern countries in Western institutions. The present move toward association on the part of Poland with the General Agreement on Tariffs and Trade should be encouraged. It is to be hoped that other Eastern European countries will follow suit. Compliance on their part with the general rules of GATT in their external trade would do much to regularize the conditions for their Western trading partners.

Most important, however, to a return to normal commercial relations, as it was for the industrialized countries of the West after World War II, is eventual currency convertibility. Every opportunity should be pressed to broaden convertibility with the rest of the world. Increased transferability among Eastern European currencies should, where possible, be encouraged as an interim step. The recent addition of $33 million of gold and convertible currencies to the fixed capital of the Comecon's bank, the International Bank for Economic Cooperation, should be welcomed. While there is little that can be done on our part to hasten this process, the U.S. Council recommends that the U.S. Government attempt to emphasize in its negotiations with Eastern European governments the benefits accruing from early convertibility. The question of Eastern countries' membership in the I.M.F. and the I.B.R.D. could usefully be restudied by member countries and by Eastern countries. It is in the interest of the United States to see these countries assume the responsibilities that are inherent in membership in these organizations.

A Reply to "Statement on U.S. Policy Toward East-West Trade"

The following letter is President Johnson's reply to the position statement by the Committee on Commercial Policy of the United States Chamber of Commerce.

THE WHITE HOUSE

Washington

March 24, 1967

Mr. Christopher H. Phillips, President
United States Council of the International Chamber of Commerce, Inc.
1212 Avenue of the Americas
New York, New York

Dear Mr. Phillips:

I very much appreciated your letter transmitting the Council's policy statement on East-West trade. I know that the conclusions and recommendations are the products of profound study. All Americans can take pride in the creative spirit in which you, Mr. Watson, Mr. Steele, and your other associates have approached this important question.

In my judgment, the statement is an eloquent expression of the case for giving the President the tools necessary to work for the improvement in East-West relations which is the best hope for a lasting peace. As you point out, increased peaceful trade with Eastern Europe and the Soviet Union will serve our broad political objectives as well as our economic interests. Peaceful economic competition builds a common stake in stability. The day that it replaces the arms race as the primary form of East-West rivalry will be a landmark in the history of man.

Of course, we shall have to feel our way carefully. The East-West trade legislation I have proposed was recommended by a distinguished group of businessmen, economists, and labor leaders; it is carefully designed to be used only when it is clear that our interests are served. It provides for trade, not aid. It does not affect the system of controls on the export of strategic goods. It does not lower our guard; it simply permits us to grant the same tariff treatment to the Soviet Union and Eastern Europe which we grant all other nations if, and to the degree that, it will further our interests.

The issue reduces to a simple question: should we be prepared to do our part to bridge the chasm between East and West which has so long threatened the peace of the world? Trade alone will not be sufficient to this task. But it will certainly be necessary. I believe, as you do, that we must be ready to respond as opportunities arise. The East-West Trade Act which I have proposed to the Congress would equip us to do so.

The policy statement of the United States Council of the International Chamber of Commerce is further powerful testimony to the wisdom of this course. Your countrymen are deeply in your debt.

My best personal regards to you and your fellow Council members.

Sincerely,

United States Export Controls

Phillip D. Grub and David A. Peterson

The realities of industrial production throughout the world have changed significantly since the present U.S. export controls were enacted. Two decades ago the United States was the sole supplier of the world's technological and advanced capital equipment. Today more than a dozen countries compete effectively for their share of this market. The following article by one of the editors, co-authored with an expert in international law, outlines various legislation that has had an impact on U.S. trade overseas.

The United States has traditionally restricted exports only during time of war and special emergency. Throughout World Wars I and II, the President was given authority to control all exports to all destinations. In all other cases prior to 1954, export controls were limited to war materials or to articles exported to countries with which we were at war or which were at war with others, or in which a state of civil strife existed.[1]

At the present time, trade between the United States and Communist countries is subject to a variety of legislative restrictions. Some of the restrictions, such as those under the Export Control Act, are discretionary; however, most are of a mandatory nature. These legislative measures may be in the form of general restrictions on trade, such as the prohibition of most-favored-nation treatment and export controls; they may be restrictions on particular commodities such as furs and bamboo pipe, or arms and other strategic items; or they may be restrictions on particular types of transactions, including transactions with U.S. government financing and private credit transactions. This paper provides a legal framework within which any relevant discussion of East-West trade must take place and is based upon an analysis of present legislative provisions in the United States pertinent to trade with Communist countries.

Trading With The Enemy Act (1917)

The Trading With the Enemy Act of October 6, 1917, has been regarded in succeeding years as an act of permanent legislation which could be applied in the event that the United States was again involved in war. Due to the increasing importance of economic warfare in World War II, the belligerents began as early as 1938 to reexamine and revise their legislation regarding trading with the enemy.[2] Great Britain, Canada, Australia, New Zealand, Union of South Africa, Egypt, France and Germany all issued new and more extensive acts.

The threshold question raised by this legislation is who is to be included within the concept "enemy." As in the Trading With the Enemy legislation of World War I, the Acts of different countries noted above, provided expressly that *government* of enemy states are to be considered "enemies."

Section 2(b) of the United States Act defines "enemy" to include "the government of any nation with which the United States is at war, or any political or municipal subdivision thereof, or any officer, official, agent, or agency thereof."[3] In 1942, the U.S. Supreme Court in *Ex parte Don Ascanio Colonna*, decided while a state of war existed between Italy and the United States, held that the Italian Government was deemed an enemy within the meaning of the Trading With the Enemy Act. An important consequence of this designation, according to the *Colonna Case*, is that "war suspends the right of enemy plaintiffs to prosecute actions in our Courts."[4]

The test determining the enemy character of *individuals* has rested upon residence within enemy territory, carrying on business in such territory, nationality and loyalty. The term "enemy territory" has been understood to include territory occupied or controlled by the enemy. "Residence," as the decisive test of the enemy character of an individual, is used in Section 2(a) of the Trading With the Enemy Act, which states: "resident within the territory. . .of any nation with which the United States is at war." This term, however, was superceded in the fields of freezing regulations and censorship of communications by replacing "resident within enemy territory" by the term "individual within the territory."[5]

With the adoption of residence or commercial domicil in enemy territory as the test to determine as "enemy" within the meaning of the Trading With the Enemy Act, the character of an enemy was no longer governed by nationality, but also

[1]See: Harold J. Berman and John R. Garson, "United States Export Controls–Past, Present, and Future," *Columbia Law Review*, (May 1967); Frederick Davis "The Regulation and Control of Foreign Trade," *Columbia Law Review* 1428 (1966); also: *Yale Law Journal* "Constitutionality of Export Controls," (Nov. 1966).

[2]Italy, though entering the war in 1940, had enacted War and Neutrality Legislation as early as 1938, which included provision on the treatment of enemy nationals and enemy goods, and economic relations with the enemy.

[3]40 *Stat.* 411.

[4]314 U.S. 510, 511, (Jan. 5, 1942). For further discussion of this see: 42 *Col. L. Rev.* 105, and 30 *Col. L. Rev.* 358.

[5]See: Note, "Foreign Funds Control Through Presidential Freezing Orders," 41 *Col. L. Rev.* (1941) 1039, 1046.

included a person of any or no nationality who is voluntarily resident or carrying on business in enemy territory.

Due to the development of economic warfare during World War II, emphasis was also placed upon loyalty, and even a belligerent's own nationals were subject to control, whether or not the individuals were enemies within the meaning of the Act. Even American citizens have been treated as enemies for certain purposes of Trading With the Enemy legislation, inasmuch as they appeared as potential enemy sympathizers in wartime. Early in World War II, it was observed that "the ideological and racial nature of the present war appears, in many respects, to have cut across national lines and destroyed the value of old distinctions based upon nationality."[6] The administrative determination of the enemy character of individuals, without regard to their nationality, is fraught with constitutional implications. The cold war context within which such questions are framed today does not make the question any less difficult.

Under the Trading With the Enemy Act of World War I, a *corporation* may qualify as an enemy according to any one of three decisive tests: (1) organization under the law of an enemy state, (2) residence in enemy territory, and (3) control by enemies.

Under American law "speaking generally, the status of a corporation as being either foreign or domestic is determined solely by the place of its origin, without reference to the residence of its stockholders or incorporators, or the place where its business is transacted."[7] The determination of the enemy character of a corporation by virtue of its incorporation under enemy law or its carrying on business in enemy or enemy occupied territory has also prevailed in various court cases and regulations issued under the Trading With the Enemy Act, as amended.

Although enacted 50 years ago, the Trading With the Enemy Act is by no means a dead issue. The Act was employed by President Truman in December 1950, following the entrance of communist Chinese forces into Korea, as the basis for regulations designed to prevent virtually all economic dealings with Communist China and North Korea.[8] In 1953, another set of regulations was also issued under the Act, controlling exports to communist countries by persons subject to the jurisdiction of the United States and of goods produced outside the United States.[9] In 1961, the Trading With the Enemy Act also provided the foundation for the imposition of controls on economic dealings with Cuba similar to those previously made applicable to China.[10]

Export Control Act (1949)

A major source of control over U.S. exports to Communist countries is the Export Control Act of 1949, as amended. Probably no other present legislation gives the President such wide ranging authority, subject to only vague "foreign policy" and "national security and welfare," criteria. It provides for discretionary authority in the President to limit or prevent the export from the United States of commodities (a) which are in short supply; (b) the shipment of which would be inconsistent with the foreign policy of the United States; and (c) the shipment of which would impair national security.

The penumbra of this Act seems to include all exports from the United States regardless of destination. The President has delegated his authority under the Export Control Act to the Secretary of Commerce, while the 1950, 1953 and 1961 regulations issued under the Trading With the Enemy Act are administered by the Treasury Department and under the Mutual Security Act of 1954, the Department of State administers the licensing system regulating the export of arms, ammunition, and other implements of war. Under present regulations of the Secretary of Commerce, most exports to the Soviet Union and the satellite countries require special licenses, and such licenses are denied for any export which is determined to make a significant contribution to the military or economic potential of the Communist countries. The general license list for the U.S.S.R. and most of the Eastern European Communist states has been expanded significantly in recent years, but Rumania and Poland have even larger lists of items which may be exported under general license. These regulations could, however, be changed by direction of the President.

In 1948, a Senate Committee investigating the administration of export controls reported that the national security aspects of our export control program are of transcendent importance, particularly in view of the present activities of the Soviet Union and its satellites. This highlighted a shift from a scarcity

[6]Note, "Alien Enemies and Japanese-Americans: A Problem of Wartime Controls," 51 *Yale Law Journal* 1318, 1337 (1942).
[7]20 *Corpus Juris Secundum* § 1784, p. 10, (1940).
[8]The Foreign Assets Control Regulations of Dec. 17, 1950, were issued in conjunction with the emergency declared by the President on Dec. 16, 1950, and included both imports and exports, and financial transactions. See: 31 *C.F.R.* §§ 500 101-808 (1968).

[9]The Transaction Control Regulations, 31 *C.F.R.* §§ 505.01-60 (1968), were issued in 1953, to supplement the export controls exercised by the Department of Commerce over direct exports from the U.S. to the USSR and Eastern Europe.
[10]The Cuban Import Regulations of February 6, 1962, were replaced by the Cuban Assets Control Regulations on July 9, 1963. See: 31 *C.F.R.* §§ 515, 101-808 (1968).

rationale to one of security controls. When armed conflict broke out in Korea in June 1950, doubts as to the wisdom of maintaining a comprehensive system of export controls were dispelled. During the 1950's and early 1960's, there was very little opposition to the systematic use of export controls as a foreign policy weapon, either in the Congress or in the business community, and while still treated as a temporary measure, the Act was renewed without amendment in 1951, 1953, 1956, 1958 and 1960. It is scheduled to come before Congress in 1969.

In 1962, the Commerce Department strongly urged that the Act be made permanent. The reasons advanced were (a) that the Act would undoubtedly be needed in the future, (b) friendly countries could be more easily persuaded to maintain their export controls at an appropriate level if a more permanent system existed, and (c) a permanent Act would attract more qualified administrators. This was during the same year in which President Kennedy referred to the Trade Expansion Act as "the most important international piece of legislation. . .affecting economics since the passage of the Marshall Plan." The Senate bill adopted this request, but the House bill granted only a three year extension, and it was the House amendment which was followed in a conference substitute.

Congress, on its own initiative, substantially broadened the scope of the controls. An amendment set forth the Congressional finding that certain materials continued in short supply at home and abroad, therefore affecting "the welfare of the domestic economy" and have "an important bearing upon the fulfillment of the foreign policy of the United States," and further that "unrestricted export of materials without regard to their potential military *and economic* significance may adversely affect the national security of the United States." Also, that requests to export "articles, materials, or supplies, including technical data. . ." "to any nation or combination of nations threatening the national security of the United States if the President shall determine that such export makes a significant contribution to the military *or economic* potential of such nation or nations which would prove detrimental to the national security *and welfare* of the United States," would be denied (emphasis added).[11] These amendments, which were opposed by the Kennedy Administration, underscored the broad economic aspects of what had come to be called "strategic," in contradistinction to "military," controls. They also marked the widespread sentiment that exports of nonmilitary items which might assist the industrial development of the Soviet Union would be detrimental to the national security of the United States.[12]

In 1962, Congress also amended the Act in an attempt to meet various problems created by the less restrictive policies of other noncommunist countries which worked in opposition to U.S. export controls. Congress, therefore, declared it to be the policy of the United States "to formulate, reformulate, and apply such controls to the maximum extent possible in cooperation with all nations with which the United States has defense treaty commitments, and to formulate a unified commercial and trading policy to be observed by the noncommunist-dominated nations or areas in their dealings with the communist-dominated nations."[13]

In 1962, a further amendment declared United States policy to be "to use its economic resources and advantages in trade with communist-dominated nations to further the national security and foreign policy objectives of the United States."[14] The Department of Commerce has given this language the following interpretation:

> . . .Having in mind that the economic resources and advantages in trade possessed by the United States obviously includes much more than the power to impose export controls, the Department construes the scope of this amendment as transcending the preexisting statutory authority and responsibility vested in the Department under the Act. . . (The Department construes this amendment as providing congressional policy authorization to vary the scope and severity of export control to particular countries from time to time, as national security and foreign policy interests require. . .[15]

The Administration sought to make the Act permanent legislation in 1965, but Congress again rejected this proposal; however, it did extend the expiration date for four years, the longest in the history of the Act, to June 30, 1969. The Act was amended at that time to include a statement that it is the policy of the United States "to oppose restrictive trade practices or boycotts fostered or imposed by foreign countries against other countries friendly to the United States" and "to encourage domestic export firms to refuse to take any action which has the effect of furthering such restrictive trade practices or boycotts."[16] The President's authority under Section 3(a) of the Act to prohibit or curtail exportations from the

---

[11] 50 U.S.C. App. § 2021 (b) (1964); 50 U.S.C. App. § 2023 (a), (1964), as amended (Supp. I, 1965). (Emphasis added).

[12] See: *Hearings on Extension of Export Control Act of 1949,* Subcomm. of the House Comm. on Banking and Currency, 87th Cong., 2nd Sess. 21, 27 (1962). Also: Berman and Garson, *op. cit.*, p. 801.

[13] 50 U.S.C. App. § 2022 (1964), as amended (Supp. I, 1965).

[14] *Ibid.*

[15] *Export Control,* 61st Quarterly Report 5 (1962).

[16] 50 U.S.C. App. § 2022 (4) (Supp. I, 1965).

United States was extended to cover "any other information," in addition to technical data.[17]

To implement the broad policy objectives surrounding the Export Control Act, the Office of Export Control has created a veritable thicket of regulations concerned with what may be exported to what countries under what conditions and by what procedures. To trace these provisions would be an exhausting task, however, the following examples give an overall view of the types of controls that do exist and illustrate the complex network of export controls in effect today. At the heart of these enormously complex regulations lies the fact that the United States exerts a substantially greater degree of control over exports to Communist countries than that exercised by any other government. This policy determination is complicated by the fact that the United States must guard against the possibility that goods or technical data permitted to be shipped to "friendly" countries may be transshipped from those countries to less friendly or "unfriendly" countries. A second factor which increases the complexity of export controls is the extreme refinement in the degree of restriction upon exports to different countries.

General and Validated Licenses

A *general license* is a general authorization to export certain types of commodities to certain destinations for which no application is required and for which no document is granted or issued.

The exporter presents to the Customs Office at the place of exit a sworn statement describing the nature and quantity of the commodity or commodities and containing the names and addresses of all parties to the transaction, including the ultimate destination and the ultimate consignee of the goods. The Shipper's Export Declaration, all bills of lading and commercial invoices must contain an anti-diversion notice stating: "United States law prohibits disposition of these commodities to (names of countries to which the commodities may not be shipped under general license) unless otherwise authorized by the United States."[18]

All anti-diversion notices under general license presently prohibit disposition of commodities to Communist China, North Korea, Communist controlled areas of Vietnam, and Cuba. In addition, diversion to Macao and Hong Kong is usually prohibited as is diversion to Communist countries of Eastern Europe and the Soviet Union, since many items may not be shipped in the first place to those destinations under general licenses. In 1965, exports to Southern Rhodesia fell under these controls.

A *validated license* is a document issued to an exporter by the Department of Commerce authorizing the exportation of a particular commodity or technical data, to a consignee in a particular country for a particular use. The applicant must be a United States exporter or the U.S. agent of a foreign importer, subject to United States jurisdiction. There must be a specific transaction contemplated and the names and addresses of all parties must be submitted not only the ultimate destination and ultimate consignee, but also the "end use" of the commodity must be submitted. Special variations of this licensing form include "Technical Data Licenses," "Project Licenses," "Blanket Licenses," "Periodic Requirements Licenses," and "Time Limit Licenses."[19]

The exporter applying for a validated license must indicate on a customs office form: the name and address of the applicant, the person named as purchaser, the ultimate consignee, any intermediate consignees, the country of final destination, the quantity shipped and a description of the commodities, unit price, name and address of any foreign principals involved in the transaction and producer of the commodities to be exported. It is also provided that the "end use of commodities or technical data covered by this application will be an important factor in determining issuance of (a) license."[20]

Anti-diversion notices stamped on the Shipper's Export Declaration, bills of lading and invoices in transactions under validated licenses are more stringent than those under a general license. It states: "These commodities issued by the United States for ultimate destination (name of country). Diversion contrary to United States law prohibited." Where distribution or resale to a second country is approved by the Office of Export Control, the notice will read: "These commodities licensed by the United States for ultimate destination (name of country) and for distribution or resale in (name of country or countries). Diversion contrary to United States law prohibited."[21]

Country Controls

The United States has increasingly sought to adapt its export restrictions to the wide variation in its political relations with various countries, relaxing or tightening controls to express the U.S. view of the economic and political developments abroad. It goes without saying that this is at best a complex task and one in which tangible results may be difficult to identify.

From 1950 until 1957, the U.S. distinguished for purposes of export control between: (a) Communist China and North Korea; (b) all other Communist countries except Yugoslavia; (c) all noncommunist countries (including Yugoslavia) not in the Western

[17] 50 U.S.C. App. § 2023 (a) (Supp. I, 1965).
[18] 15 *C.F.R.* III, 370.1, (1967); E.R. 379.10 (c) (2) (III).

[19] 15 *C.F.R.* III, 372.2, (1967), E.R. 374-377.
[20] 15 *C.F.R.* III, 372.5, (1967); E.R. 372.
[21] E.R. 379.10 (c) (2) (I) and (II).

Hemisphere; (d) all Western Hemisphere countries except Canada, and (e) Canada. Goods designated as "strategic," contained on a so-called Positive List, could not be exported without a validated license to any country except Canada, for fear of possible transshipment.

The use of country controls is illustrated by the following examples: In August 1957, after the "coup" that brought the Gomulka regime to power in Poland, export licensing requirements to that country were liberalized; and in July 1964, Rumania was given special treatment. The rationale for these two exceptions from other Communist countries of Eastern Europe was their desire for independence from Soviet domination. After the Castro regime came to power in Cuba, regulations were placed in effect "controlling all financial and commercial transactions involving Cuba or nationals thereof."[22] In 1964, controls were imposed on exports to North Vietnam by foreign subsidiaries of U.S. firms.[23] Political differences, coupled with U.S. policy against the proliferation of nuclear weapons, led to restrictions upon the export of United States made computers to France.

The Commodity Control List

In January 1965, a new "Commodity Control List," published by the Department of Commerce, replaced the Positive List and several general licenses and country groupings. This is a comprehensive export control list containing virtually all the commodities of the census classification and eliminates the need for the would-be exporter to consult several lists to see if the validated license requirement applied to his particular export.

All commodities are listed, and opposite each item there are listed those countries, symbolized by the letters T, V, W, Y, or Z, to which the particular type of product may not be exported without a validated license.

Group T: Western Hemisphere excluding Canada and Cuba.
Group V: All noncommunist countries of the world outside the Western Hemisphere and Yugoslavia.
Group W: Poland and Rumania.
Group Y: Soviet Bloc exclusive of Poland and Rumania.
Group Z: Communist China, North Korea, Communist-controlled areas of Vietnam and Cuba.

On November 14, 1966, a new group, Country Group S, was formed, consisting of Southern Rhodesia. Canada is not included in any country group. This unique position in the export control system derives from the time when the United States and Canada were engaged in joint war mobilization efforts.

On October 7, 1966, President Johnson announced that the U.S. would reduce export controls on East-West trade with respect to hundreds of nonstrategic items. On October 12, the Department of Commerce announced about 400 changes in the Commodity Control List. These commodities included: cereals and cereal preparations; sugar, sugar preparations and honey; feeding-stuff for animals; hides, skins, and fur skins; crude rubber, including synthetic and reclaimed rubber; pulp and waste paper; textile fibers; crude fertilizers; metalliferous ores and metal scrap; petroleum and petroleum products; chemical elements and compounds; medicinal and pharmaceutical products; iron and steel; electrical machinery, apparatus and appliances; and transport equipment.

While seemingly great in scope, the changes are extensively footnoted and qualified as follows: Tin oxides ("A validated license is no longer required for export of these commodities to Country X and Y, except to East Germany"); electric motors specially designed for aircraft ("A validated license is no longer required for export of these commodities to Indonesia"); and chemicals ("Bromine trifluoride and bromine pentafluoride require export authorization from the Department of State").

Technical Data

Technical data is also restricted in its exportation by the Office of Export Control. It is defined as:

> "Any professional, scientific or technical information, including any model, design, photograph, photographic file, document or other article or material, containing a plan, specification, or descriptive or technical information of any kind which can be used or adapted for use in connection with any process, synthesis, or operation in the production, manufacture, utilization, or reconstruction of articles or materials."[24]

"Exportation of technical data" is defined as:

> "Any release of unclassified technical data for use outside the United States. It includes the actual shipment out of the United States as well as furnishing of data in the United States to persons with the knowledge or intention that the persons to whom it is furnished will take such data out of the United States."[25]

Closely related to this are the regulations of the Office of Munitions Control which may come into play if the information relates to any technology which

[22] 31 *C.F.R.* 515.101-.808 (1967).
[23] 29 *Fed. Reg.* 6010 (1964).
[24] 15 *C.F.R.* III, 385.1 (a), (1967).
[25] 15 *C.F.R.* III, 385.1 (b), (1967).

advances the state-of-the-art or establishes a new art is an area of significant military applicability.[26]

Mutual Defense Assistance Control Act (1951) "The Battle Act"

United States controls on the shipment of strategic goods to Communist destinations has never been a unilateral effort of either theory or practice. Immediately following World War II the economies of Western Europe and Japan were not capable of such exports on a large scale, however, as early as 1949 the United States and six major allies formed a multilateral system of strategic controls on trade with the "Sino-Soviet bloc." Embargo lists were drawn up and a central Consultative Group, composed of export control officials of the various governments, was formed to supervise the lists. Membership was expanded in 1952 and 1953 to include Norway, Denmark, Canada, West Germany, Portugal, Greece, Turkey and Japan, in addition to the original members England, France, Italy, the Netherlands, Belgium, and Luxembourg.[27] The two major working groups are: the Coordinating Committee (COCOM), established in 1950 to deal with Eastern European trade and the China Committee (CHINCOM), established in 1952, and concerned with trade with Communist China.

In 1951, Congress passed the Mutual Defense Assistance Control Act, (called the "Battle Act" after its sponsor Congressman Laurie Battle), designed chiefly to restrict U.S. aid to nations that export strategic items to Communist countries. It created within the Department of State a Battle Act Administrator who bears responsibility for coordination with other COCOM countries.

The Act requires *inter alia* that the United States prevent export or re-export to Communist areas threatening U.S. security of those commodities falling into the categories of arms, ammunition, implements of war or other strategic items. These categories are identified in lists established by the Battle Act Administrator under Title I of the Act. The United States Government could not knowingly permit shipment of any commodities on the Title I lists to the U.S.S.R. or countries under its domination. These lists are classified, are revised from time to time, and are made available to the United States diplomatic missions in aid recipient countries to be used in controlling trade under the Battle Act. The United States is also required under Title II of the Act to regulate exports to the Communist bloc of other items which are of secondary strategic importance. The strategic value of these Title II commodities is primarily related to quantities shipped, and includes such items as certain machine tools and raw materials.

On February 20, 1968, the Assistant Secretary of State for Economic Affairs stated: "the Battle Act represents an authoritative statement of United States policy on the control of strategic trade with Communist countries. . . . The Battle Act has served as the underpinning for our negotiations with other countries of strategic controls by them in parallel with U.S. strategic controls. It provides the basis for U.S. participation in the cooperative multilateral strategic embargo program that is maintained through the 15-nation Coordinating Committee. . . ."[28]

Even without such an act it is probably true that the Department of State would have brought pressure to bear on foreign governments not to export strategic goods to Communist nations. Its major positive effect may have been to institutionalize U.S. participation in COCOM. If the Battle Act were repealed it would probably be necessary for the Department to create another office to negotiate and report on multilateral export controls.

Under the Act the administrator has drawn up two lists which went into effect on January 24, 1952. The first list, called "Title I, Category A," is composed of arms, ammunition, implements of war and atomic energy materials.[29] The second list, called "Title I, Category B," contains other strategic materials such as: electronic equipment, chemicals and petroleum products; scientific instruments and apparatus; metalworking machinery; and synthetic rubber.[30] No United States military, economic or financial assistance may be given to any nation which knowingly permits shipment of any of these items "to any nation or combination of nations threatening the security of the United States, including the Union of Soviet Socialist Republics and all countries under its domination."[31] However, as to the second list there is an exception giving the President discretion not to withhold aid from nations that knowingly permit shipments of those items to prohibited destinations, if such withholding would clearly be detrimental to the security of the United States. This authority has frequently been exercised by the President.

The effect of the Battle Act on the trade policies of other countries is hard to estimate. It is evident however, that U.S. export control policies have conflicted with those of its allies to various degrees. In 1965, the 18th Battle Act Report stated:

> While there may be differences of opinion at any given time among the countries partici-

---

[26] 31 *Fed. Reg.* 15182 (1966).

[27] Stanley Metzger, *Law of International Trade*, pp. 1059-93, (1966).

[28] LVIII, *Bulletin*, Department of State, No. 1500, March 2, 1968, p. 423.

[29] 1st *Battle Act Report* 37 (1952).

[30] *Ibid.*, at 43.

[31] 22 U.S.C. § 1611 (b) (1964).

pating in COCOM as to the details of what should be regarded as strategic, those differences have been resolved in recent years through frequent technical reviews that have preserved the basic scope of the international strategic lists. These reviews have resulted in the addition of new items of technological importance and the deletion of items which are considered to be no longer of strategic significance from the standpoint of Sino and Soviet-bloc capabilities.

Central to the policy conflicts between the United States and other COCOM countries has been the difference in philosophy concerning the relationship of international trade to international politics. In oversimplified terms, the U.S. is more willing to promote or withhold trade to accomplish specific foreign policy objectives than the British, French or Germans who view trade with the Eastern European countries in a commercial rather than a political light.

When American political objectives and European commercial objectives do not happen to coincide, as in the case of trade with the Soviet Union itself, these differences are reflected in changes in the COCOM lists. In point of fact, it is the United States that has gradually modified its strategic objectives to conform more closely to those of its allies. The 16th Battle Act Report stated in 1963, that "nonstrategic Western trade with the Soviet bloc, or the denial thereof, cannot affect basic Soviet military capability," and that "that capability is independently based on the Soviet's own advanced weapons technology and military production."

Other Restrictions

The Trade Expansion Act of 1962 in Section 231(a), directs the President, as soon as practicable, to suspend, withdraw, or prevent the application of concessions, including reductions or maintenance of duties proclaimed in carrying out any trade agreement entered into under the Act or previous authority, (such as the Tariff Act of 1930), with respect to any products of countries or areas dominated by Communism. The effect of this provision is to prevent the application of most-favored-nation treatment to products of Communist countries. The Section also may be viewed as a limitation on the authority of the President to negotiate trade agreements pursuant to the general authority contained in the Trade Expansion Act. A similar provision has been applicable since 1951, when the Trade Agreements Extension Act of that year was passed by Congress. In accordance with Section 5 of that Act, most-favored-nation treatment was suspended in 1951, with respect to the Soviet Union and the Eastern European countries, except Yugoslavia. In 1960, it was restored to Poland.

Title I of the Agricultural Trade Development and Assistance Act of 1954 (P.L. 480), authorizes the United States to make sales of agricultural commodities to "friendly countries." Section 103(d) of the Act defines "friendly country" for purposes of such sales to exclude, *inter alia*, "(1) any country or area dominated or controlled by a foreign government or organization controlling a world Communist movement," and "(2) for the purpose only of sales of agricultural commodities for foreign currencies. . .any country or area dominated by a Communist government." In addition, Section 103(j) of this Act provides (1) that the President shall exercise Title I authority "to assist friendly countries to be independent of domination or control by any world Communist movement," and (2) that nothing in the Act "shall be construed as authorizing sales agreements under Title I with any government or organization controlling a world Communist movement."

Section 103(d) of Public Law 480 states that, notwithstanding any other Act (including the Battle Act), "the President may enter into agreements for the sale or agricultural commodities for dollars on credit terms under Title I. . .with countries which fall within the definition of 'friendly country' for the purpose of such sales." As these provisions exclude only foreign *currency sales* to those Communist countries, the clause would appear to permit dollar *credit sales* to certain Communist countries. Poland was determined to be a "friendly country" for purposes of P.L. 480 by a decision of Secretary of State Dulles in 1956, and later confirmed by Secretary Rusk in 1961 and succeeding years.[32] It would appear that from a legal standpoint, such a determination could be made for other Communist countries.

Section 103(d) of the Agricultural Trade Development and Assistance Act of 1954, as amended by the Food for Peace Act of 1966, includes the following provision directed against Cuba and North Vietnam:

"(In exercising the sales authorities in title I of this Act). . .the President shall–

"(d) make sales agreements only with those countries which he determines to be friendly to the United States. . . . As used in this Act, 'friendly country' shall not include. . . (3) for the purpose only of sales of agricultural commodities under title I of this Act, any nation which sells or furnishes or permits ships or aircraft under its registry to transport to or from Cuba or North Vietnam (excluding United States installations in Cuba) any equipment, materials, or commodities so long as they are governed by a Communist regime: *Provided*, That with respect to furnishing, selling, or selling and transporting to Cuba medical supplies, non-strategic raw materials for agriculture, and non-strategic agricultural or food commodities, sales agreements

[32]L *Bulletin*, Department of State, No. 1292, March 30, 1964, p. 480.

> may be entered into if the President finds with respect to each such country, and so informs the Senate and the House of Representatives of the reasons therefor, that the making of each such agreement would be in the national interest of the United States and all such findings and reasons therefor shall be published in the Federal Register. . . ."[33]

The consequence of this provision is to make Poland and Yugoslavia ineligible for P.L. 480 sales, even though as indicated above these two Communist countries would have been otherwise eligible.

In addition, the Department of Agriculture and Related Agencies Appropriation Act of 1968, contains the following restriction:

> "*Provided*, That no funds appropriated by this Act shall be used to formulate or administer programs for the sale of agricultural commodities pursuant to titles I and IV of Public Law 480, 83rd Congress, as amended, to any nation which sells or furnishes or which permits ships or aircraft under its registry to transport to North Vietnam any equipment, materials or commodities, so long as North Vietnam is governed by a Communist regime."

The Johnson Act prohibits certain financial transactions by private persons in the United States involving foreign governments which are in default in the payment of their obligations to the United States.[34] The prohibited transactions include the making of "loans" to, and the purchase or sale of "bonds, securities, or other obligations" of, a foreign government which is within the defined category. The U.S.S.R. and all the countries of Eastern Europe with the exception of Bulgaria and Albania, are governments in default within the meaning of the statute. Yugoslavia is exempted from the terms of the Johnson Act by reason of membership in both the International Monetary Fund and the International Bank for Reconstruction and Development.

The Attorney General has ruled that the Johnson Act does not prohibit the extension of credit "within the range of those commonly encountered in commercial sales of a comparable character."[35] He also stated that the scope of the Johnson Act should not be measured in terms of distinctions among the various forms of financing export trade. According to the Attorney General financing arrangements are outside the scope of the Johnson Act "if they are directly tied to specific export transactions, if their terms are based upon bona fide business considerations, and if the obligations to which they give rise 'move exclusively within the relatively restricted channels of banking and commercial credit.' "[36]

Under Section II of the Export-Import Bank Act of 1945, as amended, transactions in which the Exim Bank participates are exempt from the provisions of the Johnson Act. However, Section 2(b) of the Act, as amended by legislation approved March 13, 1968, now states:

> The Bank in the exercise of its functions shall not guarantee, insure, or extend credit, or participate in any extension of credit—
>
> > (A) in connection with the purchase or lease of any product by a Communist country (as defined in section 620(f) of the Foreign Assistance Act of 1961, as amended), or agency or national thereof, or
> >
> > (B) in connection with the purchase or lease of any product by any other foreign country, or agency, or national thereof, if the product to be purchased or leased by such other country, agency, or national is, to the knowledge of the Bank, principally for use in, or sale or lease to, a Communist country (as so defined),
>
> except that the prohibitions contained in this paragraph shall not apply in the case of any transaction which the President determines would be in the national interest if he reports that determination to the Senate and House of Representatives within thirty days after making the same.[37]

---

[33] 80 *Stat.* 1527.
[34] 18 U.S.C. Sec. 955.
[35] 42 op. Att'y. Gen. No. 27.
[36] *Ibid.*
[37] P.L. 90-267, approved March 13, 1968.

Reconciling East-West Trade and National Security

Sherman R. Abrahamson

Dr. Abrahamson, Deputy Director in the Office of Export Control, U.S. Department of Commerce, has contributed an original article describing the historical background of the Export Control Act and its relation to East-West trade. Having drawn on his valuable practical experience in export licensing, Dr. Abrahamson has concluded that the administration of the Export Control Act is consistent with both East-West trade promotion and U.S. national security.

Introduction: Our East-West Trade Policy

Encouraging East-West trade in peaceful goods[1] continues to be an important U.S. policy. President Johnson has declared, as did each of his three predecessors, that the United States should pursue opportunities to maximize our trade in peaceful goods with the Communist nations of Eastern Europe. This policy should be followed even though we are at war in South Vietnam. "Our task," he has said, "is to achieve a reconciliation with the East. . .We do not intend to let our differences in Vietnam or elsewhere prevent us from exploring all opportunities." He believes that the intimate engagement of peaceful trade, over a period of time, can influence Eastern European societies to develop along paths that are favorable to world peace.

Peaceful trade has long been considered by the United States as a normal feature of international relations. Consistent with this general attitude, the United States placed no obstacles in the way of trade with the Soviet Union in the 1920's and 1930's even though we did not officially recognize the USSR until 1933; and at the end of World War II we treated trade with the countries of Eastern Europe no differently from trade with other countries.

The Export Control Act

Most of the special wartime controls over various phases of our economy were quickly terminated at the end of World War II, but export controls were not. Many materials and commodities, important not only to the reestablishment of consumer goods industries in the United States but also to the recovery of Western Europe, were in extremely short supply. The fear that the intense foreign demand would pull scarce goods out of the United States, plus the need to allocate the few exports that we could spare as equitably as possible among the countries whose needs were greatest, were the main reasons for continuing, on a year-to-year basis, the wartime restrictions on exports.

Postwar improvement of economic conditions both here and abroad undoubtedly would have brought about a dismantling of the export control apparatus had the Cold War not developed. The expansion of Soviet influence and control in Eastern Europe, the growth of Communist power in China, and the Berlin blockade in June 1948, convinced both Congress and the Executive Branch that the repeated extensions of the wartime controls on exports did not provide an adequate legislative basis for controlling exports in the Cold War situation. On February 28, 1949, therefore, Congress passed the Export Control Act. This Act, giving the President extensive power over American foreign commerce, provided for careful review of all exports to Communist-dominated countries and for prohibiting those that would be of military significance to them. From that time until the present, export controls have been one of the means used by the United States to combat the spread of international Communism and to reduce the danger of war.

In the Export Control Act, the Congress declared that

"it is the policy of the United States to use export controls to the extent necessary (A) to protect the domestic economy from the excessive drain of scarce materials and to reduce the inflationary impact of abnormal foreign demand; (B) to further the foreign policy of the United States and to aid in fulfilling its international responsibilities; and (C) to exercise the necessary vigilance over exports from the standpoint of their significance to the national security of the United States.

The Congress further declares that it is the policy of the United States to. . .apply such controls to the maximum extent possible in cooperation with all nations with which the United States has defense treaty commitments. . .in their dealings with the Communist-dominated nations."

This policy is carried out cooperatively with our European allies and Japan. Fourteen NATO countries and Japan, working together as a Coordinating Committee, better known as COCOM[2], maintain an agreed control list of strategic goods. These are items that

[1] Throughout this paper the phrase "trade in peaceful goods" and its variants are intended to mean transactions involving commodities, materials, and technologies that normally are used in the countries of destination for nonmilitary purposes and, according to available information, are likely to be used for such purposes.

[2] The legislative authority for U.S. participation in COCOM is the Mutual Defense Assistance Control Act (Battle Act), which was passed in 1951. Its purpose is "To provide for the control by the United States and cooperating foreign nations of exports to any nation or combination of nations threatening the security of the United States. . ." The Battle Act is administered by the Department of State.

have such potential for making a military contribution to the Communist countries as to require close control.

Section 3 of the Act authorizes the President to prescribe such rules and regulations providing

"for denial of any request or application for authority to export articles, materials, or supplies, including technical data or any other information, from the United States, its territories and possessions to any nation or combination of nations threatening the national security of the United States, if the President shall determine that such export makes a significant contribution to the military or economic potential of such nation or nations which would prove detrimental to the national security and welfare of the United States."

It also authorized him,

"to delegate the power, authority, and discretion conferred upon him by the Act as he may deem appropriate."

The President has delegated this authority, by means of an Executive Order, to the Secretary of Commerce.

Congress realized that the regulation of U.S. exports affects the responsibilities and interests of a number of departments and agencies. In Section 4 of the Act, therefore, Congress stipulated the following:

"In determining what shall be controlled hereunder, and in determining the extent to which exports shall be limited, any department, agency, or official making these determinations shall seek information and advice from the several executive departments and independent agencies concerned with aspects of our domestic and foreign policies and operations having an important bearing on exports."

These are the principal authorizing and policy provisions of the Export Control Act that relate directly to East-West trade and national security. Of interest also, is the fact that the Act applies to about 90 percent of all the goods exported from the United States. The remainder is controlled by other Government departments and agencies under other legislative authority. For example, under the Mutual Security Act of 1954, the Department of State administers export controls over arms, ammunition, war equipment, and technical data related thereto.

Attitudes in Congress–1968

Stating the policy on East-West trade, be it that of the President or that of the Congress as it is set forth in the Export Control Act, is easy. But carrying it out is quite a different matter. Congressional critics of the President's policy believe that East-West trade should not be expanded while we are fighting a war in South Vietnam. They say U.S. exports to Eastern European countries ease their supply situation and enables them to send war materials to North Vietnam. While Congress is divided on this issue, the division is not strictly along party lines. Some Republicans, for example, favor continuing trade in peaceful goods between the United States and Eastern Europe, while others believe that all such trade should be curtailed. In the Spring of 1968, the opposition of Senator Mundt of South Dakota, for example, took the form of a proposed amendment to the Tax Adjustment Act of 1968. His amendment would have penalized U.S. taxpayers that traded with Eastern Europe by levying on them a 20 percent surtax. The amendment was narrowly defeated.

Some Democrats also oppose East-West trade expansion but Senator Mondale of Minnesota, for example, favors such expansion. In 1968 he sponsored a resolution calling for modifications in the Export Control Act and the Export-Import Bank financing regulations to "promote the best interests of the United States by permitting an increase in trade in peaceful goods between the United States and the nations of Eastern Europe." Whether he will succeed in getting a majority in the Senate to support this resolution is uncertain at this time.

Export Control Policy Development

At this point a basic question arises. How is the President's policy of building bridges to Eastern Europe through peaceful trade reconciled with national security as expressed in Section 3 of the Export Control Act. This Section authorizes the President to prohibit or curtail the export from the United States of any articles, materials, or supplies, including technical data or any other information, to any nation or combination of nations threatening the national security of the United States, if the President determines

"that such export makes a significant contribution to the military or economic potential of such nation or nations which would prove detrimental to the national security and welfare of the United States."

In answering this question I should like to recall that the Congress, in the language of the Act, instructed the administrator of Export Control to seek "information and advice." To carry out this instruction on a regular basis, the Advisory Committee on Export Policy was established. Its chairman is Commerce's Assistant Secretary for Domestic and International Business. Members are the Departments of State, Defense, Treasury, Agriculture, and Interior, the Atomic Energy Commission, the Federal Aviation Agency, and the National Aeronautics and Space Administration. The Office of Emergency Planning is an observer and the Central Intelligence Agency is an advisor. The Advisory Committee, or ACEP, is convened only when difficult policy issues arise or when an especially troublesome export license application is received by the Office of Export Control that raises policy problems. Clearing away the bulk of the work is the ACEP's subgroup, the Operating Committee. Its membership is the same as that for ACEP, but at the senior staff level. The Operating Committee, or OC,

EXPLANATION OF SYMBOLS AND DESIGNATIONS ON THE COMMODITY CONTROL LIST

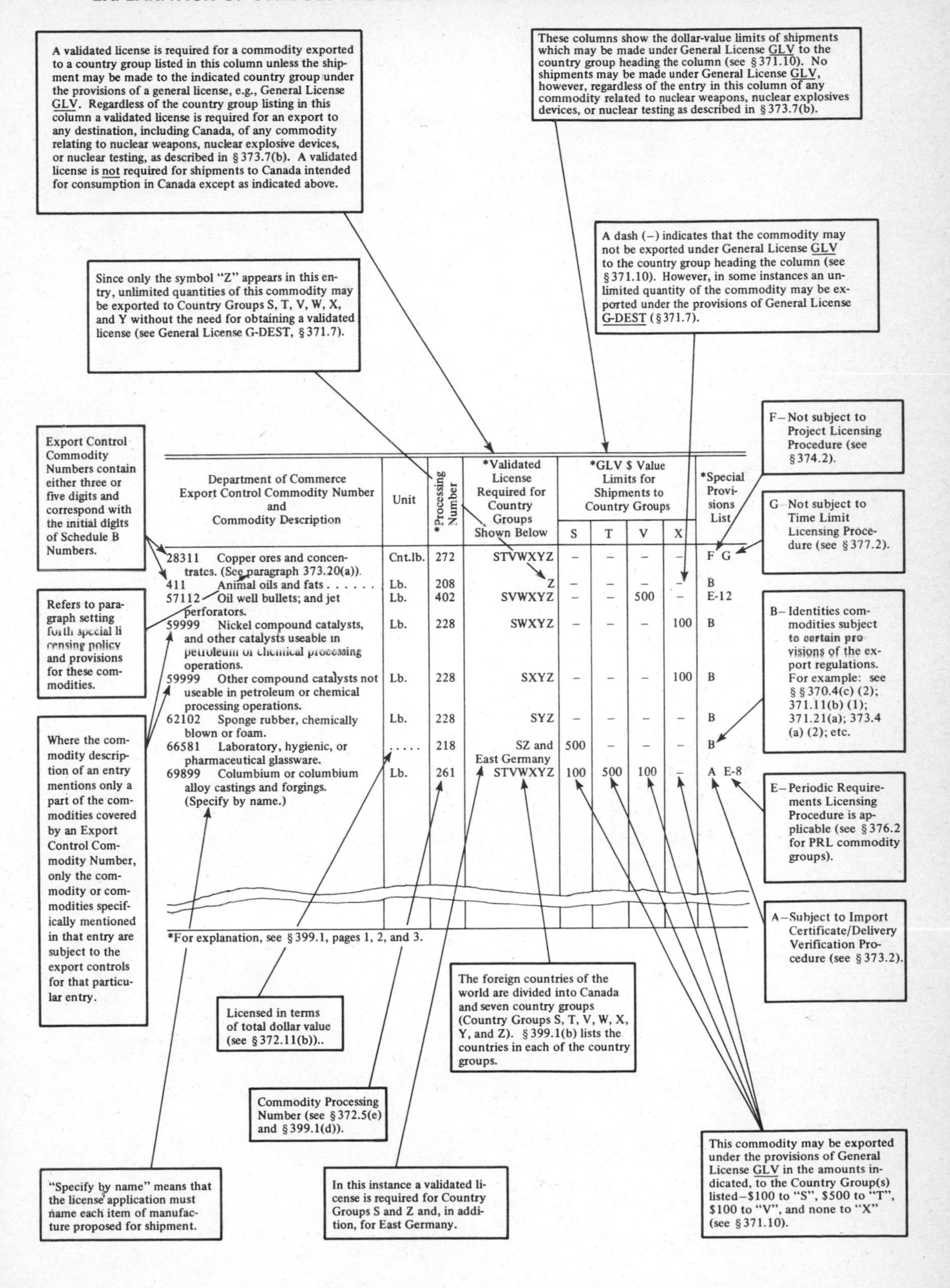

Department of Commerce Export Control Commodity Number and Commodity Description	Unit	*Processing Number	*Validated License Required for Country Groups Shown Below	*GLV $ Value Limits for Shipments to Country Groups				*Special Provisions List
				S	T	V	X	
28311 Copper ores and concentrates. (See paragraph 373.20(a)).	Cnt.lb.	272	STVWXYZ	–	–	–	–	F G
411 Animal oils and fats	Lb.	208	Z	–	–	–	–	B
57112 Oil well bullets; and jet perforators.	Lb.	402	SVWXYZ	–	–	500	–	E-12
59999 Nickel compound catalysts, and other catalysts useable in petroleum or chemical processing operations.	Lb.	228	SWXYZ	–	–	–	100	B
59999 Other compound catalysts not useable in petroleum or chemical processing operations.	Lb.	228	SXYZ	–	–	–	100	B
62102 Sponge rubber, chemically blown or foam.	Lb.	228	SYZ	–	–	–	–	B
66581 Laboratory, hygienic, or pharmaceutical glassware.	. . . .	218	SZ and East Germany	500	–	–	–	B
69899 Columbium or columbium alloy castings and forgings. (Specify by name.)	Lb.	261	STVWXYZ	100	500	100	–	A E-8

*For explanation, see § 399.1, pages 1, 2, and 3.

deals both with policy issues and exceptional export applications. Its recommendations are made to the Chairman of ACEP.

The Rule of Unanimity

The interdepartmental advisory procedure is of enormous importance in the policy planning for, and the administration of, our export controls. Fundamentally, decisions reached through this procedure govern the content and scope of our export control regulations and the make-up of our Commodity Control List.

The Commodity Control List, which is an integral part of our Comprehensive Export Schedule, lists all of the commodities under the licensing jurisdiction of the Department of Commerce. Commodities are listed in numerical order by Export Control Commodity Numbers of either three or five digits. These numbers correspond with the first three or five digit numbers shown in the Census Bureau's Schedule B, Statistical Classification of Domestic and Foreign Commodities Exported from the United States.[3] (For a more complete description of the CCL, see the enclosed diagram. The references in the diagram are to numbered paragraphs in the Comprehensive Export Schedule.)

Of special significance, however, is the fact that although the Secretary of Commerce has the authority to make export control decisions, he follows the practice of seeking unanimity among agencies advising him. If it cannot be achieved in the OC, the problem is re-examined in ACEP and agreement is sought. If ACEP cannot achieve unanimity, the issue is referred to the Export Control Review Board. Its Chairman is the Secretary of Commerce. The only other members are the Secretaries of Defense and State.

Recommendations reached by the OC and the ACEP form the basis for the broad licensing policies followed by the Office of Export Control. They make unnecessary the referral to the OC and ACEP of each the thousands of cases received annually by the Department. The practice of seeking unanimity has this important effect: Every export legitimately made to Eastern Europe under either a General License or a Validated License, or to any other destination, has the approval—general or specific—of the Executive Branch of the Federal Government.

General and Validated Export Licenses

A General License is a broad authorization that permits exports of certain commodities to certain destinations with a minimum amount of paperwork. For example, the only requirement we place on an exporter who wants to ship unlimited quantities of cleansing tissue to the USSR is that he file an export declaration with Customs at the port of shipment. A Validated License is a formal document issued to an exporter who has submitted a signed application to our office. It authorizes the export of only the commodities listed on the license under the conditions and terms therein specified. The Commodity Control List identifies for each listed commodity the destinations for which a Validated Export License is required.

When the Export Control Act was first passed, a Validated License was required for nearly all exports to Eastern Europe. You may remember that the Act was passed shortly after the blockade of West Berlin by the USSR. During the blockade, trade between the United States and Eastern Europe was negligible. There were no General Licenses for such trade, and applications for Validated Licenses were not approved.

Removal of Validated License Requirements

Since that time U.S. relations with Eastern European countries have improved gradually, but the curve has indeed had its ups-and-downs. (See tabulation.[4]) Keeping pace with the improvement in relations has been a sort of progressive removal of the Validated License requirement for a wide range of both producer and consumer goods. The first significant step was the establishment in 1956 of a list of items that could be exported to Eastern Europe on a General License basis, that is, without review of the transaction by the Office of Export Control. It was called the GLSA list and contained about 700 items in 57 different commodity areas.

The removal process is a continuing but a slow one, as the following figures indicate:

Year	*Approximate Number of Changes in the CCL Reducing Validated License Requirements to Eastern Europe*
1956	700
1960	160
1961-63	9
1964-65	188
1966	411
1967	69
1968 (5 mos.)	23

[3] The Schedule B code system is structured generally on the Standard International Trade Classification (SITC), published by the United Nations. The SITC in turn is correlated with the Brussels Tariff Nomenclature (BTN), thus providing comparability between trade statistics of the United States and those of other countries. The codes consist of 7-digits, the first of which indicates the broad type of commodity (e.g., chemicals begin with the number 5, and machinery and transport equipment with the number 7). Within these major groupings are additional subdivisions. Any commodity exported can be classified within one of these 7-digit numbers. For export control purposes, however, use of the complete 7-digit code is unnecessary.

[4] On page 11.

In the process, each commodity listing is scrutinized and tested against various strategic criteria. Validated License requirements are not removed until each commodity is carefully considered by the ACEP structure and found no longer to meet any of the strategic criteria.

APPLICATIONS PROCESSED FOR VALIDATED EXPORT LICENSES FOR EASTERN EUROPE, INCLUDING THE USSR

(VALUE IN MILLIONS OF DOLLARS)

	Approved	*Denied*
1948	73.7	NA
1949	58.4	NA
1950	0.7	NA
1951	*	NA
1952	3.7	0.7
1953	2.6	0.1
1954	18.8	49.5
1955	13.4	28.4
1956	29.0	11.3
1957	67.4	16.7
1958	33.9	20.3
1959	55.9	44.4
1960	90.0	24.2
1961	57.8	36.2
1962	49.6	48.9
1963	139.1	4.9
1964	406.1	11.0
1965	143.4	6.7
1966	153.1	3.7
1967	116.9	2.7
1968 (First 6 mos.)	81.3	5.5

*Probably less than $100,000
NA Formal records not readily available

Our basic position, therefore, is this: If a certain commodity is believed to be incapable of making a contribution to any Eastern European country that would be so significant as to be detrimental to our security and welfare (for example, cleansing tissue, tobacco products, sugar, etc.) even if it is diverted to a military or a military-oriented consignee, it is considered nonstrategic and removed from Validated License control to all Communist countries except Far Eastern Communist countries and Cuba.

Extending Validated License Requirements

Although broadening the range of goods that can be exported to Eastern Europe has been the trend, stricter licensing controls have also had to be imposed on certain commodities. During the last year or so, stricter controls have been placed, for example, on ablative materials. These permit re-entry of space vehicles at high temperatures. Tighter controls have also been placed on structural sandwich construction materials, which because of their heat resistance and high strength-weight ratios are especially useful in military aircraft and missile applications. Also subjected to tighter controls are isostatic presses, which are used in the manufacture of nuclear weapons. These items were under Validated License requirements to Eastern Europe before controls were tightened. The underlying purposes of stricter controls are to minimize the risks of unauthorized diversion and to impose special controls over the export of the technology to manufacture them.

"Gray Area" Cases

Our recent reports to Congress show that some types of commodities and technology are being approved for Eastern European countries that we were not approving to any of them a few years ago.

For example, exports to most Eastern European countries of U.S. machine tools for the manufacture of automotive vehicles generally were not approved before 1966. In 1966, however, Fiat, the Italian automobile manufacturer, signed an agreement to build an automobile plant in the USSR. The agreement called for a plant containing substantially the same automobile manufacturing equipment as in the Fiat plant in Turin, Italy. In keeping with President Johnson's desire to build bridges of trade in peaceful goods, U.S. manufacturers of machine tools normally used in the manufacture of automobiles (e.g. those that supplied equipment for the Turin plant) were advised that license applications for the export of such equipment to the Fiat plant in the USSR were likely to be approved. As a result licenses for about $30 million worth of U.S. machine tools have been issued for the Fiat-USSR project.

In the technical data field, a similar development in licensing policy has occurred. Since 1964, for example, licenses have been approved to several countries in Eastern Europe for the export of manufacturing technology for synthetic rubber of the type used in the production of automobile tires and for ethylene glycol, which is used primarily in the production of automotive antifreeze.

In arriving at these determinations, ACEP was advised that the USSR uses foreign trade to assist in meeting production plans for consumer goods. The ACEP members throught that increasing the availability of automobiles in the civilian economy and thereafter the supporting services to maintain them was a significant step towards improving the level of living of the Soviet people. Moreover, the presence of U.S. machinery and equipment in the USSR would demonstrate in a graphic way the high quality of the products of U.S. technology and indirectly the superiority of our economic system.

Important in the deliberations on the automobile machine tool cases, and also on the synthetic rubber and ethylene glycol technology cases, was the availability to the USSR of comparable equipment and technology from countries other than the United States. Although some U.S. machinery and much of our technology in a variety of fields are superior to that available abroad, the United States does not have any significant degree of unilateral control over the types of items and the technology in these particular cases. Well known is the fact that machine tools and technology of European and Japanese origin are currently being used to produce quality automobiles, automobile tires, and antifreeze. If these cases had been denied, the USSR could still have equipped its new plant with non-U.S. machinery, and tires and antifreeze could have been produced without our technology. In such event, the manufacturing plants may have been somewhat less efficient, but the loss to the United States would have been significant in terms of balance of payments and employment.

Although such applications are now being approved to Eastern European destinations, the approvals do not mean that the items or technologies are regarded as having no strategic potential, and that we are ready to remove them from Validated License control. They are still "gray area" items, meaning items that can have both peaceful and strategic uses. We are, however, able to approve *some items* in the gray area because analysis has shown that they will most probably be used in the particular instance for peaceful purposes. Where this probability cannot be established to our satisfaction, the transactions are not approved. Still other items have such strategic potentiality that we would not license them under any conditions to any of the Eastern European countries.

Criteria for Assessing the Strategic Potential of a Commodity

Each application for an export license involving a commodity that is under Validated License control to Eastern Europe is closely studied. This study is made to determine whether, in that transaction and for that stated end use, its contribution to the proposed recipient is so significant as to be detrimental to our security interests. Entering into this decision are such considerations as:

1. Is the commodity designed, intended, or capable of being used for military purposes?
2. Are there adequate substitutes available elsewhere that would make export denial by us futile?
3. Are the quantities and types of equipment appropriate for the proposed use?
4. Is the equipment an integral part of a larger package and, therefore, unlikely to be used for other than the state civilian purpose?

East-West Trade and Vietnam

Fully appreciated by the Department of Commerce and the other members of the export control community is the concern of those citizens who are apprehensive that our policy of promoting trade in peaceful goods with Eastern Europe at a time when we are engaged in a conflict with Communists in Vietnam will undermine our position. Secretary of State Dean Rusk has explained this policy when he sent the proposed East-West Trade Relations Act to Congress in May 1966. In his letter of transmittal he said:

"We are reaffirming in Vietnam—as we have on many earlier battlefields—our determination to aid free and independent nations to defend themselves from destruction by Communist aggression or subversion. But determined resistance to such force is only part of our strategy to maintain a peaceful world.

"It has equally been our purpose to demonstrate to the Communist countries that their best interests lie in seeking the well-being of their peoples through peaceful relations with the nations of the free world. We want the Soviet Union and the nations of Eastern Europe to understand that we will go step-by-step with them as far as they are willing to go in exploring every path toward enduring peace. We require only that our willingness and our actions be genuinely matched by theirs.

"We are confident that this policy is sound even when we are fighting against Communist weapons in Vietnam. Indeed, it is when we are resisting force with force that it is most important to hold open every avenue to peace. We need to make unmistakably clear to all the Communist nations in Eastern Europe that their best interests lie in economic development and peaceful trade, not in support of futile attempts to gain advantage through the use of force."

Balancing of Disparate National Interests

Our East-West trade policy and our regulation of exports pursuant to the Export Control Act represent a controversial arena in which men of good will can and sometimes do differ sharply with one another on a proposed export transaction. Experience has proved that if too few export controls are applied too leniently, the President's relationships with Congress suffer. They also suffer if too many applications for Validated Licenses are approved after only superficial review and analysis. On the other hand, if we apply too many controls too stringently, or deny too many applications "just to be on the safe side," trade promoters and trade expanders, both inside and outside Government, complain. To complicate matters even further, in nearly every proposed export transaction there are foreign policy interests that may be affected adversely or beneficially by either approval or denial depending on the circumstances. One might say, not altogether facetiously, that we have succeeded in balancing these disparate interests when we find that we have dissatisfied each to the same degree.

My contention is that our administration of the Export Control Act does reconcile East-West trade and national security. Our procedures call for review of landmark cases in an interagency forum where not only relevant information but also policy viewpoints are exchanged. The dynamics of the process progressively narrow the range of disagreement, and in the great majority of the cases, unanimity is achieved surprisingly quickly. If approval would affect adversely our national security, the application is denied. Conversely, those that are approved have been found to be beneficial to our national interests.

East-West Trade and American Agriculture

Roy F. Hendrickson

Agricultural products constitute a major portion of total U.S. exports annually. In the following statement before the International Finance Committee of the Senate Committee on Banking and Currency July 24, 1968, the Executive Secretary of the National Federation of Grain Cooperatives cites the negative impact current legislation has on U.S. agricultural trade with East Europe and how these countries have reacted with retaliatory measures against U.S. products.

Thank you, Mr. Chairman, for the invitation to report on observations I made on a mission to East Central Europe from June 17 to July 1, 1968. This mission was appointed by Secretary Freeman to help develop U.S. trade relations.

In my report to Secretary Freeman summarizing my observations as co-leader of the mission, I stated that updating applicable U.S. policies relating to the area is the first essential of agricultural trade–and other trade, for that matter–in East Central Europe is to be expanded.

In the case of agriculture this trade volume is now small–and declining. U.S. agricultural sales to the three countries I visited–Poland, Hungary, and Czechoslovakia–plus Yugoslavia and Rumania which were visited by another segment of our mission headed by Henry H. Wilson, mission co-leader, were reported by the U.S. Department of Agriculture to be only $118.5 million in the calendar year 1967. They were larger, a total of $209 million, in calendar year 1966.

This volume of sales can be substantially increased. But this can be done only if a number of policies are reformed and if serious, solid efforts are undertaken on a continuing basis to facilitate a mutually advantageous exchange of goods and services. Such an exchange would be consistent with the long history and tradition of friendship between the peoples of those nations and the United States.

In the past, agricultural exports have in many years been substantial in the case of wheat, feed grains, soybeans, soybean meal, cotton, and cattle hides.

I believe that U.S. agricultural exports to this area will decline in 1968 below the small total recorded in 1967 for reasons which I state below. This trend can be reversed if legislation proposed by the President, Senator Mondale, and others is enacted. The first need is authority for the Executive Branch to negotiate for restoration of Most-Favored-Nations status for Czechoslovakia and Hungary.

There is one very limited possibility of an increase in agricultural exports to the area. Drouth reportedly is affecting Bulgaria and the other nearby areas, including Hungary. But whether it reaches into the Soviet Union is unclear. No solid data on the consequences of drouth are available, possibly won't be until late August or the middle of September.

While Hungary has a poorer crop outlook than in 1967, its officials told us that its food cereal reserves would fill any void. Its feed grain production outlook is poor, and here reserves are low.

Poland's crop is good to excellent, and that in Czechoslovakia is better than average. Both are now counting on imports of wheat from the USSR, Czechoslovakia in the magnitude of two million metric tons. Both are also counting on substantial imports of cotton and vegetable oils from the USSR.

The best prospects for agricultural exports into these areas, if certain policy impediments to trade were removed, center on soybeans, soybean meal, feed grains, and cotton, with a lesser role for a number of other items, including wheat and tobacco.

The two major reasons for a decline in U.S. agricultural exports to the area–even lower than the low figures registered in 1967 and 1966–are: First, the very short supply of hard currency there and the higher priority given to uses of such currency for other than the import of food; and secondly, the tariffs put into effect in 1968 in two of the three countries on soybean meal or cake which was a leading item in value in 1967.

The tariffs imposed by Czechoslovakia (15 percent ad valorem) and Hungary (10 percent ad valorem) are retaliatory. They are frankly referred to as "counter-discrimininatory" measures by officials there, an answer to the refusal of the United States to reinstate "most-favored-nations" treatment for these two countries as was done in 1960 for Poland. Such treatment was withdrawn during the Korean war in the early fifties.

Nations which do not receive most-favored-nations treatment are penalized in that the U.S. tariffs and duties that apply to their exports are those that existed under the Smoot-Hawley Tariff Act of 1930. Those countries are not eligible for the major reductions in tariff rates published since, pursuant to the Reciprocal Trade Agreements Act and to GATT.

In the case of Czechoslovakia, an original member of GATT, their ineligibility for most-favored-nations status appears to be especially offensive to their trade officials.

The adamant U.S. position not only discourages trade. The U.S. attitude is resented and provides forensic ammunition for specialists in the anti-U.S. propaganda fields.

Furthermore, West Germany, France, Canada, and many other nations competing with the United States do not have similar discriminatory practices and thus have a competitive advantage over the United States.

One consequence of denial of the most-favored-nations treatment for these countries which have food deficits, especially in the case of cereals, is to rely increasingly on supplies from Russia.

President Johnson has requested authority from Congress to negotiate with these countries for a resumption of the most-favored-nations status. Favorable action by Congress is well-merited.

In the absence of authority on the part of the Executive Branch of the U.S. Government to negotiate, we can expect little or no progress in resolving a few differences which have been gathering mold on the unfinished business list for many years. These include claims of American citizens for compensation for their property incorporated into nationalized industries in the case of both Czechoslovakia and Hungary, recovery of 2-1/2 tons of gold held by the U.S. to which Czechoslovakia feels it is entitled, and return of Hungarian crown jewels, precious stones, and other property which Hungary claims are in the possession of the United States.

The recent decision of the United States to release about $5 million on blocked social security, veteran, and government annuity payments to citizens of Czechoslovakia and Hungary was announced while the mission was in Prague. It was accepted as a helpful token step in getting on with the world's mounting burden of unfinished business. In a world where unresolved tensions have tended to increase it was welcomed in Czechoslovakia which obviously is in a worrisome period of uncharted change.

I will list here other barriers to expansion of trade which the United States should remove in fairness and in its own self-interest. Before doing so, I want to indicate that I am fully aware that there are formidable potential barriers of other than U.S. origin.

First of all is the extent and range of the Soviet program to influence Eastern European policies in future years. The USSR is today the No. 1 trading partner for each of the three countries visited. The trade volume is growing annually. A pattern employing bilateral trading agreements has emerged. This facilitates clearance of trade balances with periodic reviews.

Russian power, its proximity and its dominant role in East Central Europe are facts of life that will influence the trade policies and practices of all members of the bloc indefinitely. The factor of proximity provides an advantage in lower transportation costs as compared to imports from the United States, Canada, Australia, and other overseas areas.

However, none of this should counsel inaction by this country or acceptance of the status quo. Everywhere we found evidence of a desire to trade for the best possible and oldest reason of all—mutual advantage. The ministries we visited and the various state trading companies—all were very cordial. They certainly manifested no attitudes or views that could be interpreted as unfriendly and unfavorable to an expanding trading partnership with the United States covering a very broad spectrum of goods and commodities.

There is another factor of possibly large future consequence which should not be ignored. There is evidence in East Central Europe, as well as elsewhere, of a steady drive towards greater self-sufficiency in food cereals. This drive appears to be even more a bloc objective than a country-by-country goal, especially in the case of Hungary and Czechoslovakia.

Structural change in agriculture, accenting larger farms, many state farms, has been substantial in both of those countries. They appear to be laying tremendous emphasis on development of their industrial potential, drawing surplus labor from the farms. Poland is a current exception to this trend.

These three countries now obtain most of their cotton from the Soviet Union plus Iran, Egypt, Syria, and Greece, with very limited purchases from the United States. We face an uphill fight in cotton so long as trade policies remain as at present.

Besides settling the issue of most-favored-nations recognition, the United States should, in my view, remove other barriers to trade to facilitate sales of U.S. agricultural commodities and other exports in the area.

I will list the two principal barriers: Cargo preference and the off-load requirement.

Cargo Preference and Off-Load Requirement

The Cargo Preference Act of 1954 provides that at least 50 percent of all U.S. Government shipments made under foreign aid transactions or overseas military supplies be shipped in U.S. flag vessels. Commercial exports for hard currency are exempt from this Act. The Act has tremendously increased the cost of P.L. 480 programs paid for out of CCC funds and regularly and often erroneously treated in the public prints as "farm subsidy expenditures."

For reasons never explained under the rules of rudimentary logic, this 50 percent requirement was made applicable to 1963-64 sales of wheat to the USSR, even though it paid in gold or convertible currency. The difference between foreign flag and U.S. flag rates for dry bulk cargo ranges up to nearly 100 percent.

A sale of at least two million metric tons of wheat to the USSR in 1963-64 was prevented by the Executive Branch of our Government when it extended the cargo preference requirement to the USSR although not required to do so by law. Sales by other wheat-exporting nations for cash were thus promoted while U.S. wheat remained unsold.

In another step not required by law, the 50 percent U.S. flag requirement was incorporated in the Commerce Department's Comprehensive Export Schedule early in 1964 by executive order. This was applicable to future validated export licenses for wheat sold not only to the Soviet Union but to East European countries not approved under general licenses and to all feed grains sold to the Soviet Union. Feed grains sold to East European countries were exempt from the 50 percent shipping requirement by exclusion from the Comprehensive Export Schedule covering them.

In 1965-66, a number of East and Central European countries in the Soviet bloc bought feed grains, nearly a million tons in all, from the United States. But while they paid in hard currency and were free to use other than U.S. flag vessels, they were subjected to a new trade barrier of truly nuisance character. The true origin of this requirement is shrouded in mystery. At least I have yet to find a rational explanation.

In this case, U.S. exporters in obtaining export licenses were, and still are, required to agree in writing that a parcel of each cargo will be delivered to a destination other than East Europe. This is often called the "Part Cargo Requirement." In effect, this expressed a U.S. preference for unloading at West European ports, a preference that even their port chambers of commerce had never sought. It is unjust to East European buyers, unfriendly, a costly barrier to trade, and counter to the best interests of the United States and its farmers.

We listened frequently and sympathetically in Czechoslovakia, Hungary, and Poland to repeated complaints concerning these shipping requirements. As a member of the President's Food and Fiber Commission in 1965-67, I was already on record in opposition to these barriers in reports made to the President in June 1967.

This barrier can be erased by the President. Early action is merited. In event drouth conditions result in USSR wheat purchases this fall and winter, no sales by the U.S. can be expected so long as the barrier is in force.

In Prague, officials of Koospool, including its principal officials and its specialists responsible for imports of grain and oil cake, indicated their reasoning in objecting to the part-cargo requirement.

They seek to conserve their limited hard currency resources by obtaining ocean shipping and inland rail transportation services from Poland with which Czechoslovakia has a bilateral trade agreement where balances are annually cleared without recourse to the use of hard currencies. This is surely not an unreasonable aspiration.

Soybean Meal Tariffs

In Hungary and Czechoslavakia in January 1968, tentative schedules of import duties were published as part of a new "economic reform." The United States was lumped in the "third column" class of origin countries, along with South Africa and Portugal, to which the highest schedule of tariffs applies. Officials in both countries told me that these tariffs will be canceled if and when most-favored-nations status is reinstated for them by the United States.

East-West Trade: An Avenue Toward World Peace

Alexander B. Trowbridge

Mutual confidence, a necessary condition for "peaceful engagement" requires ample amounts of flexibility and patience. Although the author reminds us of the difficulty and complexity of gaining increased trade, he is optimistically confident that the reward is worth its price. He notes the positive steps that have been taken in the USSR and he encourages national dialogue as a means to clarify the myths from the realities in East-West trade. As acting Secretary of Commerce in the Johnson administration, Mr. Trowbridge shares the latter's hope for a "mounting traffic across the bridge of commerce" in which American business is to play the primary role.

Two years ago, soon after becoming a Government official, I made a short visit to Budapest to open the U.S. exhibition at the Budapest International Trade Fair.

While there, I had an opportunity to talk with some Hungarians. They lost no time in illustrating their type of self-directed humor which has gained some fame as one method of commentary on their form of government. Their jokes take the form of question and answer. "Why," they ask, hasn't Switzerland become a Socialist country?" They answer, "Because it is too small—it couldn't afford it!"

We here in the United States are not small. As we exert every effort to build a permanent peace, we are indeed too big to be able to afford automatic rejection of any potential avenue of peaceful engagement.

"Trade," Emerson wrote, "is a plant which grows wherever there is peace, as soon as there is peace, and as long as there is peace."

United States policy is to cultivate this plant of progress and mutual benefit in the soil of peaceful engagement between the East and the West.

The administration, as President Johnson has stated clearly and often, favors the equitable liberalization of two-way trade in peaceful goods with the Soviet Union and Eastern Europe. We have taken a number of steps in this direction. We have sought congressional action to further open the way. And we have encouraged the commercial activists of the private sector to move ahead in this area, as indeed they are now doing.

This broad approach is a central element in President Johnson's policy of building new bridges of "ideas, education, culture, trade, technical cooperation, and mutual understanding for world peace and prosperity." Peaceful trade can form one of the strongest and most durable of these bridges between East and West.

And, particularly with the passage of time, this expanding trade can yield tangible, meaningful material benefits on both the Eastern and Western ends of the bridge of commerce. . . . Evolving conditions and evolving relationships in our complex, changing world demand that we be more flexible and forward looking—both in the East and in the West—in order to serve the peaceful and progressive future of all of our peoples. We know that to be hidebound and hypnotized by the divisions and antagonisms of former years is to serve only the past.

Even as we meet here today, the first industry-organized, Government-approved United States trade mission is visiting Eastern Europe and the Soviet Union. We hope that during its stay in Moscow—as well as in Warsaw, Bucharest, and Belgrade—the Minneapolis Chamber of Commerce mission firmly plants its steps on the road to commercial growth.

And in addition, a second agricultural and business trade mission from California is now preparing to leave for Moscow next week on a trip that will also take them to the cities of Kiev, Kishinev, Krasnodar, and Kharkov. Their Moscow visit will coincide, as well, with the opening of the 21-nation international exhibition there—INPRODMASH-67—at which some 18 United States companies will be displaying their food processing, packaging, and distribution equipment.

Add to this the series of industry-sponsored or Government-organized U.S. trade groups that have operated in Poland, Hungary, Romania, and Bulgaria in the past few years—plus participation in numerous trade fairs and exhibits in this period—plus the initial U.S. trade mission to Czechoslovakia scheduled for later in 1967—and I believe you see examples of what I generally call a "steady movement from the permissive to the promotional" approach by our country as we consider East-West trade.

Growth of U.S. Trade with Eastern Europe

There are, of course, numerous other dimensions as well.

One was the significant growth of United States trade last year with the Soviet Union and the nations of Eastern Europe to the highest level in the past two decades, with the single exception of 1964 when an unusually large volume of wheat shipments inflated the total by $180 million.

Reprinted from Department of State Bulletin, Vol. 56, No. 1459, (June 12, 1967)

The two-way trade total in 1966 came to something over $375 million, compared to $277 million in 1965–an increase on the order of 35 percent overall, with a slightly larger increase in U.S. exports to the U.S.S.R. and Eastern Europe than in U.S. imports from these nations. From 1965 to 1966, the U.S. export total rose from $140 million to $198 million, while the imports went from $138 million to $178 million.

Alongside aggregate U.S. two-way trade in 1966 of about $55 billion, this is not a very large total. Nor does it come to more than a small percentage of the volume of commerce that flows between the Soviet Union and Eastern Europe and other major trading nations.

For example, according to the preliminary figures that I have seen, trade between the Federal Republic of Germany and these nations last year exceeded $2 billion, contrasted to the U.S. $375 million. The figure for the United Kingdom was about $1 billion; and Japan, France, and Italy all fell in the range between $600 million and $1 billion.

The United States total does take on added perspective, however, with consideration of two additional factors.

First, United States trade figures do not include exports by the overseas subsidiaries or licensees of U.S. firms. Rather, these are reflected in the trade statistics of host nations. Although solid figures are not available, such trade between European-based U.S. subsidiaries and licensees and the U.S.S.R. and Eastern Europe appears to be growing rapidly.

Second, trade statistics are limited to commodities. Not included is the sales price or other monetary value of technical data or services. Yet such trade constitutes an increasingly important share of exports eastward by U.S. industrial and engineering firms. An increasing number of such transactions have been licensed under the Export Control Act.

There have been cases where the likely return to the U.S. firm from the export of technical data to Eastern Europe was several million dollars, and others often are known to total in the hundreds of thousands. Cumulatively, this element of East-West trade could represent a sizable addition to the value of exports reported for only the shipment of goods.

Although it is a generalization, we can say that United States participation in East-West trade is somewhat larger than suggested by the bare statistics, with a growth rate that is significant, and has a potential for future expansion across a diverse range of peaceful products.

Such expansion will not come automatically, however. Considerable effort to build and broaden and strengthen the bridges of peaceful trade are necessary at both ends of the span. And considerable effort will be necessary to increase and enhance the flow of commerce across the bridges.

Let us not underestimate the difficulties of expanding trade at the same time as we are strongly committed to resist Communist aggression in Vietnam. We have adopted what I describe as a "dual track" policy. With one hand we confront such aggression where it must be resisted, and our resolve is firm. But in a time where pressures increase on one front, we need pressure relief valves on other fronts. Hence the desire to keep open channels of communication–in education, travel, culture–as well as trade.

Trade Liberalization Measures

President Johnson, carrying forward the efforts of the past three administrations in today's evolving world environment, has acted in a number of ways to liberalize, to stimulate and support East-West trade as a part of our overall, long-term policy toward Eastern Europe and Soviet Russia.

–Export controls have been liberalized. More than 400 nonstrategic items were removed from the Commerce Department's Commodity Control List late last year. These products, which now can be shipped without a specific license, cover a broad range including consumer products, textiles, certain metal manufacturers and machinery, various chemical materials and products, and a considerable number of manufactured articles. In addition, the process of sifting, refining, and updating this list is an ongoing one. We want to make sure that our control list is realistic and unburdened with excessive or ineffective coverage.

–Commercial credit facilities have been extended. In his October 7th speech, President Johnson authorized the Export-Import Bank to provide normal commercial credit guarantees on industrial export transactions with Poland, Czechoslovakia, Hungary, and Bulgaria–as provided in July 1964 for exports to Romania. Commercial credit facilities are an important concomitant to trade that must and does receive our continuing attention.

–At the same time, the President announced that he had authorized the Export-Import Bank to extend a loan of some $50 million to the Istituto Mobiliare Italiano to finance U.S.-origin machine tools and other equipment for the automobile plant to be constructed by the Italian firm Fiat in the Soviet Union. Eximbank participation encourages U.S. businessmen to compete for these sales, assists Fiat in obtaining the finest equipment available, and tangibly expresses our support for projects designed to serve the consumer goods requirements of the people of the Soviet Union or Eastern Europe. While any equipment sold for this plant will be carefully examined to ascertain that it has basically peaceful applications, we operated from the general approach that we would rather see traffic jams of automobiles than of tanks.

—The East-West Trade Relations Act proposed by President Johnson can provide the conditions under which steady expansion can come about by authorizing the President to use nondiscriminatory tariff treatment as a bargaining element in negotiating commercial agreements with these nations. . . .

Realistic judgment does not suggest that such legislative authority in itself would set in motion an immediate flood of two-way trade. But the power to extend such tariff treatment, which currently applies only to Poland of the nations concerned, could certainly help to increase the flow of East-West commerce.

I think it is true that the implementation of nondiscriminatory tariff treatment has psychological and political overtones as well as commercial importance. But if we are serious about desiring to increase the levels of peaceful trade—which we are—then we should frankly face the impediments that exist and reduce them where possible. The Soviet Union and the nations of Eastern Europe will have to export to earn exchange to buy our products. We should recognize their need to operate under competitive conditions equal to other countries selling in our market.

Of course, agreements reached under this act would have to be based on mutual benefits. In return for the benefits of most-favored-nation treatment, the United States may seek settlement of commercial disputes, arrangements for protection of industrial property, provisions for promotion of U.S. products, entry and travel of commercial representatives, arrangements for market access and fair treatment for our goods, and settlement of claims.

Taken as a whole, as I say, these administration measures represent a broad and energetic administration approach. They are designed to reduce conspicuous obstacles to United States two-way trade with the Soviet Union and Eastern Europe.

Increasingly, we hope, the name of the game will become competition in each other's markets consistent with normal commercial relationships that extend across other international borders around the globe, and despite the differences in economic organization that exist between our countries.

The challenges, then, will be clear at both ends of the bridge. We will have to become increasingly aware of each other's market requirements, of competitive practices and conditions, of consumer likes and dislikes. We will have to develop advertising, promotional, and distribution techniques suited to the varying markets. We will have to be patient and flexible. Long and time-consuming exchanges are probably necessary in order to build the kind of mutual confidence we hope for as part of "peaceful engagement."

This problem is neither simple nor insoluble. To a considerable extent, the answer is likely to be fully realized only through experience. Such experience as has been gained by Western businessmen negotiating in the Soviet Union indicates the need for patient and skilled bargaining techniques. Experience of Soviet and Eastern European state trading agencies has probably shown them the need to adapt to the competitive demands of our free economies.

A number of approaches present themselves for the acquisition and broadening of such experience. Perhaps, to speed the orientation process, trade officials of the Soviet Union and Eastern Europe will want to broaden commercial relationships with businessmen in this country, and particularly importers. Perhaps it will be desirable in some cases to contract certain business services in the United States, at least during this orientation process.

Or again, possibly businessmen and trade officials on both sides might think in terms of general approaches to broadening communications. Trade missions or factfinding tours, such as the Time, Inc. and Business International group visits, are undoubtedly useful. The use of business publications stimulates exchange of business or marketing information. Obviously, there are a good many alternate routes that could be followed.

As well as increased sales in each other's markets, this process could also lead to further expansion in the future through exploration of new trading techniques or the reexamination of existing trade tools for application to trade between the United States and these nations. To cite one example, it may be that the technique of switch trading—which is proving useful elsewhere could have an application. As I have suggested, however, time, effort, and experience must interact before such specifics emerge.

The essential aim in this current period is to get the ball moving—to allow the dynamics of peaceful international commerce to come fully into play here as in other areas of world trade that have seen such surging expansion.

Primary Role of American Business

Past this point, I cannot stress strongly enough the primary role of American business in this whole process of growth. While the government-to-government aspects of world trade can be decisive, the fact remains that in our system there is no business without business.

From a great many indications, there is indeed at the present time impressive and growing interest in the American business community in the potentials of East-West trade, just as an increasingly favorable commercial climate appears to be emerging in the nations of this region.

International cooperative efforts under way today also hold promise of important progress in the vital field of industrial property, particularly in connection with patents.

This is a complex and difficult area where material accomplishment comes slowly, but the pluses to date are encouraging. They include:

–Soviet accession to the International Convention for the Protection of Industrial Property, or Paris Convention, the leading international treaty in the patent and trademark field.

–Subsequent U.S.S.R. and Eastern European support for the U.S. proposal, in the Executive Committee of the Paris Convention, that set in motion current detailed consideration of an international patent cooperation treaty.

–Formation of a state trading agency known as Licensintorg in the Soviet Ministry of Foreign Trade to handle foreign licensing matters including promotion of export-import arrangements in this field.

–And issuance of basic Soviet publications in this field in English translation.

These are positive steps in an area that bears particularly on trade in the new products and processes that are staples in U.S. business overseas. In particular, they stimulate the confidence that is fundamental to increased commerce.

So, in summary, what we see today throughout this broad field of U.S. trade with the U.S.S.R. and Eastern Europe are new activity, new interest, new developments. The picture is one of movement, and the direction is toward expansion and liberalization. We are increasingly talking of contracts rather than contrasts.

One very significant part of the picture is the notably increased national interest and national debate on this vital subject across the United States–by business groups, in the newspapers, at meetings such as this one, and among the general public. I applaud this, both because healthy, vigorous national dialog–pro or con–is at the very heart of our democratic process and because the views expressed by the business community and others provide important contributions to the President and the Congress in their considerations and decisions affecting East-West trade. I hope that this discussion can separate the myths and the realities of the situation and that our policy directions are based on realistic appraisals rather than emotional reactions.

All that we have said notwithstanding, I believe it is abundantly clear that the numerous diverse influences on the future of East-West trade that we have been discussing remain subordinate in impact to one single central determinant. I am referring, of course, to the general climate of relations between the United States and these nations.

In this regard, President Johnson has expressed United States hopes and intentions in a brief, historically eloquent declaration: "Our objective," he has said, "is not to continue the cold war but to end it."

In the years to come, mounting traffic across the bridge of commerce between our nations could be one very effective element in achieving this objective for our own people and all of the peoples of the world.

East-West Trade Policy in a Balanced Strategy for Peace

Joseph A. Greenwald

In this article, Joseph Greenwald, also a government official, points out the need for greater flexibility in our relations with the East. He argues in favor of new legislation, such as the East-West Trade Relations Act, if the U.S. is to take advantage of trade as an effective tool in improving East-West relations. We must appreciate the disappearance of the "monolithic Soviet bloc" and seek new means of peace strategy. The author is critical of those opposed to trade with Eastern Europe since he believes that the U.S. can take advantage of the opportunities of such trade while defending the free world against Communist aggression.

In his European policy speech, President Johnson described our task of reconciliation with the East as "a shift from the narrow concept of coexistence to the broader vision of peaceful engagement." The subject—expanded East-West trade—is one of the main tools we can use in working toward the objective set by the President.

Our East-West trade policy is part of our balanced strategy for peace. On the one hand, we will continue to defend freedom in Southeast Asia and to demonstrate that Communist aggression does not pay.

But at the same time we must be prepared to take advantage of all opportunities to widen the areas of peaceful association with Eastern Europe and the Soviet Union.

The underlying concept of flexibility and differentiation in our policy toward the Communist world calls for a special effort to achieve public understanding and support. It requires a greater degree of sophistication than some other aspects of United States foreign policy. This applies particularly to the field of trade. Since decisions to buy and sell are in the hands of individuals under our private enterprise system, a policy of expanding East-West trade can be effective only if businessmen, as well as consumers, understand and accept it.

The obvious question is: Why should we trade with any of the Communist nations when they are supporting the forces shooting at Americans, South Vietnamese, Australians, and others? President Johnson answered on Friday. Speaking of the need to work with the East to build a lasting peace, he said: "We do not intend to let our differences on Viet-Nam or elsewhere prevent us from exploring all opportunities."

Another answer to this question lies in the nature of the Communist world as we see it today. What we once knew as the Sino-Soviet bloc is no longer the monolith of Stalin's time. We know that today there are deep and bitter differences among these countries. It is no longer axiomatic that Moscow's word will be followed blindly by all of the faithful followers throughout the world. On the contrary, we find daily evidence that each of the Communist countries increasingly pursues its own national interests. It is to our advantage in this situation to deal with these countries in accordance with our own national interest—and not in accordance with an outdated concept of a Sino-Soviet bloc of a decade ago.

Finally, we do not ignore the commercial benefits from expanding trade.

Thus, as a part of our continuous search for areas of agreement with the East, as a part of the effort to balance resistance to aggression in South Viet-Nam with a peace-serving move in another part of the world, and as part of our general program of trade expansion, Secretary of State Rusk, acting on the President's instructions, submitted the East-West Trade Relations Act to the Congress on May 11 of this year. He asked the Congress to provide the President with the authority necessary to negotiate commercial agreements with the Soviet Union and other nations of Eastern Europe to widen our trade in peaceful goods, when such agreements will serve the interests of the United States. The President last Friday affirmed that the administration intends to press for passage of the proposed legislation.

Both Republican and Democratic administrations have favored expanding trade with Eastern Europe. In 1958, for example, President Eisenhower made it clear that "the United States favors the expansion of peaceful trade with the Soviet Union" and spoke of the importance of trade as a means of strengthening the possibilities for independent actions by the countries of Eastern Europe.

The United States is not alone in seeking to improve relations with the Soviet Union and other countries of Eastern Europe. Last June, after the meeting of the foreign ministers of the North Atlantic alliance in Brussels, Secretary Rusk reported that all the members of NATO have observed signs of evolution in Eastern Europe and the Soviet Union—evolution toward national autonomy, less harsh internal discipline, and the restoration of more normal relations between the peoples of Eastern Europe and those of the West.

Reprinted from *Department of State Bulletin*, Vol. 55, No. 1427 (October 31, 1966).

Most of the responsible statesmen of the North Atlantic community recognized, the Secretary said, that the facts of the world situation require that NATO remain strong and alert. At the same time, he said, "they agree that every effort must be made to improve East-West relations and to solve or blunt East-West disputes. . ."

Before President Johnson decided to seek East-West trade legislation, he had the matter studied intensively by a group of American business, labor, and academic leaders. In its report in 1965, the Miller committee concluded that the United States, having protected itself by a secure and adequate defense, can prudently seek practical means of reducing areas of conflict with the Soviet Union. The committee advocated the use of trade in peaceful and nonstrategic items as a policy instrument.

Provisions of the Proposed Legislation

The proposed East-West Trade Relations Act is based on the recommendations of the Miller committee. It would give the President positive tools to accompany existing laws which use the negative power of trade denial—the Export Control Act, the Battle Act, the restrictive provisions of other laws—to prevent trade from strengthening the Communist regimes militarily. These existing laws deny to the Communist regimes items of strategic and military value and they will continue in effect. What we propose in the East-West Trade Relations Act is to reduce the barriers to trade in nonstrategic goods.

The main provisions of the proposed legislation would authorize the President to extend most-favored-nation (MFN) tariff treatment to certain individual Communist countries instead of the very high rates of the 1930 Smoot-Hawley tariff. In other words, the President could apply the same tariff duties to individual Communist countries that are now applicable to all other countries. The authority could be exercised only in a commercial agreement with a particular country in which such MFN treatment would be granted in return for equivalent benefits to the United States.

We would seek through these commercial agreements to find ways to make it easier to carry on East-West business transactions.

Problems of interest to American businessmen could be dealt with under the consultation procedures or in the periodic negotiations to be provided for in agreements under the proposed act.

Any agreement would be limited to 3 years but could be renewed for periods not to exceed 3 years each. Any agreement could be suspended or terminated at any time on reasonable notice. MFN treatment would apply only while an agreement was in effect. The President would be directed to suspend or terminate MFN treatment whenever he determined that the other party was no longer fulfilling its obligations under the agreement or that the suspension or termination was in the national interest.

The act would apply only with regard to European Communist countries. It would not apply to Cuba, Communist China, North Korea, and North Viet-Nam, and the Soviet Zone of Germany. Existing laws and regulations will assure that no benefits of the act will be made available to these areas. Poland and Yugoslavia now receive most-favored-nation treatment under the Trade Expansion Act, and they could continue to do so.

Prospects for Trade with Eastern Europe

But even with passage of the requested legislation and conclusion of commerical agreements with a number of countries, what are the actual prospects for more trade between the United States and Eastern Europe?

In recent years, United States trade with those countries has grown relatively little compared with the growth of total U.S. trade and compared with the growth of trade between other industrial countries and Eastern Europe. Last year U.S. exports to Eastern Europe and the Soviet Union totaled $139 million, and U.S. imports from those countries were valued at $137 million. In 1964 U.S. exports to those countries totaled $340 million, but that was a year of unusually large shipments of wheat and other grains. In contrast, total free world exports to these Communist countries (excluding Yugoslavia) in 1965 reached $6 billion, and free-world imports from them totaled approximately the same amount. The Netherlands and Sweden each did more business with the Communist countries of Eastern Europe last year than the United States did.

For a number of reasons, we would not expect a sudden huge expansion of United States trade with Eastern Europe to result from East-West trade legislation and conclusion of commercial agreements. This trade historically has not been large. The availability of Eastern European goods that will find a market in the United States is a real constraint on a sizable growth in trade. Although there need not be a strict bilateral balance of their trade with the United States, the Eastern European countries will have to sell in the United States to earn some of the foreign exchange with which to pay for American products.

Another constraint, despite the Soviet theme that trade should not be affected by "differences in economic and social systems," is the fact that we do have different trading systems and it will take time before marketing techniques both ways are understood and mastered. One difficulty is the limited contact between U.S. businessmen and plant managers in Communist countries. Another is the lack of clear-cut protection for U.S. industrial property rights. There is also difficulty in identifying and providing information on products and technology which might be of interest to U.S. firms.

But we should not consider that this is a permanent state of affairs. In almost all the countries of Eastern Europe an active search is under way for means to overcome the inefficiencies and lack of incentives in the economy which are depressing growth rates and retarding improvement in standards of living. Plans for overcoming these obstacles are being advanced in almost every country of the area. The plans usually call for rationalization of investments, introduction of new incentive systems based on profits, an increase in the autonomy of enterprises, and an increase in trade with the West. The tremendous economic success of the United States and Western Europe since World War II is exerting an irresistible pull on the economists and planners of the East, just as Western standards of living sharpen the dissatisfaction of Eastern European consumers with the results of their own systems.

The experience of Yugoslavia has been closely studied by the other Eastern European countries. Immediately after the break with the Cominform in 1948 Yugoslavia dismantled its central apparatus for planning and controlling the economy, giving its individual enterprises substantial autonomy in their own management. The remaining structure of central governmental controls over investment, foreign currency transactions, etc., was intended to be temporary and, with some hesitations, has been steadily reduced. An economic reform introduced in July of 1965 was intended, over a period of adjustment, to open the Yugoslav economy to competition from outside producers, to force Yugoslav enterprises to prove their viability in competition on the world market, and to integrate Yugoslavia more closely with the free world economic system. The transformation of the Yugoslav economy is well symbolized by their acceptance last August as a full contracting party to the GATT [General Agreement on Tariffs and Trade] –an international trade instrument designed primarily to govern trade relations among countries with market economies.

It is reasonable to expect a moderate and gradual growth in U.S.–Eastern European trade. It is increasingly evident that the Eastern Europeans, including the Soviets, are intent on acquiring more advanced equipment and technology. Moreover, as their national economies turn more and more to consumer needs and desires, they will become more attractive markets. One impressive example is the recent agreement of the Fiat Company of Italy to build an $800 million factory in the Soviet Union to make compact cars for the Russians. In connection with this, inquiries have been made of U.S. companies which may lead to substantial sales of U.S. automotive equipment and services to Fiat for the Soviet plant. President Johnson in his October 7 speech announced that the Export-Import Bank is prepared to finance American exports for this plant. Other Western European countries are building or expect to build factories in Eastern Europe to produce a wide range of goods.

Two additional steps to facilitate expansion of U.S.–Eastern European trade were announced by the President on October 7. One was his signing of a determination that will allow the Export-Import Bank to guarantee commercial credits to Poland, Hungary, Bulgaria, and Czechoslovakia. This already was possible for Yugoslavia and Romania. The other was a decision, details of which the Commerce Department will shortly announce, to reduce export controls on East-West trade with respect to approximately 400 non-strategic items.

These recent actions by the President and passage of the proposed East-West trade legislation should result in a higher level of trade. While the total still would be a very small percentage of U.S. world trade, it would be important to individual industries and businesses, to farmers, and to many firms providing the services to facilitate exports and imports.

Trade Can Convey Ideas

But would increased two-way peaceful trade between the United States and Eastern European countries really have significant effect on the general policies and attitudes of these countries?

We should not expect miracles from trade, but greater exchanges of goods and increased contacts of persons involved in trade could help to bridge the gaps between us and the nations of Eastern Europe. Trade can convey ideas. Through trade and the contacts which it requires, we can communicate to others some additional elements of our national personality and philosophy and our hopes for peace. The articles of trade can transmit specifically and perhaps more convincingly than the most powerful radio station some idea of our marvelous productivity–the rich variety and efficiency and consumer orientation of our output. Perhaps we can also transmit, through trade, the idea of our own system's basic reliance on a framework of economic incentives and rewards.

As with all trade relations, it must be a two-way street. If we believe that expanded East-West trade is an essential part of our balanced strategy for dealing with Communist countries, if we want to sell more of our farm and factory output to the Eastern Europeans, if we want them to invest some of their scarce economic resources in producing peaceful specialties for our consumers, then we will have to buy from them. In the case of Communist countries, we all have a special problem of consumer education.

There is a small but active minority which apparently believes it is unpatriotic to buy from or sell to any Communist country. Some individuals and small groups, such as self-appointed "Committees to Warn of the Arrival of Communist Merchandise on the Local Scene," have tried through boycotts, threats of economic reprisals, and other methods to block legal trade in goods from Communist countries. The targets of their intimidation have ranged from small shops to supermarket chains and multimillion-dollar corporations. The goods that aroused their wrath have varied from Christmas tree ornaments and hams from Poland, and vases and ashtrays from Czechoslovakia, to baskets and tobacco from Yugoslavia. Similarly, pressure has occasionally been brought on companies not to sell to Communist countries.

Are these Americans advancing the interests of the United States? The Government of the United States does not believe so. We think they are harming the United States national interest by obstructing a foreign policy that has been developed by four administrations since World War II. We think they are still living in the late 1940's and the early 1950's—not the middle of the 1960's. We think they are out of step.

In the past, we have been able to act with sufficient flexibility to meet changing situations and exploit new opportunities. Now the situation has changed and opportunities are arising, but in our view we do not have enough authority to act flexibly in our own interest.

As we see it, it now makes good sense for this nation with its enormous economic strength and its economic involvement in every part of the non-Communist world, to use trade as an effective tool to advance our relations with the countries of Eastern Europe.

Senator Magnuson has said of the proposed East-West Trade Relations Act that "few bills can ever hope to rival this one in its potential for contributing to the peace and stability of the world in what is left of the 20th century." He urged that we look at the Communist world as it exists in actuality today, not as it took shape in our fears of 10 or 20 or 30 years ago.

Today there is no longer a monolithic Soviet bloc—nor is there a Sino-Soviet bloc. Growing appreciation of the significance of this fact should increase popular acceptance of the general proposition that an expansion of peaceful trade with the nations of Eastern Europe would serve the purposes of peace and, thus, the national interest of the United States.

Something There is That Doesn't Love a Trade Wall

Alec Nove

The clamor for increased East-West trade relations is not restricted to the Western political scene. With polycentrism in fashion and serious efforts being made to rationalize prices, the East Europeans are primed for broader trade contacts. From the east: a plea; in the west: reappraisal.

To start off: a broadly valid generalization—all Soviet bloc countries buy from the west to the limit of their export earnings, plus any available gold. To be sure, the Soviet Union prefers buying from other bloc countries, relying on the capitalist nations only for items that can't be supplied by the communist world. The trouble is so much is unobtainable that, willy nilly, the Russians are keen advocates of expanded east-west commerce.

Their smaller allies are even more unrestrained in their desire to throw open a westward door. For one thing they have higher standards than the Russians and are therefore less willing to be satisfied with second-rate goods. For another they perceive that deals with noncommunist countries provide the means for greater economic and even political independence. A communist official has said: "It is fortunate for Rumania that the new pipeline enables us to be supplied with Soviet oil, because now the Rumanians can sell their own oil in the west and have much more western currency." Rumanian political independence of Russia may well be closely connected with her ability to trade outside the Soviet bloc.

Thus the desire to trade is there. However, the means to trade are often lacking. The balance of payments of all eastern countries is in a state of chronic strain. The list of goods which they wish to buy is always much longer than the means of paying for them. Their secrecy concerning balance of payments statistics, and gold too, is beyond doubt designed to conceal weakness.

It therefore follows that the most important limiting factor in east-west trade is the difficulty of expanding eastern earnings of western currency. The sale of communist goods to western countries is impeded by two principal circumstances: the restrictions imposed by western countries, and failure to make and sell the right goods. Both are important and require some further detailed consideration.

There are a great many restrictions against communist goods applied by nearly all western countries. In some cases the import of a commodity is free from all except communist sources, whereas the communist product is simply banned. More common is the practice of assigning the communist countries a limited quota for a product, while the same import from noncommunist nations is not subject to quantitative restrictions. This quota prevents exports from the east from rising above a given limit, but sometimes impedes trade within these limits too, because it is often not worthwhile to market and service the relatively small quantities of goods (for instance, machinery) permitted by the quota.

Discriminatory quotas stimulate a great deal of bilateral bargaining. Thus France or Britain undertakes to admit a limited quantity of Soviet watches or canned fish, on condition that the USSR allow the entry of British herrings or French hats. A long list of examples of such bargaining about quotas can be collected.

There is also a tendency to insist on bilateral balancing of trade; i.e., confining trade wholly or partly to goods and quantities listed in trade agreements, so arranged that the values in the two directions are more or less equal over the year, or the period of validity of the agreement. For example, Hungary and Czechoslovakia are more or less compelled to spend the whole of their earnings of French francs or German marks on the purchase of goods from France and West Germany respectively. They are unable to earn convertible currency, and thus while they might prefer to buy a machine from A rather than B, the bilateral agreement in effect ties them to B. This practice, they point out, is inconsistent with our advocacy of freer trade. Nor is the situation improved by the fact that we sometimes read them lectures on the advantages of multilaterialism.

Western strategic controls also affect east-west trade, though not so much as was the case when a longer and stricter list was in operation. Obviously, items known to be on the list must be produced in eastern countries, and this affects their investment policies in the direction of greater self-sufficiency. Outside of strictly military items, one wonders if this is in the interests of the west in the long run. Particular harm to east-west trade is caused by uncertainty over changes in the list and by divergent application of the rules by different countries. Thus chemical machinery exported by Britain or by West Germany may contain items covered by U.S. patents, whereupon the United States applies its more restrictive definition and seeks to impede the sale, for reasons which are not too clear to me.

Steel-pipe Story

The case of the ban on exports of steel pipe is an even worse one. Steel pipe was not on the list, but was banned *ad hoc* because it was an immediate way of causing economic embarrassment. Fear of repetition of such tactics must affect the willingness of eastern planners to rely on western suppliers for important items. It may be that the cancellation of the undertaking to supply steel pipe contributed to the failure to fulfil the plan for gas in 1964, and so led to a fuel shortage. It is a matter of opinion whether this is a desirable objective of western trade policy. It is a matter not of opinion but of obvious certainty that such acts will not encourage east-west trade. The same clearly applies to the cancellation of an American contract to build a tire factory in Rumania, though in this instance it was "unofficial" anticommunism that was responsible.

There are, in addition to the above, the restrictions involved in the Common Market (EEC), which particularly affect those East European countries who traditionally sell much of their produce in the countries of the EEC. However, save in those instances in which the EEC follows a policy of imposing special restrictions on goods of communist origin, the victims of discrimination include *all* outsiders, i.e., Great Britain and the United States as well as Czechoslovakia and the USSR.

Why the West Discriminates

What is the rationale of western restrictions? The Committee for Economic Development report on east-west trade (published in May, 1965) comments, on the whole favorably, on "the unwillingness of the west to extend its own system of freedom unilaterally to the east." The key word here is "unilaterally." The question is: how to define meaningful reciprocity? If a western country grants free access (subject only to the normal tariffs) to a communist country, in other words affords it most-favored-nation (MFN) treatment, what can a state-trading communist country offer in exchange? Tariffs are either nonexistent or unimportant. The Ministry of Foreign Trade could discriminate at any time by an interoffice memorandum urging that preference be given to imports from any particular country. Even if the policy is to buy in the cheapest market, even if the trade corporations are told to behave like "capitalist" traders, there is no means of checking that this is really done. There is no satisfactory way of having any real "access" to the eastern market. No one knows why particular decisions are taken, a by-product of the fact that there are few definable criteria for decision-making in communist economies. The eastern economies recognize this problem, and efforts are being made to alter the situation, as we shall recount below. However, at the present time suspicion of discrimination, as well as the undefinability of reciprocity, stand in the way of granting MFN.

Another restraining influence on western trading policies is fear of "dumping" and "market disruption." Some believe that the USSR and its allies go in for dumping with the avowed object of disorganizing the market. Yet all known cases of communist dumping are explicable by one or more of the following circumstances:

(a) the necessity to undercut existing prices in order to get into and hold a new market—often in the face of built-in preferences for noncommunist suppliers. This tactic is not unknown to shrewd capitalist traders;

(b) ignorance, due to lack of experience on the part of the communist traders, who are sometimes outmaneuvered by slick importers anxious to make a large profit; and

(c) pressure to sell very quickly so as to meet extremely urgent bills at a time of severe shortage of foreign currency.

Dumping Is Not the Aim

Under normal circumstances (and on all occasions known to me) communist salesmen were told to maximize foreign currency earnings and sell as dear as possible, provided they did sell the available goods. Because of restrictions imposed in a number of western markets, the effort to make quick sales in the few remaining markets that were open did sometimes have a disorganizing effect, but there is no evidence that disorganization was in itself an objective. Faced with open markets and a surplus to dispose of, eastern traders would surely seek to distribute it so as to maximize foreign currency proceeds. Unless tied by import restrictions and by bilateral agreements, there is no reason why they should seek to "unload" the surplus in any one place.

Though not politically motivated, the occasional communist dumping that does take place is nonetheless damaging to the interests of domestic and foreign suppliers in the west. This damage is all the more unfortunate in its effects since the communist traders often are unable to supply these goods over the longer term, this being the consequence of having to sell such surpluses as may happen to be available, under conditions of variable supply and inflexible domestic prices. (This kind of variation also occurs in agricultural surpluses in many western countries, since prices in this sector are artificial, and this has led many of these countries to impose quantitative restrictions on each other.)

While the policies of the communist salesmen *could* lead to market disruption on occasion, I would add at once that the danger is often exaggerated, because of the limited export potential of the eastern bloc. However, since the danger does exist, it is entirely proper for western countries to maintain reserve powers, which in many instances already exist with respect to imports from any source—namely, the power to impose antidumping duties or quotas.

The Dependency Argument

Finally on the list of justifications for discrimination, there is fear of undue or excessive dependence on communist supplies. This is a point not to be ignored, and indeed operates on both sides. Thus no Soviet planner could fail to have been impressed by the effects on the Soviet pipeline program of the ban on sales of large-diameter pipe which we have already mentioned, and so will avoid such excessive dependence in the future. This whole thought pattern is a quite inevitable by-product of mutual suspicion. One must not be too vulnerable to economic warfare by the other side. This could affect not only import needs, but also export outlets. Thus it is conceivable that either side might make access to its market conditional upon political concessions. Communist China is using such tactics on Japan.

All this is, no doubt, true, but what constitutes "excessive" dependence? Is Italy, who buys a very considerable fraction of its oil from the USSR, or is Britain, who does the same for timber, in this position? One would have thought that if the Soviets attempted to use oil and timber as a means of influencing Italian or British policies, the political and economic harm done to the Soviets themselves would be disproportionate, and in such conditions, alternative supplies would speedily appear. No doubt this constitutes one reason why the Soviet Union does not follow such policies. In any case, the value of the total trade of western countries is far higher than the east's trade, and so the relative importance of east-west trade in the trade of communist countries is much the greater. Therefore, the communists stand to lose far more from a disruption of trade relations than does the west and are not likely to initiate trade warfare.

Eastern countries tend to ask, understandably enough, for elimination of western restrictions. They ask for an end to discrimination, and they claim that, since they buy to the limit of their resources, the application to them of the principle of MFN is entirely fair and proper. If pressed, they will admit that their traders might so disrupt the markets of established suppliers that reserve powers will be needed to impose antidumping restrictions. They claim that given due warning that these restrictions are being contemplated, appropriate action would be taken. They deplore various western trade blocs, from which they suffer in common with other outsiders. They suspect also that the effect of the Common Market will ultimately be to reduce still further the markets open to them. Thus agricultural deficit countries will tend to give priority to the imports of surpluses from France rather than from Poland, and there might well be pressure on Italy to buy its oil from western companies rather than from the Soviet Union. Instances have also been known of discriminatory restrictions on eastern goods being imposed by such supranational western institutions as the Coal and Steel Community.

An Open Market . . .

However, the communist countries are becoming aware that elimination of western barriers is not enough. It is obvious that sales to the west suffer from the inadequacies of their own trading and production arrangements. In this connection one must mention that communist sales have remained poor in the one country, Canada, which has virtually no restrictions of any kind on imports from eastern countries—this despite the eastern bloc's very large deficit with this country. In the case of the Soviet Union this is partly to be explained by the noncomplementarity of the two economies, since Canada itself exports many of the raw materials typically sold by the Soviet Union. But this does not apply to the other communist countries. The explanation may be neglect of this difficult market, poor salesmanship, failure to make the right goods, or all these things at once. Since Canada is so "Americanized" a market, its experience reinforces the belief that sales in the United States would also be extremely difficult to make even if there were no discriminatory restrictions. In general, it supports the view that availability of the right goods at the right price is at least as important as western restrictions in explaining the still modest level of eastern exports. But it also confirms the views of those who discount the need for restrictions. A wide-open hard currency market has *not* led to massive Soviet-bloc dumping or market disruption.

. . .But No Sales Savvy

The Soviet bloc countries organize their foreign trade along lines that obviously impede expanded east-west intercourse. Thus all trade is centered, in nearly all these countries, under the Ministry of Foreign Trade, and is undertaken by specialized trade corporations. This interposes a barrier between the customers abroad and the producers at home. The latter have few if any possibilities to study the foreign market and to make direct contacts with potential customers. Trade corporation executives and commercial representatives abroad often have insufficient technical knowledge and little commercial sense. Of course this is not always so. In some traditional lines, such as Soviet timber or furs, there is much expertise and intimate knowledge of the market. But there are many instances of inefficiency, and such trading countries as Czechoslovakia have suffered from the fact that their experienced traders have been regarded as too politically unreliable to be allowed abroad to trade.

In addition, one need only mention the oft-cited fact that in many eastern countries productive enterprises have no material interest in making any effort to produce for foreign markets, and little or no incentive to improve quality (although this is changing). By contrast there is every incentive to fulfil output plans in quantitative terms. Therefore it is easier to make goods for the less demanding domestic or other communist markets.

The difficulty of making international price and cost comparisons is a further problem. Suppose that it costs 1,000 crowns to produce a given item in Czechoslovakia which would be bought from the USSR for 125 roubles or from West Germany for 750 marks. What should the Czech planners do–import or produce? The problem seems soluble: one could devise an exchange rate, not necessarily the official one. Cost in domestic currency could then be compared with foreign exchange earnings from sales, less the import content of the exported items. This might help to determine the desirability of importing and the choice of a trading partner. However, there are several reasons why such calculations break down. One is that domestic prices and costs are not particularly meaningful. So far, these prices do not even pretend to reflect relative scarcities, opportunity costs and quality. Since the price of a material does not mirror the fact that it is in very short supply, the assessment of the costs of production of a product which uses this material will not correctly reflect real costs for practical purposes. Lacking reliable measures of real costs, it becomes impossible to determine whether it is wiser to produce or import a given item.

Then there is the complex question which arises because Comecon-country currencies are not convertible into western currencies. Shifting the location of our example, if at a cost of 100 zlotys the Poles could earn either 100 U.S. dollars or 90 roubles, this would represent an identical sum at the official rate of exchange, and indeed might well represent an equal purchasing power at actually existing prices, since this exchange rate was chosen because it is fairly realistic. However, with dollars the Poles could buy almost anything they wanted, anywhere; whereas the roubles would buy only the goods which the Soviet Union was able and willing to supply. In a similar situation in the early postwar years, the British planners used different criteria for earning so-called "soft currencies" and "hard currencies," but since they never devised a workable quantitative measurement of degrees of softness or hardness, it was all very rough and ready.

Finally communist agricultural deficiencies reduce exportable surpluses of farm produce. Failure to invest adequately in agriculture is one example of neglecting export potential in favor of domestic (industrial) development. In fact imports of food and fodder, rendered necessary by agricultural short-comings, are a drain on the balance of payments of several eastern countries.

All of this indicates that deficiencies in the trading arrangements of communist countries are a major factor in limiting east-west trade. However, in a number of eastern nations, experiments are being conducted which could vastly improve these countries' ability to sell in western markets.

Russian Focus Is Domestic

In the case of the smaller communist countries these reforms are directly related to the need for expanded foreign trade. In the Soviet Union, however, the motive of reformers is predominantly to achieve greater efficiency in internal planning. This is hardly surprising, since exports make up only about 3% of the Soviet Union's national income. The need for change has arisen because the old system of administrative instructions and allocation of inputs, with inflexible and economically meaningless prices, has become increasingly unable to cope with the needs of a large and modern industry. Reforms have at least two objectives. First, the planners must be able to choose rightly, in the sense of using resources (especially investment resources) with maximum effect and minimum waste. Secondly, planners must be freed from the futile and time-consuming effort of issuing commands on detailed matters of output, inputs, deliveries, wages, finance, etc. For both these purposes, it is essential to devise appropriate criteria in monetary terms, and on this basis to let subordinate bodies choose much more freely.

Though the focus of Soviet reforms is domestic, the gains in foreign trade planning would be useful by-products. If the measurement of the cost of alternative courses of action helps Moscow to compare the advantage of producing something in Minsk against producing it in Omsk, logically it could facilitate a similar comparison with Prague or even Düsseldorf. If, in order to encourage production and discourage consumption of some scarce material, its domestic price were raised so that it reflected its scarcity, calculations of relative advantage of imports and exports would be facilitated. And, finally, if, in order to operate the reformed system, enterprises (or trusts, or combines) are given greater freedom to place orders for their requirements within the USSR, it might bring nearer the day when they can also place orders in another country, subject perhaps to a permit or license, or to import duties. This would be a decisive breach in the present narrow interpretation of the state monopoly of foreign trade. It would place the western importer and exporter in a very different situation and give him new opportunities. It must be emphasized that in the case of the USSR this may not happen for some years after the adoption of reforms because of the strength of the tradition that the Ministry of Foreign Trade and its organs should conduct trade, and also because of shortages of foreign currency and their effects on the minds of the planners. Like British officials in the first years after the war, these planners think in terms of priorities, and will probably regard it as natural that they should be in a position to give preference to "essential" imports by issuing appropriate orders.

Conforming to Capitalist Prices

As noted, in the smaller countries gains in foreign trade are no by-product but the chief object of reform. Thus in Czechoslovakia, Poland and Hungary, there is much talk not only of allowing more enterprises direct access to foreign markets, but also of aligning at least some prices to "world" (i.e., capitalist, or American) prices. The argument is put in the following terms. In the case of goods which are either imported or exported in appreciable quantities, the opportunity cost of the use of the domestic product must be seen as the export earnings foregone, or the import expenditure incurred. Therefore the domestic price should be aligned to the external price. It is interesting to note that such considerations militate against the emergence—often talked about—of a specifically "socialist" market price for use by Comecon countries. To avoid complications, it would be more logical to make Comecon prices conform rather more closely to "capitalist" market prices and to bring domestic prices into line with them. Obviously, this would greatly alter the conditions under which production and trade would be planned, to the considerable advantage (so one would think) of all concerned. However, the logic of such prices must eventually extend to the economy as a whole. For virtually everything is, at least potentially, either exportable or import-saving. This is particularly evident in making choices between alternative investments. Even in the Soviet Union this point has been the subject of published discussion, though not until recently.

An Overview of Reforms

But this is running ahead of decisions actually taken. What has happened so far is important and indicates the shape of things to come, but has not yet had much influence on foreign trade. The reforms thus far are in a number of instances merely experimental, and they differ widely from country to country. This is not the place for a detailed analysis. However, in view of the possible effects on foreign trade, some remarks are called for.

In the Soviet Union, much has been heard of the profit motive as the criterion of managerial decision-making. There have been other proposals too, and the authorities have based their recent experiments on a compromise between a number of different approaches to the problem. Thus the profit motive is by no means the sole criterion, since increased output (sales) must also be achieved. The reforms announced by Kosygin in September, 1965, are not clear about the extent to which the composition of output is still to be regulated by the planners, and how much freedom there will be to purchase inputs. Nor is there yet freedom to alter or fix prices, though there is somewhat greater flexibility, at least with respect to new products or designs. Reforms will probably be introduced gradually and cautiously.

Nonetheless, it does seem that enterprises will be left freer to make their own plans, based on what they think they can sell. They will have a wider range of choice in placing orders for the materials, components, and goods that they want, instead of having to apply for allocations to planning offices. Plans for labor, costs, and profits all become the responsibility of the management. This, if extended further, would represent a major departure from past practices. Great stress would now have to be placed on contracts, on sales and therefore also on salesmanship, a notoriously weak spot in a country where it has been all too easy, for a generation, to sell anything, Obviously, greater attention will have to be paid to the requirements of the user, and therefore to quality. This is, of course, an important part of the motivation of the reform. Production for global output statistics, instead of for the customer, has been (and still is) a major cause of waste and inefficiency.

The reluctance to go all out in this direction is based on a fear that the center would lose command over the macroeconomic magnitudes, resulting in intolerable overstrain, shortages, and even chaos. These fears are far from being groundless. Thus it is hard to see how the center can retain control over major investment decisions without being able to guide the production program of enterprises which make investment goods (e.g., building materials, machinery and the like). Yet many such enterprises (and many such materials and machines) can be used to make consumers' goods, in other words are inputs for those sectors of the economy which would no longer be subject to stringent central control.

Therefore we may find, for several years at least, that in the USSR the "liberalization" is confined to consumers' goods and to materials used to make them (cloth, leather, etc.). Production of, and foreign trade in, most capital goods (for import or export) is likely to remain chiefly centralized. Certain traditional Soviet exports—timber, furs, grain—will also remain under existing arrangements, since these are probably rational and have their counterpart in "capitalist" countries.

In this respect as in many others, reforms will not follow any single pattern. The Soviet type of economy has suffered for too long from a bureaucratic standardization of organizational forms. What is needed is diversity. The west, after all, has all kinds of production and trading organs. Some are nationalized, some are giant corporations, and some are quite small and independent. The units comprising the big corporations have a variable degree of autonomy in making decisions, including decisions involving foreign trade. Sometimes it is considered convenient to negotiate trade deals directly; sometimes it is more sensible to use specialized agencies. Gradually, this need for variety is being understood in eastern countries. Thus some Soviet enterprises are being unified for commercial and planning purposes into a species of trust, now called *firma*, or "firm." These *firmy* are a Soviet reaction to the fact that, for commercial purposes, many Soviet enterprises are too small (and too ill-informed as to needs) to be given autonomy. In some instances the *firma* (or trust) may cover a whole industry. For example, four Soviet phonograph record enterprises are now part of the single *firma*, called *Melodiya*.

This trend toward large trusts is also to be observed in Czechoslovakia and Poland. In both countries there has been a great deal of discussion about the granting of much wider commercial and planning freedom to productive units, but it is Czechoslovakia that is now (1965) taking a major step in this direction. As in the Soviet Union, production is to be more closely geared to demand by basing the plans on negotiated contracts. Incentives to management and labor are to be directly related to profits. Indeed, as in Yugoslavia since 1959, the Czech system intends to base the level of wages and of managerial salaries on the total "net revenue" of the production unit, this being defined as total revenue from sales less purchases of materials and fuel, plus depreciation. There is already strong pressure to allow the trusts, into which enterprises are being merged, greater freedom to make deals with foreign countries. They are likely to be allowed greater scope to study foreign markets, to make contacts (if not contracts) with customers and suppliers abroad, and, last but not least, they will be rewarded for success in exporting.

It is feared by some that the new trusts will be economic ministries in all but name, and so the essence of the traditional system will remain. However, the intention seems to be genuinely to avoid such a result. The trusts are expected to act commercially and not try to fulfil global output plans laid down by the government and the central planning offices. If it tells its constituent enterprises to produce for the customer, the trust need be no more "ministerial" than is the head office of a western corporation, which similarly distributes tasks to its factories. The western exporter and importer may therefore find himself dealing with a much more responsive trading partner than were the foreign trade corporations, dealing with men with greater technical knowledge, who are closer to production and more interested in the economic consequences to the given sector of the economy of foreign trade decisions. But there would be little or no competition between exporters, insofar as the trust would usually (and in smaller countries perhaps always) cover all the given country's output of the commodity in question. There is less likelihood of this kind of monopoly situation in the case of imports, since many items (for instance, trucks, typewriters, machine tools, metal) can be used in many different parts of the industrial structure.

New Forms of Regulation Needed

Autonomy in buying and selling across frontiers, as and when it comes, must be accompanied by new methods of central regulation of foreign trade. As already mentioned, some system of differential import duties and licensing and a more realistic exchange rate will have to replace the present highly centralized system of operating the foreign trade monopoly.

It is worth mentioning that in Hungary the reform is taking a rather different road. Oddly enough—since Hungary has gone far toward liberalization in many respects—the Hungarian reforms have been the least radical, at least on the surface. Economic ministries have been preserved, and some of these continue to control "their" enterprises as tightly as ever. Nonetheless, there is now much greater stress on economic rationality, on commercial advantage and on the customer. A few large enterprises, with a significant role in foreign trade, have for many years been allowed to make direct deals with foreign countries.

In some ministries in Hungary, enterprises are given a greater degree of autonomy. One way of doing this may perhaps be adopted in other communist-ruled countries and may have an effect on foreign trade. This consists of giving an enterprise a plan closely defining part of its activities, and leaving it free to sell and buy with respect to the rest.

It is, in my view, wrong to regard these trends as an evolution toward market capitalism. Profits may become much more important, in the sense of being treated as indicators of efficiency, as criteria for microdecision-making, as the basis on which bonuses are computed, but they still belong for the most part to the state, and the enterprises and trusts will not become in any sense the private property of the management. However, the move toward a more rational price structure and a study of comparative costs will facilitate both the planning of trade (and investments) within the Comecon and the calculations involved in east-west trade. The institutional changes which may accompany the reforms could well have the effect of reducing the objections, voiced by many in the west, to a more liberal and multilateral approach to trade with communist countries.

It appears that the west can contribute to the expansion of east-west trade by adopting more liberal policies, and the east by so altering its system as to facilitate the adjustment of output to consumer demand, abroad and at home. Thus, in conjunction with investments geared to expand output of items which have a promising export potential, better marketing could lead to a major increase in sales. Since the communist countries' imports are only limited by their earnings of western currency (plus gold production, if any), any increase in their sales is bound to lead to a proportionate rise in their purchases. There are many urgent requirements on which they would like to spend the currency they would earn.

What the West Can Do

What specific steps should the west take? In the case of the United States, the immediate measures would seem to be obvious, since her discrimination against imports from most communist countries hits them hard, and the American "strategic" list covers far more purely civilian items than does the list used by her allies. Obviously, if the goal of expanded trade were accepted, the United States would try to eliminate these barriers, which were erected at a time when east-west trade was regarded with distaste.

But the United States is not in itself a promising market for communist goods, even if there were no discriminatory restrictions at all. In the natural course of trade, one would expect the USSR and most of its allies to run a deficit with the U.S., and to cover it with surpluses earned elsewhere. Strict bilateralism, therefore, is not in America's economic interest, nor in the interest of trade expansion generally.

It would obviously be of help if western countries agreed to a *joint* abrogation of discriminatory measures and to abandon any bilateralism, while retaining necessary powers agains market disruption. Discriminatory bargaining over quotas is justified because the others do it. It is a form of competition between *western* countries for privileged access to eastern markets. If the French or the Italians were not insisting on a quota for their hats, or cars, or footwear, there would be no reason for the British or the West Germans to do so, and vice versa. This would, of course, require agreement among the major western trading nations, perhaps within the Organization for Economic Cooperation and Development.

What would be the objections to, or the risks involved in, such a step? There is no doubt that it would facilitate "commercial" behavior by the eastern bloc's foreign trade corporations, and also by any enterprises or trusts allowed to buy and sell across frontiers. They would try to buy cheap and sell dear. True, the old bilateral habits may persist, but it is surely for the west to discourage them, not to insist on their retention. Yet there is opposition to such measures.

There is, first, the usual objection to MFN: that the communists will discriminate secretly, or in some other way not grant reciprocity. Yet if, as seems reasonable, we can expect them to spend the western currency they earn, obviously their exports will result in more imports. They would import, in the main, from a western country, or on occasion from a developing country which, like Malaya or Argentina, derives most of its imports from western countries.

Even if the communist country that earns a surplus in francs or sterling expends it in purchases from one of its own allies, this would present no particular problem, since, through procedures already in theory available within the Comecon Bank, the other country would use this western currency to finance its own purchases. True, western currency is at present so scarce that eastern countries are very loath to transfer any to one another. This has led some western analysts to deny the possibility of multilateralism in east-west trade. I must confess myself unable to see the point. Surely the eastern countries could be placed in a position of treating all their resources of western currencies as freely interchangeable. They could then use a surplus in francs to cover deficits in marks, or sterling surpluses to pay Italy, Swedish crowns to pay Britain, and so on.

It is true, of course, that the Czech crown, the Polish zloty, and the Russian rouble are not convertible. That is to say, it is not at present possible for a western country to convert a surplus in one eastern currency. But for multilateral trade to occur it is not necessary that eastern currencies be made convertible. Accounts between eastern and western traders are not settled in eastern currencies. To finance east-west trade, to pay for their imports, the communist countries use western currency. In other words, the multilateral arrangements I have in mind do *not* mean that any country runs up a surplus of inconvertible zlotys or roubles, but that Poland and the USSR can pay in any western currency. And while the net effect of this scheme on any given western country's exports *may* be less favorable than under the system of bilateral balancing, there is no inherent reason why any country should expect this to happen, unless it is pessimistic about the competitiveness of its exports.

To work, such a system might well need an intergovernmental committee to keep an eye on how things are going, to warn the Soviet side if the rules of the game are not being observed, and especially to keep a joint eye on possible market disruption. So far, the more go-ahead countries in east-west trade have regarded suggested western organizations for the conduct of such trade with understandable suspicion. It was thought that they would increase rather than decrease restrictions. However, a joint effort to *increase* trade would be quite another matter.

One common argument for bargaining about quotas is the need to persuade the planners of communist countries to buy what they regard as "nonessentials," i.e., consumers' goods. I am not sure that it is particularly important for us to tell the partners to trade negotiations what they *must* buy. However, if such an attempt is desirable—and it may well be—it could be incorporated in the multilateral arrangements suggested above by introducing some kind of global quota, a sum which the country concerned is free to spend on these so-called nonessentials anywhere in the west (or perhaps even in such a country as India or Japan). Such an arrangement would probably require complex international (multilateral) negotiations, but the possibility exists.

The Question of Credit

What of credits? The eastern countries have been asking in many instances for long-term credits, and the Soviet Union in particular wishes to buy capital goods in this way. Presumably we are referring only to such credits that seem to be in the commercial interest of the country granting them, at the proper commercial rate of interest. No one, so far as I know, is proposing aid—though the United States has in fact granted some aid to Yugoslavia and Poland. No one is proposing artificially favorable terms. Therefore, credits must be considered as an integral part of mutually profitable trade. For example, a Hungarian economist argued for long-term credits to buy fodder to build up a Hungarian export trade in beef. The beef would relieve shortages in the west and would therefore be desirable. These *have* to be long-term credits, because it takes many years to build up beef cattle herds. What is wrong with this? Credits have the effect of relieving immediate shortages of foreign currency on the part of the recipient. If strain and shortage in communist-ruled countries are desirable objectives, then credits should not be granted, but neither should trade be expanded, since we may be sure that communist countries try to obtain by way of trade many items which relieve strain and shortage. The point is that if one accepts the idea of expanded trade one ought concomitantly to raise no barrier to the granting of credits.

But a very real question mark does arise. Suppose the west decides to relax restrictions on trade and on credits. Should it exact a price? By this is meant, of course, a political price. Implied in this formulation is the belief that communist countries derive more benefit from east-west trade than the west does. This view seems to be held, for example, by so balanced and serious a scholar as Gregory Grossman. It would seem to follow that the sale of an item worth, in world markets, $1 million is worth more than that to the USSR, who should therefore be charged more, i.e., a million dollars *plus* political concessions. Certainly a "trade" of this kind should not be excluded. Thus the USSR could be given to understand, privately, that some act of theirs would facilitate the conclusion of a highly desirable trading arrangement. There was, it is believed, such an informal agreement between East and West Germany, involving the release of political prisoners by the former. But this would seem an exceptional situation. We cannot, for instance, expect to "trade" MFN for a Soviet troop withdrawal or for a public criticism of Ho Chi Minh. And my own view is that trade is mutually advantageous. I see nothing in the trading methods and practices of the communist countries to suggest that they are capable of extracting more advantage from trade deals than do hard-headed "capitalist" businessmen. In fact statistical evidence, cited by Pryor and by Holzman in their researches, suggests the contrary.

Differentiating within the Bloc

Should there be differentiation between the countries of the communist bloc—if indeed there is a bloc nowadays? To some extent the United States does differentiate, "rewarding" those who seem likely to take an independent line, while imposing stringent embargos on any trade with China and Cuba. The correctness or otherwise of such policies in the present political situation raises questions which it is unnecessary to pursue here. They concern issues of political-economic warfare. Thus, apart from the rather special cases of China and Cuba, the arguments for discriminating among communist countries are based on the hope or need to weaken the cohesion of the bloc. This may be a perfectly legitimate political objective, which can be effectively pursued by economic maneuvering, among other ways. However, the too-obvious use of economic weapons to drive wedges between the Soviet Union and its allies may backfire, impede the political détente and limit the possibilities of expanding trade.

It would be desirable, however, to devise such rules as will encourage the tendency toward reform and flexibility in communist countries. By this is meant nothing so crude as to make the lifting of trade restrictions conditional upon the adoption of this or that reform of the planning system. This would surely delay change. The point is rather to make the rules for east-west trade such that the trade corporations, trusts and enterprises can make calculations of relative advantage and can base their trading in investment decisions upon such calculations. This will facilitate trade and bring the trading procedures closer to what we in the west would regard as normal. A profit-maximizing "communist" exporter would, no doubt, be a state organization. But it could behave commercially, try to sell at an advantageous price and to buy in the cheapest market. For reasons already stated, this tendency may well be linked, for good internal reasons, with a major reform of the planning system and to greater attention to economic rationality generally. It is a criticism of the present western insistence on what amounts to bilateral barter that it helps to keep the traditional communist institutional structure in being. After all, how can a Czech trust be allowed to buy a given commodity on commercial principles if the foreign currency has been earmarked in laborious trade negotiations for the purchase of this item from, say, France? Obviously, this tends to strengthen the practical arguments for the retention of the Ministry of Foreign Trade and its specialized corporations as the sole authority allowed to deal with foreign countries.

There are a number of other outstanding items on which tough negotiations may be desirable: patent protection and arbitration procedures are two of them. Neither is an insuperable obstacle. Indeed, I have heard of a number of businessmen who like arbitration awards to be decided in a communist capital, because, in their anxiety not to be considered prejudiced, the arbitrators bend over backward to be fair. There are exceptions to this, no doubt, but the problem is not a difficult one.

Patents are a matter of careful inquiry. It must not be assumed that the record of communist countries is so very bad. They are not the only ones to have copied other countries, and they have paid considerable sums for know-how. Their own hope of securing payments for their own discoveries has led the Russians to offer to sign international agreements in this field. More difficult are copyright and royalties on books. Here most communist countries prefer to save scarce currency by disregarding their duty to pay. This is deplorable, and they should be urged to mend their ways. Certainly pressure to achieve this result would form a useful part of east-west trade negotiations. However, the conclusion of such an agreement would not be an unmixed blessing, as it could give the Soviet authorities the right of veto on the kind of Russian books which should be translated in the west. This, clearly, ought to be avoided.

It is not for a moment suggested that the task of facilitating exchanges between different economic systems is an easy one. All kinds of tough obstacles exist in both east and west. The above ideas represent a few possible approaches which could lead to progress. And there are very few areas in which progress is as desired as in this. It would, of course, be absurd to expect that trade would or could by itself eliminate international tensions. Nonetheless, the growth of commercial interdependence and mutual confidence can contribute to the lowering of political barriers, and so help create an atmosphere conducive to a durable political détente.

Chapter 2

EAST-WEST TRADE IN CONTEMPORARY POLITICAL ENVIRONMENT

United States Policy in East Europe

Michael B. Petrovich

In the following survey, Professor Petrovich of the University of Wisconsin points to the polycentric changes which have recently occurred in Eastern Europe giving it the form of an alliance rather than a bloc. Regional economic progress has encouraged the East European nations to seek a détente with the West to which the United States should respond positively. The author concludes that "poor politics rather than good business stand in the way of increased American trade with that area."

As an East European official recently observed, "The trouble with you Americans is that you are about two years behind the times in your view of this part of the world. You think that Rumania and Hungary are the fastest changing countries in Eastern Europe, when actually they are Bulgaria and Czechoslovakia." It is true that developments are moving so fast in East Europe that even well-informed Americans may have trouble in keeping up. Indeed, by now even the opinion of that East European official may be out of date.

Yet the real trouble is that some Americans may still see the communist countries of East Europe as they were in the Stalin era—a monolithic bloc subjected to a Soviet-imposed uniformity. Such Americans may be reacting in ways which may have been appropriate one or two decades ago, but which are no longer relevant or effective.

Though *Current History* devoted its March, 1965, issue to "East Europe in Flux," it is not too soon to take another look at those eight countries—East Germany, Poland, Czechoslovakia, Hungary, Yugoslavia, Rumania, Bulgaria and Albania—whose hundred million people live between the Soviet Union and the West, with a view to determining what American foreign policy in East Europe is and what it might be.

Behind any American policy toward East Europe is the basic American dislike of communism. The vast majority of Americans are opposed to communism as an ideology and dislike the manner in which communist regimes have seized and maintained power. As United States Secretary of State Dean Rusk has put it, "We view communism as a system incapable of satisfying basic human needs, as a system which will ultimately be totally discredited in the minds of men everywhere. We believe that the peoples who have been brought under Communist rule aspire to a better life—of peace, economic opportunity, and a chance to pursue happiness."

Nevertheless, most Americans have come to realize that the communist regimes of East Europe are not transient interludes, like the fascist regimes of Mussolini or Hitler, but are here to stay. If not even the death of Stalin in 1953 or the ensuing rebellions in Poland and Hungary in 1956 could unseat the communist rulers of East Europe, the prospect of a sudden violent overthrow of those governments seems unlikely. Certainly the hands-off policy of the United States during those uprisings served notice that military intervention against the communist regimes of East Europe is not a part of American policy. Every American administration has sought to avoid any confrontation with Soviet power in East Europe that

Reprinted with permission from *Current History*, Vol. 52, No. 308 (April 1967).

might lead to war with the U.S.S.R. Only recently, in October, 1966, President Johnson again stressed this policy when he stated, "Our purpose is not to overturn other governments. . . ."

Polycentric Communism

American policy toward East Europe has also been forced by certain events to recognize that the East European countries are not to be regarded as the helpless satellites of the Soviet Union. In 1948, some Americans found Yugoslavia's break with Moscow so unbelievable that they suspected trickery or connivance. Surely, the uprising in East Germany in 1953 and the uprisings of 1956 in Poland and Hungary awakened Americans to the realization that the solar system of Eastern Europe was in disarray, and that the satellites were not orbiting as they used to do. Albania has left the Soviet camp altogether and has declared its solidarity with Red China. The other nations of East Europe are carrying out their disengagement from Moscow in a quieter manner. It is highly important to realize that the degree of dependence of each East European country on post-Stalin Russia varies greatly, and that all are freer of Soviet control today than they have been since World War II. Indeed, today one can no longer speak of a Soviet bloc in East Europe, but rather of an alliance which is being made looser all the time as each bloc member pursues its own interests.

This situation takes on special meaning as we come to realize that the unity of the international communist movement has been destroyed, especially by the Sino-Soviet schism. "How much meaning can even the phrase 'world communism' have," Under Secretary of State Nicholas deB. Katzenbach asked recently, "when Red Guards riot at the Soviet Embassy in Peking and the Chinese Communists charge the Soviet Union with conspiring with the United States to betray North Viet-Nam?" In Europe itself, the communist parties in the West do not figure in the Warsaw Pact of East Europe but carry on independent policies. And apparently this is not being done in defiance of Moscow, but with Soviet acceptance. Today the communist universe is not heliocentric but polycentric.

It is becoming increasingly apparent that the dead hand of Stalinism did not do away with the differences which have always marked East Europe. There have always been deep cultural divergences which have separated the East European countries from one another. These have been exacerbated by conflicting territorial ambitions which still exist—as in Macedonia or Transylvania. Historically, Poland has been more a part of Western civilization than Spain: the border between Poland and Germany is a changing political one, but that between Poland and Russia is a cultural iron curtain of a millenium. One can hardly understand the vagaries of Tito's Yugoslvaia without realizing that the Yugoslavs have been straddling the boundary between "East" and "West" since the sixth century. Americans who tend to think of East Europeans as being all the same, either culturally or ideologically, are making a serious mistake. Despite communism, the old nationalisms are not dead.

On the other hand, one must not make too much of what has been called "national communism" in East Europe. This communist "nationalism" arises from a simple practical necessity: communism must be suited to the specific needs and temperament of each country. However little the communist leaders of a given East European country are politically responsible to their own people, they wish even less to be responsible to any authority outside their own country. Least of all do they wish to be tied to an arrangement which makes them dependent on others to their own detriment.

At the bottom of all this is a revolution which has overtaken the communists of both the Soviet Union and the West European countries: the ideologists have become managers, and those who have not made the change are being replaced. Anyone who reads the "state of the union" message of any East European leader gets the feeling that the state is less a newly converted sector of the communist religion than it is a vast economic corporation. This is not to say that the communist faith is dead in East Europe; it is rather that the old-time religion no longer seems relevant to modern problems. Economic efficiency has taken precedence over Marxist ideology. No longer is reality twisted so frequently to fit any rigid conception of Marxism, but Marxism is stretched to fit new realities. This practical approach and flexibility make the "red executives" of East Europe far more accessible to Westerners. It is precisely this emphasis on economic progress rather than dogmatism that has encouraged the East European countries to seek a détente with the West.

U.S. Policies in East Europe

It may be said that during most of the period since World War II the United States has not had an active policy for East Europe. The postwar policy of "containment" arose in response to a severe Soviet threat to West Europe and accomplished little in East Europe other than to give cautious aid to Tito's Yugoslavia after that country's rift with Moscow. Rather, the emphasis was on saving Greece and Turkey from communism under the Truman Doctrine. The policy of "liberation" in President Dwight D. Eisenhower's first term was shown to be an empty pious hope when the United States failed to intervene in the uprisings in East Germany, Poland and Hungary.

It was especially after Wladislaw Gomulka's Poland showed its ability to withstand Soviet pressure—even though Poland remained in the Soviet bloc—that United States policy became formed around the idea of fostering evolutionary change in East Europe. That policy of "gradualism," furthered by President John F. Kennedy, has now reached new emphasis under President Lyndon B. Johnson. It has already received a handy name—"peaceful disengagement" or, to use the President's term, "building bridges." First enunciated by President Johnson on May 31, 1964, this policy has been repeatedly voiced by him ever since. For example, he declared in a public address on September 5, 1966: "In Europe our partnership has been the foundation for building bridges to the East. We and our friends in Western Europe are ready to move just as fast, just as far, as the East is prepared to go in building those bridges of friendships."

What "building bridges" means to President Johnson and his administration is no mere exercise in international friendship. Rather, it is meant to be a serious and far-reaching effort, in the President's own words, "to help the people of Europe to achieve a continent in which the peoples of Eastern and Western Europe work together for the common good, a continent in which alliances do not confront each other in hostility, but provide a framework in which West and East can act together to assure the security of all."

The most ambitious goal and expression of this policy is nothing less than "the reunification of Germany in the context of a larger peaceful and prosperous Europe." Under Secretary for Political Affairs Eugene V. Rostow made clear the intimate connection between these problems when he declared, in a statement on November 25, 1966, that there could be no détente in Europe without German unification, and no German unification without a détente.

To implement the policy of "building bridges" to the East, President Johnson proposed the following steps, on October 7, 1966: (1) To remove "hundreds of nonstrategic items" from the list of American goods barred from shipment to the communist countries of East Europe; (2) To permit the Export-Import Bank to guarantee commercial credits to Poland, Hungary, Bulgaria and Czechoslovakia; (3) To ease the burden of Polish debts to the United States; and (4) To liberalize rules for travel by Americans to communist countries. This last proposal referred only to Albania, among the East European countries, since Albania is the last European country to remain off limits to Americans by order of the State Department.

In the past two or three years the United States government has undertaken many and varied measures to build bridges to the East. For example, in 1964 the governments of the United States and Rumania reciprocally elevated their diplomatic missions to the rank of embassies. Similary, on November 28, 1966, the White House announced that the United States legations in Bulgaria and Hungary had been raised to the level of embassies. This symbolic move had some significance since these two diplomatic missions had been retained as the last two American legations in the world to show American disapproval of previous anti-American policies in Hungary and Bulgaria.

More concretely, the United States has negotiated settlements with several East European countries concerning the property claims of American citizens—with Bulgaria in 1963, and with Yugoslavia in 1964. Rumania was persuaded to allow several hundred "dual nationals" and relatives of American citizens to travel to America.

In the field of cultural relations, in 1964 Yugoslavia was included in the exchange of Fulbright scholars. Moreover, on December 31, 1965, the United States National Academy of Sciences and the Council of Yugoslav Academies concluded a three-year program of scientific exchanges, including reciprocal visits of American and Yugoslav scientists for research and teaching. This was the first such agreement between learned bodies in the United States and any East European country except the Soviet Union. The Inter-University Travel Grant Committee and the Office for International Education—to mention but two American organizations—have greatly expanded scholarly exchanges with Bulgaria, Czechoslovakia, Poland and Hungary. The writer was one of three American professors involved in the first such exchange with Bulgaria, in 1963-1964. Cultural exchanges with Rumania have also risen markedly.

The United States has made several gestures of goodwill toward Poland. Not the least of these was the appointment, in November, 1965, of former Postmaster-General John Gronouski as ambassador to Poland. What made the appointment unusual was that Gronouski, a native of Wisconsin, is of Polish descent on his father's side. His arrival in Warsaw was attended by a large crowd of cheering admirers. In 1965, too, the United States financed a children's hospital in Poland. In 1966, the Chicago Art Institute featured an exhibit of art treasures from Poland marking the celebration of a millenium of Polish statehood. The United States Post Office also issued a stamp commemorating the official establishment of Christianity in Poland a thousand years ago.

A physical bridge to East Europe was inaugurated in 1965 when Pan-American World Airways established a direct service to Czechoslovakia, the first such service in almost 20 years. In the field of communications, it is noteworthy that since 1963, when the Soviet Union stopped jamming the broadcasts of the Voice of America, practically all East European countries have followed suit.

To be sure, incidents continue to mar relations between the United States and various East European countries. For example, some East European countries—most recently Hungary and Czechoslovakia—have place curbs on the travel of American diplomats, in retaliation for similar restrictions on those countries' diplomats in the United States. Anti-American demonstrations over our involvement in Vietnam have taken place in several countries. Occasionally East European officials still flee to the United States for political asylum, as in 1965, when the second secretary of the Hungarian legation in London and the head of the Polish military mission in West Berlin sought American protection. Incidents involving espionage also crop up. In late December, 1963, about 3,000 Bulgarians demonstrated outside the United States legation in Sofia, smashing windows and overturning American cars, as a result of a treason trial in which Ivan-Asen Georgiev, a member of the Bulgarian delegation to the United Nations, was convicted for supplying secret information to the United States Central Intelligence Agency.

On the other hand, the United States was highly embarrassed when Yugoslav diplomatic missions in several American cities were simultaneously bombed by unknown persons in late January, 1967. The Yugoslav press not only blamed Yugoslav political exiles in the United States for the deed, but reproached the C.I.A. for supporting some of the exile groups. More recently, a naturalized American citizen, Vladimir Kazan-Komarek, was snatched from a Soviet plane which made an unscheduled stop in Prague, and he was tried as a spy. Though sentenced to eight years, a relatively light sentence by Czech standards, he was released immediately and returned to the United States within 24 hours. Apparently the Czech government did not consider the matter worth risking reprisals from the United States. Perhaps, too, it indicated Czech desires for improved relations in the future.

Expansion of Trade

There is no avenue of intercourse with the West to which the East European countries are so receptive as increased trade relations. It would be difficult to name any single element in international relations which can contribute more effectively to the breakdown of barriers and to the maintenance of peace than mutually profitable commerce. Yet in 1965, Holland and Sweden did more business with East Europe than did the United States. In that year the free world exported about $6 billion worth of goods to communist East Europe (excluding Yugoslavia), and it bought almost the same amount; the American share of this was only $139 million in exports and $137 million in imports. While one should not exaggerate the importance of East Europe as a market for the United States, the fact is that poor politics rather than good business stands in the way of increased American trade with that area.

One of the chief problems is that, at present, only Yugoslavia and Poland have received the most-favored-nation treatment we give to the other countries of the world. As Under Secretary of State Katzenbach recently admitted in an address to the National Association of Manufacturers, "I might add that I have never understood the reason for the phrase. All that 'most-favored' means is 'non-discriminatory treatment'." It was in 1951, at the height of the cold war, that the United States withdrew this policy from the communist countries of East Europe and imposed on them the very high rates of the Smoot-Hawley Tariff Act of 1930.

Undoubtedly hoping to convince the American public and Congress, in early 1965 President Johnson appointed a committee of distinguished business, labor and academic leaders to study the problem. He placed the committee under J. Irwin Miller, chairman of the Cummins Engine Company. This committee concluded that peaceful nonstrategic trade "can be an important instrument of national policy in our country's relations with individual communist nations of Europe." Despite the Miller committee's findings, Congress would not act on the proposed East-West Trade Relations Act which the administration requested in 1966. However, the administration has indicated that it will try again during 1967.

There are at least three basic questions which complicate this problem in the minds of many: (1) Will trade increase the military strength of the communist countries? (2) Is it really good business? (3) Is it good policy diplomatically?

The Johnson administration's answer to the first of these questions is *no*; to the other two questions, it is *yes*. To begin with, the export of strategic goods is already strictly controlled by law. Besides, the military might of the Soviet Union is not dependent on imports but on that country's own resources and production. As for trade with East Europe being good business, one need only observe the increasing trade the West European countries are developing with East Europe. In answer to the last question, Foy D. Kohler, deputy under secretary for political affairs and recently United States ambassador to the Soviet Union, replied, in an address before the Florida department of the American Legion on December 10, 1966:

> Trade is not just commercial, but also political. It is a two-way street and one of the channels of communications with these countries. Let me put it to you this way. Who here would not sooner have people in Yugoslavia growing tobacco rather than producing munitions? Who among us would rather not have Soviet workers making passenger cars instead of missiles? Isn't it better for us all for Poland to devote increased resources to production of high quality pork and ham? Who does not think it useful that Romanian resources be devoted to an automobile-tire industry rather than to production of jet fuel?

One of the obstacles to American trade with Eastern Europe is the pressure exerted by various right-wing groups in the United States. On January 4, 1965, Secretary of State Dean Rusk disclosed that the Firestone Tire and Rubber Company of Akron, Ohio, and the Universal Oil Products Corporation of Des Plaines, Illinois, had agreed to build a synthetic rubber plant and a petroleum plant in Rumania, in accord with a United States-Rumanian economic and trade agreement signed on June 1, 1964. The American press described this as a major breakthrough and as the first direct entry by American private industry into a communist country since the Second World War. However, the Firestone Company cancelled its contract after a right-wing organization threatened a boycott. Other American companies, most recently American Motors, have since been forced to have second thoughts about trade with East Europe.

In the last few years "Committees to Warn the Arrival of Communist Merchandise on the Local Scene" have been formed in various places throughout the United States to organize campaigns against the sale of East European products.

U.S. Policy Goals

What policy and goals one would set for the United States in East Europe depends basically on how one views the nature of the confrontation between the Western democraticies and the communist countries.

John C. Campbell of the Council on Foreign Relations, former State Department specialist for East European affairs, has outlined three alternative courses for United States policy in Western Europe.

The first course attracts those Americans who still think in terms of the cold war of the 1940's and 1950's. To them the idea of "building bridges" seems foolish and dangerous. Their view would be, instead, to step up political and economic warfare against both the Soviet Union and the East European "satellites" as a whole and to take advantage, by all means short of war, of any disunity in their ranks in order to free the captive peoples of the Soviet empire. All means possible, including radio communication and underground activities, would be used to help organize popular resistance to communist rule. In this task, an important role would be given to exiled East European political leaders now living in the West. In military policy, the emphasis would be on the maintenance of the strongest possible military establishment in Europe. As for economic relations, only the most rigidly controlled trade would be permitted, and then largely to place pressure on communist regimes to make specific concessions. Cultural relations would be reduced or even discontinued on the premise that cultural exchanges can only benefit the communist countries by lending them prestige or even opportunities for espionage.

The second line of policy would be based on a distinction between the communist countries of Eastern Europe and the Soviet Union. It would aim at loosening their ties by encouraging the national interests of the East European countries and by rebuilding the historic ties between the West and the East European states. Instead of any major showdown, this policy would look to a gradual change in which other East European countries would approach a status like that of Yugoslavia, or even Finland and Austria. In diplomacy, the goal would be a détente on the one hand, relieving pressures in Central Europe, and getting the East European countries more independently involved in the United Nations and in international bodies in general. In propaganda, while the United States would go on contesting communist falsehoods, the accent would be on urging independence versus dependence for the communist countries. Militarily, the goal would be a gradual reciprocal reduction of forces in Europe. Trade and even aid would be used to open the doors to greater Western influence. The same argument would apply to increased cultural exchanges.

A third approach is similar to the second, except that it would treat the Soviet Union and the East European countries alike. It would assume that further liberal changes are taking place in both the Soviet Union and the rest of communist East Europe, that they, unlike the Red Chinese, really want and need "peaceful coexistence," and that they would welcome an easing of tensions.

It is obvious that the Johnson administration has chosen to follow a combination of the second and third courses. It is doing so not out of any "softness" toward communism. Rather, it is led by the conviction that this is the more practical policy, the one which will come closer to achieving the general aims of American policy.

In 1965, Professor Brzezinski listed the following specific goals which he thought the United States should pursue in the immediate future:

> 1. To convince the East Europeans, particularly the Czechs and the Poles, that the existence of East Germany limits their freedom without enhancing their security. . . .
> 2. To promote a German-Polish reconciliation, somewhat on the model of the Franco-German reconciliation of the fifties. . . .
> 3. To lessen the Russian obsession with Germany. . . .
> 4. To relate the expansion of economic ties to more extensive cultural and social contacts. . . .
> 5. To promote multilateral ties with West Europe and East Europe.

The question naturally arises as to why the United States should be actively engaged in any policy in East Europe, especially when we are still so deeply involved in Vietnam. Why not let the countries of West Europe, who are closer to the problem, deal with East Europe?

This may be precisely the way in which France's Charles de Gaulle sees it. His slogan of "Europe to the Urals" was meant to convey something of this idea.

France's recent successes in establishing new contacts–and reestablishing old ones–in East Europe are significant. De Gaulle's eleven-day tour of the Soviet Union in early July, 1966, coming as it did at precisely the same time as France pulled out of NATO, was a stunning show of French independent policy in Europe. The resumption of ties between France and certain East European countries, especially Rumania, recalled France's traditionally strong role in that region.

Similarly, especially after control in West Germany passed from Konrad Adenauer to Chancelor Ludwig Erhard, the West German government also pursued a more active policy in East Europe, one based on the recognition of evolutionary changes in East Europe. This policy was only intensified with the advent of the new chancellor, Kurt Georg Kiesinger, and Foreign Minister Willy Brandt in November, 1966. The most startling result of Bonn's new approach was the establishment of diplomatic relations between West Germany and Rumania, on January 31, 1967. When Foreign Minister Willy Brandt shook hands with Rumania's Foreign Minister Corneliu Manescu to seal the agreement, in effect he scrapped the Hallstein Doctrine. Once a cornerstone of West German foreign relations, the Hallstein Doctrine proclaimed that West Germany would not recognize any country that had diplomatic relations with East Germany, except the Soviet Union. With the demise of this policy, the road is now open for similar agreements between West Germany and other East European countries, especially Hungary, Bulgaria and Czechoslovakia, much to the openly declared displeasure of the communist regime of East Germany.

That the United States government welcomes such steps may be gathered from the whole trend of United States policy in Eastern Europe today. Significant, for example, is the statement made on November 25, 1966, by Under Secretary for Political Affairs Eugene V. Rostow at a meeting of the ministerial council for the Organization for Economic Cooperation and Development. He stressed that it was not the American view to urge the member nations of the O.E.C.D. to promote a common position with which to confront the countries of Eastern Europe. Rather he hoped that they would share views on steps to be taken singly by each member, with the goal of bringing the East European countries into the O.E.C.D. as well.

It is Brzezinski's view, nonetheless, that the United States must take the lead in the whole task of restoring the unity of Europe, precisely because it is not a European power.

The Revival of Trade Between the "Communist Bloc"and the West

Anthony M. Solomon

In the following article, the Assistant Secretary of State for Economic Affairs argues that the United States as a global power concerned with preserving peace and reaching an accommodation with the U.S.S.R. should not deliberately refrain from expanding its economic relations with Eastern Europe, which our West European allies have been intensifying. While the author is aware of existing difficulties, he suggests some measures how to promote U.S. commercial contacts with Eastern Europe so as to render them mutually beneficial. He stresses that the transactions which American firms shy away from are engaged in by their European subsidiaries and affiliates.

Abstract: Since the death of Stalin, trade between the Western democracies and East European Communist countries has been on the increase. The economies of the Communist countries are evolving in a direction of lessened rigidity and greater diversity. The countries of West Europe, with a greater dependence on trade than the United States, have pursued trade with the Communist countries more than has the United States. The policy of the United States government is to expand East-West trade in peaceful goods. There are political as well as economic advantages to be gained by such trade. The President needs legislative authority to be able to best use trade relations with East Europe most effectively in the national interest. Such legislation would permit the United States to negotiate a removal of tariff discrimination in return for benefits from the Communist countries, such as nondiscriminatory treatment for United States businessmen, with respect to market and trading access, and agreement on settlement of disputes. Meaningful agreements between a free market system and state trading systems will not be easy to reach. However, the free market countries of West Europe have worked out agreements that have been mutually profitable. There is no reason why the United States cannot do the same, to our economic and political advantage.

Both the Communist world and the free world have shown a growing interest in recent years in increasing trade between themselves. The revival of trade has been primarily between western Europe, Canada, and Japan on the one side, with eastern Europe, including the Soviet Union, and, to a lesser degree, Communist China on the other. Trade statistics indicate that the revival of trade with eastern Europe has indeed been under way, with little fanfare until a few years ago, for some thirteen years—or, interestingly, since 1953, the year Stalin passed from the scene.

Since that time, but especially during the 1960's, important changes have taken place in the Communist world. "Communist Bloc" is a convenient term to describe collectively geographic areas under one kind or another of government calling itself Communist. But, when we look at some of the Communist countries separately—Yugoslavia, Poland, Romania, Red China; when we see the changes and experiments made or planned in some of their domestic economies; when we note the variation among them in relaxation of police controls and widening of cultural contacts with the West; and, finally, when we hear the Soviet and the Chinese Communists castigating each other in the vocabulary once reserved for the United States and other capitalist countries—then we can be sure that there no longer exists a political bloc. Indeed, perhaps it never was the monolithic structure it seemed to be in Stalin's day before the defection of Yugoslavia.

Before discussing current trends and future prospects, it might be useful to examine the history of trade relations between Communist countries and the West, and to identify some of the major influences on this trade.

In the years following World War I, United States–Soviet trade was a rather one-sided affair. Soviet purchases of United States goods during the years 1919 through 1934 came to almost three-quarters of a billion dollars, while United States purchases of Soviet goods were only $155 million. Thereafter, there was a sharp break in United States exports to the Soviet Union, to less than $13 million in 1932 and less than $9 million in 1933. This reflected the drop in world raw material and agricultural prices that deprived the Soviet Union of the foreign exchange which it needed to buy the machinery and agricultural equipment sought in the West. Beginning in 1935, a series of United States–Soviet commercial agreements provided Soviet undertakings to increase their purchases in the United States, and for the period 1935–1941, Soviet purchases averaged more than $50 million a year, while United States purchases from the Soviet Union averaged over $23 million a year.

At the end of World War II, there were virtually no goods to be traded as Communist and capitalist countries alike struggled to recover from the devastation of war. When it became clear that the Soviet Union under Stalin had no interest in co-operating to develop a peaceful world, the United States, concerned

Reprinted with permission from the *Annals of the American Academy of Political and Social Science,* (Vol. 372 (July 1967)).

for its own security and determined not to contribute to the Soviet Union's potential for aggression, established licensing controls on exports to the Soviet Union and the Soviet-dominated countries of eastern Europe. In 1948, the United States consulted with friendly industrial countries with a view to adoption of parallel controls in the interest of joint security. This led in 1949 and 1950 to the multilateral export control system established under the Paris-based Co-ordinating Committee (COCOM), of which all North Atlantic Treaty Organization (NATO) nations (except Iceland) and Japan are members.

In 1953, free world exports to eastern Europe and Communist Asia totaled $1,389 million, and imports from Communist countries, $1,631 million. In 1965, the exports totalled $7,557 million and imports, $7,856 million. Even allowing for inflation and the general increase in world trade, these are significant increases. More significant, however, is the increased share of total world trade claimed by Communist-free world trade. In 1953, free world exports to Communist countries were only 1.9 per cent of total exports, and imports, 2.1 per cent. By 1965 these proportions had increased by more than 200 per cent, to 4.6 per cent and 4.5 per cent, respectively, of total world trade.

United States trade with Communist countries has been of much smaller dimensions. The United States enforces a virtual embargo on trade and financial transactions with the East Asian Communist world (Red China, North Korea and North Vietnam), as well as with Cuba.

Our postwar trade, (both exports and imports), with the eastern European countries, including the Soviet Union, was at a low point in 1953. United States imports from eastern Europe have been moving slowly upward, in step with the expansion in our over-all imports. From a low of $36.4 million in 1953, our imports have risen to $142 million in 1965. For 1953, this represented 0.3 per cent of total imports; during the period 1955-1964, imports from Communist countries were stabilized at 0.5 per cent of total imports, rising to 0.7 per cent in 1965.

TABLE 1–Free World Trade with Eastern Europe (Millions of Dollars)

Time Span	Exports	Imports
January–June 1965	3,107.3	3,165.1
January–June 1966	3,941.9	3,800.0

Source: Department of Commerce

United States exports to Communist countries display a less continuous pattern. A low of $1.8 million was exported to eastern Europe in 1953. Exports have trended erratically upward since 1953 to a peak of $340 million in 1964, and $139 million in 1965. The 1964 figure was inflated by an unusual volume of wheat shipments, amounting to some $140 million.

Exports to eastern Europe as a per cent of total exports have been erratic. The trade has been at such a relatively low level that a single transaction, such as the large wheat sale in 1964, has a substantial effect on a year's figures. During 1953-1955 exports to eastern Europe were less than 0.05 per cent of total United States exports; in 1956 they reached 0.1 per cent and thereafter ranged between 0.5 per cent and 1.0 percent until 1964 when the wheat transaction raised them to 1.3 per cent a total exports. 1965 exports of $139 million represented 0.7 per cent of total United States exports.

The comparatively low level of United States trade with eastern Europe is a reflection of several factors. First, historically and traditionally, we have not been a major trading partner of that part of the world. There exist barriers of distance and language, and of mutual disinterest on the part of sellers. In this country, there are the impact of public opinion and even active boycotts to be dealt with. United States businessmen have found it more profitable and easier to deal with more familiar markets, closer at hand. In addition, there are problems that flow from the differing trading systems of East and West.

The Cold War has had a greater adverse impact on United States trade than on that of other free world countries. We are less dependent on foreign trade than our allies. Our total imports amount to only about 3 per cent of our gross national product (GNP), while other industrialized nations such as the United Kingdom, Germany, and Japan have imports amounting to 12 to 17 per cent of GNP. These countries have a greater incentive than we to sell where they can. They have not been inclined to let the political emotions of the Cold War interfere with trade, which is so vital to their well-being.

American sellers find it difficult to do business with the State trading companies with which they must deal in Communist countries. Frequently, there are bureaucratic layers to be overcome before a purchasing decision can be made. Fear of criticism for a possible wrong decision results in a spreading of the decision-making process in Communist countries that makes for cumbersome dealing. On the Communist side, officials sometimes become impatient with administrative delays caused by United States licensing restrictions and will buy a plant or a product from a European competitor even though it may not be quite as good as what the American firm has to offer.

American firms that handle consumer products sometimes find that trade in Communist-origin goods creates for them a public relations problem and the threat of boycott from a small but articulate minority which claims that any trade constitutes aid to the

Soviet Union. The government has taken a strong stand against such boycotts, but the threat of action against his company is bound to be a factor in a businessman's decision to trade or not to trade with Communist countries. (There are two interesting ironies in the position of those who oppose trade with Communist countries. First, from the standpoint of Communist China and North Vietnam, the Soviet Union, or any other eastern European country, is "aiding" the United States by carrying on trade with us. Second, a look at the items that move in trade between the Soviet Union and the United States suggests that, insofar as there is a significant strengthening of the strategic-industrial potential of either country, it is probably the United States which reaps the advantage. For example, in 1965 our principal exports to the Soviet Union were in the agricultural area, consisting of oils and fats, soybeans and cattle hides, while approximately two-thirds of United States imports from the Soviet Union consisted of chrome ore and scarce platinum group metals. In 1966 our imports of these and other essential metals and minerals were also large.)

It is worth noting that the apparent low level of United States trade with eastern Europe reflected in the discussion above is, in a sense, exaggerated. Although business done by firms located in the United States is small, there is an element not shown in the bare United States trade figures. This is the trade carried on with eastern Europe for foreign subsidiaries and affiliates of American companies. While the extent of such trade is difficult to measure accurately, it seems clear that exports by subsidiaries and affiliates to eastern Europe are at least several times as great as direct exports of manufactures from the United States, which, in 1965, amounted to only $21.3 million.

Prospects and Problems for the Future

Trade between the Communist countries of eastern Europe, including the Soviet Union, and the West will probably continue to expand, perhaps at an accelerated rate. The developing economic changes within the East European Communist countries are, perhaps, the most significant elements suggesting continued expansion.

The shift from a rigidly controlled economic system began in Yugoslavia, coincident with that country's break from the Soviet Union. Although Yugoslavia has come only part way to anything like a "free-market" economy, the country is committed to moving as rapidly as possible to liberalize government restraints on the economy and to the operation of free economic forces in trade and investment.

Similar trends are under way in Czechoslovakia and Hungary and, to a lesser degree, in Poland and the Soviet Union. These countries have all been influenced by Western economic thought in the field of resource utilization and the resultant social benefits. The principal impact of these changes will be internal. However, they are related in an important way to foreign trade:

> . . . the importance of foreign trade in preparing the ground for the reforms must not be underrated. All the European Communist countries have continuously found serious shortages of foreign exchange, and for all of them, except the Soviet Union, rapid industrialization without relatively large importations of goods—whether raw materials or highly fabricated goods (especially machinery) or both, depending on the particular country—is impossible. Extensive credits are difficult for them to obtain. Thus, they must export on a large scale, both to the East and to the West. In doing so they submit their goods to a severe competitive test in terms of quality and technological modernity; and their economic institutions undergo a similar test in terms of adaptability to changing external conditions and over-all effectiveness. Frequently they have found both their goods and their institutions wanting on these scores. In all the countries, with the exception of the U.S.S.R., a major argument for thoroughgoing economic reform has been the need to render their economies more effective in both the "capitalist" and "Socialist" world markets.[1]

Insofar as their reforms make headway, these countries will be pushed into world markets, both by the need to obtain foreign exchange and to obtain goods on the economically most efficient basis. Indeed, the smaller East European Communist countries have an example in the Soviet decision to turn to the West to expand the Soviet automobile industry. There can be little doubt that the Soviet Union could develop its own auto industry without recourse to the West—but at what cost in time and efficiency? Clearly, it is more efficient for the Soviet Union to use raw-material exports to purchase a "turn-key" plant from Italy that will turn out 600,000 cars a year when completed, about 1970. With the autarkic policy of Stalin no longer fashionable, and the Soviet Union setting an example in the Fiat transaction, the other Communist countries need feel no ideological restraints on turning to capitalist countries in the interests of economic efficiency.

Complementary to the East European disposition to expand foreign trade, the apparent slowdown in the West European economy is likely to generate still greater interest by western Europe in the eastern market. Taken together, these factors should insure at the least a continued growth in both the absolute volume of trade between East and West, and in the proportionate share of East-West trade in total world trade.

The United States should share in the benefits of expanded East-West trade. Such trade can be of no little economic importance to us, even though the factors mentioned earlier in this article will probably keep such trade from ever being very great. It is at such a low level now that it can hardly do anything but increase. But to permit an increase, our posture must

[1]Gregory Grossman, "Economic Reforms—A Balance Sheet" in *Problems of Communism*.

be changed from one of discriminating against imports from Communist countries, to treating their imports as we do imports generally.

Congressional action is required before the President can remove the existing tariff discrimination applied to the Soviet Union and other European Communist countries except Poland and Yugoslavia. This discrimination applies the prohibitively high Smoot-Hawley tariff rates of the 1930's to imports from those countries. President Johnson has urged East-West trade legislation that would provide authority to negotiate, country by country, the extension of nondiscriminatory tariff treatment in exchange for benefits to further the United States national interest.

There would be problems to confront in seeking a balanced reciprocity between the state trading systems of Communist countries and the free private trade that controls United States commerce. These problems would not, however, be insoluble. The countries of western Europe, with their free trading systems, have been successful in expanding trade substantially, to mutual advantage.

The benefits we seek might vary from country to country. An obvious requirement on the United States side, in exchange for the removal of tariff discrimination, would be nondiscriminatory treatment for United States exports to a Communist country. There would be insistence on treatment for United States businessmen equal to that of their foreign competitors in such matters as travel facilities, office space, and access to government or trading company representatives. There might be a value of quantity purchase commitment with respect to imports from the United States, as provided in United States–Soviet commercial agreements during the 1930's. Tied to such a purchase commitment there would have to be an assurance of payment to United States sellers in dollars or other hard currency. Other benefits might include agreement on settlement of commercial disputes, protection of industrial property rights, and assurances against injurious trade practices.

There would be hard negotiating involved in reaching agreement satisfactory to both sides, but self-interest on both sides and a basic commitment to trade expansion should facilitate the negotiations. Both sides have much to gain from the traditional advantages that flow from international trade.

Economic advantages are only a part of the benefit. Removal of tariff discrimination in these circumstances would, hopefully, prove to be a step towards better over-all relations with the European Communist countries, particularly the Soviet Union.

The Administration's policy of seeking to expand East-West trade has enlivened the interest of American businessmen in such trade. This is a healthy development. It stems naturally from the sound business conclusion that these markets are worth going after, and from an increasing awareness of the need to "get a foot in the door." Communist purchasers like to come back to the seller on whom they know they can depend, based on past experience. This gives the company that does a good job on an initial transaction an advantage that later competitors find difficult to overcome. Fortunately, United States equipment and technology enjoy a high reputation in the Soviet Union, and in eastern Europe generally.

On the part of the East European countries, there is a need to learn a great deal about the United States market. The scarcity economies that have prevailed in eastern Europe do not produce able and energetic salesmen. These countries have to sell in the United States if they are to buy here. To sell here, they must study the American market and learn to compete in it. There are signs of an increased awareness of the highly competitive nature of the United States market, which should lead to increased promotion and sales here.

Yet, at a time when our soldiers are fighting in Vietnam, there is a temptation to damn all those countries with governments labeled "Communist" and to have nothing to do with them. If there were to be an early settlement in Vietnam, trade with Communist countries would not be subject to the same emotional and psychological hazards that beset such trade today. However, as a great power with awesome global responsibilities, the United States, in relations with Communist countries, must look to the future and make progress where progress is possible, as in the trade area. We have seen what a small role East-West trade plays in our over-all economic activity; we have also seen that, in our recent past trade with the Soviet Union, we have been buying goods of greater industrial significance than we have been selling.

There is a larger end to be gained in an expanded trade with the Soviet Union and other eastern European countries. It is a factor in our ultimate objective of reaching an accommodation with the Soviet Union and other Communist countries that will lead us to a peaceful world.

The conclusion seems clear—the United States does have a very direct interest in the revival of trade with the Communist countries of eastern Europe. This interest is both economic and political. Unless we can begin soon to advance our national interests constructively in this area, we shall forfeit the leadership we should be exercising in this important area of East-West relationships.

The Recent Course of East-West Trade

Leon M. Herman

On the basis of a thorough statistical analysis, an eminent American expert in East-West trade produces in the following article impressive evidence of the continuously expanding commercial ties between Eastern Europe and the industrially developed Western countries. While both these trading partners benefit from their exchange of commodities, the analysis shows that the flows of goods are relatively much more important for the East than for the West.

Overall Proportions

In terms of its aggregate volume, commodity trade between East and West now looms larger than ever before. Expressed in dollars, the value of exports from the entire "West" to the whole of the "East," as these shorthand terms are usually defined, reached a figure of 8.5 billion dollars in 1966 (the latest calendar year for which such figures are at present available). The import side of this trade, in keeping with recent trends, came to a somewhat larger value in the same year, namely 9.0 billion dollars.

In recent years, as shown by the record, this segment of international commerce has expanded at a somewhat faster pace than world trade in general. As a result, trade with the communist areas of Europe and Asia came to account for 4.7 percent of all foreign trade transactions of the non-communist countries by 1966. This represents a measurable improvement over 1960, when the share of the East in the total trade of the West amounted to 3.8 percent.

In general, therefore, the growth of East-West trade during the current decade has been rather impressive. In the case of both exports and imports, the annual dollar figures approximately doubled between 1960 and 1966, which reflects a yearly growth rate of 12 percent. In dollar terms, exports to the East increased from $4,425 million to $8,509 million; imports rose from $4,462 million to $9,047 million.

Major Participating Areas

The largest single trading nation in the East, throughout the recent past, has been the USSR, which in 1966 absorbed $2.8 billion worth of merchandise originating in the West. This comes out to somewhat more than 30 percent of all commodities moving from West to East in that year. As has been the case right along, the six small countries of Eastern Europe, as a group, did far better. They accounted in the same year for $4.2 billion worth of Western exports, or 52 percent of all goods sold to the East. Sales to Mainland China in 1966 came to a figure of 1.4 billion dollars, representing 17.5 percent of all exports from West to East. As might be expected, the import side of the commodity flow showed the same percentage distribution among the three major geographic areas making up the East.

TABLE 1

Relative Importance of East-West Trade to the Participating Areas
(Percentages)

Industrially Developed Countries

	IMPORTS			EXPORTS		
Year	Total	From E.E.	Percent	Total	To E.E.	Percent
1964	113,279	3,048	2.7	180,984	3,210	2.9
1965	124,633	3,588	2.9	119,990	3,195	2.7
1966	138,453	4,048	2.9	132,720	3,853	2.9

Eastern Europe

	IMPORTS			EXPORTS		
Year	Total	From Dev. Countries	Percent	Total	To Dev. Countries	Percent
1964	19,500	3,210	16.5	18,680	3,048	16.3
1965	20,600	3,195	15.5	20,000	3,588	17.9
1966	21,700	3,853	17.8	21,210	4,048	19.1

As far as the West is concerned, the main component areas have also remained unchanged in recent years. Western Europe continues to be the most active participant in East-West trade, reflecting the fact that this region has been traditionally a natural market for the major export commodities of Eastern Europe and, at the same time, a readily accessible source of industrial products of the kind regularly imported by the East. In 1966, specifically, Western Europe contributed some 55 percent to the total value of the exchange of commodities between East and West. All the industrially developed countries, taken together, i.e., the nations making up the O.E.C.D. group, have emerged in recent years as the principal factor in this two-way trade, accounting for 70 percent of the entire trade turnover between East and West. This leaves 30 percent for the share of the less developed nations as participants in East-West trade.

Commodity Composition of East-West Trade

A. *Trade Between East and West in Europe.* The historic pattern of trade between the countries of Western and Eastern Europe has not changed materially in recent years. As in the past, the Western group of nations continue to import from the Eastern half of the continent primarily raw materials and foodstuffs, while exporting, in turn, finished products of metal and other materials.

On the import side, the group of foodstuffs imported into West Europe for example, accounted for, respectively, 21.3 and 22.9 percent of all goods purchased from the East in 1964 and 1965. Included among these were: meat and dairy products, cereals, fruits, vegetables, and sugar.

Next, the broad group of crude materials, which includes fuels and base metals, represented 49.7 and 58.2 percent respectively, of all goods moving from East to West in Europe. The most prominent, clearly identifiable commodities in this group were: petroleum, coal, coke, timber products, and base metals.

Finished products make up the third, and least important, broad group of import commodities of Eastern origin that have been finding their way into Western Europe in recent years. This group as a whole accounted for 17.0 and 16.8 percent, respectively, of all such imports into Western Europe during 1964 and 1965. More specifically, it was represented by such commodities as chemicals, transport equipment, and industrial machinery. The dollar value of the machinery category of imports, it may be noted, added up to only 5 percent of the value of all merchandise imported from the Eastern half of Europe.

To sum up, four commodity categories stand out most prominently in the range of imports from Eastern Europe. These are: meat and dairy products (10.7 percent of all imports in 1965); timber products (16.5 percent), mineral fuels (20.0 percent), and base metals (9.2 percent). Added together, foodstuffs, crude materials, fuels, and base metals, added up to 81 percent of all Western Europe's imports in this trade, with "manufactures" and "miscellaneous" making up the remainder.

On the export side of this exchange, i.e., the movement from West Europe to the Eastern half of the continent, the product mix has been quite different. Here, finished goods, as a broad group, accounted for the largest share of the commodity flow, namely 59.6 and 58.0 during 1964 and 1965. The three principal components of this group have been: industrial equipment, ships, and chemicals.

The second group of importance among West Europe's exports to the East has been that of crude materials. The share of this group came to 24.6 percent of all export to the East for both years under review. Most prominent among the commodities in this group were: base metals and such industrial raw materials as synthetic rubber and fibers. By way of contrast, exports of mineral fuels from West and East in Europe account for less than 0.5 percent of all recorded shipments.

Foodstuffs, as a group, have been of least importance in the composition of West Europe's exports to its trade partners in the East. During the two years under review, the major commodity categories in this group were grains, meat, fruits and vegetables.

B. *General Economic Character of Trade With the East.* As illustrated briefly above, by means of the commodity content of East-West trade in Europe, the trade pattern of the communist countries, both on the export and import side of the exchanges, is that of an industrially underdeveloped group of economies. Basically, they tend to exchange crude materials and farm products for manufactured goods in general and machinery in particular. In this regard, the most characteristic feature of the exchange is illustrated by the fact that some 30 percent of West Europe's exports to the East consists of productive machinery, whereas the commodity flow in the reverse direction contains only 5 percent of industrial equipment.

One significant development of the past few years has been the decline in the momentum of machinery imports into the Soviet Union from the West in general. After a steady rise through the early sixties, Soviet purchases in this category of goods began to level off, with the result that machinery imports were only marginally (6 percent) larger in 1966 than they were in 1962, as may be seen in the figures below: (in $ million).

	1961	1962	1963	1964	1965	1966
Dollars	474.4	601.3	588.1	620.4	505.2	638.0

TABLE 2

Trade of Industrial West* With East Europe
(In millions of U.S. dollars)

	IMPORTS			EXPORTS		
	1964	1965	1966	1964	1965	1966
Food and live animals	576	724	805	924	628	760
Beverages and tobacco	30	31	36	40	47	56
Crude materials, inedible except fuel	775	893	973	290	330	432
Mineral fuels, lubricants and related materials	645	650	735	15	13	11
Animal and vegetable oils and fats	31	46	54	40	56	36
Chemicals	147	171	202	325	411	467
Manufactured goods	549	719	831	531	664	763
Machinery and transport equipment	147	180	208	939	918	1,239
Miscellaneous manufactured articles	138	155	183	67	102	155
Commodities and transactions not classified	10	18	21	38	26	25
TOTAL	3,048	3,588	4,048	3,210	3,195	3,853

*All members of O.E.C.D.

Source: *Commodity Trade*, Series B. January-December 1966. Vol. 6, O.E.C.D. Paris. pp. 6-7.

TABLE 3

Geographic Distribution of East-West Trade: Viewed From the West
(In millions of dollars)

	Exports From the West			Imports Into the West		
	All Comm. Areas	Comm. Areas in Europe	USSR	All Comm. Areas	Comm. Areas in Europe	USSR
Total West						
1965	7,668	6,296	2,749	8,098	6,539	2,949
1966	8,509	6,967	2,769	9,047	7,166	3,175
Developed Countries						
1965	4,998	4,262	1,536	5,190	4,573	1,891
1966	5,995	4,995	1,674	6,000	5,210	2,150
Western Europe, NATO						
1965	2,677	2,347	592	3,163	2,857	1,086
1966	3,265	2,824	578	3,577	3,206	1,204
Western Europe, Other						
1965	1,324	1,280	548	1,307	1,264	513
1966	1,396	1,334	544	1,484	1,427	585
Developing Countries						
1965	2,559	1,958	1,160	2,666	1,740	936
1966	2,514	1,972	1,095	3,047	1,956	1,026

Source: U.S. Department of Commerce

The recent decline in Soviet imports of industrial equipment from the West is assumed to have been caused by a tightness in the supply of hard currency, and in particular by the urgent need on several recent occasions to maintain a trade surplus with the countries of the Industrial West in order to pay for the wheat purchases. The smaller countries of Eastern Europe, on the other hand, have continued to expand their procurement of machinery in the West. In Western Europe alone, for example, they purchased $442 million in 1964, followed by an import value of $535 million in 1965. From the West as a whole, imports of machinery into the smaller countries of East Europe rose from $549 million to $687 million during the two years in question.

The Outlook

The economic evidence at hand tends to support a forecast of continued steady growth of the present volume of trade between the East and West. There are a number of evidently strong economic incentives at work on both sides of the exchange to expand both direct commodity trade and other, newer forms of industrial cooperation between private firms in the West and the state enterprises of East Europe.

For the industrially developed countries of the West the pull of the East at present appears to be of a long-term character. The economies of the Western nations will, without a doubt, continue to be substantially dependent upon the world market as a means for supplementing their own resources with substantial quantities of imported commodities of a wide variety. As far ahead as we can see, therefore, the industrialized countries will continue to seek abroad the kind of fuels and mineral materials that are normally exported by the East. If the latter countries should, moreover, improve their surplus position in some categories of foodstuffs, these too could presumably be absorbed by the expanding economies of the West in larger quantities than at present. The plain fact is, moreover, that the Western countries as a group have a substantial and continuing interest in helping the East to market more of their commodities and thereby improve their hard currency resources as potential importers of Western goods.

As traditional producers of industrial surpluses, the Western trading nations, furthermore, cannot afford to ignore a market having the kind of characteristics that Eastern Europe has displayed during the past two decades. According to the recent record, some two-thirds of all the goods imported by Eastern Europe from the O.E.C.D. countries have consisted of finished industrial goods. Given the present disparities in the levels of industrial technology in several branches of production between the two regions, the tendency for more advanced types of equipment, products, as well as synthetic materials to flow from West to East may be expected to continue for the foreseeable future. The hard fact is, after all, that the industrial labor force of the developed countries of the West, and presumably the scale of industrial activity in general, are at least twice as large as in Eastern Europe.

If we add to this the fact that a number of the major trading nations of the West are now extending long-term credits to the East and, on a substantial scale at that, we may reasonably conclude that (a) financing facilities for the expansion of imports into the East are likely to be better than in the past; (b) the current foreign exchange earnings of the East should improve steadily in the near term.

TABLE 4

Dollar Value and Percentage of East-West Trade
(In millions of dollars)

	Exports From the West			Imports Into the West		
Year	Total Exports	Exports to Communist Areas	Percent	Total Imports	Imports from Communist Areas	Percent
1960	113,700	4,425.1	3.9	119,600	4,462.1	3.7
1961	118,800	4,966.6	4.2	124,800	4,987.1	4.0
1962	124,900	5,172.2	4.1	132,800	5,517.8	4.2
1963	136,100	5,622.1	4.1	144,000	6,240.6	4.3
1964	153,300	6,814.9	4.4	161,800	7,072.3	4.4
1965	166,200	7,667.7	4.6	176,100	8,097.6	4.5
1966	182,000	8,508.7	4.7	193,400	9,047.1	4.7

Source: U.S. Department of Commerce.

The economic forces at work in the East also appear to be operating in favor of expanding the volume of trade with the industrially developed market economies. To the extent that the centrally planned economies are gradually discarding the purely ideological approach to trade and economic development in general, they have come to recognize the nature of the conditions under which technical progress is generated in the world today. They are aware, for example, that the main theatre of operations and research in industry is located in Western Europe, North America, and Japan. By their own reckoning, in fact, the countries of East Europe today account for only some 30 percent of the global output of industry, while the bulk of the world's industrial output, including its research and development, is to be found among the nations that make up the O.E.C.D. grouping.

In addition, it needs to be borne in mind that economic ideas of an operational character have begun to take strong root in East Europe within the past few years. These practical ideas have come to be widely accepted in the region as a result of a steadily growing interest in ways and means to develop a more effective system of domestic production and external trade. Thus, for example, there is now wide acceptance in the area of the view that only large scale production, based on the best tested technology, can achieve the universally desired objective of quality production at steadily lower average real costs.

There is also now fairly general acceptance in East Europe of such propositions, to cite just a few, as the following: (a) that comparative costs are the most important factor in calculating the rationality of a country's participation in international trade; (b) that international trade decisions based on the physical ability to produce the commodities in question rather than their cost and utility tends to reduce the total output and income that could be derived from the finite supply of resources available within a national economy; and (c) that autarky, whether national or regional, is nothing more than a potential source of waste in the use of national resources; that it imposes an unnecessary diffusion of national skills and capacities, and, hence, leads to low productivity and economic weakness rather than strength.

While we can expect the countries of Eastern Europe to continue to expand, and to refine, the present pattern of their intra-regional trade, there is nonetheless good reason to believe that in the course of this process of refinement they will also earnestly seek ways and means to introduce certain practical modifications in the established commodity composition of this trade. These modifications are, of course, likely to take a variety of forms. But they may be reasonably expected to include the gradual elimination from the range of goods exchanged with other trade partners in Eastern Europe such materials and finished goods, including machinery, that are produced either under less than optimal economic conditions or according to specifications of quality and utility that are perceptibly below existing world standards. If this process of adjustment is guided largely by considerations of economic effectiveness, as they are very likely to be, the outlook would seem to be favorable for a steadily expanding exchange of goods with an ever wider range of industrialized trade partners, based on a more rigorous calculus of real costs of production both at home and abroad.

A Reappraisal of U.S.-U.S.S.R. Trade Policy

Harold J. Berman*

This article by a noted Harvard Law School professor provides an excellent survey of the economics and politics of East-West trade. The author covers the subject from a pragmatic viewpoint and he makes a special effort to underline the problems that are likely to arise because of the differences between the U.S. and Soviet economic institutions. He recommends a study of the governmental and intergovernmental arrangements as well as of private contractual arrangements available for conducting the U.S.-U.S.S.R. trade.

A great deal has been said recently about the politics and economics of East-West trade. At the White House Trade Expansion Conference in September 1963, attended by some 200 leading American businessmen, strong voices were raised for a "reappraisal" of our policies concerning exports to the Soviet Union and to Eastern Europe. The subsequent sale of large quantities of American wheat to the Soviet Union has touched off a nationwide discussion of why we should or should not trade with some or all of the Communist countries.

The springboard for the debate is the realization that our allies are in fact trading rather vigorously with the East, and there is virtually nothing we can do about it. In crude terms, Americans are torn between two traditional antipathies: we hate to trade with our enemies, but we also hate to be played for suckers. Beneath the surface there lurk deeper issues: (1) our need for increased foreign trade in order to meet our balance-of-payments deficit, and (2) our belief in international trade as an instrument of peace and a bulwark of world order. Secretary of Commerce Luther Hodges has several times in the past year referred to the "schizophrenic situation" which requires him, on the one hand, to promote exports and, on the other hand, to restrict them. In February 1964 Secretary Hodges said at a conference at Duke University, "Trade even with the Soviets is a good thing. It comes nearer to making peace than anything else one can do."

Despite the very considerable attention which has been given to these matters, the institutional aspect—how trade between Communist and non-Communist countries is actually carried on, and how it should be carried on—has been strangely neglected. Yet the institutional aspect is linked inextricably to the political and the economic aspects. Without an understanding of the governmental and intergovernmental arrangements and also of the private contractual arrangements available for conducting trade, we shall not be able properly to assess the political and economic advantages and disadvantages of increased commerce with the Communists.

One reason why the institutional aspect has not been widely discussed is that the issues have been formulated chiefly by those who would like to see East-West trade reduced to a minimum. The question is put: "Why should we trade with the Communist countries at all? Such trade will only help them in their desire to surpass us economically and ultimately to attend our funeral." This is the political formulation of the issue. This position is bolstered by the economic argument that these countries have very little to offer us. It is argued that there is no quid pro quo—they will get our machinery and know-how, and we will get nothing in return except caviar and furs.

¶ Both the British and the French have exported airplanes to Communist China, and the Japanese have recently sold a textile plant on liberal credit terms to Communist China.

¶ The Communist countries have been developing a rather substantial export trade in industrial goods to the countries of Asia and Africa, in return for foodstuffs and raw materials.

Moreover, all signs point toward an increase in East-West trade in the future. In 1962, 47% of Soviet imports of machinery came from the West; Khrushchev's program for expansion of the Soviet chemical industry calls for an investment of $46 billion in the next seven years. It is not unlikely that much of this will be spent in the West.

Awakening to Realities

Meanwhile, U.S. trade with the Soviet Union in 1962 amounted to about $30 million worth of imports and exports—out of a total U.S. export-import trade of over $36 billion. And with the other Communist countries, chiefly Poland, we did only another $170 million worth of export and import trade.

Thus it appears that our friends in Western Europe and Japan—including many subsidiaries of American corporations—are deriving considerable economic advantages from trade with Communist countries, while we are biting our fingernails. The realities of this situation which has been developing for at least ten years, have more or less suddenly dawned

---

*AUTHOR'S NOTE: This article is based on my speech delivered at the University of Rochester College of Business Administration, as a part of its Sperry & Hutchinson Lecture Series, March 12, 1964.

on us, as our economic need to expand exports has become more acute.

In addition, virtually all Western countries except the United States *believe in* trade–except in military goods–with the Communist countries. They believe it is ultimately to their own, and Western, *political* advantage to expand such trade. They say:

(1) Trade is an important avenue of communication with the Communist countries.

(2) Trade makes the Communist countries more dependent on the West and thereby gives the West more leverage, more bargaining power, in resolving political conflicts.

(3) Trade contributes to a higher standard of living in the Communist countries, which is a good thing politically, since, in Prime Minister Home's words, "a fat Communist is a less aggressive Communist."

(4) The stability of international relations requires, as a matter of principle, that countries refrain from waging economic warfare with other countries with which they are at peace.

But will Western exports of machinery, machine tools, and factories enable the Soviet Union to overtake and surpass the West economically? The Europeans reply that the Soviets will always be behind us so long as they import from us, for by the time they acquire our know-how on one type of machine, we shall have gone far beyond it. Thus we export a systematic economic lag. As one Western European businessman puts it, "We are building obsolescence into their system."

Semi-Economic Warfare. The fact is that on the issue of East-West trade we have been outvoted. This might have been less material ten years ago, when Europe was economically weaker and there was a dollar shortage; but today to be outvoted on this issue is to lose it. Our "semi-economic warfare" (as it was called recently in *The New York Times*) does not really hurt the Communist countries (it probably never did hurt them very much), since they can simply trade elsewhere or produce themselves what we withhold.

Growing Soviet Trade

This view–I think we may call it, without exaggerating, a negative view–of the politics and economics of East-West trade has received some rude shocks. The rudest shock, perhaps, was the Soviet proposal to purchase from us some $250 million worth of wheat. Wheat is a far cry from machinery and know-how, and $250 million at one stroke could have done a great deal to ease our critical balance-of-payments problem. (Actually, the Soviets purchased some $125 million worth of wheat from us; and while nobody is quite sure why they decided not to order more, it seems safe to conclude that if we had acted more quickly and more rationally in the matter, they might well have purchased the balance. Indeed, they purchased $500 million worth of wheat from Canada in 1963–the largest wheat sale in history.)

The wheat deal, however, is only a small part of the whole picture. The principal shock is the realization that Soviet trade with the rest of the world, especially with Western Europe, is substantial and that it is growing. Thus:

- In 1950 total Soviet exports and imports amounted to less than $3 billion, of which only $550 million was trade with non-Communist countries.
- In 1963 Soviet exports and imports amounted to about $15 billion, of which about $4 billion was trade with non-Communist countries.
- Also, in 1963 trade between non-Communist countries and Communist countries of Eastern Europe *other* than the Soviet Union amounted to an additional $5 billion.

Economic Significance–It is true that trade between Communist and non-Communist countries in 1963 represented less than 3½% of total world trade. But such statistics can be quite misleading. For one thing, a large part of total world trade is made up of intra-European trade, which from some points of view might be considered as a unit, just as we tend to treat Communist-bloc trade as a unit. Also, 3½% of world trade is a large amount. If the United States could capture 50% of the export market in Eastern Europe and the U.S.S.R., we might be much farther on the road to solving our unemployment problem.

The fact is that the $9 or $10 billion worth of total Communist exports to and imports from the non-Communist world is a more than negligible factor in the economies of many countries:

¶ West Germany exchanges about $1 billion worth of goods with Communist countries.

¶ Japan's trade with Communist countries in 1962 amounted to $400 million worth of exports and imports.

¶ Italy would be very unhappy to lose its imports of oil, coal, and wool from the Soviet Union and its Soviet market for Italian synthetic rubber, woolen goods, nylon stockings, shoes, and industrial machinery and equipment. Soviet-Italian trade amounted to $260 million worth of exports and imports in 1962, and Italy expects to increase that trade to $400 million per year by 1969.

¶ The British import Soviet timber in large quantities and export sizable amounts of machinery.

The total British exports and imports to and from all Communist countries in 1963 amounted to about $650 million. We have recently read of the British agreement to export $10 million worth of buses to Cuba. "If

America has a surplus of wheat," a British manufacturer is quoted as saying, "we have a surplus of buses."

Meanwhile we sit and sulk or, worse, make picayune reprisals against our friends, such as cutting off infinitesimal amounts of military aid, as we did in February 1964 to France, Britain and Yugoslavia for permitting their ships to carry goods to Cuba. If such military aid was not in our interests, we should have cancelled it anyway; if it was in our own interests, we were only cutting off our nose to spite our face. As Senator J. W. Fulbright, in a recent speech calling for review of the U.S. trade policy toward Communist countries, said:

> "What we terminated with respect to Britain and France . . . can hardly be called aid; it was more of a sales promotion program under which British and French military leaders were brought to the United States to see–and to buy–advanced American weapons."[1]

Even worse, however, was Secretary of State Rusk's suggestion–later qualified–that American consumers might want to boycott goods from foreign firms trading with Cuba. This would be abdicating the conduct of our foreign economic policy to the American buying public. And again, who would be hurt? Chiefly the American consumer, who would be foregoing more desirable imports (such as British cars) for the sake of a doubtful principle.

Congressional Restrictions

Although the economic and political arguments for expanding our trade with the Soviet Union and other Communist countries are not totally rejected in the United States, only recently have we begun to take them seriously. The Executive Branch of our government has for the past 15 years consistently reiterated that it "favors trade in peaceful goods" with the Communist countries–except China, North Korea, North Vietnam, against whom we have a total embargo on all commercial and financial transactions, and except Cuba, against whom we now have a partial embargo. Moreover, the Executive Branch has favored the expansion of trade with Poland and Yugoslavia and has removed most restrictions on such trade, for the very same type of political reason that Western European countries offer in support of trade with all Communist countries.

Congress, however, especially since 1951, has consistently taken a different view. It has placed severe obstacles in the path of trade with Communist coun-

In addition, there are a variety of minor legislative restrictions on trade with Communist countries.

¶ One of the least defensible of these is the prohibition against the import from the Soviet Union of certain kinds of furs, but not of others. We cannot import any Soviet ermine, fox, kolinsky, marten, mink, muskrat, and weasel furs or skins; but we can and do import Soviet sable, squirrel, and Persian lamb. This, of course, is simply "special interest" legislation.

¶ Another example which defies rational explanation was our determination that Soviet crabmeat could not be imported because it is a product of forced labor. This restriction was finally removed by Presidential action in 1961.

¶ Finally, and most important, Congress has, by the Export Control Act of 1949, as amended in 1962, authorized the President to establish an elaborate system of export licensing directed primarily at Communist countries. It is forbidden to export goods or technical data to "any nation or combination of nations threatening the national security of the United States" if the government decides "that such export makes a significant contribution to the military or economic potential of such nation or nations which would prove detrimental to the national security and welfare of the United States."

Although these Congressional restrictions do leave a considerable amount of leeway to the Executive Branch, particularly in regard to export controls, Congressional attitudes and the political forces which they are thought to reflect have not encouraged the Executive Branch to use that leeway boldly. The Department of Commerce lawyers emphasize that under the language of the statute an export that makes a significant contribution to the military or economic potential of a Communist country might nevertheless not prove "detrimental" to the United States if in fact the Communist country can easily obtain the product from another country. Indeed, in that case, to export it

tries. It has withdrawn most-favored-nation treatment of imports from all Communist countries except Poland and Yugoslavia, thereby restoring the 1930 tariff rates for those imports, amounting generally to three times the tariff level for imports of the same goods from other countries. Soviet vodka, for example, carries a 35% higher duty than liquor from Western Europe. Soviet manganese is subject to a duty four times as high as that on manganese imported from other countries. It is only by very great effort that Congress has been persuaded to give the Executive Branch discretion to exclude Poland and Yugoslavia from this discriminatory policy.

Congress has also imposed certain credit controls on trade with Communist countries, especially with the Soviet Union. Under the Johnson Act of 1934, loans cannot be made by Americans to governments which are in default on their debts to the U.S. government, and this law has been construed to apply to the Soviet Union and to prevent the giving of long-term commercial credits to Soviet import agencies, although short-term commercial credits are permitted.

from the United States might be beneficial to us, for it would help our balance of payments, our shipping, and our employment of labor and resources. In practice, however, the Department of Commerce is very sensitive to Congressional attitudes toward export controls

---

[1] *The New York Times*, March 26, 1964, p. 13.

and is very loath to permit exports of industrial goods. It has recently denied license applications for export of automotive parts and machine tools to the Soviet Union, although such products are easily available from England and West Germany.

The whole system of export controls is extremely discouraging to trade even in so-called peaceful goods. With some exceptions, the American exporter cannot apply for a license until he has a firm contract. But it is expensive to negotiate contracts—in the case of plant and equipment, very expensive indeed; with the possibility of denial of a license hanging over the negotiations, most businessmen are not very interested. Moreover, even after a license is granted, it may later be revoked if new facts appear which make delivery seem undesirable to the U.S. government.

The fallacy of our export controls is in the concept of "peaceful goods." Goods are not peaceful or warlike. Only people are peaceful or warlike. Goods are inherently neutral. Any goods may be used either for peaceful or for warlike purposes. Shoes might seem at first to be peaceful, but on the feet of marching soldiers they might seem less peaceful. Therefore, I think it would be a mistake to *give* the Soviets shoes, or wheat to fill their stomachs, or anything else—since they all might be used against us. The question, however, is not whether we should "give" them goods but whether we should "sell" them goods. The basic distinction seems to be lost on many Americans.

But what is the difference between giving and selling, it is asked, if we do not need their money? The question betrays a certain naiveté concerning money. We do need their money; we can make armaments with it, or support foreign bases if nothing else. But even assuming we do not need it, the question still remains: Where do they *get* their money? It does not require a profound knowledge of international economics to realize that they get their money only by producing goods for export. If we sell, and not give, our goods to them, they must pay for those goods by producing and selling goods to us or to others.

Two explanatory notes may be required at this point:

(1) The Communist countries do all their foreign trade with Western countries in Western currencies—or gold. The ruble is a purely internal Soviet currency.

(2) The Soviets have large but nevertheless limited supplies of gold, and they are quite careful about spending them. Theodore Shabad, the very competent *New York Times* correspondent in Moscow, who is himself a professional geographer, reports that it costs the Soviets the ruble equivalent of $60-$65 an ounce to mine gold, whereas the world price is about $35 an ounce.[2] This figure may be wholly erroneous. Nevertheless it illustrates the point that when the Soviets pay in gold, they are not getting the goods for nothing. They must redirect manpower and allocate other resources for the production of that gold.

Our restrictions on trade with the Communist countries are designed primarily to prevent the export of goods which would substantially help the Communist economies. A more subtle but equally effective way of accomplishing this objective would be to balance the benefits which they obtain from our exports against the costs which they incur in exporting to us (and to others). Our Western European friends are willing to sell to the Communist countries certain goods which we are unwilling to sell to them—just because they *are* able to balance their exports against imports from the Communist countries, and hence to calculate the costs reflected in the prices which the Communist countries pay.

Institutional Arrangements

Here we come to a crucial question: If we balance Soviet exports of caviar and furs to us against our exports of chemical plants and textile machinery to them, the American exporters will presumably be getting a cash equivalent. But will not the Soviet economy as a whole be getting an incomparably greater advantage?

This takes us to the problem of arrangements, the problem of institutions.

The foreign trade of each of the Communist countries is a monopoly of the state and is conducted as part of a state system of integral (or "global") economic planning. If we take the Soviet Union as an example, we find that all Soviet exporting and importing is conducted by 31 state agencies, which procure goods for export from Soviet state enterprises and purchase goods abroad for resale to Soviet state enterprises. The 31 export-import agencies operate under a plan prepared by the Soviet Ministry of Foreign Trade, which is part of the national economic plan of the Soviet government. It is the direct aim of the Soviet importing or exporting agency, therefore, to procure or sell goods in conformity with the national economic plan, and hence in conformity with the interests of the Soviet state.

The Soviet export-import agency ("combine") appears on the world markets as a legal entity, with capacity to enter into contracts and to sue and be sued. It is willing to adapt itself to international trade custom and law. It will seek agreement to submit disputes to arbitration in the Moscow Foreign Trade Arbitration Commission (which has a good reputation among Western traders), but it may also be willing to submit to arbitration in Sweden, Switzerland, or elsewhere. In all this it will be pursuing not only its own interest but also that of the Soviet state, which benefits in many ways from the use of "bourgeois" law.

The individual European, American, or Japanese trader who deals with the Soviets, however, is only indirectly interested in promoting the national interests of his country. He considers that he is successful if he makes a profit, even though conceivably the state may have suffered a net economic, political, or military loss from his transactions. He relies on the market, or his government, to adjust any such losses.

Thus there is an absence of reciprocity in trade between a Western business firm and a Communist state trading agency. The advantages obtained by each may be quite different in kind. The Westerner derives a direct individual advantage; the state trading agency derives a direct national advantage.

It is because of this absence of national reciprocity that our government has imposed a system of controls to protect the national interest, even as the Soviet system protects Soviet national interests. Indeed, the Soviet system is far more restrictive than ours. The trouble is that the controls which we have imposed have been entirely negative and have served only to restrict trade. It would also be possible to impose controls which would foster trade; and this is what virtually all other countries have done.

If we study the way in which England, France, Germany, Italy, Belgium, Sweden, Argentina, Brazil, Nigeria, and most other non-Communist countries trade with the Soviet Union, Poland, Czechoslovakia, and the other Communist countries, we find that such trade is carried out on the basis of bilateral trade agreements containing programs of exchanges of particular goods in particular quantities over a period of years. Such programmed trade agreements are particularly convenient for planned economies, since the so-called contingents of goods, that is, the lists contained in the agreements, can help form the basis for plans of domestic production and consumption. The trade agreements are, in one sense, part of the national economic plan.

At the same time, from the point of view of the Western country, an intergovernmental agreement establishing contingents of exports and imports is a means of preventing the export of those goods which for various reasons the Western government does not wish to export to a Communist country. The Western government promises to issue export licenses to its private exporters only for the goods listed in the agreement. At the same time, the Western government, in negotiating the agreement, has the opportunity to bargain for particular Soviet exports. Thus the mutual advantage of both countries, each viewed from its own national standpoint, can be achieved.

In June 1958 Soviet Premier Khrushchev proposed such a Soviet-American trade agreement in a letter to President Eisenhower, and in March 1964 Deputy Premier Kosygin renewed the proposal. Here is the essence of that proposal:

¶ Khrushchev's 1958 letter listed types of industrial products which the Soviet Union would like to purchase in the United States and types of products which the Soviet Union would offer to sell in the United States. The proposal stated that it was not directed to trade in armaments or plant equipment for military production but to trade in industrial equipment for production of consumer goods and in nonmilitary industrial products and finished goods, including refrigeration equipment, installations for air conditioning, equipment for the cellulose, paper, wood-processing, textile, leather-footwear, and food industries, television equipment, equipment for manufacture of packing materials, automatic vending machines, pumps and compressors, machinery for the mining industry, machinery for the manufacture of building materials, pipes for city gas lines, and several other types of machinery, as well as various chemical products, medical equipment, medicines, and certain consumer goods.

¶ Khrushchev said that the Soviet Union would be willing, in return, to export manganese and chromium ores, cellulose and paper products, ferrous alloys, platinum, palladium, asbestos, potassium, salts, lumber, certain chemical products, furs, and other goods, "as well as a number of types of modern machinery and equipment which could be of interest to American firms." Also, his proposal stated that "if American firms manifest an interest, the Soviet Union could also consider the question of developing the extraction of iron ore for delivery to the U.S.A."

¶ Khrushchev also proposed that American specialists be sent to the Soviet Union and that licensing arrangements be made in individual cases. He suggested that a very large expansion of Soviet-American trade would raise questions concerning the possibility of long-term credits, but added, "Of course, it is possible to begin the development of commerce on the basis of reciprocal deliveries."

¶ Khrushchev continued: "It is also obvious that development of trade between the U.S.S.R. and the U.S.A. will require the creation of the requisite contractual and legal basis. The question of creating such a basis, as well as that of implementing a program for purchases of American goods and deliveries of Soviet goods, and also payments for them, could, provided the Government of the U.S.A. consents, be subject to intergovernmental negotiation."

President Eisenhower replied that "the United States favors the expansion of peaceful trade with the Soviet Union," but he rejected the bid for an intergovernmental agreement:

"As you know," the President wrote, "United States export and import trade is carried on by individual firms and not under governmental auspices. There is no need, therefore, to formalize relations between United States firms and Soviet trade organizations. Soviet trade organizations are free right now, without any need for special action by the United States Government, to develop a larger volume of trade with firms in this country."

The President added: "I am asking the Department of State to examine the specific proposals contained in your letter and to communicate further with your government." No such further communication seems to have been made.

Less than a year later, in May 1959, the Soviets negotiated a five-year trade agreement with the United Kingdom very similar to that proposed to President Eisenhower.

In fact, it is doubtful whether Soviet-American trade could be substantially expanded without any changes in existing American governmental or legal policies or practices. Even the recent wheat purchases seemed at least to require new law, namely, Congressional authorization to the Export-Import Bank to guarantee commercial credits extended by our exporters, and a new interpretation of the Johnson Act by the Attorney General permitting the extension of commercial credits up to 18 months (previously, the act was interpreted as limiting such credits to 6 months).

Although for the most part the products which Khrushchev proposed in 1958 to buy from American firms, and which the Soviet Union is still interested in buying from us, are not on the "positive list" of strategic exports, they require validated export licenses. This means, as I have already indicated, that in many cases the American exporter would have to incur the very large expense of negotiating a contract without assurance that he will ultimately be permitted to make the export. Moreover, some, though not all, of the goods which Khrushchev proposed to export to us are subject to a tariff rate much higher than that which is applied to the same products imported from other countries; and even those which are duty-free may fall within various other restrictions–the antidumping laws, the prohibition of products of forced labor, the provision of added "countervailing" duties on imports which are subsidized by the foreign government, and the provision for added duties to "equalize costs of production."

Promoting U.S. Interests

By a trade agreement of the kind proposed by Khrushchev, we could insist–

... on the elimination of those Soviet trade practices which are obnoxious to us;

... that the Soviets refrain from purchasing very small quantities of machinery simply for the purposes of copying it–so-called "prototype" purchases;

... on protection of our patents and on compensation for our know-how;

... that there be no dumping;

... on the establishment of a fair method of arbitration of commercial disputes–perhaps by establishing a joint American-Soviet arbitration tribunal, as the Italians have done with the Poles;

... on diversification–in terms of consumer goods and industrial goods–of Soviet imports from us and exports to us.

And we could establish our controls of strategic exports by the trade agreement itself, so that our manufacturers would know in advance just what products will be licensed for export and what will not.

Perhaps such an agreement would not expand our trade very much; that would depend on many factors. But it would guarantee that such trade, whatever its volume, would be conducted on the basis of mutual national advantage.

It makes no sense to keep saying that the Soviets "really have nothing to sell us" when in fact they have made us an offer which we refuse even to explore. If their offer is a bluff, then the best answer is to "call" it. If it is not, the best answer is still to put down our chips.

And it makes no sense for our government to keep saying that American private business is free to trade with the Soviets if it wants and that American private business is not interested in such trade, when private business–perhaps to its discredit–is looking to the government for leadership. On March 12, 1964, *The New York Times* quoted the general manager of Du Pont's international department as saying: "E. I. du Pont de Nemours and Co. is completely guided by Government policy in trade matters relating to the Soviet Union." This is by no means an isolated attitude.

It is possible that underlying our reluctance to trade with the Soviets is a vague feeling that they will get the better of us, that they will outsmart us. We insist that they are unscrupulous–though in fact they have shown no signs of unscrupulousness in commercial matters. Such timidity is hardly worthy of the most powerful nation in the world. Surely we can be as smart as they are in business matters, and surely we can protect ourselves commercially against any unscrupulousness.

Conclusion

It may be asked: "Why is it important for us to go out of our way to do business with the Communists? A trade agreement like that proposed by the Soviets is contrary to our ideal of multilateral trade, and would involve complex relationships between government and business which are subject to great abuse. Why not leave East-West trade to other countries that need it? We can get along without it."

It is, of course, true that we can get along without their trade–and that they can get along without ours. Also, a trade agreement does indeed involve risks; we would have to be as wise as serpents in negotiating it and in implementing it. Further, such a trade agreement would require a high degree of cooperation between government and business in determining what exports and imports to provide for. For us, it would be a virtually unprecedented way of conducting foreign trade.

The overriding importance of Soviet-American trade is that it would help to integrate the Soviet economy into the world economy. It would help to create economic bonds between the two countries which in the long run can prove stronger than the autarchic tendencies of the Communist economic and political system.

The Soviets give limited acceptance to the principle of comparative advantage which underlies international trade. To a limited extent they will import goods which are cheaper to buy abroad than to produce at home and will export goods which are more profitable to sell abroad than to consume at home or not produce at all. The extent to which they are willing to partake of the economic benefits of the international division of labor can be measured fairly precisely by the amount of their international trade—approximately $15 billion in 1963 (out of a gross national product of approximately $300 billion). This $15 billion worth of trade is too much to be called merely political, but it is not enough to satisfy the real economic needs of the Soviet Union, even allowing for the long-range economies which can be effected in the huge Soviet market by protection of Soviet infant industries.

It is very much in the interest of a stable world order to stimulate the Soviet Union to increase her foreign trade and, in particular, to increase her allocation of resources for production for export. At present the Soviets plan their imports carefully, individual plant managers study foreign techniques and products to determine what should be imported and submit import applications to superior planning and administrative authorities. Exports, however, are treated as a necessary evil, an inescapable means of earning the foreign exchange required to pay for imports. Procurement for export is initiated from Moscow. Plant managers do not study foreign markets for their own products, and exports are not planned from below; in a sense they are not planned at all. It is very doubtful that the Soviet foreign trade officials, or indeed any Soviet officials, have a clear idea of what the Soviet Union has to export to the West, apart from what it has exported in the past.

An example is scientific testing equipment in schools:

> Several years ago a Boston importer discovered quite by chance that the Soviets mass-produce such equipment and had surpluses stored in warehouses. He bought large quantities at relatively low prices and made large profits, at the same time benefiting American school children. But without the initiative of an American businessman, the Soviets would never have known of the existence of an export market for those goods, simply because all foreign market studies are made by a few agencies in Moscow.

The United States should send over a series of trade missions to study Soviet export and import possibilities. Such missions could uncover possibilities for Soviet exports to the United States which would surprise the Soviets themselves. It should be borne in mind that the more resources which the Soviets allocate to production of goods for export, the fewer, relatively, they can allocate to production of military goods.

Even if we should prove unable to exert a substantial influence on Soviet investment policy, trade with the Soviets—on the basis of mutual advantage—can help to persuade them that their own long-range interests are linked with the stability and integrity of the international economic order. In the 1920's and 1930's one of the principal charges levied against the Soviet leaders was that they had withdrawn from the world economy, that their foreign trade system was inherently restrictive and discriminatory, and that their goal was self-sufficiency. In the 1950's and 1960's the Soviet leaders have come out of their shell, have abandoned their earlier tendency toward economic isolationism, and have sought to establish firmer economic ties with the West. It is strange indeed that they should now be able to charge the United States with subverting economics to politics, with refusal to trade, and with discriminatory trade practices.

Have we lost our faith in the economic interdependence of all countries as one pillar of world order?

Why We Should Trade With the Soviets

Theodore C. Sorensen

Thus far very few articles about the boon to the United States of trading with the U.S.S.R. have been published which duplicate Sorenson's tolerant, conciliatory, and perhaps even idealistic spirit. Unavoidably, the author is opposed to the existing "arbitrary" discriminatory restrictions employed in U.S. trade with the Soviets. His contention that these restrictions do not deny anything to the U.S.S.R. is one of the three arguments for the encouragement of these relations. The other two arguments concern Sorenson's view that by trading with the Soviet Union, the U.S. can advance its national interest globally as well as in Vietnam, and that in the long-run, trade will moderate the existing conflict with the Russians.

Trade between the United States and the Soviet Union is unlikely ever to reach mammoth proportions, regardless of political considerations or even economic systems. It is equally unlikely that either nation would ever consider such trade economically indispensable or even significantly beneficial. Nevertheless, the tendency in some quarters in the United States to dismiss both the prospects and the political importance of such trade should be less readily accepted.

It is inconceivable, in fact, that the United States could not, if both parties were willing, gradually achieve a substantial exchange of goods with a massive, modern nation, now largely urbanized and industrialized but needing far more equipment and technology to fulfill its potential; a market of some 250 million people with much the same needs as Western Europe but insufficient productive capacity to meet all of those needs; a nation with eight cities of over a million populations, with an increasing level of education and living standards that now finds television and other appliances in millions of homes, and with increasingly restive consumers (whose comparatively low wages are somewhat offset by free or subsidized medical care, housing, education and other services); a potential trading partner which has demonstrated its economic and technological maturity in space, medicine, aviation, biology, electric power and nearly every basic industry.

The Soviet attempt last year to bid on six giant new turbines for the Grand Coulee Dam—a bid prevented largely for political reasons by a startled U.S. Government—is but one demonstration of the folly of our continually asserting that trade between us will always be miniscule because the U.S.S.R. produces nothing worthwhile for us to buy. On other occasions the Soviets have talked of building in this country metallurgical plants with equipment superior to our own, of licensing new medical inventions, of selling us new kinds of industrial tools.

Soviet-American trade today is miniscule. Except for the special sales of American wheat authorized by President Kennedy in 1963 and implemented under President Johnson in 1964, it has been miniscule since the early days of the cold war. Indeed, it has never been large; but the barriers have always been—and remain today—more political than economic. No doubt some American businessmen will always refuse to trade with a communist country on grounds it is immoral. No doubt some critics of communism will always be convinced that, without our trade, the Soviet economic system will ultimately and inevitably collapse. No doubt there remain in Moscow disciples of Marx and Lenin who fear that such trade will only postpone the demise of American capitalism and pollute the purity of Soviet communism. But these are minority voices at best. The largest single obstacle to the growth of U.S.-U.S.S.R. trade to a level of hundreds of millions of dollars is the obsolete, arbitrary network of discriminatory tariff, credit and export restrictions imposed by the U.S. Government. These restrictions were imposed largely when the cold war was both hotter and more pervasive than it is today, then elaborated in the days when Stalinism and a more unified communist bloc in Europe appeared to make aggression a clear and present danger; they are justified today on the grounds that the Soviet Union is a supplier and supporter of our enemies in Viet Nam.

We refuse most-favored-nation tariff treatment to Soviet goods, thus forcing American importers to pay the excessive Hawley-Smoot tariffs of 1930 and inviting like retaliation on American goods. (This gap between what the Soviets must pay and what their West European competitors must pay to bring goods into the United States will grow even larger as the new Kennedy Round agreement is carried out.)

We ban seven kinds of Soviet fur in favor of U.S. domestic interests which ask protection in the name of anti-communism.

We ban the export to the Soviet Union of not only military and genuinely strategic goods but also goods which are now freely available for purchase in both Eastern and Western Europe.

Reprinted with permission from *Foreign Affairs*, Vol. 46 (April 1968).

We prohibit the Export-Import Bank from financing any sales to the Soviets other than agricultural goods.

We prohibit the sale on credit of surplus agricultural commodities under Public Law 480.

We will not permit, under the Johnson Act, private banks and businessmen to extend long-term credits similar to those granted by our West European competitors.

We impose costly restrictions and delays on Soviet vessels seeking clearance to enter our ports.

Some of these barriers could not be eliminated entirely and some relate to long-standing questions involving Tsarist World War I debts and Lend-Lease World War II debts. But all would be susceptible to early reduction if the necessary will prevailed on both sides.

Other obstacles to Soviet-American trade must not be underestimated, including those inherent in doing business with a communist state. Trading with a state is not easy for private businessmen in any case, and Soviet bureaucracy can be even slower and more disorganized or over-organized than our own. The problems of delivery, distribution, servicing, procurement of spare parts and foreign exchange are all immense. Differences in currency, in concepts of competition, in measurements, standards, traditions, trademark and patent protection, in the use of arbitration for disputes, and even in language cannot be swiftly swept aside. Until the Soviets earn more dollars by sales to us, they may often require American exporters to take payment either in Soviet goods for resale by professional "switch dealers" or in credit balances which the Soviets have in a third country (or they may simply stipulate American components in goods which they purchase from countries whose currencies they hold). Some American businessmen may be deterred by the inconveniences of Moscow hotel service, by the need for unusual advance planning for each business trip, by the inefficiencies of the Soviet postal and telephone systems, by the lack of easy access to buyers or sellers and to plant managers or technicians, and by the need to be patient and precise on every possible point in negotiations.

Nor are the political objections confined to one side. Communist doctrine makes a virtue of economic self-sufficiency. In the midst of a business negotiation, the Soviet representatives have been known to stiffen their attitudes and their terms very quickly when the cold war suddenly turned for the worse. The war in Viet Nam has at least dampened the Soviet desire to trade. Clearly, the Kremlin has its own share of "hawks," who ask whether the Soviet Union should be trading with the United States while it is bombing their North Vietnamese allies; who regard their current sale to us of strategic metals as "trading with the enemy"; who believe President Johnson's "bridge-building" is a devious method, to quote one Soviet official, of American "ideological penetration"; and who want no Soviet resources or currency reserves diverted to Western imports, and especially to Western consumer goods, when they could be used instead for a greater Soviet military build-up.

Nevertheless, the U.S.S.R. has not been deterred by the Vietnamese war from selling to this country items which we tell our allies have too great a military potential to be exported to the Soviets—items such as the extremely rare, light, durable metal known as titanium, which we use, as the Soviets well know, almost exclusively for our outer space vehicles and for the supersonic aircraft we fly in Viet Nam. In the course of a long talk last year with Soviet Minister of Foreign Trade Patolichev and other Soviet officials I became convinced that the Soviets today desire, despite Viet Nam, to buy American goods as well as to sell their goods to us. This desire springs not from any pressing economic need—for they can obtain all the goods and markets they really need elsewhere—but from their belief that trade can help keep doors open and normalize relations.

President Johnson and his Administration, recognizing the value of such exchanges from the American point of view, moved some time ago to remove several hundred items from the export control list and to increase Export-Import Bank financing of sales to Eastern Europe; and the President condemned extremist-sponsored consumer boycotts against East European goods. His proposed East-West Trade Bill of 1966 would have authorized a wholesale liberalization along the lines recommended by a blue-ribbon advisory committee of businessmen. That bill, however, was bottled up in the Congress without even serious consideration and was not resubmitted by the President last year.

Also in 1967 the Senate amended the Export-Import Bank Extension Bill to prohibit loans and guarantees by the Bank to any nation furnishing supplies to Hanoi and to prohibit in particular loans to the Italian credit agency financing the new Fiat automobile plant in the Ukraine. Debate on the amendment related primarily to its effect on the war in Viet Nam and showed that the war is in fact the major obstacle to a liberalization of policy. It is easy to talk about expanding trade with Russia after the war or about trading now with the East European countries in order to lessen their dependence on Moscow. But the really tough question is whether the United States Government should encourage increased two-way trade (in nonstrategic goods) with the Soviet Union so long as that nation is shipping weapons and other supplies to our enemies in Viet Nam.

That is a question fraught with emotion and uncertainties. Former Secretary of Agriculture Benson has compared such trade to financing Hitler, and suggests that by allegedly promoting communism by such trade the President may be open to impeachment. One Democratic Senator calls it trafficking with the enemy and another describes it as giving aid and comfort to those killing our boys overseas. A Republican Senator compares it to Northern speculators purchasing Southern cotton during the Civil War; and a Republican Congressman says such trade places dollars ahead of lives.

Nevertheless, the question must be faced up to, and my answer is that this trade is desirable for three reasons:

First, such trade can actually advance our national interest in Viet Nam as well as in the world at large. The war in Viet Nam is a time-bomb ticking away in a nuclear world. In this period of tension, the United States and the Soviet Union must deal with each other outside the channels of cold-war manœuvring and hot-war threats and deterrents. We should make every effort to increase understanding and minimize misunderstandings and demonstrate that there is hope for peaceful coexistence. We must show that the United States is not out to eradicate communism from the face of the earth and that methods other than aggression can make progress. Any other counsel tends to escalate the risks and prolong the length of the Vietnamese war. No one advocates that we put dollars ahead of lives; and existing Commerce Department controls on the export of strategic goods will prevent any businessman who wished to from doing so. But neither in a nuclear world can we put all our hope in armaments.

This is not "trading with the enemy." The Soviet Union, for all its contrary interests and adverse actions, is not a declared enemy in Viet Nam nor do we want it to become one. Trade can neither solve nor prevent the conflicts of interest and ideology that divide us there and elsewhere; but by increasing contacts and providing experience in working together, it can help create a climate in which peace may perhaps be more readily achieved.

Bilateral trade strengthens the economies of both countries and any Soviet diversion of foreign exchange to the purchase of nonstrategic goods from us can only be to our advantage. On the other hand, restrictions on East-West trade only draw the communists closer together in increased mutual dependence.

Second, restrictions on Soviet-American trade in nonstrategic materials cannot affect the flow of Soviet arms to Viet Nam. Obviously our trade is not of sufficient importance to the Soviets to affect their determination to supply North Viet Nam; equally obvious is the fact that they can buy all the goods they want from our friends in Western Europe and from Japan.

Although East-West trade is still small, it has grown in recent years even more rapidly than Western trade as a whole. American participation in this growth has not equalled that of even some of the smallest European countries. In fact, the latest figures available indicate that, despite some increase, we are trading with the Soviet Union less than we did a generation ago; our sales of hides and skins, foods and fibers, and a variety of other items comprise considerably less than 1 percent of our total exports, while we are buying even less–mostly high-grade chromite, platinum-group metals, furs, aluminum scrap, diamonds and window glass. Meanwhile, our friends and allies–especially Britain, France, West Germany, Italy, Finland and Japan–compensating for recent sluggishness in their domestic economies, have been expanding their sales to the Soviet Union by means of long-term credits for machinery, equipment, rubber, transportation items and fabrics, purchasing in return even larger amounts of Soviet fuels, tools and raw materials for their industry, as well as some items for their consumers.

In short, our restrictions on nonstrategic trade do not deny anything to the Soviets. They do deny our businessmen an equal chance to sell in that vast market, to make the most of our technological applications and to reap the rewards in jobs, profits and an improvement in our balance of payments. They deny American farmers and producers who are disappointed with the results of the Kennedy Round in terms of West European markets a fair opportunity to develop markets in Eastern Europe. And they deny American consumers an equal chance to buy low-cost Soviet watches or bicycles or other goods now produced in the Soviet Union more efficiently than by other suppliers. It takes time for our businessmen to develop a new market, particularly one where we have no well-established trade pattern. But we have virtually abandoned the Russian and East European market to the West Europeans and the Japanese; and the longer we stay out the more established Soviet acceptance of other patterns and standards will become. In the name of anti-communism we are not hurting the communist nations but ourselves.

Trade is not aid. If we sell the Soviets more than we buy, our balance of payments benefits. Even if we grant them long-term credits, sooner or later they will have to come up with the gold or the dollars. As stated by the U.S. Council of the International Chamber of Commerce: "Trade by definition does not take place unless benefits accrue to both parties. If one nation refuses to participate, in so far as the second party can find another trading partner, the loss is entirely sustained by the country refusing to do business."

An example of this kind of shortsightedness was the Senate's 1967 amendment to the Export-Import Bank Bill prohibiting the Bank's participation in the sale of American equipment to the Italian Fiat Motor Company for use in its new Soviet plant. Credit was to be granted not to the Soviet Union but to the quasi-official Italian credit agency. Some $50 million worth of American machine tools would have gone into that plant and opened the door for still more American exports. The Departments of Defense, Commerce and State, supported by General Wheeler of the Joint Chiefs, all declared that this loan and plant, as well as the resulting increased Soviet appetite for cars, could not help but result in a diversion of Soviet resources into consumer goods instead of military. The U.S.S.R. is to expend several hundred million dollars of its own on this project and between twenty and forty thousand workers will be employed. There is no possibility, in view of our export control checks, that the smaller, lighter cars this plant will produce in the 1970s could be sensibly used in Viet Nam or any other battle; and it is very clear that both Eastern and Western Europe can supply any of this equipment that we fail to supply.

Nevertheless, in what Secretary Trowbridge called "a fruitless exercise in self-denial without corresponding advantages to the United States," the Senate adopted an amendment which could only antagonize the Soviets, irritate the Italians, deny profits and jobs to our own industry and lose what little influence that sale might have brought us in Moscow—all without interfering in the slightest with the building of the plant in question, with the flow of Soviet supplies to Viet Nam, with the progress of the Soviet economy or with the length of the Vietnamese war. The House having already this year adopted an even broader amendment barring all Export-Import Bank transactions relating to any communist country, it is apparent that Western Europe will supply these nonstrategic items to the Soviets and its businessmen and labor will reap the gains, while our balance of payments—as well as our reputation for common sense—will suffer. Perhaps the Senators who voted for the amendment intended it as a symbolic slap at the Soviet Union and felt better as a result. Perhaps the torrent of emotions which compared the proposed transaction to our building "a munitions plant in Moscow" or creating an "RFC for communist countries" had too strong a demagogic appeal to be resisted. But every Senator should have known that the amendment was futile and foolish.

A third reason for trade with the Soviet Union in nonstrategic goods has to do with our long-term interest in moderating the conflict with the Russians. It is often charged that the Soviets use trade as an instrument of policy in the struggle between our two systems. They do and we should. World peace, as President Kennedy said, does not require that we love our neighbors; and world trade likewise does not require that we love our trading partners. While both the ideological differences and the national conflicts of interest between the United States and the U.S.S.R. are too real to be ignored, present U.S. restrictions on trade with the Soviet Union are a handicap in the ideological struggle and run contrary to our foreign policy interests.

The United States should not emerge from the struggle in Viet Nam to find itself wholly out of favor in Europe and wholly out of touch with Moscow. The gradual reconciliation of Eastern and Western Europe seems destined to proceed, whether we like it or not—and most of us do. Eastern and Western Europe are developing a great network of economic relations, trade routes, pipelines, power grids, shared technology and coöperative production agreements. We are already somewhat isolated from this process by the Viet Nam war and an appearance of uncompromising cold-war militancy. We should not add to our isolation by inflexibility of East-West trade.

It is in our interest to see the Soviets invest more of their resources in consumer goods and less in their traditional sectors of heavy industry, space and defense. Already Soviet leaders show an increased if cautious recognition of consumer demand, of the complaints about shortages, the desire for cars and better homes and clothes. The economic reforms launched by the Kremlin more than two years ago do not go as far as those in several other East European states in experimenting, decentralizing and paying more attention to market factors. But more responsibility and initiative are now permitted at lower levels; bonuses, profit incentives and other forms of capitalism are beginning to appear; and the balances between production and demand and between prices and costs are becoming more realistic.

Centralized planning is still responsible for unnecessary rigidities and delays. But once their State Planning Committee has decided that the nation's long-range priorities and hard-currency reserves permit the importation of certain goods, their Foreign Trade Ministry and its operating subsidiaries will seek the lowest possible price in the most arduously negotiated contract.

If our businessmen are to make the most of the vast Soviet market, if we are to influence the evolution of Soviet external political attitudes and internal economic reforms and are to resist the ambition common to Kosygin and de Gaulle to exclude our influence from a reunited Europe, then the Congress should remove our outmoded, discriminatory barriers against nonstrategic trade with the Soviet Union; authorize most-favored-nation status for all of Eastern Europe; and remove these latest restrictions imposed upon the Export-Import Bank. The Administration should remove from export controls those commodities which no longer are strategic in the sense that they are unavailable elsewhere; and the Export-Import Bank should grant short-term commercial credits for industrial exports to the Soviet Union without requiring of the Kremlin anything more than is required of other nations to prove their credit-worthiness.

The traffic on bridges to the East, as Senator Dirksen has said, should move both ways. The credits and concessions should be reciprocal and the expansion should be bilateral. Chinese opposition as well as the Vietnamese war may inhibit Russia from accepting our offers for the moment. But our efforts should outlast the Vietnamese war and outgrow the cold war. Trade is a force for friendship, understanding and peace. We should use it, not thwart it.

The Long-term Credit Strings Attached to Trade With The Soviet Union

Norman A. Bailey

Rather than analyzing long-term credit to the U.S.S.R. as such, Mr. Bailey cautions the United States on the primary and ultimate objectives of Soviet promotion of East-West trade. He states bluntly that unless the U.S. believes that the U.S.S.R. has renounced its goal of world domination, intensification of economic relations with this power "does not make sense." The author contends that Soviet economic weakness has caused the U.S.S.R. to seek expansion of commercial contacts with the West.

In eary 1963 the Russians began the latest in a long series of "détentes," periods of relative relaxation of tensions in the Cold War. Economic policy is always an important aspect of détente, and expansion of East-West trade has been particularly stressed in the 1963-64 period, with great and growing success, particularly in Western Europe. Nevertheless, the Soviets have apparently decided that the time is also ripe to open up the greatest of the world's markets, and the greatest of the world's sources of supply, the United States. A severe wheat shortage caused by internal mismanagement and compounded by scattered droughts provided a perfect opening into the American market, through our own best example of internal mismanagement, agriculture.

We Open the Road to Long-Term Credit

• When the Soviet Union offered to purchase large quantities of wheat in the United States, the prospect of reducing our enormous accumulated surplus was too tempting to be turned down and the wheat was sold. More importantly, the wheat was sold *on credit, long-term credit*, permitted by a one-vote margin that the Senate was induced to provide in the immediate aftermath of the tragic assassination of President Kennedy.

–In this way, not only was the wall of the American market breached, but it was breached in such a way as to constitute a precedent for a *sine-qua-non* of communist trade, the provision of long-term credit.

This initial success was immediately followed up by an intensive campaign to induce the United States to abolish its remaining barriers. Businessmen on junkets to Moscow were told that Russia was in the market for hundreds of millions of dollars worth of chemical equipment, construction equipment, farm tools and other manufactured goods. Construction equipment makers and the Manufacturing Chemists Association were invited to exhibit their wares in Moscow.

In return long-term contracts were offered for the supply of iron ore, manganese, chromium and other raw materials, a far cry from the "caviar-furs" type of trade common until the present time. All of this trade is to take place on the basis of long-term credit, preferably more than five years (the French recently signed a trade pact with the Soviet Union providing for terms up to seven years, thereby violating agreements with their NATO allies).

• In April of this year [1964] the then Deputy Premier and now Premier of Soviet Russia, Alexei Kosygin, told a visiting delegation of U.S. government officials and businessmen that the two countries should sign a long-term trade pact, and that the U.S. could "name its needs and we will fill them." Significantly, Kosygin stressed the Soviet desire to buy whole plants and the rights to American manufacturing processes, all on credit. The delegation was impressed.

–In referring to whole plants, Kosygin may well have had in mind the recently-opened textile mill in Kalinin, built by the American company Intertex International Inc., which will provide Russia with 15 million yards of woolen suiting, 5 million yards of cotton-synthetic blends and 2 million pounds of yarn yearly. The head of Intertex is a government consultant.

American Business Pricks Up Its Ears and Goes to Russia

–Most important of all, the campaign gradually began to find echoes in the organized business community in the United States, which for years had stood idly by and watched European and Japanese firms walk away with large Soviet and communist-bloc orders they were unable to compete for.

At the 47th annual convention of the International Executive Association, members listened to a panel advocate increased trade with the Soviet bloc. The members of the panel most enthusiastically in favor of liberalization were all businessmen. Most recently, the consulting firm, Business International, organized a trip to Moscow by about a hundred top corporation executives, who made it clear to now-Premier Kosygin that they wanted to sell. Mr. Kosygin happily replied that Russia was ready to buy–on Russia's terms. In a lyrical vein, a spokesman for

Reprinted with permission from *The Magazine of Wall Street* (December 12, 1964).

Business International toasted Premier Kosygin in the following words: "The assurances you gave, and even more the way in which you gave them, convinced any who were still in doubt of the sincerity of your country's desire to live in peaceful coexistence and to see a steady and rapid development of trade, for the benefit of every one."

The Danger in Long-Term Credits on Plants and Rights to Manufacturing Processes

Whatever the reaction of the American executives in Moscow, there are some who are still in doubt about the peaceful intentions of the Soviet Union and its desire to conduct nonpolitical trade. In discussing Soviet strategy in the current phase of the Cold War the British expert J. M. Mackintosh wrote: "Economic penetration . . . may come to appear in Moscow (though not necessarily in Peking), *as the only possible policy for the Soviet Union in the next two decades*."

And lest anyone think that the problems of East-West trade are in any way new or unique, the great master of strategy, the eighteenth-century Prussian strategist Karl von Clausewitz wrote in his classic treatise On War: "Disarm your enemy in peace by diplomacy and trade and you will conquer him more readily on the field of battle."

The trade policy of governments–and all Soviet trade is government trade–is adopted for internal or external policy reasons, for the furtherance of the domestic or international goals of that government. The Soviets understand this very well, and they are under no domestic pressure by independent economic groups to deflect their purpose.

If we believe that the Soviet Union has renounced the goal of domination of the world by communism, our present headlong drive towards expanded trade makes sense. Otherwise it does not.

A Policy Without Strategy

It is, perhaps, a misunderstanding of this basic equation that has resulted in the vacillation of American and allied policy with reference to East-West trade since the beginning of the Cold War. On the one hand we have proclaimed a policy of trading with *some* communists in order to make money, further political aims, or for humanitarian reasons, while refusing to trade with *other* communists because they are supposedly more aggressive, addicted to violence or intransigent.

Were we to follow the classic rules of strategy, of course, we should assist and trade with China, the weaker of our two great enemies, rather than with Russia, which is infinitely stronger, but be this as it may, our policies have had precious little to do with strategic analysis.

Can We Ever Trust Russia to Pay Up?

–Our task here is to show that the Soviet Union trades for political reasons having to do with the eventual demise of the Western political and economic systems, and having determined that speculate on the appropriate policy response.

There is no doubt that in an economic exchange free from coercion and fraud, both sides gain. That is, if Guatemala trades a quantity of bananas in return for a quantity of wheat from the United States, it is because Guatemala would rather have the wheat than the bananas and the U.S. would rather have the bananas than the wheat. Only if there *is* coercion or fraud involved in the exchange does one side have the advantage over the other. Thus if the United States forced Guatemala to give up bananas it wanted to keep and forced upon it wheat it did not want, the advantages of the exchange would be entirely on the side of the United States. This is, of course, often the result of bilateral barter agreements such as those signed by the Soviet Union and its satellites after the war. If there is fraud in the transaction it will also not exhibit the characteristics of a free exchange. Thus if the United States gave Guatemala rotten wheat in exchange for good bananas, then again the advantages of the exchange would be completely on the side of the United States.

Soviet Practices Economic Warfare

Economic warfare as conducted during the Cold War by the Soviet Union exhibits precisely these factors of coercion and fraud, which is to say that the ordinary laws of economics and the market do not apply.

In other words, if the Soviet Union were to change its trade policies so as to follow these economic laws, it would then be as advantageous for the West as for the Soviets to trade, and thus any form of embargo would make no sense economically. *In fact, however, the Soviet Union trades for primarily political, not economic reasons, except under duress, and then usually on long-term credit. If it finds that the political results hoped for do not occur, it will cease trading and apply its resources otherwise.*

This is not to say that economic warfare does not impose a cost upon the Soviet Union. Economic warfare, as any form of conflict, has an economic cost. It has a cost not only directly in economic terms, as when the Soviet Union accepts goods it does not want in order to control a market, but also in psychological and perhaps political terms, through an indefinite delay in substantial improvement of the standard of living of the Soviet people.

–Should the West begin to apply economic warfare measures in earnest, there would also be an economic cost involved, of course, although the West is much better able to bear the cost than the communist nations. There would then be a political calculation involved as to comparative advantage, rather than an economic calculation. *As it is now, however, with one side calculating largely economically and the other side completely politically, it is clear where the overall strategic advantage lies.*

†† Two principal economic elements are to be found in the détente pattern of Soviet strategy. The Soviet Union adopts détente when it is relatively weak, rather than when it is strong. This is as true of the economic situation as it is of the estimate of relative military strengths. Thus it would appear that economic weakness is an element of détente which, in combination with other factors, forces the Soviet Union to seek a period of respite, either to prevent further widening of the strategic gap, or to permit transferral of resources from military to economic uses.

Soviet Economy Occupies Second Place in Red Strategy

Soviet economic problems have theoretical bases with practical results. We are not going to examine here the theoretical reasons behind Soviet economic failures. The excessive centralization, the lack of a price system, the difficulties of the economic calculus, the lack of incentives, and other problems are well known. *What is perhaps not so well known is the fact that these theoretical difficulties have resulted in a rate of economic development far below the panicky Western estimates of a few years ago, not to mention official Soviet statistics.*

Even before the Central Intelligence Agency made public in early 1964 its estimates of the downturn in the Soviet growth rates, many observers had concluded that Soviet development, though creditable, was neither fantastic nor miraculous. The pattern of retardation, moreover, is accelerating. Indices of industrial production and intercity freight traffic were lower in the second half of the fifties than in the first half and lower again thus far in the sixties.

Turning Over a New Leaf to Correct a Bad Situation

The Soviet drive for industrialization at all costs has resulted in a situation of accelerated obsolescence of plant and equipment, and industrial sectors essential to an advanced economy have been neglected. With its inherent weaknesses, the Soviet economy may have to move backwards before it can move ahead again. For the final push in the satellite and rocket programs, resources were drained from the agricultural sector, and the results are only too obvious now.

—In other words, unless it is bailed out, the Soviet economy is in a state of acute crisis. Unfortunately, there is an army of Western businessmen anxious and eager to provide that bailout. It is doubly ironic that this should come at a time when many communist economists are questioning the viability of their own system.

The United States vs Soviet Union

One of the road blocks inhibiting forceful American action on the international scene is the psychological association of the word "conflict" with bloodshed and violence, whereas it applies equally to political steps taken, that can be just as devastating and dangerous. When the action is political, the relative advantages to the various combatants must be carefully considered in order to adopt the economic strategy necessary to conform with international reality. For example—a policy of embargo makes sense only if imposed on the weaker country by an economically stronger power, with the purpose of forcing political concessions in return for softening the embargo.

It is clearly evident that the Soviet Union has staged its trade offensive precisely because it is weak, and therefore the wide policy for the West—and particularly for the United States—would be to act in accordance with recognition of this truth.

The challenge which détente poses to Western strategy in the field of economics, arises from the inevitable pressures on governments and private entrepreneurs to divorce economic power from political goals—in an attempt to conduct relations with communist countries solely or primarily for economic profit. Thus, if Western resolve remains strong during the period of détente in the years ahead, the Western states can use their growing margin of economic superiority over the communist world, to limit the military power of their principal antagonist, the Soviet Union, and weaken its expansionist foreign policy. For—if we permit them to lead us around by the nose, we will end up doing exactly what they want us to do, and suffer the consequences of being outsmarted.

The United States, the West, and the Future of Eastern Europe

Jerzy Lukaszewski

Professor Lukaszewski of Bruges, Belgium, views U.S. trade and economic aid to East Europe as an instrument capable of advancing the emergence there of "as more pragmatic, more humane, and more European socialism." The United States should fully understand East European nationalism because it has an important role to play in those countries for which "America remains the promised land of affluence and freedom." The author observes that East Europeans have a spontaneous desire for broad contacts and cooperation with the West.

The Aftermath of Soviet Hegemony

As Soviet hegemony in Eastern Europe has been eroded, and as Communism in Eastern Europe has sunk into sterility and contradictions, unable to cope with the problems of the industrial societies whose formation is precipitated, the direction of the development of newly autonomous Eastern Europe has become of utmost importance. The alienation of the Communist parties from society, in particular from the intelligentsia and youth, has become increasingly manifest. Various oppositions have emerged within the parties, and the most devastating criticism of the Communist system has been formulated by Communists from the Eastern European countries. Under the circumstances it is vitally important to determine the alternatives that will succeed the obsolete ideology: will it be the revitalization of the present totalitarianism by a massive injection of nationalism, or will it be the emergence of a more pragmatic, more humane, and more European socialism? In a few years the old Communist leaders, intellectually and morally degraded by Stalinism, haunted by fear and suspicion, and prisoners of dogma, will be replaced by men of a younger generation. The political options of these new men will be a matter of great concern.

The erosion of Soviet hegemony in Eastern Europe has also created the conditions for a greater Western role in that region. Italy has achieved spectacular results in developing her trade with the Eastern European countries. Germany, after rejecting the dogmatic application of the Hallstein Doctrine, embarked upon an active Eastern policy under the Kiesinger-Brandt government, a venture that cannot but profit from the considerable influence of the German economy on Eastern European markets. France, under General de Gaulle's leadership, has actively stimulated developments in Eastern Europe through the multiplication of contacts with the People's Democracies and by the creation of precedents in the Western world that these countries are expected to imitate within their own orbit.

Against this background of change, a clear definition of American policy intentions with respect to Eastern Europe could effect important consequences. Because of the weight and responsibility of the United States in international affairs, such a definition could crystallize the common long-range political objectives of at least a number of the Western powers. This in turn would greatly enhance the impact of Western influence upon the evolution of the Eastern European countries, for the powers of Western Europe with the exception of France, seem so far to have been guided in their Eastern policy only by a day-to-day pragmatism and to have pursued not necessarily convergent goals.

A clear definition of American policy toward Eastern Europe could also provide a strong impetus for the crystallization of political goals and attitudes within the region. This would be a natural result of the great prestige America enjoys among an overwhelming majority of the Eastern European populations, including segments of the membership of the Communist parties. For the Czechs, Poles, Hungarians, and other Eastern Europeans, America remains the promised land of affluence and freedom, the country which has accepted millions of their compatriots and offered them a better life, the home of scientific and technological wonders, and the only power capable of defying the Soviet giant.

What then should be the long-range American policy objectives in Eastern Europe? It is the conviction of this observer that the United States should stimulate and support the economic and political integration of Eastern Europe by a continuation and extension of the action designed by General Marshall twenty years ago.

Analyzing East European Nationalism

At present, differences of opinion exist within the United States with regard to the future of Eastern Europe and the policy to be adopted vis-à-vis that region. For the most part, these differences result from

Reprinted with permission from the *Journal of International Affairs,* Vol. 22, No. 1 (1968).

divergent assessments of the role of nationalism in Eastern Europe. For example, Ambassador Averell Harriman stated not long ago: "Although nationalism among the nations of Eastern Europe has led to their demand for greater independence from Moscow, there is reason for our recognizing that cooperation among the countries of Eastern Europe can contribute to the health of the entire continent." Zbigniew Brzezinski, formerly of the State Department's Policy Planning Council, considers nationalism in the People's Democracies a harmful phenomenon: "Nationalism in East Europe is now becoming a conservative force and is expolited by the new elites in order to maintain themselves in power, to protect the status quo . . . I am convinced it would be idle, and probably counterproductive, to concentrate on stimulating East European nationalism or hostility to the Soviet Union. . . ." However, Mr. Foy D. Kohler, Deputy Under Secretary of State and a distinguished expert on Eastern Europe, affirms: "We have encouraged the powerful forces of nationalism by positive programs of developing constructive relations with the countries of Eastern Europe."

Various processes taking place in Eastern Europe during the last years and generally understood as a powerful upsurge of nationalism have met with immense interest in the West and have given rise to interpretations by statesmen, diplomats, scholars, and journalists, that, in this author's view, were mostly wrong. A correct understanding of this nationalism is vital to the formulation of American policy objectives in Eastern Europe.

Just after the war, the extreme weakness of the Communist parties in the newly founded People's Democracies–except for Czechoslovakia and, in a somewhat different sense, Yugoslavia–induced those parties, exalted by war experiences, to identify themselves with nationalism in order to find a common denominator with the societies. Of course the anti-Russian component of the nationalist traditions was dampened by all means available but other components were enchanced according to place and circumstance: the anti-German in Poland, the anti-Hungarian in Rumania, etc. Later, the anti-Semitic component was stirred in almost all Eastern European countries. Moscow eagerly sponsored this operation that, on the one hand, augmented the chances of Communism in Eastern Europe and, on the other hand, helped to maintain the fragmentation of that region, thereby facilitating Soviet hegemony. Soviet specialists in ideology and propaganda have taken great pains to glorify the "national state" in Eastern Europe and to present it as a progressive historical form. This glorification has been particularly intense in the field of historical interpretation, especially with regard to the multinational Hapsburg empire that was dismembered in 1918.

The causes of the recent intensity of nationalism are many. One of the most important is the search of the Eastern European ruling elites for a political alternative to the outdated and sterile Communist ideology. The elites' choice of nationalism as an alternative to Communism has been to a great extent determined by their own sociological and intellectual character. The older generation of Marxist intelligentsia, with strong internationalist convictions, has been decimated by time and by Stalinist purges. Consequently, the center of gravity in the leading Communist strata has shifted to half-educated elements, quite often of peasant origin, for whom rudimentary nationalism has always been, in addition to simplified Marxism, a strong ingredient of the *Weltanschauung.* It is not surprising that to these elements an appeal to nationalist emotions and an identification with nationalist traditions appears as the surest methods of reinforcing the social basis of the regime, shaken by the crisis of Communism.

There is no doubt that grievances toward the Soviet Union play a part of the recurrence of nationalism in Eastern Europe. The amputations of territories for the benefit of the U.S.S.R. and the ruthless economic exploitation by the U.S.S.R. in the first decade after the "liberation" have not been forgotten. The frictions in COMECON nourish misgivings and dissatisfaction. At first in Yugoslavia, then for a short period in Hungary and Poland, and most recently in Rumania, the anti-Soviet trends have risen to the surface.

This was one of the principal reasons why the recent intensity of nationalism in Eastern Europe has been applauded in the Western countries. What is more interesting, however, is that the Soviet Union has not in the least departed from its policy of strong support for the "national state" and from its benevolence toward nationalism in Eastern Europe. Zbigniew Brzezinski provides an explanation of this seemingly surprising fact: "Nationalism not only inspires but also fragments East European opposition to the Russians, and helps the Soviet leaders in maintaining their predominance in the region by resorting to the ancient device of *divide et impera* . . . There is no doubt that the inability of the East Europeans to overcome their own national antipathies makes them much weaker in their efforts to reassert their independence." The last Hungarian Communist Party Congress supplied a striking illustration of that truth when Mr. Kadar resorted, under Mr. Brezhnev's benevolent eyes, to the arguments and terminology of prewar Hungarian revisionism to attack the "imperialist dictation of Trianon" and to sling a dart at Rumania.

The convulsions of isolated nationalisms may be a source of trouble for Moscow, but they cannot seriously challenge the Soviet domination in the region. An Eastern European state determined to attain real independence of the U.S.S.R., regardless of the attitude of its immediate neighbors, would inevitably become a burden for the West and might turn into an artificial Cuba-like bridgehead. The stimulation and backing of nationalisms should not be the essence of the policy of the United States and of the West in general toward Eastern Europe. One must be aware that it does not represent a real alternative to the Soviet policy in that region. One also must not overlook the fact, as is generally done in the West, that the multiplication of the symptoms of nationalism in the internal and external affairs of the Eastern European countries represents more an evolution of the Communist parties and ruling elites than a change in the basic attitudes of the population. It is true that the nationalism of ruling elites has sometimes met a favorable response among the population, particularly when it engaged in anti-Soviet policies. However, it is the conviction of this author, based on a long observation of Eastern Europe, that the recent tendency of the Communist elites toward closer identification with nationalism is contrary to the basic trends and ideas taking shape among the societies. In fact, this divergence is one of the expressions of the growing alienation of the parties from the societies.

The citizens of the People's Democracies do not fail to realize that, between the two wars, nationalism had plunged Eastern Europe into chaos and prepared the way for foreign domination. Their claustrophobia, produced by long years of hermetic isolation within the frontiers of the "national state," leads to a strong, spontaneous desire for broader contact and cooperation with foreigners. They watch the experiment of the European Economic Community with the greatest interest and respect. The shortages they endure impress upon them the idea of a more rational and more efficient economic organization, one similar to the model which emerged in Western Europe. In brief, there are strong reasons to believe that the idea of an economic and political union of Eastern Europe is in the process of crystallization among the population of that region, particularly among the intelligentsia that has been the catalyst of all important social and political processes during the last century.

A Marshall Plan for Eastern Europe

The considerable potential of spontaneous social support for the integration of Eastern Europe is one of the reasons that should induce the West, and the United States in particular, to define this integration as their political objective. Such a clarification of Western policy would, in turn, greatly stimulate the pressure of public opinion in Eastern Europe to achieve that objective.

It has to be emphasized that public opinion in Eastern Europe has been gaining in importance since the collapse of Stalinism, and the governments are less and less able to neglect it. Old-style Communist authoritarianism has been declining and seems to be doomed as a consequence of the social evolution. Public opinion and its pressures are constant components of the socio-political reality of the Communist orbit, whereas the ruling elites and the "lines" they represent are subject to change, as recent history has shown. When, in a few years, leaders of the new generation replace the old guard, they may identify themselves, of necessity if not of conviction, with the ideas prevailing in the society.

It is necessary to observe that despite the nationalistic leanings of the present ruling elites, some degree of useful economic integration of the People's Democracies has been attained as a result of the endeavors of intelligent and efficiency-minded technicians. This is important, for the more extensive the common infrastructure, the more likely it is that a common institutional and political superstructure will develop.

The economic and political integration of the People's Democracies would be beneficial not only for these countries, but also for Europe and the world. Integration would be the surest means of doing away with the remainders of the Soviet hegemony established by Stalin. The forces generated by union would inevitably lead to independence and this, in turn, would considerably augment the chances of stability in that area. It was the humiliation, dissatisfaction, and hatred nourished by Soviet domination that led to dissent, violence, and bloodshed in the past. As the Chinese giant becomes an increasing menace to the U.S.S.R.'s Asiatic confines, the Soviet interest in stability on their Western front may force a recognition that a united, independent, and stable Eastern Europe is a better partner for friendly and fruitful cooperation than the conglomerate of uncertain statellites. Moscow's accommodation to a nonhegemonistic pattern of relations with Eastern Europe will certainly evolve with difficulty, for it implies a reorientation from dogmatism to pragmatism among the Soviet leadership. But this difficulty will not be overcome so long as the tendency toward hegemony is nourished by the confusion and weakness inherent in the microcosm of nationalisms and "independent national states" in Eastern Europe.

The emergence of that region as an autonomous, third segment of the continent, between the Soviet and West European poles, would in itself be an important step towards overcoming the split of Europe sustained today by the aritificial East-West dichotomy. The economic and political integration of Eastern Europe would give its peoples a feeling of security in the face of Germany and thus remove one of the important obstacles to rapprochement with Western Europe. Closer relations with the EEC and other Western nations would, on the one hand, counter-balance the connections with the Soviet Union that are much too unilateral at present, and on the other enable Eastern Europe to assume the useful role of a bridge between the U.S.S.R. and the West. Such a development would act in favor of a gradual reunification of the continent.

It is evident today that the endless economic difficulties of Eastern Europe, with all the hardships they imply for the populations, stem to a great extent from the original decision of the Communist ruling elites to construct their economies as miniatures of the Soviet autarky. The integration of Eastern Europe would create the indispensable conditions for the economic and technological progress likely to elevate the standard of living of the region.

As a prerequisite to independence vis-à-vis the U.S.S.R., to security vis-à-vis Germany, to rapprochement with the West, and to economic progress, the integration of Eastern Europe is more likely to captivate the imagination of the societies, set meaningful goals for the ruling elites, and constitute a more viable alternative to decaying Communism than nationalism. The latter is, in fact, as outdated a proposition for each developed society as Communism itself. The emergence of a viable political alternative in Eastern Europe is an urgent necessity for there have been more and more symptoms of unrest and mounting tensions in recent years. Eastern Europe should be spared violence. A peaceful and organic development moving toward a more prosperous and more democratic society should be promoted.

How could the United States precipitate the emergency of an integrated and hence independent Eastern Europe? First of all appropriate use should be made of the existing stock of knowledge on Eastern Europe—greater than in any other Western country—and of the incomparable facilities for further study of that area. It would be of great importance if American experts and specialized institutions would inquire into the problems of regional integration in Eastern Europe and draw up relevant propositions. Such studies could stimulate the gestation of corresponding ideas and projects in the countries concerned despite the present unfavorable official climate.

The intensification of economic relations with Eastern Europe would also be of great importance. Any easing of the present excessive economic dependence of the People's Democracies upon the U.S.S.R. could only facilitate their freedom of political maneuver and their search for solutions best suited to their own interests. The United States is lagging far behind the West European powers in trade with Eastern Europe, and there certainly are possibilities for augmenting this trade.

Still more important would be a generous program of economic assistance for Eastern Europe as soon as it would be practicable for the United States. Such a program, possibly designed and carried into effect jointly with the EEC, could decisively assist the integration and independence of Eastern Europe in the same way as did the Marshall Plan for Western Europe. The economic situation of the People's Democracies is difficult; their needs for credits and investments are immense, and the necessity to improve their standards of living is pressing. The U.S.S.R., itself in the grip of serious economic and political difficulties, is unable to meet all the needs of these countries. In such a situation, the governments of Eastern Europe would welcome a large-scale Western aid program despite all the doctrinal reservations. The U.S.S.R.'s control over the region is not so unrestricted as it was twenty years ago, and Moscow is no longer in a position to prevent the People's Democracies from accepting Western aid as she prevented them from participating in the Marshall Plan.

Finally, the future integration and emancipation, of Eastern Europe could only be stimulated by the continuous, strong support of the United States for West European integration. The EEC has developed into a potential source of economic assistance to its eastern neighbors. It is also a most eloquent denial of the Marxist dogma of the inevitable and suicidal contradictions in capitalism, and thus supports the tendency toward pragmatism among the Communist ruling elites. The existence and progress of the EEC produce, as a chain reaction, movements of integration in other regions of the world.

It is unlikely that Eastern Europe will resist the idea impressed upon it by the EEC example. It is also unlikely that it will postpone for a long time the transformation of its present relations with the U.S.S.R. into a partnership on the basis of equality, similar to that which unites an integrated Western Europe and the United States.

Problems of East-West Relations

Václav Kotyk

Mr. Kotyk's analysis of East-West relations is a serious and frank attempt to make the West appreciate that East Europe is indeed in the process of transition and reorientation toward world-wide economic cooperation. He shows, among other things, that the economic development of a number of socialist countries makes it necessary for them to seek mutually beneficial contacts with the West. He also approves of President de Gaulle's new concept of "Europa." Mr. Kotyk is a member of the Czech Institute International Politics and Economics in Prague, where he is Director of the Department of Socialist Countries.

Today there is little doubt that a process of profound change is occurring in the relationship between East and West, between the socialist and nonsocialist countries. It is a complex process in which the tendencies of the past are intertwined with those of the present. Today we stand at the beginning of this process of change, and that is one of the reasons why our thinking about this new relationship is marked so heavily by the political past.

The tendency to judge new developments and needs in terms of old concepts is a characteristic of contemporary international politics. It is essential to recognize that the increasing cooperation between East and West is a product, above all else, of the objective conditions and needs of current international developments. It is a process of a permanent, inevitable nature, independent of the intentions and conceptions of political leaders and scholars. While we must not in the least underestimate the significant role of the subjective factors in the development of this process, we must seek our answers to the fundamental East-West questions in the historical conditions that are at the root of the new relationship.

It is certainly difficult to analyze in a brief article the important characteristics and factors of the contemporary East-West rapprochement. However, it is possible to begin by noting that in the voluminous literature about this East-West theme there are many valuable and suggestive studies that one could only repeat. Therefore, may I as a scholar of the Eastern bloc, be permitted to express my opinion about some important aspects of the socialist countries' approach to the problems of East-West relations, and in doing so elucidate the conceptual elements of the foreign policy of the majority of these socialist states. This attempt may not be entirely superfluous. Western studies of the East-West relationship—even studies notable for their originality of thinking—frequently show a surprising lack of understanding for the motivation of socialist foreign policy. This misunderstanding is occurring at a time when mutual understanding and truthful interpretation of the West's policy in the East and the East's policy in the West are important prerequisites to rapprochement and the elimination, step by step, of the mistrust that has characterized relations between socialist and non-socialist countries in the recent past. Scholarly research has an unquestionably large, and so far unexplored, opportunity in this area. It is difficult to overestimate the potential significance of the scholar's contribution in creating an objective outlook about the contemporary world and in formulating political concepts that correspond with the real world of today.

I

A number of Western scholars, publicists, and politicians—consciously or perhaps unconsciously—continue to present a thesis that focuses on the expansionist nature of the foreign policy of the socialist countries, particularly of the U.S.S.R. Even if the thesis is not always openly expressed, it nevertheless forms an undercurrent of the studies about Eastern political concepts and goals, and it is from this point of view that certain concrete facts and statements are often interpreted. It is important to understand the *foundations* of the foreign policy of the majority of the socialist countries, so that we may understand the *meaning* of Eastern efforts to develop economic, cultural, and political contacts with countries of the West. Should Eastern efforts to cooperate with the West be understood as a temporary and insincere tactic, as a mood of the moment? Such an interpretation would not exclude some contacts between the East and the West—contacts were not completely suspended even in the years of the Cold War—but it could hardly become the basis of an all-out and ever increasing process of cooperation.

In analyzing the socialist states' approach toward cooperation with the West, we must first of all be aware of the substantial *change* in the Soviet's concept of "peaceful coexistence" that occurred in the second half of the 1950's. It is senseless to try to prove the sincerity of the socialist countries' efforts to cooperate

Reprinted with permission from the *Journal of International Affairs*, Vol. 22, No. 1 (1968).

with the non-socialist countries by a mechanical listing of the numerous examples of cooperation in the economic, cultural, and political fields. Nor would it be sufficiently convincing if the vital Eastern interests in peaceful cooperation with the West were deduced only from the fact of the existence of the socialist order in these countries. Of decisive significance, however, is an analysis of the domestic as well as international political developments that condition and influence the peaceful policy of the East. Such an analysis proves that the Soviet Union, practically from the moment of its birth, pursued a policy of peace. This policy was a result of the objective conditions of the inter-war period, the characterization of which would go beyond the limits of this article, but which did not allow the Marxists to move beyond the state of coexistence. To the Soviet Marxists, peaceful coexistence was simply a part of the transitional era that was to precede a new period of international conflict and revolutionary upheaval.

When, therefore, Stalin stressed in a 1936 interview with Roy Howard that, "American democracy and the Soviet system could live in peace and mutual competition," this was not the same as N.S. Khrushchev's similar remark twenty years later. Those twenty years, during which the face of the earth completely changed, have enforced a conception of politics that corresponds to new developments in the world. Stalin had in mind–in harmony with Lenin's belief that there can be no permanent peace as long as socialism and capitalism exist side by side–a *specific* peaceful coexistence, not the possibility of excluding war from the life of society, but the possibility of excluding a *specific* war. That Stalin maintained this theory even in the postwar years is suggested in his well-known 1952 work, *The Economic Problems of Socialism*.

However, this theory of the provisional nature of peaceful coexistence between countries with differing social systems–and this is essential–is *not* a current concept in the foreign policy of the Eastern socialist countries. The theory of the provisional nature of peaceful coexistence lost its validity in the last decade. Profound changes that occurred in the development of international relations, particularly the qualitative changes in the development of modern armaments, made it possible for the socialist countries to understand peaceful coexistence as a period of *permanent* peace, not as a period of temporary good relations. Moreover, peaceful coexistence between countries of differing social and political systems may be logically understood in a much broader sense. Peaceful coexistence may be seen as a way to promote the further development of world socialism, indeed, as the *only acceptable* means of widening the sphere of socialism.

It is difficult to exclude altogether the possibility of the victory of socialist forces, by way of armed struggle, in a country of the developing world. However, this is, and will be, an exceptional situation. From the point of view of the vital interests of socialism, emphasis upon anything other than peaceful interaction between the countries of East and West cannot be a part of the conceptual basis of their foreign policy. In particular, it cannot be a concept of the East's policy toward the industrially developed states of Western Europe and toward the United States of America. Even if the conditions of a particular situation require an emphasis of this or another aspect (for example, the current policy of the socialist countries is to emphasize the unity of the socialist world), the fundamental concepts of the foreign policy of the Eastern countries remain unchanged. These concepts are determined by the long-range, basic tendencies of world economic and political development, particularly by the requirements of the forthcoming scientific-technological revolution. If we must think about the relations between East and West in terms of the struggle between various social systems, then today this struggle is taking place in the areas of production and technological and scientific progress. Only in this area can one think about overcoming the social system of capitalism. This is, in my opinion, an entirely acceptable avenue for the development of relations between East and West, an approach that would eliminate, step by step, mutual mistrust, interference, and violent methods of solving disputes.

Interest in a peaceful solution to the East-West conflict, even if it is not motivated by identical purposes, is being stressed increasingly in both the East and the West. The view which stressed, from the birth of Soviet foreign policy, the hostility between socialism and capitalism–which undoubtedly had and still has a certain justification in reality–is today different, emphasizing peaceful forms for ending antagonism. Even if the recent socialist programs for economic competition between socialism and capitalism were to a considerable degree exaggerated and contained an unrealistic evaluation of the possibilities of socialism, they nevertheless expressed a certain tendency to transfer the struggle between socialism and capitalism onto a peaceful plane.

However, it would be a mistake to limit this struggle between social systems to the field of economics, even if that area is decisive. One must not forget that there is also an ideological challenge, a competition of ideas. This competition is also a form of struggle that does not exclude, but on the contrary assumes, a mutual exchange of views, discussion, and even polemics.

Obviously, a policy focusing upon permanent peaceful cooperation is not a matter for one party alone; it is a task for both parties, East and West. Certain political concepts and foreign policy acts can encourage the development of these relations; others may hinder it. This is true for both sides. After all, we are aware that even within the socialist system forces can exist that do not understand–and in the objective conditions of their environment probably *cannot* understand–the new historical situation that categorically demands peaceful contacts in a divided world. Such forces with similar goals, it is well known, also exist within the system of capitalist states. The existence of such forces indicates that the development of relations between the East and the West will probably not be free of recriminations. As far as the approach of the majority of the socialist countries is concerned, however, the development of relations between East and West derives from its own logic and necessity, and from the knowledge that the fate of mankind largely depends upon it.

II

In addition to the analysis offered here of the origin and character of the relations between East and West, it is necessary to note other more concrete tendencies and interests within the socialist world, particularly the need for economic development, that are encouraging the current orientation. New circumstances in the evolution of international relations, noted above, have made it possible for the internal economic policies of the U.S.S.R. and the other socialist countries to be re-oriented toward peaceful economic cooperation. For example, the basic direction of the Soviet Union's five-year plan for 1966-1970–compared with the preceding five-year plans–is to emphasize the development of science and technology in its application to production. Considerable effort is also being made to bring the production of capital goods and consumer goods substantially closer together, as well as to bring closer together the lagging agricultural production and industry. Even if the preferential production of capital goods remains intact, the proportions of capital goods to consumer goods production in the national economies of the U.S.S.R. and some socialist states have begun to change gradually. This factor is of extraordinary significance in light of the economic needs of the Eastern countries, and, even more important, in light of their foreign policies.

The requirements of economic development compel a number of socialist countries to seek and to exploit all possibilities of mutually favorable and equitable economic cooperation that exist in the sphere of East-West relations; this is essential because the existing system of economic relations within the socialist bloc is of itself unable to create a satisfactory economic stimulant for the effective development of some socialist countries. At this moment only the more developed states of the economic commonwealth of the socialist countries understand the need for a more complete international specialization and cooperation in production. Participation in the development of more sophisticated forms of economic cooperation and in an international economic association has become a matter of vital importance for these states, and the expansion of relationships within a framework of the European and worldwide economy has become part of their economic policy. Thus many socialist countries have shown a more realistic attitude toward Western European integration and a sympathetic understanding of efforts to find a common solution to some problems of an all-European nature.

It is not, therefore, surprising that Czechoslovakia, one of the more economically developed countries of Eastern Europe, is especially interested in the activities of the European regional organization of the United Nations, the Economic Commission for Europe. Czechoslovakia's interest in European organization was expressed, for instance, in "The Memorandum Toward the Development of an All-European Economic Cooperation." In this Memorandum, submitted by Czechoslovakia at the Twentieth Plenary Session of the Commission, it was stated that:

> . . . a full exploitation of the powerful development of science and technology that characterizes the contemporary phase of development requires an integrated effort of large human collectives which can be achieved within the framework of the contemporary world relationships by way of cooperation among nations.

Czechoslovakia is interested in studying and solving some of the problems of an all-European nature, such as energetics, regulation of raw materials and resources, transportation, interconnections of waterways, and similar projects.

Other socialist states have also indicated interest in developing patterns of economic cooperation with West European countries, even if, understandably enough, their potential for participation in economic cooperation and international division of labor is presently restricted. At the same time, the improvement of the systems of planning and direction of the national economies of the individual socialist countries creates–and will create in an ever-increasing measure–economic conditions for cooperation between the countries of East and West.

The fact that stimulants for the further development of European cooperation have appeared in the countries of Western Europe is also a necessary condition for this East-West cooperation. As recently as 1964-1965, a number of West European countries, including France, Great Britain, Sweden, Denmark, and Italy, reduced restrictive measures against the import of some products from East European markets. The mixed Soviet-French commission in 1966 led to the establishment of similar commissions between other East European countries and France; it is the goal of these commissions to prepare concrete measures leading to East-West cooperation in the traditional as well as new sectors of economic development.

III

Another important factor in East-West détente is the process of differentiation among the socialist countries. This is the result of the constantly more marked influence of specific objective conditions within the individual countries, as well as within the Communist and workers' parties, and is equally deeply rooted in the subjective conditions and needs of the socialist world. The concept of the relatively recent past that extolled the monolithic unity of the socialist states is being replaced by a concept of unity based upon a *recognition of the differences* in their policies. There is no doubt that this process, also taking place in the West, although on a somewhat different basis and in a somewhat different form, has created entirely new possibilities for the development of contacts between the East and the West. We are witnessing a process that is creating socialist nations independent of one another in the full sense of the term, that is, pursuing internal and external policies that correspond to their own specific national interests. This does not necessarily mean, however, that the policies of individual countries of the East are neglecting the common interests of socialism. But this process has opened new possibilities, particularly for the development of bilateral relations between countries of the East and the West; it has created conditions for concluding a number of rather definite agreements, particularly about economic and cultural cooperation, and there are numerous and well-known examples to prove this.

If we truly desire peaceful cooperation between the countries of the East and West, we should view this process of differentiation in the socialist world *exclusively* in the light of its possibilities for détente. It is difficult to see wisdom in the fact that some governments and certain political forces in the Western world approach this process primarily with intentions of exploiting it, of deepening the conflicts among socialist countries by exploiting to the maximum the difficulties which some socialist countries are experiencing, and above all else, of weakening socialism as an entity. The development of economic, cultural, and political contacts between the East and West is being subordinated by some Western interests to a concept of "selective coexistence," which attempts an all-out development of contacts with certain socialist countries and the isolation of others. The period when the East and the West saw each other as enemies is not so distant that it is impossible to partly understand such thinking, related as it is to the political concepts of the past. This approach has subordinated the development of economic and cultural contacts to the political concepts that are related, though different in form, to the political ideas of the West current in the early 1950's. Such an approach cannot but create mistrust in the East about the basic goals of the "policy of building bridges." Such an approach would be only the continuation of the policy of the past to present times when the real problems of the East and West are of an entirely different nature.

IV

There is no need to reiterate the reasons why the socialist countries of Europe have endeavored since World War II to create an atmosphere of peaceful cooperation and mutual security on the European continent. The effort to achieve peace, pursued on a continent that has been divided for a long time by Cold War and suffering from continuous tension, is entirely legitimate and is finding an ever-increasing response. For West European governments, particularly for the French, the current threatening situation in Vietnam has not prevented further development of peaceful cooperation and détente in Europe. If American intervention in Vietnam limits the possibilities of cooperation between the socialist countries and the United States, this does not affect socialist contacts with the countries of Western Europe. Europe, which until only recently provoked feelings of fear and uncertainty, may now play a positive role in easing the conflicts of the contemporary world. This new climate of an all-European rapprochement is taking place, as far as the West is concerned, largely because of the influence of President de Gaulle's concept of Western European emancipation from American leadership. This reorientation of the previous political alignment is one of the elements that, combined with the long-range effort of the socialist countries to improve the political atmosphere of Europe, has created a new situation today—a situation which invites study of the possibility of creating an all-European system of cooperation and security. The development of bilateral relations between the countries of Eastern and Western Europe, particularly in the economic and cultural fields, has become a reality. Despite certain political problems, there is still considerable room for further development of these contacts. One can therefore expect more progress in the bilateral relations between East and West, a development which cannot remain without influence upon the general political atmosphere inside, as well as outside, the continent of Europe.

Solution of the complex political problems in Europe must stem from the acceptance of certain realities: 1) the question of boundaries that was created after the Second World War and that must be considered unchangeable; 2) the existence of two Germanies in Europe, a fact that must be recognized, as disagreeable as it is for certain circles. A majority of the Western countries have already expressed, more or less clearly, their positions on the question of European boundaries, so the question of recognizing the existence of two German states remains the greatest bone of contention. It is certainly possible to refuse to recognize for various reasons the existence of the German Democratic Republic; it is possible to have many varied views on the circumstances of its origins, for example. However, this does not mean that this state does not exist. The German Federal Republic and the German Democratic Republic (DDR) are realities of contemporary Europe. The reality of the DDR may be ignored in theory but it cannot be ignored in any effort to solve fundamental political problems in contemporary Europe. A belief that the unification of Germany is a pre-condition to an agreement on the broader questions of European political cooperation is just as unrealistic as the belief of certain circles that other socialist countries of Europe may abandon, under certain circumstances and for certain concessions, their interests in the existence of the DDR. These views misinterpret the changes taking place within the socialist world. A number of Western politicians and scholars continue to look at the DDR as though it were still 1953, and, under the influence of West Germany's reasoning, they have failed to comprehend the material changes which have occurred in the DDR during the past decade.

The socialist countries are endeavoring to normalize and extend relations with both German states. The East is following with extraordinary attention the *ostpolitik* of the Grand Coalition of the Federal Republic. Czechoslovakia, for example, is highly interested in the normalization of relations with the German Federal Republic. But in this current period, Czechoslovakia can undertake this step only on the assumption that the government of the German Federal Republic will disavow all revisionist claims against Czechoslovakia, and that it will show a basic willingness to accept the principles of peaceful coexistence with all European countries, regardless of their social systems. In the past few years, there has been a rapid and far-reaching development of trade relations and cultural exchange between Prague and Bonn. This development is unquestionable creating conditions capable of overcoming certain mistrusts—mistrusts that, given a recollection of Czechoslovakia's relations with West Germany, are not always entirely unfounded—and, in the long run, it is helping to solve questions of a political nature.

When we talk about Europe, we must keep in mind the full meaning of the term, *Europa*. We must think of the whole continent, of the more than half a billion people who live there, of their problems in life, of their economic and cultural development, and of their freedom and security. We must keep in mind the manifold nature of their styles of life and of their economic, social, and political systems as they have been created in a rich history, during which these peoples have frequently stood on the forefront of human progress. It is therefore necessary to develop the relations among the nations of Europe in such a way that they may grow in peace, independence, and freedom, as well as in harmony and cooperation with hundreds of millions of people in other parts of the world. Thus they may develop their great talents, capabilities, and the wealth of their culture forged in centuries of effort, for the benefit of all mankind.

The Future of East-West Trade

Vladimir Velebit

At the time of this printing, Vladimir Velebit is the Executive Secretary of the U.N. Economic Commission for Europe. He has been Yugoslav Under-Secretary of State for Foreign Affairs and Ambassador to Italy and the United Kingdom. In this article, he surveys some of the forms of cooperative arrangements in East-West trade, and emphasizes those recommended for the ECE Expert Group. He appears convinced that the contemporary economic reforms, inaugurated by some East European countries, make an expansion of East-West trade relations possible. However, the author also believes that no "explosive" growth of this trade is likely because, through their Council for Mutual Economic Assistance (COMECON) the Soviet bloc nations have succeeded in establishing a self-contained "second world market."

Political and economic relations are mutually dependent but not parallel variables, neither rising nor falling with equal intensity. As functions, they are *correlated* rather than *coordinated*, influenced by a number of separate and independent determinants that cause relative differences in their levels.

It is useful to analyze postwar relations between Western and Eastern European countries from this perspective. East-West *economic* relations have markedly intensified in the last twenty years and are in terms of trade many times the volume recorded two decades ago. But this has not meant that *political* relations have improved to the same extent, although it suggests that there has been *some* favorable change.

The extraordinarily low level of economic relations between the two groups of European countries in the early 'fifties was not solely the result of the Cold War, although the importance of this factor cannot be contested. One must also consider the substantial transformation that occurred after the war in the international trading system. Before the war, there was one world commercial circuit, embracing all countries except the Soviet Union, which as an outsider accounted for only about one percent of world trade. After the war, the political links between the Eastern European countries and the Soviet Union gave rise to a new commercial circuit. This "second world market," comprising the Soviet Union and the countries that established in 1949 the Council for Mutual Economic Assistance, developed according to its own internal logic. Based on trade needs generated by the development programs of the participating countries, it became a new element of great importance in world trade. Although it caused a significant reorientation of the prewar trade flows of the newly established People's Democracies, it brought considerable benefits to them.

This reorientation had two immediate and clearly discernible effects. First, it brought the Soviet Union into a system aiming at an international division of labor, thereby ending the period of economic isolation dating from the October Revolution. Soviet foreign trade rose sharply above the level reached before the war, and the first signs of a tendency to depart from the principle of full economic self-sufficiency appeared. Second, it changed the geographical pattern of the trade of the Eastern European countries from participation in the old commercial circuit through their established trade links with Western Europe to participation in the new circuit set up in association with the Soviet Union. The countries in the Council for Mutual Economic Assistance succeeded, through intensification of mutual trade, in raising their share of total world trade to approximately twelve percent, considerably above prewar levels. Primarily for extra-economic reasons, the COMECON group created a specific market having only subsidiary or supplementary trade relations with the rest of the world, and consequently formed its own trade circuit, the socialist market. The political reasons underlying the appearance of a "second world market," coupled with the particular institutional factors deriving from the similarity of the economic structures of the countries involved, engendered new trade habits and practices which in turn created strong economic links and imperatives tending to widen gradually the existing cleavage between the two markets.

This observation provides a point of departure for examining the often heard and frequently repeated statement that East-West trade is inadequately developed, and that the volume of this trade is lagging behind its real possibilities. Those who criticize the existing level of East-West trade in such terms base their argument on the volume of trade between Western countries having an economic structure, degree of industrialization, and per capita national income comparable to that of the Eastern European countries. They point to the fact that the average level of trade between such Western countries is far superior to that between them and the group of Eastern European countries, and reach the conclusion that East-West trade is too small compared with the standards they

Reprinted with permission from the *Journal of International Affairs,* Vol. 22, No. 1 (1968).

have set. By similar reasoning, a very interesting and instructive paper prepared by the UNCTAD Secretariat for the fifth session of the Trade and Development Board draws the conclusion that East-West trade is "far below its potential."

This conclusion, however, tends to disregard the all-important changes of a political and economic nature which took place in Eastern Europe after the Second World War. The potential volume of East-West trade cannot and should not be assessed without first understanding that a second circuit in world trade was set up which absorbed, from its beginning, the major part of the foreign trade of its participants. The relatively small part of their trade which was not immediately drawn into the newly established circuit was in many cases of marginal interest to countries outside the group and thus constituted a rather meager starting-point for revived trade in the postwar period. Due consideration must be given to the fact that on the average sixty or seventy percent of the trade of eastern European countries was earmarked for their own closed circuit, and that an elaborate net of long-term trade agreements and arrangements for industrial cooperation or for supply of essential raw materials established a closely connected self-sufficient trade pattern. An abrupt change was neither possible nor desirable.

For these reasons endeavors to assess the "potential" of East-West trade by generalized and rather static determinants, such as the size of the economies concerned, their level of industrial production, or their shares in world production and trade, prove misleading. East-West trade must be seen as a dynamic process and studied in its progressive development over the past twenty years. Such an approach is firmly based on measurable values and provides a means of explaining the development of East-West trade in a rational manner.

Trade between planned economy countries and countries with market economies commenced on a very low level, but despite a generally adverse political climate and far-reaching differences in the economic systems of the countries concerned, it recorded a larger rate of increase over the twenty-year period than world trade in general. The high rate of increase in East-West trade over the twenty-year period was only slightly lower than the rate achieved by the countries of the European Economic Community in their trade among themselves. In addition, the growth of East-West trade was relatively stable, registering only mild fluctuations never greater enough to impair the general upward trend of growth. According to the "Economic Survey of Europe for 1966," published by the United Nations Economic Commission for Europe, the share of East-West trade in total Western European trade increased in 1966, following a long-term trend of a modest but steady rise, from 4.2 percent the previous year to 4.3 percent. Correspondingly, the share of this trade in total Eastern European trade increased from 18 percent in 1965 to 18.9 percent in 1966.

There is no doubt that the share of East-West trade in total Western European trade is not very significant, but the fact that this share is growing slowly but steadily despite rather unfavorable circumstances demonstrates that there is further scope for an enlarged exchange of merchandise between Eastern and Western European countries. The countries involved in this trade would do well to further its development, not only because a larger volume of trade might serve to overcome, or at least soften, some of the existing political tensions, but also because increased trade, as the recent past has shown, serves the economic interests of both sides. Obviously there is no method of determining a "normal" or "satisfactory" volume of East-West trade, but the countries concerned would be well advised to work toward conditions which would favor trade.

What are the prospects of such a policy, one might ask, and are some measures in that direction already under way, or at least being studied or envisaged? The United Nations Economic Commission for Europe (ECE) is the only international organization in which Eastern European countries meet regularly with their Western European trade partners on a multilateral platform. The ECE offers a means of improving the basic trading conditions prevailing among the member countries, supplementing agreements concluded on a bilateral basis. In 1946, after considerable difficulties and some delay, the ECE countries set up a Committee for the Development of Trade. Besides keeping under close examination the current development and prospects for intra-European and specifically East-West trade, the Committee searches for new trade possibilities and facilities to improve trade, and provides a forum for the confrontation of commercial policies. In this latter field, repeated attempts have been made to discover ways to remove obstacles to trade and harmonize trade relations. At the ninth session of the Commission, in March, 1954, a resolution was adopted which called on ECE countries to study, among other questions, the possibility of removing obstacles to foreign trade of an economic, administrative, and trade-policy character. Seven years later, at the sixteenth session, the Commission noted that the possibilities of expanding trade among ECE member countries were hampered by obstacles, and suggested that the Committee on the Development of Trade give particular attention in its work to the preparation of recommendations which would help remove these obstacles. It was obvious that ECE governments were reluctant to tackle these difficult policy questions in a multilateral body, for in their bilateral negotiations substantial progress was being made in expanding their trade.

It was only in 1963 that the Commission set up an ad hoc Group of Seven governmental experts with instructions to examine: 1) the role of customs tariffs in the trade of member countries with different economic systems, and the bearing of pricing and taxation policies on external trade; 2) the most favored nation principle and nondiscriminatory treatment, as applied under different economic systems; and 3) the possibility of establishing multilateral trade and payments.

It is unfortunate that neither the Trade Committee nor the plenary session of the Commission have been able to formulate recommendations, based on the work of the Group of Seven, which would serve as guidelines for the settlement of these trade policy questions. Nevertheless, it would be defeatist to consider the effort of the Group of Seven an utter failure and a waste of time. On the contrary, this Group accomplished a great deal, if only by defining more precisely certain problems and, more particularly, by elaborating a new concept of effective reciprocity which could be used to overcome the thorny problem of application of the most-favored-nation clause between countries having different social and economic structures.

A renewed attempt to draw up policy recommendations acceptable to ECE governments was made in September, 1967, by an Expert Group consisting of representatives of all ECE countries, but it was not successful. It is difficult to resolve issues of principle in multilateral negotiations when governments feel that they risk losing some of the bargaining points they may need in bilateral negotiations. But it should be borne in mind that most of the countries concerned are preoccupied by the problem of a multilateral code of conduct for East-West trade, and that they have all pledged themselves to work toward a removal of the obstacles hindering such trade. As in many similar cases, the practical needs encountered in carrying out trade, together with a certain passage of time, may help bring this problem to a state of maturity where a solution can be found.

Important among the factors which will certainly have a beneficial influence on East-West trade in the not too distant future are the economic reforms presently being undertaken in Eastern Europe. Certain aspects of these reforms constitute an important contribution toward facilitating trade with the rest of the world. The basic ideas and principles on which these reforms are based might be summarized as follows:

1. Improvement of planning techniques through the introduction of modern mathematical methods, together with a greater accent on medium and long-term planning.

2. Changes in and reduction of the number of centrally planned indicators which are mandatory for enterprises, together with greater emphasis on gross income (i.e. net value added), profit, and rate of profitability, as criteria for evaluating the success of the enterprise.

3. Expansion of decentralized investment funds available to enterprises and larger economic units, a greater use of bank credits, and the extension of credits by increasing application of normal banking criteria.

4. Introduction of a capital charge on the fixed and working assets of the enterprise.

5. Strengthening of economic incentives (often amounting to important changes in the wage system) by establishing closer ties between the remuneration of employees and the enterprise's performance.

6. Promotion of direct contracts between economic units which, in contrast with the old system, are no longer envisaged as simple instruments for implementing centrally planned decisions, but rather as the means of guiding the plan itself.

7. Price reforms, including changes in price relations as well as in the price-fixing mechanism.

8. Concentration of industrial enterprises into larger units (sometimes comprising a whole branch of industry), with administrative responsibility but also operating as relatively independent business organizations.

Most of the measures included in these reforms have a direct or indirect influence on the foreign trade of these countries with Western countries of differing economic systems. The reforms will most certainly lend greater flexibility to the foreign trade mechanism, for producing enterprises will be allowed to participate directly in foreign trade operations, by-passing the hitherto omnipresent foreign trade enterprises. This may help end an often repeated complaint, heard from trade experts in Western countries, that direct contacts between producer and end-user are hampered by the obligatory interposition of specialized trade organizations. Producing enterprises in socialist countries will, moreover, retain a part of their foreign exchange earnings which they may freely dispose of either in buying machinery and equipment or in covering part of their commercial expenses for establishing adequate services, advertising of business travel. In turn, the desire to utilize freely available funds may act as a powerful incentive to increase the volume of exports.

Furthermore, the price reforms envisaged should gradually eliminate the need for governmental subsidies. These have been distributed with a great deal of bureaucratic formality, discouraging beneficiaries from utilizing them more often than absolutely necessary to fulfill the prescribed export plan. Also, it might not be too bold to assume that the disappearance of the differences between foreign and domestic prices will pave the way for the establishment of uniform and economically sound foreign exchange rates and a subsequent convertibility with all its inherent benefits for the multilateral organization of trade and payments.

It should not be foregotten that, since the war, the Eastern European countries have achieved a considerable change in their economic structures. From countries which, with a few exceptions, derived the greater part of their national income from agriculture and forestry, they have transformed themselves into full-fledged industrial countries. Consequently their trade pattern must adjust itself to this new industrial orientation. But, perversely, the pattern of exports to the developed Western market economies has remained concentrated on nonindustrial goods. At present, just as twenty years ago, the Eastern European countries export raw materials and agricultural produce to the West and import machinery and other manufactured goods from the West. Such a state of affairs is not only unnatural under present conditions, but leaves a very limited scope for the increase of the volume of trade, since trade in raw materials and agricultural produce is notoriously sluggish and does not lead toward dynamic trade expansion. On the other hand, as the imports of the socialist countries from the West are determined and limited by the possibility of earning convertible currency, the outlook for the future would not seem to be very bright unless Eastern exports of manufactures can increase. It appears therefore to be the primary task of the Eastern European governments to put into motion, without further delay, measures designed to change their present pattern of exports. Needless to say, such a change would be conducive to a larger and more dynamic flow of East-West trade and would therefore be in the interest of all those who participate in that trade. The Western European countries have an equal stake in the change of the Eastern export structure and would be well advised to encourage any action taken in that direction.

In this connection, it is important to note that the recent experiments in industrial cooperation between Western and Eastern countries may illustrate one of the desirable ways to contribute to this end.

Only a modest number of industrial cooperative agreements has been concluded in the past three or four years, but a larger number is likely to follow if present trends continue. These agreements are, in fact, of a far greater importance than the actual amount of business involved would indicate. As each individual case is separately negotiated, the agreements reached reflect the specific interest of the partners, as well as the skill and toughness of their negotiators. Although the agreements are different in form and substance, certain common features may permit the identification of several kinds of arrangements. The ECE's "Economic Survey for Europe in 1966" distinguishes four broad types of East-West industrial cooperation. These four types do not exhaust all of the existing individual cases, as some would hardly fit any of the groups.

The *first* type is a long-term delivery contract. The Eastern partner undertakes to produce and deliver to his partner in the West an agreed quantity of semi-manufactured goods. The buyer provides the technical documentation and know-how for production of the goods. The product is custom-made to fit the exact specifications of the purchaser. For example, the ECE Survey cites an agreement according to which a Polish enterprise furnishes, for an agreed period of five years, castings and other semi-manufactures to a company in the United Kingdom. A number of Yugoslav and Bulgarian firms have similar agreements, particularly with partners in Italy and Austria. The Eastern firm acts as a subcontractor of a Western assembly plant that produces the final product under its own name and responsibility and organizes the distribution of the end product. No relationship is established between the subcontractor and the purchaser of the final product, so that this type of arrangement is the most rudimentary form of industrial cooperation.

The *second* form resembles a cartel agreement. Here the contracting parties agree on product specialization to cover the needs of markets they have previously serviced. Today, when economies of scale play such an important role in lowering productiion costs, small and even medium-size producers are at a marked disadvantage if they seek to satisfy the entire range of needs of markets they are eager to keep for themselves, for this involves a great number of different specifications. Constant retooling requires frequent interruptions in the production process and impairs the full utilization of installed capacity. In such cases, in order to allow the production of larger series, industrial cooperation makes possible a production plan in which each partner specializes in only one part of the specifications required and satisfies its market demands by exchanging a part of its production. Such arrangements are found between steel rolling mills in Austria and mills in Hungary and Czechoslovakia. Chemical and pharmaceutical industries in Hungary and Austria have recently begun similar practices.

The *third* type of industrial cooperation arrangement provides for the production of components for a product by both partners, who exchange the components needed so that each of them can assemble the final product independently. The final product may be the result of research and experience of both partners, in which case they exchange documentation and know-how for the manufacture of the components. On the other hand, one experienced partner may furnish the whole documentation and know-how, which he confides to the other for the production of a certain number of components. Both partners may utilize different sub-contractors for the assembly of the end product.

While the final product in such an arrangement may be primarily destined for the partners' respective home markets, foreign trade transactions are frequent. In some cases the export part of the arrangement is subject to a special agreement of the partners. The final product is sold under the trademark and sole responsibility of each partner. The arrangements between the Yugoslav car factory, Zastava, in Kragujevac, and Fiat in Turin enter into this category, as well as those between Citröen in France and the Yugoslav firm, Tomos, in Kopar. An agreement between Polish organizations and the British Steelfounders and Engineers is another example. In this deal, concluded for a period of seven years, the joint production of cranes on the basis of British know-how is envisaged.

The provisions of the recently concluded agreement between a Polish car manufacturing concern and the Fiat works are not yet known, and it is impossible to say whether that arrangement will have the characteristic features of this category. On the other hand, the well publicized Soviet agreement with Fiat does not seem to be of this type, for the U.S.S.R. acquired the documentation and technology for the production of the Fiat prototype 124, but is not furnishing component parts of that car to its Italian partner.

The *fourth* category comprises cooperation for exports to third markets. The underlying reasons for the conclusion of such arrangements are sometimes economic advantages and, in other cases, political expediency. This type of arrangement is closely related to the previous one, the main difference being that the efforts of the participants are focused on the expansion of exports, while in the former cateogry their principal interest is the domestic market. The existing political alignments of nations on bilateral trade patterns established through clearing sometimes makes it difficult for an enterprise to enter the markets of a particular country. It is therefore most convenient to conclude an arrangement with an enterprise in a country which enjoys facilities in the coveted market. Such examples are becoming more frequent, particularly with respect to countries of the developing world.

Current trends indicate that the diversity of trade arrangements will continue to grow. In some recent arrangements the desire of the Eastern countries to acquire specialized technological information to produce equipment and consumer goods for the home market seems to be the main characteristic; in others, the cooperation is intended to diversify and thus increase the production pattern. The latter is obviously the more important for international trade, as it implies improving the export structure of the socialist countries in their trade with the West.

The total impact of all these agreements on East-West trade is still very modest. It is nevertheless interesting to note the continuously growing feeling on both sides, particularly in business circles, that the two different forms of economic systems can profitably cooperate. New forms of cooperation which increase the mutual interdependence of the two systems are constantly being devised. Last April at the session of the Economic Commission for Europe, which is to some extent a barometer of East-West relations, the participating countries encouraged the search for new methods for exchanging scientific and technological information and for furthering cooperation.

Yet there is no gound for expecting that even in the most favorable political circumstances East-West trade will accelerate "explosively." It is impossible to overcome rapidly the rift brought about by the experiences and changes, both political and economic, of the past twenty years. Nevertheless governments are increasingly aware that more liberal trade policies do not conceal hidden dangers but, on the contrary, bring both political and economic gains. There will, of course, be opposition from those who wish to protect themselves from competition and from those who fear increased contacts or the growth of joint interests. But the realization is likely to grow on both sides that a more harmonious cooperation can only produce mutual advantage.

Eastern Europe and The West

I. Orlik

It should not be without benefit for Americans to read a Soviet assessment of United States changing and changeable policy toward the East European countries. Orlik points to Western attempts to normalize relations with the socialist nations, in part because of the failure of the old "liberation policy," in part because of Western realization that trade, diplomacy and cultural exchange represent a more constructive approach in dealing with the East European area which, in the author's opinion, is irrevocably committed to socialism.

New trends are increasingly evident today in the attitudes of the Western Powers towards the Socialist community. They result from the further consolidation of world Socialism and the recognition of the Socialist countries' power by many realistically-minded politicians in the West. Also, they are additional proof of the crisis now hitting imperialist foreign policy.

In the last few years, the imperialist concept of foreign policy has been somewhat modified; this is attested to by their attempt to find a "differentiated" approach to the Socialist countries and by the search for a new policy and fresh tactics in relation to the Socialist world as a whole and the East European Socialist states in particular.

"Renovation" of Strategy

"There has been no more frustrating field for American diplomacy in the past two decades than Eastern Europe." This conclusion by John Campbell also applies to the diplomacy of the other imperialist states, for prior to the 1960s they pursued roughly the same policy towards Eastern Europe. Based on the hapless "liberation" doctrine, U.S. foreign policy towards the Socialist countries has reached an "apparent dead end," to quote American journalist Sulzberger.

Indeed, attempts to isolate the East European countries, severance of economic ties with them, the system of "strategic control" established at the turn of the 1950s, ideological sabotage, military provacations and threats to use "NATO and its common defence force" "for the recovery of national identity in Eastern Europe" have not prevented Socialism from growing and gaining in strength.

Towards the end of the 1950s, the economic basis of Socialism was laid in the East European states, and their peoples moved to the next stage of building a new society—the struggle for the complete construction of Socialism. The political and military might of these countries and their role in world affairs have grown immensely, thereby compelling many imperialist strategists to overhaul their concept of relations with the Socialist states. "The 'liberation' policy of the 1950s," James Fulbright, Chairman of the Senate Foreign Relations Committee, notes, "failed because it purported, in its ill-defined way, to roll back the iron curtain by forcible means of one sort or another. It therefore came up against the realities of the nuclear age."

This assessment of the cause for failure of the "liberation" policy is of course far from complete, for it ignores such an important factor as the triumph of Socialist relations in Eastern Europe. Nonetheless, even such an appraisal is very indicative: it admits that the imperialist foreign policy plans cannot be accomplished by military means and stresses the need for a change in Western policies towards the Socialist countries.

But the extreme Right-wing elements among the imperialist politicians fail to reckon with the lessons of recent history. Reproaching them with this attitude, George Kennan, well-known American diplomat, writes that "these failures of understanding represented less an inability to absorb and learn the lessons of this decade than to remember those of earlier ones." A realistic reappraisal of policy compels George Kennan to arrive at the conclusion that "the West has no choice but to accept the quest for peaceful co-existence as the basis for policy toward the countries of the Communist world."

In the general anti-Socialist policy of the imperialist Powers one can discern four "regional trends" reflecting the specific features of the West's policies towards individual Socialist countries. In his statement before the Senate Foreign Relations Committee, Secretary of State Dean Rusk said that U.S. foreign policy should be adjusted "to the differing behaviour of different Communist states" in four regions: the U.S.S.R., Eastern Europe, the Far East and Cuba.

To a lesser or greater extent the other imperialist Powers adhere to a similar "division." Leaving aside the characteristics of each of these "regional trends" in imperialist policy, it should be noted that the Western Powers have particularly livened up their policies in relation to the East European Socialist states. Relations with Eastern Europe has become a very acute problem for the West not only as far as its relations with the Communist world are concerned, but also as a factor exacerbating contradictions in the capitalist world.

Two tendencies are patently evident in the Western Powers' attitudes to Eastern Europe: one is opposed to normal relations or any ties whatsoever; the other favours them.

The first tendency is not new and its aim is quite clear: to take the most extreme measures up to and including an "anti-Communist crusade" and war. What are the strategic aims of the proponents of the second trend? What are its prospects?

The answer may primarily be found in U.S. policy. The general notion of American East European policy, modified after the "liberation" doctrine, was formulated in Foreign Affairs, July 1961, and termed as a policy of "peaceful engagement" with Eastern Europe.

In his address at the dedication of the George C. Marshall Research Library in Lexington (Virginia) on May 23, 1964, President Johnson put forward a somewhat modified formula for U.S. policy with regard to the East European Socialist countries. He proposed "to build bridges across the gulf which has divided us from Eastern Europe. They will be bridges of increased trade, of ideas, of visitors and of humanitarian aid." He announced this policy of "bridges" as a common policy for all the Western Powers: "... Identity of interest and the prospects of progress for Eastern Europe lie in a wider relationship with the West."

"Bridge" policy is in fact a more concrete version of "peaceful engagement." Its first item—expansion of trading ties with the Socialist countries—is not new either.

As far back as the 1960 election campaign John Kennedy suggested that limitations on trade with the East European states be reduced. One of the first steps he made as President was to deliver an official statement in Congress that U.S. trade policy in relation to the Socialist countries had to be reconsidered.

For over four years this question has been under review in various Senate committees. A struggle is going on over the normalisation of economic relations with the Socialist countries. It has found its way into the American press: "Time for a new look;" the old policy "plainly isn't working." In 1964, Congress began to discuss the problem of "liberalising" U.S. policy in relation to the Socialist countries. During this discussion, which still continues, the problem of extending economic ties is also being dealt with.

In his first message to Congress, on January 4, 1965, President Johnson, while describing the prospects for U.S. East European policy, declared that the Administration "is exploring ways to increase peaceful trade with these countries and the Soviet Union."

Meanwhile, the West European states have already started normalising relations with the Socialist countries. Britain, France, West Germany and Italy are displaying a great deal of activity in this direction. Latest events, particularly the conclusion of numerous East-West economic agreements in the last couple of years, show that the course steered towards the lifting of trade limitations is gaining the upper hand.

In the last two years, trading ties between Western and Eastern Europe have considerably expanded.

Britain has concluded trade agreements with Rumania, Czechoslovakia and Bulgaria and other Socialist countries. Transactions are being signed to cover 10, 12 and even 15 years.

France has cut the list of "strategic" goods for her trade with Eastern Europe. The time limits for, and the amounts of, credits to Socialist countries have been substantially increased. In 1964, long-term trade agreements were signed: with Rumania—for five years, and with Yugoslavia—for six years. In the same year, trade between France and the German Democratic Republic amounted to 62 million francs; in 1965, it will reach 110 million.

Trade between West Germany and Eastern Europe has also considerably expanded. Under the three-year agreement (1963-1965) with Poland now in force, mutual deliveries of goods are increasing. West Germany and Poland have opened trade missions in the respective capitals; and West Germany now has trade missions also in Budapest, Bucharest and Sofia.

Although West German statesmen insist that trade with the Socialist world does not conflict with the Hallstein Doctrine, more and more people in West Germany are coming to the conclusion that "new relations are breaking through the barrier Bonn had set up by its declaration that the Hallstein Doctrine was applicable to West Germany's Eastern policy."

What is new about East-West relations is the exchange of visits between statesmen. Commenting on the Socialist desire to normalise relations with France, Le Monde emphasised the great importance of the visits to Paris by the Foreign Ministers of Bulgaria, Hungary, Rumania and Czechoslovakia. "France is continuing to step up her activity in the direction of Eastern Europe," the newspaper wrote on January 14, 1965.

In the United States, too, voices are being heard more often in favour of better relations with Eastern Europe. There have been many protests against the 1959 Act under which "Captive Nations Week" is marked every year. This annual hate-campaign against the Socialist countries, like the raising of the "Hungarian question" in the United Nations (only last year the United States dropped it at long last), puts American statesmen in an absurd position. The marking of these weeks, the *Washington Post* wrote on July 11, 1964, "is only an annual advertisement of our impotence."

Increasingly sharp criticisms may be heard in the United States over the strict censorship of mail from the Socialist countries. Last November the U.S. Federal Court made unconstitutional the 1962 Act which introduced this censorship.

All these facts, insignificant as they may seem individually, testify to certain changes in U.S. public opinion, and to a tendency towards normalising relations with Eastern Europe.

What lies behind this "liberal" trend in Western policies?

First, the recognition of the strength and stability of Socialism as a social system.

"We must acknowledge, however regretfully," Senator Fulbright has said, "that it is not open to us to remove the threat of Communism from the world." Further: ". . . We must pursue a policy of building bridges of accommodation with the Communist world, not because this approach is inherently more desirable than one of total victory for American interests but because there is no acceptable alternative in the nuclear age."

Second, internal difficulties are compelling imperialist politicians to reconsider certain aspects of their foreign policies. In the opinion of the *U.S. News & World Report*, the slowing down of the boom in Western Europe (particularly in France and Italy) makes the need for trade with the Socialist countries more imperative. This problem for West Germany is no less acute. "Many German businessmen feel that East-West trade is a form of insurance against overproduction and lagging sales in times of recession at home." Similar difficulties are also being greatly felt in Britain. Continuous unemployment and her decreasing share in world exports force Britain to look for ways to stop her rapid decline as a world Power.

The West European desire to expand economic ties with Eastern Europe, however, has for a long time been counteracted by the United States. In the autumn of 1963, when tendencies to extend East-West economic ties began to show, the "strategic control" system was in danger of being eroded. U.S. ruling circles, worried by the fact that their West European allies were taking more radical steps than they had expected, hastened to take several containing measures. U.S. Under-Secretary of State Bowles visited London and Paris to persuade the allies against any substantial expansion of trade with Eastern Europe.

The Bowles mission in fact failed because of economic competition which can no longer be halted by manipulating political levers. Western Europe is in this sense escaping U.S. control. Two or three years ago the imperialist Powers largely pursued similar policies towards the East European Socialist countries, whereas today U.S. policy clearly differs from that of Western Europe. The United States is not as influential as it was before. Moreover, the U.S. attitude towards Eastern Europe is increasingly dependent on the degree of liberalisation of Western Europe's policy regarding her Eastern neighbours.

Situations arise in which the United States has to "plead guilty." For instance, last January some American firms entered into negotiations with the German Democratic Republic with a view to selling a synthetic fibre plant. The U.S. Department of Commerce had licenced the export of the plant without consultations with the West German Government. As soon as the news reached Bonn, the American Chargé d'Affaires was summoned urgently to explain the matter to the West German Foreign Ministry, while the West German Ambassador to Washington asked the State Department for explanations.

Although the policies of the West European countries towards Eastern Europe are similar in class content, they differ in their external manifestations. They are affected by numerous contradictions, particularly by competition in foreign markets.

Aims Remain the Same

In their desire to normalise relations with their Western neighbours, the Socialist countries clearly realise that the new aspects of Western policies in no way mean that imperialism has changed its spots. The strategic aims of the imperialist remain the same. Alongside the "new" means of achieving their aims they are also using the old ones.

Here is what the New York Herald Tribune wrote about the aforementioned address by President Johnson: "President Johnson's proposal to build bridges between East and West would resume the work initiated by Gen. George C. Marshall. . . ." As for the aim of the policy of "building bridges" the newspaper added: "If the time has now become propitious to pursue this purpose, it is because the West has learned it cannot achieve the liberation [?!] of Eastern Europe by force of arms."

This policy was described in greater detail by Senator Fulbright in a speech in Dallas on December 8, 1964. Supporting the idea of "liberating" Eastern Europe, he nonetheless suggested that this aim should be attained gradually by means of trade, diplomacy and culture. "The skillful use of trade and diplomacy and educational and cultural exchange can do far more to bring about the liberation of Eastern Europe than all the brave and hollow words that used to be uttered about 'rolling back' the iron curtain."

It would be wrong to think the imperialist Powers have dropped the military means from their policy towards the Socialist countries.

George Kennan, who is considered in the West to be an expert on Eastern Europe, has written that the Western Powers "have exhibited no very convincing evidence of any disposition to place effective limits on the rearmament of Western Germany, where one restriction after the other, established in earlier years, has quietly gone by the board, and where the [West] Germans are now, in the view of everybody in Eastern Europe, well on the way to becoming in all essential respects a full-fledged nuclear power." Moreover, the

United States increasingly links its policy with that of the Bonn revenge-seekers; this is evidenced by the plan to create a "nuclear belt" along the West German frontiers with the German Democratic Republic and Czechoslovakia.

True, in the United States itself there are two points of view on the use of armed force against Eastern Europe. In a speech in Congress at a subcommission on Europe last year, the then Under-Secretary of State, Averell Harriman, declared that military operations to liberate Eastern Europe were unfeasible and that the American people did not want nuclear war for the sake of "liberating" Eastern Europe.

But there are other very influential voices advocating just the opposite.

In view of the war threat from the imperialist camp, one must consider all the other means used by the Western Powers in pursuing their policies vis-à-vis the Socialist states.

The expansion of the ideological campaign against the Socialist community is an important element of imperialist policy. Western ruling circles do not deny that "bridge" strategy aims to disunite the countries of the Socialist camp. Bourgeois ideologists hope for the "resurgence of nationalism" in Eastern Europe.

János Kádár, First Secretary of the Central Committee of the Hungarian Socialist Workers' Party, said last December: "If the imperialist hope that enhanced national awareness can give rise to anti-Communist and anti-Soviet sentiments, they are sadly mistaken. We remain true to the principles of proletarian internationalism and friendship with the Soviet Union." The imperialist must accept Hungary as she is, i.e., as a loyal friend of the Soviet Union and a member country of the Council for Mutual Economic Assistance, the Warsaw Treaty and the Socialist community.

The imperialist leaders base their ideas about the future of Eastern Europe on internal forces. If Truman and Churchill, who in their day counted on internal counter-revolution in the East European countries, could not delay the people's democratic revolutions, then on what internal forces can the imperialist strategists count today? There are no such forces, nor can there be in countries where a new generation of people building Socialism has grown in the last twenty years. "Our mistake," French historian Lavergne writes, "lies in failure to understand the fact that a very great number of people in countries that have recently embarked upon the Socialist path of development sincerely believe this radical renovation to be advantageous."

Some bourgeois politicians regard internal developments in East European countries, testifying to greater economic efficiency and wider democracy, as virtually "degeneration" and a "return to the capitalist way of life." These "hopes" and "prophecies" are out of touch with reality. These Western ideologists are doing their imperialist clients a disservice and are misleading them about the real state of affairs in Eastern Europe.

Those in the West who seriously study Eastern Europe have made conclusions to the contrary. A large group of experts, appointed to U.S. Congress, has for some time been studying processes occurring in the Socialist states. Their report on changes in the Socialist world concludes that the Socialist nature of these countries remains unchanged, that the leading role of their Communist parties is as great as ever, and that the ultimate aims of the Communist movement remain the same.

Socialism is Not for Negotiation

Lenin often spoke of the need to discern two trends in the policy of the imperialist Powers towards Socialism. One disunites the imperialists, the other unites them. The former has of late increased, first, due to growing interimperialist contradictions and the further strengthening of Socialism and, second, to the prospects of peaceful coexistence of states with differing social and economic systems.

Today the imperialist Powers are being compelled in some measure to normalise relations with the East European Socialist countries. "Imperialist leaders have, whether they like it or not, to accept the prevailing balance of forces between the Socialist and the capitalist world," Wladyslaw Gomulka, First Secretary of the Central Committee of the Polish United Workers' Party, has said.

The imperialist ultras are trying to use trade relations with the Socialist countries to obtain political concessions. For instance, on the eve of trade negotiations with Rumania, Senator Pell demanded in the U.S. Senate that Rumania be told to make certain changes in her home policy. Many realistic bourgeois commentators clearly see the futility of this. Geneviève Tabouis, well-known French journalist, for instance, wrote about Socialist-capitalist trade agreements that "no signatory of these agreements abandons its ideology or loyalty to the alliances concluded in the West or in the East."

The Socialist countries will continue to expose the imperialist aims of the Western Powers. This, however, does not mean that they will refuse to improve economic and cultural relations with the West European countries or the United States, or to expand their economic ties. The Polish Zycie Warszawy wrote the following on February 5, 1963: "Brushing aside all political speculations which certain American circles would like to connect with the development of trade relations, we have always regarded these relations as the translation into reality of the principle of peaceful coexistence of states with different social systems."

Being eager to expand trade with the Western Powers, the East European countries are naturally interested in long-term agreements and credits which would enable them to plan their trade turnover. These agreements would serve as a guarantee of lasting and normal economic ties, as long as their provisions are strictly observed. Experience shows, however, that Western trade partners are not always reliable, particularly when they try to obtain political concessions from Socialist countries.

Evidently, it is only by political considerations that one can explain the U.S. Congress decision to prohibit the sale of agricultural products to Poland and Yugoslavia for their national currency. Congress has also decided to tighten up the terms for granting credits to Poland.

Relations between the Socialist and capitalist countries are a complicated international problem. In making their contribution to these relations, the East European states and the Communist and Workers' parties proceed from the tasks of building and strengthening their new society and pursue a policy of peace, democracy and Socialism.

East-West Trade

Y. Shipov

The record of growing economic contacts between the East and West European nations speaks for itself, as the statistics and commentary of this Soviet author indicate. Although some obstacles to these contacts–motivated by Cold War attitudes–cannot be dismissed, Shipov acknowledges an "objective necessity" for East-West commercial ties and concludes that their obvious advantages impel Western nations to lift politically inspired restrictions.

East-West trade is becoming an increasingly important factor in the economic development of the countries concerned. In 1965 it reached an all-high, topping $11,000 million. In the past eight or ten years, East-West economic ties have become a major and most dynamic part of world trade. In 1953-1965 world trade annually increased by an average of 6.9 per cent and East-West trade by 11.8 per cent.

Despite the impressive absolute figures, East-West share in total world trade is very low (in 1965 slightly over 3 per cent), although these two groups of countries account for the overwhelming bulk of the world's industrial output. The reasons are well known. They are, first and foremost, U.S. imperialism's cold war and its policy imposed on the West of isolating the Socialist countries from the world market.

For instance, there is still the notorious list of "strategic" goods whose exports to the Socialist countries are forbidden. As for imports from the Socialist countries, they are governed in the West, especially in the United States and Federal Germany, by a system of strict licensing and quotas. Even when trade agreements and treaties contain a most-favoured-nation clause, many Western countries put their Socialist trading partners in a disadvantageous position in relation to other countries insofar as customs tariffs and other factors are concerned, thus substantially affecting the competitiveness of goods from the Socialist countries.

Because of objective necessity, however, East-West economic ties are developing successfully. The process is especially lively in Europe. Trade between the European Socialist and capitalist countries already accounts for about 70 per cent of total East-West trade. In 1965 goods from the Socialist countries accounted for 8.5 per cent of Italy's imports, 6.6 per cent of Federal Germany's, 3.4 per cent of France's, 4.7 per cent of Britain's, 18.9 per cent of Finland's, and 12.4 per cent of Austria's. In this same year the Socialist countries' markets absorbed 21.1 per cent of Finland's exports, 17.9 per cent of Austria's, 7.3 per cent of Italy's, 6.2 per cent of Federal Germany's, 4.3 per cent of France's, and 3.5 per cent of Britain's.

In assessing these figures, one should bear in mind that foreign trade is an important channel by which many West European countries realise their national product and that countries with a highly developed foreign trade, like Britain, Federal Germany, Italy and France, are among the biggest trading Powers in the world. In 1964 Western Europe accounted for more than 40 per cent of total world exports (Federal Germany, for instance, for 9.4 per cent, Britain for 7.2 per cent, France for 5.2 per cent, and Italy for 3.5 per cent).

Western countries absorb a large proportion of the Socialist countries' exports. In 1964, for instance, the West European markets took 25 per cent of Rumania's exports, 21 per cent of Hungary's and 18 per cent of the Soviet Union's. The West European share of the Socialist countries' imports is substantial too: 23 per cent in the case of Rumania, 20 per cent in the case of Poland and Hungary, and 15 per cent in the case of Bulgaria and the U.S.S.R.

West European countries are now the main purveyors of industrial equipment and ships to the Socialist countries, who accounted for 36 per cent of their exports in 1964. As a rule, they offer equipment that meets present-day demands and conforms to the latest achievements in technology. Another reason why orders are often placed with European firms is that they sell their goods on easy instalment terms–a system now widespread in international trade in industrial equipment.

The biggest suppliers of complete plant to the Socialist countries are Britain, Federal Germany, Italy, France and certain other West European countries. The most important deals in the past few years include Britain's sale of chemical fertiliser equipment to Czechoslovakia ($11.1 million) and Hungary ($7.4 million) and of equipment producing dacron-type fibres to the U.S.S.R. ($87.1 million); Belgium's sale of a chemical fertiliser plant to Bulgaria ($38.5 million) and complete chemical plant to Hungary ($7.2 million), and Italy's sale of an iron and steel works to Czechoslovakia ($10 million).

A major step towards expanding trade between Western and Eastern Europe is the refusal of Western countries to abide by the rules of the Berne Union (a Western agreement recommending its signatories not to grant credits to the Socialist countries for periods of over five years).

The credit blockade was breached in 1964 by Britain, the first country in Western Europe to grant a long-term credit (fifteen years) to the Soviet Union.

That example was followed by Italy (with a twelve-year credit to Czechoslovakia), France (with a new trade agreement with the Soviet Union providing for credits for seven years), Federal Germany (in 1965 her Government decided to extend the credit period to eight years), and others.

Other important Western Europe exports to Eastern Europe include iron and steel (more than 10 per cent of the latter's imports), foodstuffs (about 15 per cent), and chemicals (about 10 per cent). The West European countries' exports to Eastern Europe thus consist mainly of equipment and other manufacturing industry products.

The bulk of the Socialist countries' exports is made up of raw materials. The share of equipment in 1964 came to less than 10 per cent and that of ready-made goods to about 20. One of their most important tasks is to increase the proportion of ready-made goods.

The large share of raw materials in the Socialist countries' exports is partly a consequence of the old European traditional division of labour typical of pre-war years. Improvement in the situation is hampered to a certain extent by the Western countries' discriminatory measures against imports of ready-made goods from the Socialist countries, which noticeably weakens their competitive power on Western markets.

Some goods from the Socialist countries play a prominent part in West European imports. In 1964, for instance, Western Europe imported from Socialist countries 21 per cent of its imports of solid fuel, about 11 per cent of oil products, more than 30 per cent of its unsawn timber and about 30 per cent of its sawn soft wood.

A new factor making for stable East-West economic relations in recent years was expansion of scientific, technical and production ties. The East European and Western countries have concluded numerous agreements on increased trade in licenses and patents and on promoting direct trade and production co-operation between Socialist enterprises and certain Western firms. As a result, exchange of scientific and technical documentation and specialists and joint work on projects are becoming a regular practice.

Confronted with growing competition on the capitalist market, Western firms are highly interested in obtaining new markets for their goods, and are prompted to seek new forms of economic co-operation with Socialist countries. Noteworthy in this respect are some of the co-operation agreements in trade and production. Poland and the West German Krupp-Grundig group have signed an agreement to build on Polish territory an assembly works which will produce about 100,000 tape recorders a year. Poland will pay for the Grundig license with ready-made products. Czechoslovakia has concluded an agreement with British A. E. Callaghan & Son on the joint production and sale of automatic textile equipment in almost all the countries of the world. The machines, British-made, will have additional Czechoslovak devices for processing cotton fibre.

Another increasingly widespread practice is that of Socialist countries founding establishments in Western countries with the participation of local capital. Bulgaria, for instance, has set up more than ten such establishments in the past two years. Most of them are foreign trade organisations and agencies, and some are manufacturing enterprises.

Speaking of new forms of East-West economic ties, one must mention the agreement between the Soviet Union and Fiat for the construction of a plant making up to 600,000 cars a year. The cost is to come to $800 million, of which $350 million will be supplied by the Italian firm in the form of equipment and other materials, to be repaid in instalments.

The obvious advantages of East-West trade and its prospects impel the Western countries to ease and lift politically inspired restrictions, as several of them have done in respect to imports from Eastern Europe in the past two or three years. Britain, for instance, has followed up negotiations with Bulgaria, Hungary, Poland and Czechoslovakia by abolishing the system of quotas and individual import licenses on a number of items insofar as those countries are concerned. Italy has included in her bilateral agreements with members of the Council for Mutual Economic Assistance lists of goods which can now be exported in unlimited quantities and, moreover, has simplified the license-granting procedure. Similar steps have been taken by Sweden, France and other countries.

Chapter 3

EAST-WEST TRADE IN WESTERN EXPERIENCE

East-West Trade: Myth and Matter

Joseph A. Kronsten

While commenting on some misconceptions in British evaluation of commercial contacts with the Soviet bloc countries, Dr. Kronsten provides a comprehensive review of the principal aspects of doing business with Eastern Europe. To some extent, he draws on similar experience of other West European nations. The author, an economist and export consultant, considers East-West contacts beneficial, and states that a sound basis for long-term economic cooperation between the two groups of nations does exist.

One can hardly think of a subject area more littered with misconceptions, economic and commercial irrelevancies, political clichés, strategic *non-sequiturs* and general misinformation than that of East-West trade. Depending on their political colouring and emotional involvement, many, otherwise possessed of balanced judgment, still regard East-West trade either as a panacea for all the major actual or possible scourges of contemporary mankind, including a Third World War, the spread of nuclear weapons, world famine and disease, and lack of international understanding, or as a deadly weapon in the Communist armoury, facilitating political subversion and cultural infiltration–in short, a high road to Communist domination of the world. Nevertheless, since the death of Stalin, and with the spread of the political thaw in the East, East-West trade has begun to be accepted as something desirable but rather dicey, like a very potent, unproven antibiotic.

Successive British Governments have been no less aware of the news value of East-West trade. For party political purposes, they have used the subject as an absolutely reliable gimmick of high publicity resonance. Whenever the foreign or home economic policy front has needed galvanising, or when some embarrassing issue has cried out for a diversion, some new plans for expanding or improving East-West trade have been produced. Both the present and past governments are equally guilty in this respect.

Political or other kinds of gimmickry in the field of East-West trade are harmful whether coming from the Left or the Right, and whether the gimmicking government appears as a Coppelius, a Dr. Miracle or a Dapertutto. Whatever Mr. George Kennan may have said on the inseparability of politics and trade in East-West relations, Britain's interests, at least, are best served by trade with the Communist countries which is of as politically neutral a nature as possible.

On the other hand,successive British Governments, including the present one, have done more than is commonly realised to help those directly engaged in East-West trade to help themselves. The Board of Trade is operating a wide range of constantly expanded and improved export services: informatory, advisory, promotional, financial, and of many other specialised kinds; a comprehensive export credit insurance and financial support system has been brought to a high pitch of efficiency by ECGD (Export Credit Guarantee Department). By improved trade negotiation techniques, by constantly pressing for relaxation in the strategic embargo, and in many other ways, the government departments concerned have been clearing the ground for the expansion of our trade with the East.

In addition, full official support is being given to public bodies concerned with Britain's trade with the Eastern bloc. Here the pride of place belongs to the London Chamber of Commerce, most active in this

Reprinted with permission from *International Affairs* (London), April 1967, and the author.

field, and one should welcome the recent establishment of the National Export Council's East-West Trade Committee which, unlike its opposite numbers, covers both exports and imports.

* * *

The whole subject of East-West trade being beset by misconceptions of its nature, operation and effects, an analysis of some of the more prevalent of those misconceptions may prove useful.

Let us first consider some political misconceptions. To quote Mr. Dean Rusk, East-West trade is a field in which doctrinaire extremes seem to flourish. Even in the United States, however, the John Birch Society co-exists with Cyrus Eaton, and there has been, over the last year, a visible shifting both of official policy and public opinion towards a more liberal approach to East-West trade.

Canada, perhaps surprisingly, ranged herself quite early with the strong advocates of East-West commercial rapprochement. This attitude may have been influenced by her enormous sales of surplus Canadian wheat to China, the U.S.S.R., and other Eastern European countries, but the interest shown by Canada in Communist markets far exceeds that country's current stake in East-West trade.

East-West Trade: A Symposium, edited by Philip E. Uren,[1] with academic, parliamentary and governmental contributions, analyses the subject on well-reasoned, practical lines. The approach is, for obvious reasons, somewhat theoretical, but in its support of East-West trade it takes up a position which the United States may not reach for some time yet.

In Western Europe 'The Myth,' to quote Senator Fulbright, 'that trade with the Communist countries is a compact with the Devil,' has faded out nearly everywhere. In some circles, however, it is accepted only as a necessary evil which, in addition, can and should be turned into a major strategic weapon. Here one might quote from a work on *Die strategische Bedeutung des Ost-West Handels* by Dr. Michael von Berg, a NATO scholarship holder.[2] The author regrets the absence of a NATO-inspired and controlled common East-West trade policy and formulates some of the guidelines of such a policy. Dr. von Berg further calls for concerted efforts to stop the de-politicisation of East-West trade by Communist countries; to face the Eastern bloc with a united front on economic policies, and resolutely to use East-West trade, more extensively than before, as a means of political pressure.

Dr. von Berg thinks such action is feasible because none of the Western countries is economically dependent on trade with the East (with the sole exception of Finland, a special case). Ignoring the principle at issue, the weakness of the argument lies in the fact that, otherwise than in exceptional circumstances, like the agricultural crisis of 1963-65, the East is not economically dependent on trade with the West either.

Another, though less harmful, fallacy is the belief, or hope, that by intensifying East-West trade exchanges, in the widest sense of the term, including financial, technological and scientific co-operation, the West will drive a wedge between the Soviet Union and the remaining East bloc countries, and perhaps succeed in drawing some of them into the Western orbit.

I do not share this view, regarding it, if anything, as a confusion of cause and effect. The eccentric forces operating within the Eastern bloc for the last 10 years or so have come into being independently of Western policy, with their roots perhaps in the very foundations of the social, political and economic order established throughout Eastern Europe. Western trading or other influences have been as little responsible for the politically centrifugal and economic decentralisation trends in Eastern Europe as they were for the present Sino-Soviet hostility, which no amount of Western efforts, or even sacrifices, could have caused.

Even closer East-West contacts may, perhaps, accelerate further economic reforms in the East, but such contacts will as always, remain catalysers and not agents of the process.

A Western concern entering some large and important co-operation agreement with, say, an East German State Organisation, or supplying a few complete factories to Bulgaria, would be naïve to think that, as a by-product of their business deal, the customer country might weaken its Warsaw Pact or even Comecon links.

* * *

Just as naïve, in the realm of economic misconceptions, is the school of thought which sees in a rapid expansion of this country's Eastern trade a panacea for all our economic ills.

Whenever some British industry is facing structural difficulties, or finding its home and export business insufficient to absorb its production, indignant protestations invoke Communist countries' business as an automatic and, indeed, permanent solution.

The shipbuilding industry is a case in point. How often have we heard that if only the Eastern bloc countries were encouraged to build their ships in this country, our shipbuilders would be full up with orders for many years to come. The truth is that the Eastern customers have had every reasonable encouragement to place orders with British shipyards, and have, indeed, done so; but the majority of their imported ships are built elsewhere, even in Japan. The reason is exactly the same as with non-Communist foreign shipowners—

[1] Toronto: Canadian Institute of International Affairs. 1966.
[2] Leyden: Sijthoff. 1966.

British shipyards have apparently not been competitive enough. One hopes that the position will change, but just as the world at large does not owe Britain a living, the Communist countries do not owe it to our shipbuilders either. Moreover, all the Communist countries are intensively expanding and modernising their own shipbuilding facilities, and, of course, under CMEA rules, a Comecon country must give preference to its other members' shipyards before going shopping in the West.

Even so, there is no reason whatever why Communist countries should not be continuing, and increasing, their industrial imports from this country. The more industrialised a country, the greater, in effect, not only its exports but also its imports of industrial equipment, accessories, components, instruments and so on. This presupposes a correspondingly rising standard of living, which is now safe to assume in relation to European Communist countries. China (and her European satellite, Albania), does not necessarily come under the same terms of reference, as her internal political ferments, and 'rocking' external policies may well lead to a period of siege economy harmful to her foreign trade. In any case, it would take more than my courage to forecast political and economic developments in China over the next year or two.

So far as Eastern European imports from Britain are concerned, these should continue to rise, but their content is likely to go on changing as well as diversifying. Industrial equipment needs will become more sophisticated, agricultural requirements will go on growing, and consumer goods–quotas for which have hitherto had to be bitterly fought for–are likely to become almost as 'respectable' as capital goods, and no longer mere stopgaps to make good some plan under-fulfilment, or an irritating local shortage. This development should prove a blessing to some British consumer goods manufacturers, but by and large, to maintain and increase its sales to Communist countries our industry and trade will have to try hard to be competitive in every sense.

An associated misconception implies that the Communist countries' sentimental, to say, historical, political and cultural links with this country guarantee us a certain commercial preference. These links no doubt exist, but there is precious little evidence of their having any effect on our trade with the East. Britain's sacrifices in the Second World War, even where fully acknowledged, have been confined to history books. Conversely, no one who had seen German-occupied Europe, both during and soon after the war, could have expected a restoration and, indeed, the enormous expansion of the formerly occupied countries' trade with West Germany in the lifetime of the same generation. The 'trade is trade' principle operates, however, in Communist, just as in capitalist countries.

This comment is intended, not as a criticism, because this country has, as usual, been leading the field of World War Two 'forgivers and forgetters,' but merely to stress the virtual absence today of any emotional preference for British goods where Eastern, or indeed many other buyers, are concerned. The goods must stand, or fall, on their own merit.

* * *

Next, let us turn to some financial misconceptions. Shortage of international liquidity, balance of payments difficulties of developing and already developed countries, and other factors, continuously increase the credit element and the length of credit cover period where large and even medium-small capital goods exports are concerned. This state of affairs is endemic in sales to the East, where credit facilities may be required in consumer goods sales as well.

We were at one time quite incapable of matching our Western European and Japanese-American competitors in length and cheapness of credit, the range of credit guarantee and general credit terms. With Britain sticking religiously to the rules of the game, that is, to the Berne Union's five-year maximum credit limit and other restrictions, whereas many other members did not, the British exporter was naturally up against an enormous handicap. This goes back, however, to the middle fifties, since when the Export Credit Guarantee Department has made enormous strides in the right direction. Mention need only be made of its policy of matching foreign competitors' credit terms, introducing financial guarantees on loans granted by British financing institutions to foreign customers, increasing limits, relaxing restrictive policy clauses and introducing many new and specialised types of guarantee. In addition, British merchant and clearing banks and insurance companies are now providing very substantial resources for financing large industrial and construction projects over considerably extended periods.

Certain gaps in export finance guarantee facilities still remain, especially in the range of £10,000-£50,000 transactions where East European clients expect–and get elsewhere–attractive credit terms, but by and large, British export finance and guarantee facilities are today competitive against most of the world.

The cost of an ECGD guarantee still perhaps compares unfavourably with similar charges in some other countries, but its trend over here has been steadily downwards (25 per cent decrease over the last two years).

Nevertheless, with sterling vulnerable and the financial squeeze on, the British exporter finds the provision of credit facilities a harder problems than most of his Western European and overseas competitors. Eastern sales to Britain are made to a much larger extent on a cash or very short credit basis, mainly because of the smaller capital goods element involved. But an analysis of the percentage of credit sales to that of total exports to the Eastern bloc shows that the proportion of the former is considerably higher than in the case of others of Britain's export zones.

This country's financial position is, of course, basically sound, at least in relative terms, but whilst our long-term balance of payments shows a healthy surplus, there is a big deficit on the short-term account. It follows, unfortunately, that while long-term credit-assisted exports are naturally very useful and worthy of encouragement, they contribute inadequately to our current international payments problem and bring no immediate relief to our sick currency patient.

Britain's trade balance with the Eastern bloc has been, is, and very likely will remain, adverse, especially with the U.S.S.R. and Poland, where the enormous bulk of raw materials, and food (in the case of Poland), and proves impossible to counter-balance by industrial equipment and similar exports. The deficit on the Polish account has shrunk considerably of late, but in the case of trade with the U.S.S.R. it has remained strongly against us. In 1966 Britain imported goods worth some £125 m. against exports of only £50 m. Even accepting the Soviet figures which reduce the gap by some 10 per cent to allow for the U.K.'s invisible exports, the adverse balance is still large enough. In explanation, Russian and other East European spokesmen stress that most of their new sterling earnings are also spent in this country on purchases of raw materials from the sterling area, such as wool, rubber, copper, and so on. Mr. Douglas Jay, President of the Board of Trade, said: 'Purchases of goods from other parts of the sterling area emphatically do not contribute to the United Kingdom's balance of payments.' They do, in fact, but only in a very small proportion.

The remaining European Communist countries usually either run up manageable positive trade balances with Britain or alternate between reasonably-sized favourable and adverse ones, arising mostly from the extent of deliveries of large industrial plant swelling Britain's overall export figures or on the East partner's temporary inability to supply some major commodity item to reduce the value of Britain's imports in the given year. Hungary has been the only one of these countries to present this country with a constant, though modest, surplus on the trading account.

Thus Britain's trade with Communist Europe as a whole shows a regular and substantial deficit, which in the case of the U.S.S.R. and Poland is traditional and possibly even structural, and hence is unlikely to be eliminated by increased exports. In part, of course, this is the price we pay for our open market policy, by which we allow raw materials and food to come in largely on Open General Licenses in order to keep down the cost of living and to assure a competitive raw material base for our industry. It is very difficult to imagine any British government trying to wipe out adverse trade balances by harshly restrictive measures against such imports. This attitude is based not only on economic policy reasons–Britain's bargaining position as one of the world's largest import markets being very strong indeed–but on what one might call ideological and psychological factors. The Free Trade principle, deeply engrained in the British character, has been elevated in this country to the status of a moral commandment. Should we ever have a truly protectionist President of the Board of Trade, his own permanent staff would soon re-make or break him!

By way of consolation, and possibly as proof that trading deficits with some of the East European countries are of a structural character, Britain's main West European competitors suffer from similar adverse balances in their trade with the U.S.S.R., selling only about half of what they buy from her.

* * *

A review of commercial and general misconceptions about East-West trade would require a book rather than an article, for they range from points usually covered by a travel brochure to various aspects of commercial tactics and procedures, and applied psychology in general. A few deserve some comment.

One misconception relates to the so-called strategic embargo and its related restrictions on exports. Over a number of years now these have been gradually pruned and, where remaining in force, they have been redrafted more closely and less restrictively, with obvious benefits to the volume, content and smoothness of the West's export trade with the East.

The original embargo net was far too wide, with a mesh resembling a patchwork quilt. Each of the NATO member countries participating in the Paris COCOM naturally tries to administer the restrictive regulations in accordance with its own interests.

Under the 'special national interest' clause the British Government–like other COCOM members–have been granting exceptional export licenses in deserving cases. Otherwise, Britain's electronic computer and other automation system sales, very successful and even more promising, would have never got off the ground. However, a lot of the latest, and some even less-advanced, British electronic and other equipment uses some U.S. licences or components and is, therefore, not exportable to Communist countries except under not only a British but also a United States export licence. Once the latter has been refused, British-American agreements forbid the export of goods 'with an American content,' unless the latter can be replaced, and this is often unpractical or impossible. This factor can also vitiate co-operation between British and Eastern bloc countries in large-scale industrial projects where, with today's technological progress, new processes and production methods are based on a complexity of interlocking British, and other, including U.S. patents.

The United States Government are, however, under very strong pressure from manufacturing and export interests to re-align themselves with the tendencies towards embargo relaxation supported by European members of COCOM, and it seems to be only a question of time before they do. This, of course, will mean the appearance, in force, of American competition in East bloc markets, when U.S. manufacturers will be free at last to throw in all the weight of their gigantic technical and capital resources. In the field of computers and advanced electronic equipment generally, this should prove a very serious challenge to British exporters to Communist countries.

By and large, however, current embargo restrictions as applied by the British authorities cannot be regarded as a major obstruction of East-West trade, although they hamper some sectional British exports. There remains, of course, some scope for further pruning of the restrictions, as well as for their re-definition in a more practical and specific sense.

Barter trade is another issue clouding popular conceptions of East-West trade, often to the extent of being identified with it.

Like all countries engaging in bilateral trade, the Communist states have had to employ barter methods at times, or to meet certain conditions. These conditions occur most frequently in trade with under-developed countries which are either short of foreign exchange or trying to dispose of otherwise unsaleable raw material or food surpluses. There are also cases where, to utilise a bilateral trade balance, one or more barter transactions present a better solution than, say, triangular clearing, a purely financial operation which does not involve any exchange of goods.

Barter is frequently used to enable capital goods exporters to sell to countries short of foreign exchange, offering as payment some of their–or occasionally another country's–surplus goods. Naturally enough, only 'soft' goods, that is, those not easily saleable in world markets, will be offered as barter payment, and their barter-buyer often has to dispose of them at a loss. This loss must be covered by increasing the price of, or reducing the profit margin on, the goods sold in barter. Should the country paying in barter with some 'soft' commodity decide at the same time to dump more of it on the world market at a very low cash price, its barter customer will be left with goods which he neither needs nor can sell, except at a grievous loss.

A technically simpler, and less risky, variation of barter are so-called 'reciprocal sales,' with two separate, although mutually conditional transactions, each paid for, taking place instead of a simple swap of goods with no money changing hands. These trading methods do not owe their invention to the now so numerous 'barter and switching' specialists but, in fact, date back to Dr. Schacht who made them so popular in the thirties.

Over the last few years, some of the East bloc countries have often made the counter-purchase of some of their own equipment a condition of placing large equipment orders, with the former representing some 5 to 20 per cent of the main contract value. The purpose of these 'encouragement purchases' is to force the Western manufacturer either to use in his own work, or to re-sell, some new East bloc machinery not hitherto known in the West. Sometimes this kind of approach succeeds, opening the Western market for future sales of the Eastern machinery concerned once a prestige and pioneering sale has been achieved. In other cases, the Western buyer has no use for it and will sell it as well as he can. One the whole, this seems to be an inefficient way of introducing technical equipment to a discriminating market, but countries without a machinery construction tradition are finding it very hard to overcome the buyers' initial prejudices.

As their trade with the West becomes more regular and covers a wider range of commercial co-operation, Eastern bloc countries use barter less and less. Some of them, such as Czechoslovakia, have, for reasons of economic policy, always been reluctant to do so. Barter would become still less important in East-West trade were the CMEA (Comecon) Bank, established in 1964, to make greater progress towards some measure of external convertibility of its members' balances. The difficulties and risks involved in such an achievement–at least for some Comecon countries–are, however, obvious enough. The effect on East-West trade would be that of an unmixed blessing, but such a development does not appear likely in the near future.

* * *

In Eastern European markets Britain has been generally overtaken by West Germany, in some of them by France and Italy as well, while in Yugoslavia–enjoying, in terms of the strategic embargo, a quasi-NATO status–the United States has built up an immensely strong position. However, Britain's trading achievements in Eastern Europe are, both in absolute and relative terms, no worse than in her other markets, and the question of our inferior *savoir faire* on the Communist commerce front does not obviously arise.

West Germany started her post-war Eastern trade very late, and with embarrassing political handicaps. But these obstacles were counterbalanced by her pre-war trading primacy in that area, by the traditional bias in favour of German goods, and, of course, by geographical proximity. As elsewhere, West Germany has been doing magnificently in East European markets, and new dangers for British exporters may stem from the Kiesinger Government's policy of political rapprochement with Communist countries, *vide* the recent establishment of diplomatic relations with Roumania. This development is quite likely to be repeated with some other East European countries. On the other hand, the German economic miracle seems to have run its course, and with the West German labour front no longer a haven of peace and sweet reasonableness, German exports may begin to lose some of their competitive edge.

France has been coming up fast over the last few years, even before General de Gaulle launched his independent policy *vis-à-vis* the East bloc. The French diplomatic and trade offensive has scored in a very big way on the Russian front, where French exports have, with strong Soviet encouragement, been doing extremely well. The great prize, the Renault motor-car factory supply contract, is now to be doubled in size, and, following the recent Franco-Russian trade negotiations, France is reported to have been allowed to establish her own Chamber of Commerce in Moscow, the first time a Western country has been permitted it since 1918. There are other plans for very close industrial and scientific co-operation between French firms and Soviet enterprises. All this, bearing in mind France's technological progress and reasonably well-maintained price stabilisation, may represent a formidable danger to British export interests in the whole of this area, as the French initiative is not, of course, limited to the U.S.S.R. Yet it remains to be seen how these 'Great Expectations' will fare in the next few years. France's similar overtures to China had, of course, a disappointing outcome.

Italy's success in Eastern Europe follows largely on her heavy imports of Russian and Roumanian oil, and represents the (posthumous) rewards of the policies of Professor Mattei, the late dictator of ENI, the State-owned oil, steel and engineering concern. The ENI-controlled SNAM Progetti have been responsible for many petroleum industry and associated projects throughout Eastern Europe, with most of the equipment being supplied by other ENI works. The gigantic plan for a gas pipe-line leading from the Siberian gas-fields to Trieste may also fall into ENI's hands, and the latter's willingness to buy the Soviet gas represents a powerful bargaining counter.

The United States is, so far, fighting the East trade battle—except in Yugoslavia—rather half-heartedly. Not only are U.S. exporters greatly handicapped by their country's very severe restrictions on exports to Communist countries, but a number of leading American concerns are purposely holding off East bloc markets, not wishing to annoy the U.S. Defense Department, their largest customer. As long as the Vietnam war goes on this situation may well remain unchanged. Once, however, the United States decides to go all out to get East European business, British and other West European exporters will have their work cut out to contain the American challenge.

Japan must not be forgotten. She started her export expansion in Eastern Europe, and in a much bigger way in China, not so long ago, and has already scored very heavily. Much of the Japanese export effort is American financed or technologically buttressed, but, even so, the highest credit is due to the commercial activity and efficiency of Japanese salesmen and engineers. Operating in markets hitherto unknown to them, and at great distances from their home base, the Japanese have often beaten Western competition in European Communist countries merely by giving earlier deliveries. Whilst unlikely to threaten British exports to East bloc countries on a broad front, Japan will remain a dangerous competitor, even if in only a few but very important sectors.

* * *

More fuss is made about commercial contacts and human relations than perhaps over any other aspect of the West's trade and general exchanges with the East. True, trading with, say, Bulgaria will show vastly different features from trading with, say, Holland, and there are great differences in the way business is done with East and with West Germany. The differences are, however, merely consequential to, and concomitant with, the political and social principles on which the economies of the Communist countries are based. If these differences are compared with the national and zonal peculiarities, which foreign traders find no less baffling in this country, there really is no gound for the fuss often made about trading with Eastern Europe.

Foreign buying and selling in Communist countries is, with some exceptions, in the hands of State Import-Export Corporations, each responsible for a specific range of goods or services. The only major exception is found in Yugoslavia, where several such corporations cover one sector on what is meant to be a competitive basis. These corporations, by their very character highly-centralised and subject to all the consequent disadvantages, nevertheless only act for the final users or producers, like state works, government departments, and so on, and they depend on the latter's final decision on the relative merits of a foreign offer or bid received. Covering enormous sectors of the national economy, and having to compete for skilled personnel with industry and other state agencies paying higher wages, the Export-Import Corporations face a very difficult task, and they can seldom offer their Western trading partners the speed and efficiency to which these are accustomed in dealings with other capitalist enterprises. The long gestation period of most business with Communist countries is, of course, due less to administrative delays than to factors inherent in their foreign trade system, such as imports and exports having to follow the directives laid down in the National Economic Plan and temporary, or not so temporary, foreign currency shortages. In fact, it is often forgotten that the Export-Import Corporation fulfils a double role: besides selling for the producer and buying for the end-user, it is also used to implement the Government's commercial policy.

In some of the Communist countries concerned there also exist State Agency Corporations acting as local agents for foreign exporters and remunerated by the latter. Their services are optional, and differing views are held on their ability to perform functions associated in the capitalist world with a local agent in a foreign market. Whilst their functions are quite different from those of the Export-Import Corporations, the State Agency Corporations are also instruments of Government commercial policy.

The Western exporter—and importer—must, however, try to establish and maintain contacts, especially on a technical level, not only with the State Import-Export Corporations but also with the final users of the product he sells, or producers of the goods he buys, as well as with the numerous State Research Institutes, one usually serving a given branch of industry. These institutes, responsible for technical developments and improvements of their fields, are the true creators of demand for new technical products, local as well as foreign, and as such they are of tremendous importance to the Western exporter. The latter's direct contacts with the end-users, producers and Research Institutes, frowned upon in the early days, are now allowed in most Communist countries, and, indeed, very wisely encouraged by some of them. More producers, final-users, Service Companies and so on are now being given direct export and import privileges which pre-suppose direct contacts with Western business men.

As anywhere else, friendly human relations are an important element in successful business in East bloc countries. One deals exclusively with people who are employed directly by the state and consequently more formal in their approach to foreigners, especially those from capitalist countries. Any reserve should, however, start melting on regular contacts.

The language barrier acts, of course, as an insulator and inhibitor as well, but in Britain as elsewhere this is now being more widely understood. An obstacle even greater, but easier to overcome, is the ignorance of the history and background of the country visited, an ignorance which also robs any business trip of much interest and pleasure. A little preparatory reading is greatly to be recommended.

Saving some major political setback, East-West trade shoud go on expanding. Some new factors are, however, bound to affect its volume, direction and content. The most important ones as seen today appear to be the following:

Internal changes in Eastern Europe. These are political and economic. Besides Yugoslavia, which remains part of Communist Eastern Europe only in the vaguest sense, Roumania has, for some time, been pursuing a strongly independent line, though not stepping outside the magic circle of orthodox Marxism. Poland maintains her mutually-agreed margin of freedom of movement and Hungary seems to veer in the same direction. The die-hard countries, Eastern Germany, Czechoslovakia, and Bulgaria, are fast thawing out, internally and externally. The first two are, in fact, in the vanguard of a sweeping economic reform movement aimed at a practical recognition of the profit motive in society, at a gradual adoption of market economy principles, decentralisation of industrial and other enterprises and so on.

International developments and groupings. Whilst continuing to perform a useful role in furthering economic and technical co-operation between its members, Comecon appears to be less and less likely to become the East zone's economic superstructure. To quote Mr. Kosygin in his pre-Premier days, 'CMEA implements the economic co-ordination measures of its members without being their common planning organ.' This in turn further widens the Comecon members' terms of reference in their trading with the West.

So far as new forms of East-West economic collaboration are concerned, these developments and trends favour industrial, technological and purely commercial co-operation between Western concerns and industrial associations, other economic groupings and, indeed, even individual enterprises, in Communist countries. 'With it' large and even smaller British firms have by now forged many such links throughout Eastern Europe, some of great importance, some of a self-perpetuating kind. In the East bloc's new economic climate, coupled with internal political relaxation, this type of co-operation should go on from strength to strength. At the same time, new forms of even closer co-operation will develop, such as joint production by Western and Eastern partners of equipment destined for one or both, and even for third countries. Vehicles of all kinds, power station and other electrical equipment, heavy construction machinery, and chemical and petro-chemical plant, are already, or will shortly be, the subject of such arrangements. Very important, too, are long-term agreements under which the Eastern partner supplies components for equipment built by the Western one or vice versa. Yet another type of steadily-expanding East-West co-operation is seen in joint tenders for industrial, construction and other large projects in developing countries where, depending on commercial or sometimes political considerations, the Eastern or Western partner acts as main contractor and the other as his supplier.

With most of the East bloc countries subscribing to the Paris Convention, and the U.S.S.R. reported to have joined it, East-West sales and exchanges of manufacturing licenses, patent rights and so forth are gradually becoming an important and profitable new avenue of East-West trade. This co-operation will, no doubt, also branch out into many highly-specialised services like international engineering, petroleum, chemical, aviation, shipping and other consultancies, technical designing, project and study bureaux and many others. For Britain, having to live mainly on special skills and intensive trade, the widening and diversification of her commerce with the East is highly desirable. Whilst in very general terms still behind this country in technology and international trading *savoir faire*, the East bloc countries can additionally contribute redeployable labour and spare industrial capacity, both of which are likely to become quite plentiful when their economic reforms really start biting.

A sound basis for long-term economic co-operation truly exists and, though the West will remain West and the East will remain East, here the twain should meet and meet again.

Trade Between Market and Centrally Planned Economies: Australia's Experience with the Communist Bloc

J. Wilczynski

Together with Dr. Stermann's article immediately following, this abbreviated account by Professor Wilczynski of Australia's trade with East European countries sheds much useful light on the most important procedural aspects of doing business with the Communist economies. To some extent Wilczynski's exposition complements Professor Berman's article reprinted here, too. With reference to Australia, the author has succeeded in showing that despite the impression of confusion and economic contradictions, which allegedly prevail in the East European foreign trade systems, Communist policies and practices have patterns of rationality.

In the face of the changing pattern of Australia's imports and exports, and the rising Communist importance in world affairs, trade with centrally planned economies acquires new significance. In the last decade Australia's traditional markets in Western Europe have declined from over 60 per cent to less than 40 per cent of Australia's total exports. But the Communist Bloc has been emerging as an increasingly important market for this country's exports, the proportion having quadrupled in the last decade–from 3 per cent to 12 per cent. As far as Australia's imports from the Bloc are concerned, they have settled at 1 per cent of the total.

Trading with centrally planned economies is now a well-established and vital feature of world trade. One would be deluding oneself in expecting that Communist regimes will collapse in these countries in the near future, or that central planning will be displaced by some form of free enterprise. In fact, most underdeveloped countries have already adopted some elements of State trading similar to that practised in the Communist Bloc, and it is difficult to see what these countries can do in the future but spread the practice further. The centrally planned economies of the Communist type now claim 5 per cent of the foreign trade of the countries operating under market economies.

The purpose of this article is to bring out the main features and problems with which market economies are confronted in trade with centrally planned economies, and in that light to analyse and appraise Australia's trade experience with the Communist Bloc.

General Distinguishing Features of Foreign Trade under Market and under Centrally Planned Economies

Fundamentally, each system (naturally) regards foreign trade as a means towards the maximum improvement of social welfare. But the concept of social welfare, the extent to which foreign trade is to be employed and the framework within which foreign trade is to be conducted differ considerably in each case.

In market economies the course of foreign trade is essentially determined by the market mechanism. Trade decisions are made predominantly by private firms guided by their own profit motive and operating normally under competitive conditions. Even where State agencies directly engage in foreign trade, they are in general subject to the same market forces and commercial considerations as private traders. In practically all market economies nowadays, governments intervene in the market to modify the prices paid or obtained through tariffs, subsidies and in some cases manipulation of exchange rates. But governments essentially endeavour to achieve their objectives through the ordinary market forces, without interfering with the market mechanism as a system. Government intervention may also assume the form of quantitative import (or export) restrictions, or in some cases complete prohibitions. Where such direct controls exist, they are normally regulated by the Rules of G.A.T.T. or the Articles of Agreement of the I.M.F., of which most countries with market economies are members. A special case of direct government intervention is that of embargos and controls on exports of strategic significance.

Subject to these conditions created by government intervention and to restrictive practices by certain private trading interests, the volume, composition and direction of the foreign trade of the market economies are basically governed by differentials in current prices, that is by the law of comparative advantage.

In the centrally planned economies of the Communist type, the market mechanism is superseded by planning. Foreign trade is subject to long-term (10-20 years, varying with countries), medium-term (5-7 years) and short-term (3 month and 12 month) plans. Whereas in the developed market economies the main

Reprinted with permission from *The Economic Record*, Vol. 41, No. 96 (December, 1965).

emphasis appears to be on exports, in the centrally planned economies it is imports that occupy the focus of attention. Imports are planned first, being regarded as indispensable to meet production targets (or releasing domestic resources), whilst exports are looked upon as essentially a sacrifice to secure the required imports. The foreign trade plan is dovetailed into the general economic plan, and its fulfilment becomes all-important.

By what criteria are the planned volume and composition of foreign trade determined? The top planning authority has to work within the broad objectives laid down by the Communist Party which determines socially desirable goals by reference not only to current commercial but also to political, cultural, military and long-run economic considerations. Within these objectives the central planning authority determines and reconciles targets in the light of past data and current information. The decisions are quantitative, on the basis of the so-called "material balances" (a form of input-output procedure) which are now, in general, worked out with the aid of the so-called "foreign trade profitability coefficients." Current costs (however defined) are only one of the criteria taken into account. Communist economic theory rejects the law of comparative costs which is regarded as unscientific and serving as a theoretical justification for the Western economic domination of the less developed countries. Competition is, of course, incompatible with central planning of the Communist type. To many Western observers, the foreign trade of the Communist Bloc countries presents a picture of confusion and economic contradictions. However, in the context of their objectives and circumstances, the Communist foreign trade policies and practices assume definite patterns of rationality.

The role assigned by the Bloc countries to foreign trade is generally small—particularly to trade with market economies. Extra-Bloc trade now constitutes only one-third of their total foreign trade, while before the war the proportion stood at about 85 per cent.

Institutional Framework

All Bloc countries have displayed a predilection for trade on a bilateral agreement basis because, in the context of central planning and other conditions prevailing in the Communist Bloc, this form of trading has several advantages. A study by Mikesell and Behrman has shown that in 1957 there were 240 bilateral agreements between the Bloc countries and the rest of the world. Three-quarters of the Bloc's imports from, and 67 per cent of its exports to, the countries with market economies were covered by these agreements. Although of a relatively narrower scope now, this form of trading is still an important distinguishing feature of East-West trade. However, as far as Australia is concerned, there have been no bilateral trade agreements with any of the Bloc countries since World War II. All trade has been conducted on a non-agreement basis, and practically all payments have been multilateral.

The only Bloc country with which Australia has a Treaty of Commerce is Czechoslovakia. The Treaty was first signed in 1936, re-negotiated in 1947 under the terms of G.A.T.T. when the two countries became members, and supplemented in 1948 at the time when Czechoslovakia's exchange rates were altered. The Anglo-Russian Treaty of Commerce and Navigation of 1859, which was honoured by Russia and Australia in their trade up to 1918, was repudiated by Soviet Russia later. When Mr. Hasluck visited Moscow towards the end of 1964, Soviet authorities expressed interest in a trade treaty with Australia, but at the time of writing no such treaty has been signed.

Of the total of forty Australian Trade Commissionerships operating in twenty-nine countries, none is in the Communist Bloc. Australia's commercial interests in the Bloc are normally handled by her trade post closest to the Bloc country concerned, or through the foreign representatives in Australia. Thus, the Trade Commissioner in Stockholm was formerly also accredited to Poland and Czechoslovakia, and the new Commissionerships created in Hamburg and Vienna in 1964 take care of commercial matters in Eastern Europe. The Trade Commissioner in Hong Kong advises the Government and businessmen on trade with Mainland China. None of the Bloc countries has a permanent trade mission in Australia. But Czechoslovakia, Poland and the U.S.S.R. each have a commercial counsellor (now all situated in Sydney) attached to their diplomatic missions in this country. In addition, most Bloc countries have unofficial agents operating in the leading commercial centres in Australia.

In each Bloc country complete State trading is the rule, that is, external trade is nationalized and the Ministry of Foreign Trade is vested with the monopoly of all foreign trade transactions. Its policies are put into operation through foreign trade corporations. There are over 200 of them in the Bloc, the number ranging in each country from one in Mongolia to forty-one in Hungary. Each corporation is an independent legal entity, with a monopoly of imports and/or exports in a clearly defined category of products in each country. Because of this institutional set-up, Western traders sometimes complain of the corporations' superior bargaining power and inflexibility.

Although the foreign trade corporations are large State-owned monopolies in their respective fields, the nature of their trade with, and the marketing peculiarities of the relevant products in, Australia have largely prevented them from exercising their otherwise inherently superior bargaining power. First of all, Australia's dependence on imports from the Bloc is negligible—only 1 per cent of the total. Besides, as all the Bloc countries (except East Germany, Hungary and Mongolia—but they are very minor traders) incur trade deficits with Australia, they are anxious to expand their exports to this country. In this, they have to contend with the well entrenched Western suppliers controlling superior and well-established distribution, spare-parts and servicing networks. Secondly, the marketing of wheat, barley and wool in Australia is such that it does not place a Bloc corporation in a monopsonistic position to deal separately with private traders or growers. The Australian Wheat Board and the Australian Barley Board are in a sense not unlike the Bloc foreign trade corporations. The bargaining power cannot be exercised at the wool auctions either. These three commodities constitute over nine-tenths of Australia's exports to the Bloc.

Criticism is sometimes levelled against the corporations by Australian importers, who occasionally complain of time-consuming negotiations, non-delivery, and late or faulty shipment of goods.

Fluctuations

Trade among the Bloc countries, especially within COMECON, lends itself to precise planning, and the commodities to be traded appear in the import plan of one member and in the export plan of another. Fulfilment of targets is regarded as being of the utmost significance, so as not to upset the plans of the partner countries.

But trade with the market economies is treated as unreliable and largely residual. Commitments can be renounced without serious repercussions on the fulfilment of the general plan. Other factors that may contribute to abrupt fluctuations in trade are the ability and readiness of the government to use trade for non-commercial ends and the superior bargaining power of the monopolistic foreign trade corporations. Mikesell and Behrman showed that the free market economies' trade with the Bloc was more unstable than their trade with other market economies.

To make comparisons of fluctuations in trade over different periods or with other trading partners is an ungrateful task. It appears that the share represented by trading partners in Australia's exports and imports is the only practical basis of comparison. Thus, as compared with a "normal" pre-war period, the fluctuations in Australia's exports to the Communist Bloc have increased very substantially. Fluctuations in Australia's imports from the Bloc have never been large, but under central planning in the Bloc Australia's imports have become even steadier, rising only at the same rate as Australia's total imports.

Is the market for Australian exports in the Bloc more unstable than in the market economies? Although the answer cannot be provided in precise terms, the general conclusion is in the affirmative. As borne out by experience since 1950, the amplitude of fluctuations in exports to the Bloc has been greater than would be warranted by that size of exports. Table I illustrates the point.

Table I

Australia's Exports to the Communist Bloc and other Leading Trading Partners

(£ million)

Year	Communist Bloc*	E.E.C.	United Kingdom	Japan	United States
1950-51	29	226	321	62	149
1951-52	7	153	208	49	77
1952-53	11	193	359	84	58
1953-54	41	191	301	57	56
1954-55	16	170	286	59	52
1955-56	16	171	257	86	55
1956-57	27	233	278	139	66
1957-58	34	183	221	103	59
1958-59	31	145	262	102	62
1959-60	52	179	247	135	76
1960-61	66	161	232	161	72
1961-62	94	184	206	187	109
1962-63	93	167	201	173	133
1963-64	161	214	259	244	148

*Adjustments were made by the author for the major territorial changes which affected the Bloc during the period.
Source: Commonwealth Bureau of Census and Statistics, *Oversea Trade Bulletin,* Nos. 48-61.

Imports from the Bloc are very small and they have followed a remarkably steady course as compared with those from outside the Bloc.

Of the twelve Bloc countries, the widest fluctuations from year to year are displayed in Australia's exports to the U.S.S.R., whilst the Czechoslovakian market has proved the most stable and has expanded gradually. Imports from Rumania have followed the most erratic course, but those from Mainland China have been marked by a steady upward trend.

Exchange Rates

All the Bloc countries pursue the strictest form of exchange control. Their exchange rates are generally fixed, although the U.S.S.R. now allows her official rate to fluctuate within very narrow limits. Most of the Bloc countries, in a limited sense, employ multiple exchange rates. In addition to the uniform commercial rate, applicable in visible trade, one or more non-commercial rates may be operated. The latter are more favourable to non-residents, the purpose being to encourage foreign tourists, diplomats or emigrants (including those sending cash and parcels subject to import duties) to exchange their currencies for the local Bloc country's currency.

Thus Poland officially operates two exchange rates—a "basic" one in visible trade: £A1 : 13·97 zlotys, and a "special" one for tourists and others: £A1 : 83·85 zlotys. Other Bloc countries, namely Albania, Bulgaria, Czechoslovakia, Rumania and Mainland China, follow similar schemes to increase their earnings of foreign exchange.

Australian banks do not quote exchange rates for the currencies of the Bloc countries. When necessary, the respective exchange rates are established on the basis of their sterling quotations in London. Almost all dealings with the Communist Bloc are in sterling, and thus from the Australian traders' point of view there is little need to use direct exchange rates. From a Bloc country's standpoint, the exchange rate is of minor significance in determining the total volume and composition of visible trade and in the allocation of domestic resources.

Tariffs

All the Bloc countries continue to administer their national tariffs in their trade with the market economies, and some of them even in intra-Bloc trade. To an outside observer, their tariff schedules appear very liberal and the level of tariffs is very low. However, under central planning and with the trading and pricing policies pursued, protective (and revenue) tariffs lose their conventional significance. Quantitative planning, the monopolization of foreign trade and the State planning of prices offer more complete, direct and flexible methods of protecting local industries or raising revenue. Political, military or long-range economic objectives may override commercial considerations based on price differentials. However, changes in tariffs may affect the "profitability" of the foreign trade corporations which are expected, within the confines of the foreign trade plan, to buy in the cheapest market. Thus, as the quantitative regulation of foreign trade is the rule (and not, as in the market economies, the exception), the tariffs have virtually no influence on the level of foreign trade, and only a limited influence on its geographical distribution.

In such a context, tariffs are of secondary consequence. They have been retained by Communist regimes mainly for the purposes of negotiating commercial treaties, reciprocating minimum tariffs, extending Most Favoured Nation (M.F.N.)treatment and giving preferential considerations to intra-Bloc trade. It is largely for these reasons that few Western nations extend full M.F.N. treatment to the Bloc countries.

Australia has not specifically discriminated in tariffs against the Communist Bloc. All the Bloc countries are classified as "foreign," and consequently they are subject either to the Intermediate or the General tariff (and not to the British Preferential). M.F.N. treatment is extended to most Bloc countries: Bulgaria, Czechoslovakia, Hungary, Poland, Rumania, the U.S.S.R., Mainland China and North Vietnam. This means that over nine-tenths of Australia's imports from the Bloc is subject to the Intermediate tariff. Imports from the remaining Bloc countries—Albania, East Germany, Mongolia and North Korea— consequently carry the General tariff.

Officially, all the eight M.F.N. countries reciprocate with Australia. But the Department of Trade and Industry is fully aware of the possibility of the Bloc countries evading full reciprocity. If M.F.N. treatment is understood as being related to import duties only, reciprocity is accorded. But if the M.F.N. is interpreted in a wider sense, the very nature of the pricing and trading practices—such as those associated with fixing exchange rates, State trading, non-commercial motivation—makes it impracticable for those countries to accord full reciprocity. A similar problem exists for Australia in obtaining full reciprocity with Czechoslovakia and Poland under G.A.T.T., of which the former is a full, and the latter an associate, member.

Prices

Central planning of foreign trade and the almost complete insulation of domestic from external prices in each Bloc country prevent market forces from operating to regulate trade between centrally planned and market economies. Price differentials do not necessarily govern the volume, composition and direction of exports and imports. A centrally planned economy of the Communist type has no simple mechanism, corresponding to the market mechanism, to ensure the most gainful flow of trade. The shortcomings of this system are now well appreciated in the Bloc, especially in Eastern Europe. In the past decade most Bloc countries have been using foreign trade profitability coefficients, which have been applied mostly to determine the optimum structure of exports to pay for the required imports envisaged in the plan.

Bloc countries are sometimes accused of exploitation of their trading partners, of price discrimination, and of dumping. A foreign trade corporation is usually a very large organization and its power is not unlike that of a monopsonistic buyer or a monopolistic seller. As traders facing these corporations are mostly small and unorganized, they can in addition be dealt with separately in accordance with the principle of a discriminating monopsony or monopoly. Dumping by Communist countries has been a grievance of long standing ever since 1929. A centrally planned economy lends itself better to this practice than does a market economy. On account of the pricing confusion which still prevails in all the twelve Bloc countries, some of the costs are not reflected (such as certain natural resources) or are unusually low (e.g. capital charges).

It appears that, in general, there has been nothing extraordinary about prices in Australia's trade with the Bloc. From the available information, the conclusion is warranted that the foreign trade corporations have been fair and reasonable traders. When the course of prices appeared unusual, it was not necessarily due to the fact that these countries have centrally planned economies.

Payments and Finance

Although the bilateral form of payments has been such a characteristic feature of the Bloc countries' trade since the war, only multilateralism has been practised in their trade with Australia.

The organization and methods of financial settlements in Australia's trade with the Bloc countries are conditioned chiefly by Australia's exchange control. The exchange control regulations affecting the Bloc are the same as those applicable to any country outside the Sterling Area, and there appears to be no discrimination in the administration of the Regulations against any Bloc country. None of the Bloc countries' currencies is regarded as freely convertible. In practice, almost all transactions are conducted in sterling. Quite apart from the Australian exchange control regulations, this is the most convenient medium in view of the networks of trade developed by the Bloc and by Australia. In fact, it is known that some Bloc countries either regularly (e.g. Czechoslovakia) or occasionally (e.g. the U.S.S.R.) buy Australian products directly for sterling in Britain.

At government level, Australia has never offered credit to, or sought credit from, any Communist country. Nonetheless, short and medium-term credits have been used on a considerable scale. Australian credit financing has been mostly concerned with exports to the Bloc, rather than imports from it. This is what one would expect, and the position is no different in trade with other countries. Credit is normally available on much the same basis as to non-Communist countries. In fact, stricter limitations apply to financing exports to certain non-Communist countries. Australia is, of course, not the only country extending credits to the Bloc. Practically all Western countries have been doing so in the past decade and for periods up to thirty years.

From the information available it appears that there have been no payment defaults by any of the Bloc countries since World War II. On this score, these countries have established a better record than the non-Communist countries. It appears that in this respect there is an advantage in selling to a Bloc corporation because a contract with one is in effect with its government.

Of all the Bloc countries, Mainland China has caused most apprehension as to her credit worthiness and ability to pay, particularly over the past five years when she has been receiving credits on a scale without precedent in Australian trading history. But in fact, China has so far paid to the last penny, and usually well before due dates. In view of her economic plight, China's payment performance must be regarded as a financial miracle of recent times.

Credit is available in Australia for imports from the Bloc, again on the same basis as for imports from non-Communist countries. The Bloc countries themselves, on principle, do not extend export credits. But some of them, notably Czechoslovakia, in exceptional cases make short-term credit available to Australian importers—mainly when it is necessary to meet competition from other foreign suppliers.

Apart from the abnormal year 1951-52, Australia has been earning increasing trade surpluses (averaging £90m. annually since 1960) from the Bloc ever since World War II. The Communist Bloc as a whole fairly consistently earns surpluses in trade with the United Kingdom, and in fact elsewhere in the Sterling Area as well. Australia, on the other hand, incurs regular trade deficits with the United Kingdom. Thus the Bloc countries as a whole use their surplus with the United Kingdom and other parts of the Sterling Area to offset their deficit with Australia.

Trade Disputes

Most of the Bloc countries established foreign trade arbitration tribunals in the years 1949-56 to handle not only the disputes in intra-Bloc trade but also those with capitalist countries. As such, the tribunals are concerned with foreign trade disputes only, their jurisdiction is conditional upon the voluntary consent of the parties, and the arbitrators act as judges, not as prosecuting or defending counsel. This set-up contrasts with that prevalent in the West, where disputes are handled either by ordinary courts or by tribunals concerned with both domestic and foreign trade, whilst those concerned with foreign trade only are under the auspices of some international body.

In the 1950s, the period which coincided with the Bloc's trade offensive with the non-Communist world, two major criticisms were levelled against the Communist system of foreign trade adjudication.

(a) Juridically incestuous relation between the Communist State and the tribunals. Being generally attached to their respective Chambers of Commerce, the tribunals give the appearance of being detached, independent bodies. But fundamentally, it is difficult not to see them as government administrative instrumentalities. In all cases they were created by government legislation, just as the Chambers of Commerce were. The tribunals are under the express supervision of the Ministry of Foreign Trade. The arbitrators are invariably eminent national figures in their fields, and are either members of the Communist Party of persons otherwise owing their success to the regime, the

majority if not all of whom would be employed by the State. The Communist basic theory of law is that it is an active weapon in the hands of the State. Lenin emphasized that Communist law plays a fundamental part in carrying out the policy of the Communist Party and in consolidating the dictatorship of the proletariat. When in effect the same monolithic State is both a party to the dispute and—however remotely—an arbitrator, it is difficult for a non-Communist trader to feel reassured that his case is not prejudiced. But it would be difficult for the injured trader to prove any prejudiced intention on the part of the Bloc country, since a particular act may be merely a logical and legitimate consequence of the political and economic set-up in force.

(b) The insistence by the Bloc countries on domestication of foreign trade litigations. Beginning in the later 1950s, most Bloc countries have endeavoured to introduce clauses into trade contracts with traders from non-Communist countries stipulating that controversies must be submitted to the Bloc country's tribunal and not elsewhere.

In the light of East-West trade experience in the past decade, it appears that these fears can easily be exaggerated. It is generally conceded in Western commercial and legal circles that arbitration is the most appropriate method of settling trade disputes between countries with different political and economic systems, and in fact the Communist foreign trade arbitration tribunals are acquiring a growing degree of acceptance from foreign traders, courts and governments. Neither the Department of Trade, nor the Commonwealth and State Attorney-General's Departments, nor certain semi-government business undertakings reported knowledge of any such dispute. According to the Department of External Affairs, up to the middle of 1963 no instance of a sufficiently serious nature had occurred to cause the Department to lodge a protest with a Bloc country against unfair treatment by a foreign trade corporation.

It seems unlikely, however, that there have been no trade disputes with a Bloc of twelve different countries—countries which subscribe to a different social philosophy and which organize their trade on a completely different basis from that accepted in Australia. It is possible that disputes have occurred but were either of a minor nature and perhaps were settled without recourse to arbitration or courts, or if there have been any of a serious nature that were few and received no publicity. The Consul Commercial for Czechoslovakia stated that to his knowledge there had been "practically no trade disputes" between his country and Australia; there were some cases of misunderstanding but they were settled informally on a friendly basis, without reference to arbitration. The Polish Chamber of Commerce reported that there had been no trade disputes between Poland and Australia except that in 1963 a case to which an Australian firm was a party was referred to the "College of Arbitrators Attached to the Polish Chamber of Commerce." No details were given.

From the available data, it is difficult to generalize on whether the Bloc countries insist on domestication of commercial litigations with Australian traders. None of the authorities referred to before were aware of such insistence. But, of course, in private trade contracts such a stipulation may be included and no authorities would necessarily be aware of them. One source reported that some Bloc countries, notably China, in general insert clauses in the contracts of sale stipulating arbitration in the Bloc country concerned. According to a statement received from the Polish Chamber of Commerce, the latter "only recommends" to its members (that is, to the foreign trade corporations) to insert such clauses; otherwise it is "quite usual" to specify in the arbitration clause that a dispute be referred to a permanent tribunal, or to an *ad hoc* body, "situated in the defendant's country to ensure a speedy enforcement of the award."

In this writer's opinion, the incomplete evidence suggests that if any Bloc countries have insisted in trade contracts that trade disputes be referred to their own tribunals, they must have been rare cases, and have caused no uneasiness to Australian traders in the past. Similarly, there have probably been no serious trade disputes. Such disputes as did occur in the past have not caused any concern to public authorities.

* * *

In Australia's search for markets, stimulated by the declining role of Western Europe in her trade, the communist Bloc has not received much attention. The government has largely followed a passive role, the reason for which appears to be not Communist obstruction but Australia's indifference, no doubt conditioned mainly by political considerations. The Bloc's increasing role in Australia's trade is due not so much to her own initiative as to that of the Bloc countries.

Any speculation as to what the future holds in store is likely to be unrewarding. Judging by the experience of the recent past, Australia need not feel apprehensive in expanding trade with the Bloc. But one does not have to be a prophet to recognize at least two inherent problems. First, the Australian economy has now been geared for a long period to receiving substantial trade surpluses from the Bloc to pay for substantial deficits with other partners. As we know, the Bloc's trade with market economies is characterized by its unpredictability. Should its imports suddenly drop, Australia may find herself in an embarrassing balance of payments situation. With common markets developing throughout the world, it may not be easy to find alternative markets elsewhere.

The second problem, related to the preceding one, is the vulnerability of the wheat industry. In the 1950s (up to 1959) annual wheat production averaged 160m. bushels. But owing to increasing yields and expanding acreage, the production has steadily been increasing to reach 380m. bushels in the 1964-65 season. Because of the practically constant domestic consumption, the wheat industry has become increasingly dependent on export markets–about three-quarters of production has recently been available for export. Of this, about one-half has been absorbed by the Bloc–and most of it by one country, a country which has refused to enter into long-term contracts with the American Wheat Board, and whose leaders can hardly be described as champions of "peaceful coexistence" between the two systems.

Austria as a Model for East-West Trade

Walter Stermann

This Viennese expert does not believe that Austria's intensive trade relations with Eastern Europe can serve as a model for other Western nations. He explains this by the fact that his country's heavy dependence on this trade is exceptional, based as it is on historical, political and other specified reasons. Stermann describes in considerable detail not only how Austria's trade with its neighbors is conducted and why the country holds a strong creditor position vis-à-vis Eastern Europe, but also the drawbacks of unilateral trade liberalization, including the granting of the MFN treatment.

The transition from the cold-war period, when also the economic relations between East and West had been almost frost-bound, to peaceful co-existence has brought about the Western industrial nations' growing interest in East-bloc markets, and along with it a continuous expansion of trade. This tendency became even more pronounced after, in the last years, economic reforms had started in almost all East-bloc countries–reforms, that by integrating elements of a free market economy intend to promote the national economies' performances without on principle changing the adherence to the socialist planned economy. It is a common feature of these reforms that apart from a certain new interpretation of the cost accounting system they introduce decentralisation and with that a delegation of responsibility and competence to the individual managements, that thus are enabled to exercise more influence also on the purchasing of their productive equipment and primary material. The result of all this is the possibility and even necessity of direct contacts with the suppliers. The Western seller does no longer deal exclusively with the official of a public foreign trade association in a monopoly position, but he is also offered the opportunity of talks with the producer interposed in distribution.

As is well-known, quite some time ago Jugoslavia has taken the lead regarding these decentralisation tendencies, and they resulted in such extensive changes that due to its present economic order this country is no longer considered an East-bloc country proper (Jugoslavia is but an observer, not a full-member of COMECON). In the most important East European countries these tendencies appeared in various forms, different intensity and with differing results.

Individual Prerequisites

In consequence of the political thaw the European industrial nations' Eastern trade increased constantly. Regarding this trend, apart from economic aspects, strong political motives were doubtlessly decisive, thus e.g. the influence of de Gaulle's European policy or the Federal Republic's concentrated efforts for an agreement with the East-bloc.

Of course, the change of the political climate has not been without influence on the Austrian Eastern trade, but its longer-term and more constant development is based on individual prerequisites. As shown by Table 1, from 1958 to 1966 it has only about doubled as compared with the stronger trade expansion of the EEC countries.

Table 1.
Development of Austria's and the EEC's East-West Trade

Year	Imports in Million $			Exports in Million $		
	Austria	EEC	Including Fed. Rep.*	Austria	EEC	Including Fed. Rep.*
1958	133.6	677.7	266.6	140.7	625.7	277.3
1959	149.5	823.3	323.2	156.2	710.7	314.2
1960	186.5	975.0	380.5	196.7	991.9	440.3
1961	178.5	1,077.3	412.5	211.1	1,098.5	476.4
1962	196.8	1,201.8	472.2	221.5	1,170.5	504.2
1963	233.7	1,362.8	453.2	232.7	1,079.7	438.6
1964	227.7	1,359.5	486.7	253.5	1,212.6	551.2
1965	259.0	1,572.9	589.2	285.2	1,416.0	587.7
1966	277.1	1,797.0	650.4	302.9	1,670.8	695.8

*Without interzonal trade.

Sources: Austrian Statistical Central Office and Statistical Office of the EEC.

Three components are influencing the development of Austria's Eastern trade: a historical one, a geographical one and one pertaining to international law. From the times of the Austrian-Hungarian monarchy–although five decades have passed since its dissolution–stronger traditional ties are still existing with those socialist countries, that, completely or in part, had belonged to this monarchy. This applies above all to the Danubian states Jugoslavia, Czechoslovakia and Hungary. These traditional relations are human ones, family bonds, but also cultural and economic ones. They are being promoted by the geographical position of Austria, that, politically and according to its conception of the world belonging to the West, in a way bridges the ditch between East and West. This function is facilitated politically by the country's voluntary status of unceasing political neu-

Reprinted with permission from *Intereconomics,* No. 5, (May 1968), pp. 146-149.

trality. As regards Austria's particular relation to the USSR there is the additional fact that this country as an occupation power and co-signatory of the Austrian State Treaty of 1953 to a large extent has influenced Austria's development after the last war.

Although these three components give Austria's relations to the East European socialist countries their peculiar character, on the other hand their influence should not be overestimated. For, when all is said and done, it is economic realities and the trade-political advantages offered–which Austria makes every effort to accomplish–that are decisive for trade relations between two countries.

Growing Importance of East-West Trade

In Austrian foreign trade business with the East-bloc plays a much more important part than in all other Western countries. Comparable relations are to be found only in Iceland, Finland and Greece. In 1966 all industrial nations' foreign trade with the East-bloc amounted to about 3 per cent, that of the West European states to about 4 per cent of their total foreign trade volume, while in the same year for Austria this proportion was 11.5 per cent with imports and 17.7 per cent with exports. To make a comparison possible, it should be mentioned that 1966 Austria's trade with the other EFTA states amounted to 15.9 per cent in imports and 20.1 per cent in exports. It is quite obvious that Austria's trade policy makes allowance for these facts all the more since the country's progressing discrimination by the Common Market, with which Austria carries through more than half of its foreign trade, enforces a change-over to other markets. In the first half of 1967 Austria's exports to the Common Market proportionally decreased from 46.5 per cent to 41.6 per cent, those to the Federal Republic from 27.9 per cent to 21.5 per cent even. However, a considerable expansion of Austrian trade with the East-bloc is impeded by the same obstructions as met by the other Western nations, i.e. above all bilateral transactions, which are made allowance for also by the trade and payments agrements with East-bloc countries. The individual countries' share in the total volume of Austria's Eastern trade in 1966 is shown by Table 2.

Most liberalised are of course trade relations with Jugoslavia, with which, as a full-member of GATT, practically the same trade-political relations are existing as with other developing countries belonging to GATT. Goods and payment transactions are contractually regulated since 1948. Austria applies GATT liberalisation and GATT preferential tariffs vis-à-vis Jugoslavia and this country in return grants the minimum rates of its customs tariff, that already now is employed in its traditional function. Payments are made in Austrian shillings or other freely convertible currencies.

Table 2.
Individual Countries' Share in Austrian East-West Trade

Country	Imports	Exports
	In Million Austrian Shillings	
East Germany	652	791
Bulgaria	431	648
Poland	1,105	922
Rumania	432	677
CSSR	912	1,145
Hungary	982	1,012
USSR	1,268	1,542
Total of COMECON States	5,782	6,737
Jugoslavia	1,167	998
Albania	14	4
China	239	121

Source: Manual of Austrian East-West Trade, 1967.

Trade Agreements and Payment Transactions

Bilateral long-term agreements (in most cases covering 5 years) which are renewed at any given time, are existing with all COMECON countries. For reasons pertaining to international law in the case of East Germany the partner is not Austria but the Federal Chamber of Industry and Commerce. Trade in products is wound up on the basis of quota lists, if it is not a question of import goods liberalised by Austria. Payments transactions are carried through by way of bilateral clearing in clearing dollars via accounts kept with the Austrian National Bank (for East Germany with the semi-official Control Bank) and with the Central Banks of the partner countries involved. Payment transactions are taken care of by the commercial banks. The Central Banks grant each other technical credits ("swings") up to the maximum amounts as fixed in each case. This is done in order to avoid in this bilateral payment system a longer-term blocking of goods trade caused by the indebtedness of one of the partners. The socialist countries' demand for goods and the difficulty of placing sufficient quantities of products supplied by the East-bloc lead to the result that globally the clearing accounts are permanently showing Austria's strong creditor position, although the individual East-bloc countries' positions are frequently exposed to considerable fluctuations (Table 3).

Table 3.
State of Accounts as per December 31, 1967
(in 1,000 clearing dollars)

Country	Dec. 31, 1967	Swing
Bulgaria	+ 284	1,500
Poland	+2,182	3,000
Rumania	+1,353	1,500
USSR	+2,670	5,000
CSSR	−2,475	3,500
Hungary	+1,507	2,500
Eastern Germany	+ 750	3,300

+ = Austria's claim. – = Austria's debts.

The unilateral de facto liberalisations vis-à-vis Czechoslovakia, Poland and Hungary are advances made in the hope that with a progressing easing of economic policy in these countries, counter-considerations will become possible some time. True, this exemption from any quantitative limitation of imports does not constitute a true bilateralisation e.g. as applies to imports from OECD countries. What takes place is a licencing after a previous examination, above all of prices, thus being similar to the different formalities of the import system used in the other West European states. This price control proves to be necessary in view of the volume of the quasi-liberalised imports from the four countries in order to avoid serious market distortions caused by low-priced foreign products. To what extent this main reason for licencing will cease to exist, if in the course of economic reforms also the East-bloc countries will work with comparative costs and thus with true export prices, of course cannot be predicted at all today.

The operation of the licencing system is sufficiently informal and short-term, and this way does not effect a delay of the flow of goods. The level of quasi-liberalisation is about the same as the West European one, with Poland it amounts to 70 per cent, with Czechoslovakia and Hungary to 66 per cent in each case.

Little Interest in Barter Transactions

Apart from clearing transactions the barter and package deals as formerly practised frequently in business with the East-bloc have declined much, although Eastern partners like to force them by giving that Austrian supplier the preference over others, who is in a position to link up at least part of his supplies with return deliveries. This attitude is caused by the partner's wish to save foreign exchange used for clearing transactions. Austria, however, is little interested in these business transactions, since they are quite problematical for the import market and do not improve the partner's chronic debtor position. They remain essentially confined to such large-scale skeleton transactions as e.g. are carried through by VOEST in its steel deliveries to the Soviet Union in order to receive regularly iron ores in return. More frequent is the form of package deals in the so-called "switch," in which the placing of import goods in the domestic market or in a third country will be made easier as regards pricing by a premium to be paid by the exporter. There exist the most differing variants: in case the export goods originated from a third country—and these must be paid in freely convertible foreign exchange, while they yields only clearing dollars—the Austrian National Bank itself imposes the requirement of a switch-premium.

Austria's position at the line of intersection between East and West predestinates this country to act as intermediary for the export oriented economy of the West. It is therefore understandable that the transit trade via Austria plays a major part. Moreover, in Austria the West itself is establishing points of contact with the East. It is quite significant that recently also the Chase Manhattan Bank established itself in Vienna by purchasing the majority of a Vienna commercial bank in order from here to provide its American clients with information on trends and chances of business with the East-bloc. Vice versa the Hungarian economist, Professor Bognar, recently suggested the establishment of an East-West bank in Vienna. This city also plays a major role as a market for free trade with Eastern currencies, and the turn-over of East-bloc currencies, above all for tourists, is estimated to amount annually to 50 million Austrian shillings.

No Model for the West

If now, considering everything that has been stated above, the question arises whether Austria's East-bloc trade would be a suitable model for the Federal Republic of Germany and other EEC countries, too, this question should be answered in the negative. For one thing, the prerequisites to the relatively large share of business with the East-bloc in Austria's total foreign trade are quite particular ones and cannot be transferred to other circumstances. For another, although the applied clearing system is rather expedient in the present situation, it nevertheless opposes the general endeavours aiming at a worldwide multilaterality of trade, into which the East-bloc countries are supposed to be integrated. Its acceptance by other Western countries would be a step backward. The realisation, however, that only the best possible opening up of one's own market to goods from the East-bloc creates the prerequisites to the expansion of one's own deliveries to this area, has become common knowledge in the West. This is proved by the EEC countries' progressing efforts for liberalisation vis-à-vis the East-bloc. For the rest also the chances of Austria's Eastern trade should not be overestimated too much. The general obstructions impeding an expansion of East-West trade are of course valid for Austria, too. The future development of this trade does certainly not only depend on the West's continuing the elimination of all differences between trade with the East and that with other countries, but also on the problem to what extent the East-bloc will meet the West halfway by a gradual adjustment of its foreign trade practices to those of the West.

East-West Trade

Economic Research Division, Chase Manhattan Bank

The question of expanding trade relations between the centrally-planned economies of Eastern Europe and the market economies of North America, Western Europe and Japan has generated considerable interest, as evidenced by the frequent Congressional hearings. This report examines the past importance of such trade and considers the possibilities for, and obstacles to, its future growth.

Although the volume of East-West trade remains a relatively small part of total world trade, its growth has picked up significantly in recent years. West Germany, Britain and Japan have been particularly successful in expanding their trade with the East. And, while the Eastern countries are anxious to enlarge their imports from the West, especially of capital equipment, such trade is held back not only by the U.S. Government's export restrictions, but also by the limited ability of the Eastern European countries to earn sufficient foreign exchange to pay for those imports that are available from the West. The trade expansion that has taken place up to now reflects, to a large extent, modifications in the economic controls of some of the Eastern economies; further loosening of controls would likely expand trade even more.

The volume of trade between the countries of Eastern Europe (Soviet Union, Bulgaria, Czechoslovakia, East Germany, Hungary, Poland and Rumania) and the rest of the world has more than doubled in the last decade. This is a faster growth than either trade within the Communist countries themselves or trade among the Western countries. Still, such trade, totaling some $13 billion in 1966, accounts for only 4-1/2% of the world total, compared with 16% generated by the United States alone, and 18% by the European Common Market.

Significance for the East

For the Communist countries, trade with the West is of secondary importance, although by no means insignificant. Imports from the industrial countries of the West comprise about 20% of the East's total imports and are an important supplement to domestic production. The pattern of trade is still basically that of Communist imports of machinery and, when necessary, of food, in exchange for exports of raw materials, fruits and semi-manufactures. The Soviet Union is the largest trading partner with the West, accounting for over 40% of the Communist countries' exports and about 30% of their imports from the developed countries of the West (i.e., those specified in the accompanying charts). Its total trade with these countries exceeded $3 billion in 1966. East Germany and Poland also maintain a large trade volume with the West, exceeding $1 billion for each country.

Still, the intra-regional trade pattern that was forced on Eastern Europe at the end of the Second World War remains the basis of trade for this region, with the exception of Yugoslavia. The Soviet Union has made considerable efforts to strengthen its economic ties with the other members of the Council of Mutual Economic Assistance, better known as COMECON. It entered into a number of extensive agreements on bilateral economic cooperation, including extension of industrial credits, gold and foreign exchange loans, and bilateral trade pacts that are mainly formalized barter arrangements for balanced trade.

These efforts were eased somewhat in 1963 by a system of regional payments on the basis of "transferable rubles" that were linked to gold or convertible currencies and by the establishment of an International Bank for Economic Cooperation. As a result, the other Communist countries are to a very limited extent brought on to the gold and dollar standard of trade in the world market and made slightly less dependent on bilateral trade with the Soviet Union.

Indeed, it appears that the effectiveness of efforts to direct the trade of the other Eastern European countries to the Soviet economy may have passed its peak. Rumania, in particular, has shown signs of opposition to gearing its economy to specialized fields of economic activity, such as raw materials production, that are required by the Soviet Union. Thus, Rumania and other Communist countries are slowly looking Westward for trade relations. The result has been their signing of a few commercial agreements with the West that would have been unthinkable only a few years ago.

Although in this report Yugoslavia is not included among the other Eastern European countries because of its closer ties with the West (as seen by its membership in GATT), an account of its recent trends may be in order. Two major differences separate Yugoslav trade from that of the COMECON countries. For one thing, trade with the Western countries

Reprinted from *World Business*, January 1968; published by the Economics Research Division, The Chase Manhattan Bank, N.A.

represents a major part of Yugoslavia's total foreign trade: 64% of its exports and 62% of its imports in 1966. Trade with the European Common Market in particular has been growing rapidly, with imports in 1966 up 23% and exports up 24%. Another difference is that industrial products hold the foremost place in Yugoslavia's trade, accounting for 82% of all exports and 84% of imports.

Significance for the West

For the industrial countries of the West, trade with Eastern Europe is generally of marginal importance, ranging between 2%-6% of their total foreign trade. This trade is thus much less significant to the Western than to the Eastern countries. The United States is the least involved in East-West trade. Germany is by far the largest Western trader with the East, with its Eastern trade accounting for 17% of the West's trade with Eastern Europe.

The growth of East-West trade between 1960-66 is marked by a tenfold increase in Canadian exports, a result of heavy wheat sales to the Soviet Union. Japanese exports rose over fourfold, from $63 million to $274 million, as Japan continues to penetrate the Soviet market. Italy doubled its exports to the East, while other substantial gains were made by Germany and France. In the first half of 1967, West Germany's exports to Eastern Europe (excluding East Germany) rose by 42%, reflecting the accelerated German export drive to the Eastern markets in response to a recession in the internal German market.

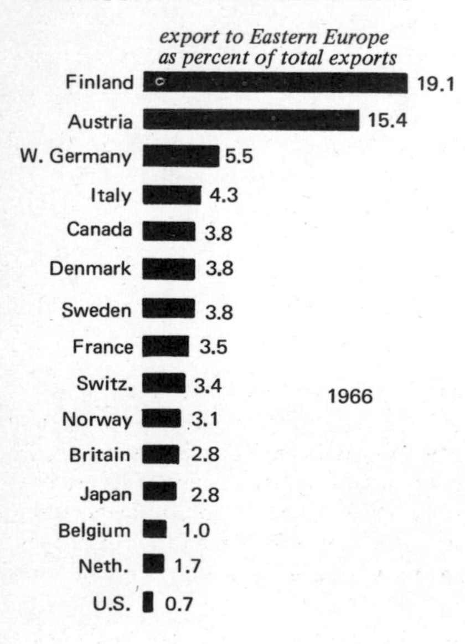

Source: OECD

U.S. Trade with East Europe

U.S. trade with the Eastern European countries is very small. For the United States, this trade represents only 0.7% of its total foreign commerce. For Eastern Europe, such trade accounts for 4.7% of its trade with the 15 developed countries of the West. During the sixties, the United States has consistently experienced a surplus in its trade with the East, although this has narrowed recently.

U.S. exports to Eastern Europe have averaged between $100-$200 million annually since 1959, excluding 1964 when wheat sales to the Soviet Union boosted the total to $340 million. No upward trend is evident in U.S. exports, although sales to Czechoslovakia and Rumania, while still relatively small, have been picking up steadily since 1962. Indeed, Czechoslovakia is now the third largest Eastern European purchaser of U.S. goods, behind Poland and the Soviet Union. Roughly two thirds of these U.S. exports consist of food and raw materials and the remainder are manufactured products. Of the latter, shipments of nonelectric machinery have been increasing rapidly—more than doubling in 1966 alone.

U.S. imports from Eastern Europe are divided into food and raw materials (40%), metals (30%) and manufactures (30%). Total imports have been rising steadily since 1962, especially of meat products and iron and steel. The 23% average annual import increase between 1962-66 was shared by most Eastern European countries, although Poland, the Soviet Union and Czechoslovakia still account for some 90% of the region's sales to the United States.

The prospects for a substantial expansion of U.S. trade with Eastern Europe are not good. In addition to the economic obstacles affecting overall East-West trade that are discussed in the next section, many people in the United States are in opposition to this trade on grounds of ideology and national security. In

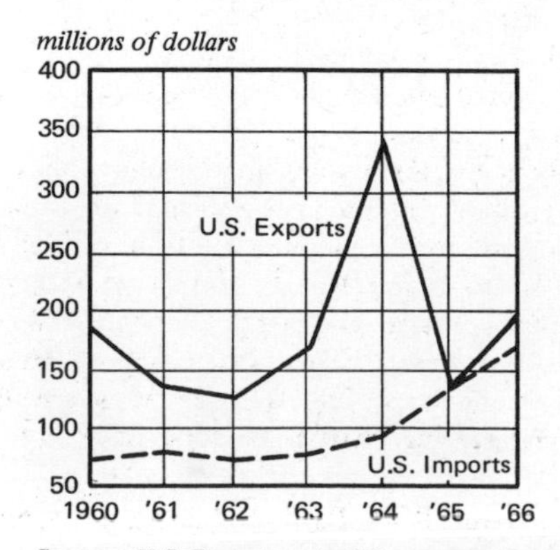

Source: U.S. Department of Commerce

contrast to most Western European governments, the U.S. Government has a more extensive embargo on strategic goods to Communist countries, stricter export controls and does not give these countries most-favored-nation treatment in its tariff reductions. Further, it enforces a stricter credit control policy on government participation in and guaranteeing of private commercial credits to any Communist country.

To some extent, trade figures do not give a total picture of U.S.-East European trade. Some U.S. companies are selling to Communist countries through their foreign subsidiaries in order to take advantage of lower transportation costs or of more lenient credit conditions in trade with Eastern Europe available in some Western European countries. Although it is not possible to quantify the extent of these sales from subsidiaries, it is generally believed that they are quite small, but growing steadily.

Question of Payment

Significant economic obstacles, aside from political considerations, have prevented the volume of East-West trade from rising substantially above its relatively low level. It may be convenient to separate those obstacles into those related to the East's ability to pay for imports from the West and those stemming from the way the Eastern European countries conduct this trade, although both factors are obviously interrelated.

As the Communist demand for Western capital goods increases, so have the pressures to find the means to pay for these imports. Either the Eastern countries must expand their exports to the West, enlarge their gold sales, or obtain increased access to suppliers' and other credits. The Communist countries, however, have found considerable difficulties in enlarging their exports to the West, either because the quality of their products is inferior and does not conform to Western specifications, or the type of goods they offer has limited potential for expansion—wood, coal, iron ore and cotton. To be sure, Eastern Europe's oil exports have been growing continuously and now account for about 10% of Western Europe's oil imports. Nevertheless, the spectrum of Communist exports remains limited.

The Soviet Union, in particular, has a problem of financing its large import volume. Although it has an overall trade surplus with the Western European countries, nearly all of this goes to finance its trade deficits with Canada, Australia, New Zealand and the less developed countries of Asia, as well as to pay foreign shipping charges. This leaves little margin for overall import growth, and when unexpectedly large foreign purchases are required, the Soviet Union has been forced to draw down its gold reserves and obtain credits from Western countries.

The foreign exchange reserves of the Eastern European countries are considered to be at a minimum "consistent with maneuverability in foreign trade." If temporary financial difficulties arise because of a shortage of funds, these countries can make limited use of the loan facilities of the Soviet-controlled banks in London and Paris, as well as the normal commercial credit facilities available for six months from Western banks.

Western credits to the Communist countries have primarily taken the form of credits extended by Western firms that export capital goods to the East. These suppliers' credits are normally granted through local banking institutions and are usually guaranteed or insured by government-supported export credit insurance organizations in the exporter's country.

During the last few years, the Common Market countries, Britain and Japan have been granting more and longer export credits. In the last three years, more than 500 deals worth over $2 billion have been financed in the Common Market alone by export credits extended longer than five years, with France, Belgium, Italy and the Netherlands often extending credits for 10 years and more. The result is that Eastern Europe has received some 25% of the Common Market's total long-term export credits, and this has helped stimulate the growth in the Common Market's exports to the East.

How Trade Is Conducted

Growth of East-West trade has been held back by the way Soviet bloc countries conduct foreign trade. Like other important economic activities, foreign trade is centrally directed and subject to national economic planning. The trade components of the national economic plan are the export and import plans and the foreign exchange plan. However, production shortfalls, such as of Soviet grain, and political tensions within the Communist countries have in the past caused actual trade results to differ markedly from the plans. In addition, plans are usually transmitted to the respective foreign trade organizations connected with the various industrial ministries and it is these organizations that do the trading, not a prospective supplier or user.

In general, imports are mainly required to cover what planners consider to be national deficiencies, and exports to pay for these imports. The lack of a market orientation to trade plus the bureaucratic problems that frequently arise from the rigidly run state-trading monopolies restrict the volume of trade as well as distort its pattern and composition.

The absence of convertible currencies in Eastern Europe necessitates a bilateral pattern of trade, where the total trade volume is limited by the country with the smaller exports. This contrasts with the multilateral basis of trade in the Western world, where a surplus

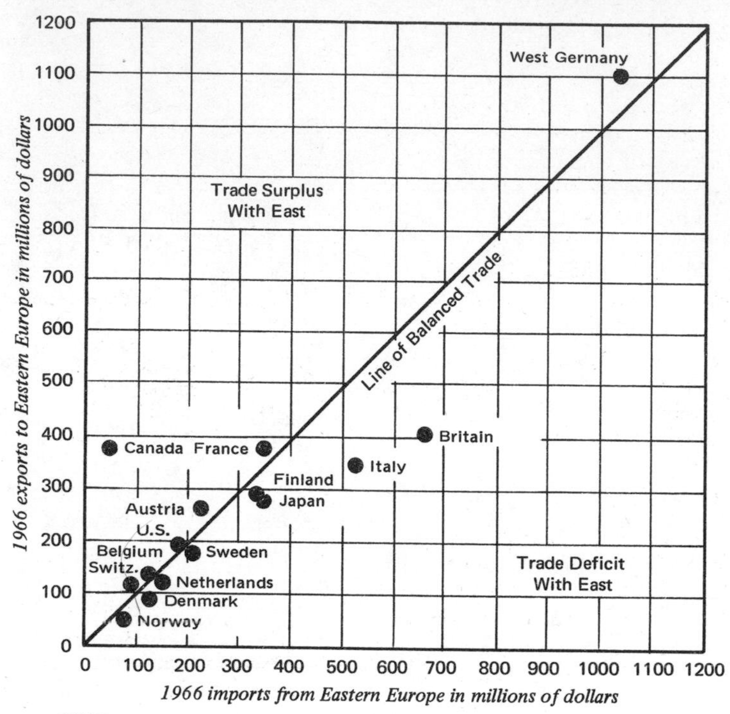

Source: OECD

with one country can be used to cover a deficit with another, so that there is no necessity to balance trade with each country. In addition to restricting the type of goods that a country can purchase, bilateral trade often involves inflated sales prices and the shipment of low quality goods.

The Communist countries have formalized this bilateral pattern, which in theory fits well into their system of planning, by using bilateral commercial treaties and agreements to cover the exchange of goods and the regulation of payments. Since it is recognized that Western markets may not be willing to absorb the commodities the plan requires, the state-trading companies are allowed a wider latitude in dealing with non-Communist countries than with the Communist ones.

A number of the agreements, particularly with the more industrialized countries, specify that payments shall be effected in convertible currency. Others are conducted on the basis of clearing accounts or barter arrangements designed to eliminate, or at least to minimize, the need for settlements in hard currency.

Signs of Easing

Although economic obstacles to trade remain strong, the last few years have witnessed some signs of easing—and this has partly resulted in the recent expansion of East-West trade. In particular, the quotas on goods which can be purchased under bilateral trade agreements have been widened considerably and given a liberal interpretation. Also, some of the Communist countries are allowing greater contacts between local firms and foreign businessmen, thus by-passing the central planners who are often unaware of the possibilities of the outside market. As a result, European manufactures are beginning to purchase goods directly from Western suppliers, instead of through the state-trading organizations.

There is little doubt that as a result of ambitious industrialization programs, there exists in Eastern Europe a large demand for products and technology that cannot be satisfied from Communist sources of supply. This is leading to more concern for exports and, as a result, to a recognition of the need to improve product quality and use resources more effectively.

Another change in policy is the growing concern of the Communist governments to raise living standards, which are still considerably below those of Western Europe. As these governments become more responsive to consumer requirements, product prices become more related to costs of production and consumer goods imports, ranging from automobiles to bowling alleys, are beginning to be bought from the West. Indeed, the Eastern European countries are increasingly buying complete factories from the West. The

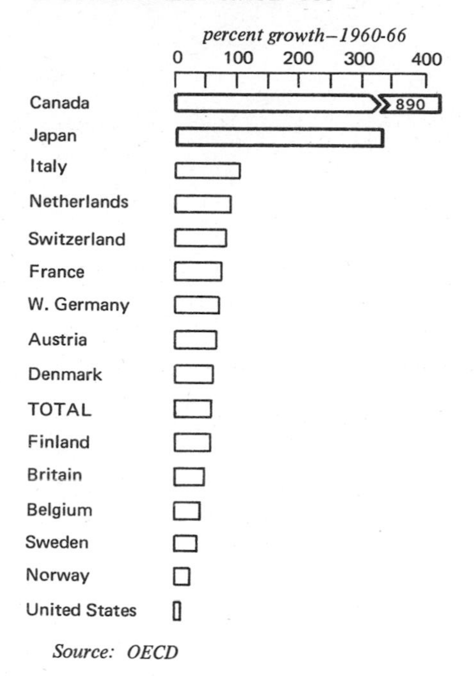

Western firms that put up these facilities often train the staff to operate them and help in the marketing of the finished products in the West.

Because of the shortage of foreign exchange in the Eastern European countries, Western firms have utilized various sales techniques to penetrate this market. In many cases, they offer credit terms of 8-15 years on multi-million dollar orders. Some Western sellers are willing to accept local goods as part payment for goods sold.

All the countries of Eastern Europe are attempting to increase their exports in varying degrees through "parallel trade"—a form of barter. Parallel trade is not a direct exchange of two commodities, but an agreement made by a Western seller to buy from an Eastern country the equivalent, or a fraction, of the worth of his exports. These offers to take part of the payment in goods vary from country to country and from deal to deal. At times, parallel transactions take the form of joint ventures, where the Western firm takes some the output of a plant as all or part payment for the sale of that plant. Another form is switch transactions, which are similar to parallel trade, but more complicated since they involve three or more countries.

A recent technique of Western firms to penetrate the Communist market has been the creation of joint ventures between Western companies and a ministry, foreign trade organization, or manufacturing enterprise in a Communist country. Usually, the joint venture provides for a subcontracting arrangement in which the Western firm agrees to buy on a long-range basis certain products, components or finished goods that are manufactured in an Eastern country. The Western firm provides some technical knowhow or some of the machinery necessary to produce the goods.

Future of East-West Trade

In the final analysis, the future volume and direction of East-West trade will be determined by the policies of governments, of both the East and the West. On economic grounds, two opposing cases can be made. The pessimist see Eastern Europe as still being dominated by concern for national self-sufficiency. If so, imports are needed only to fill the gaps in national production, and no substantial trade expansion can be expected. The optimists see a fundamental shift taking place in Communist trade philosophy, with a recognition that imports are desirable even if there is domestic output, provided the imports are cheaper. If so, Eastern Europe may try to break out of its bilateral trade pattern and, with this region regarded as one of the last large undeveloped markets, the future for East-West trade would be bright.

Although the reality is probably somewhere in between, there is really no way of judging which side will be the closest. As much depends on emerging political attitudes as on future economic circumstances.

Chapter 4

EAST-WEST TRADE AND AMERICAN BUSINESS

An Economic Profile of Eastern Europe

Karel Holbik

The following survey indicates the principal differences between the Soviet bloc economies, comments on these nations' recent economic policies, and assesses the role played in regional economic relations by the Council for Mutual Economic Assistance (COMECON). The article contains general background information for the more specific selections on East-West Trade.

For the past two decades Soviet influence throughout Eastern Europe has given the region the appearance of an international unit, especially in political relations. However, in fact, these countries, i.e., Bulgaria (BG), Czechoslovakia (CZ), East Germany (EG), Hungary (HU), Poland (PL), Romania (RO), and the U.S.S.R., differ conspicuously, as the outside world has also come to conclude from the growing centrifugal nationalism alone. Differences among these nations exist in terms of history, political development prior to World War II, cultural background, and economic potentialities. (Yugoslavia is excluded from Eastern Europe since she is not a COMECON member. Neither is Albania.)

As regards international trade and economic cooperation, to lump the East European countries together is not only unrealistic, but also contrary to their own appraisal of existing conditions. Neither does the attempt to divide them into two groups, the northern group including East Germany, Czechoslovakia and Poland, and the southern group incorporating Hungary, Romania and Bulgaria—with the Soviet Union holding a separate position—do justice to what unites and disunites the area. Again, recent years have supplied much evidence to support the contention that an economic cohesion of all these countries is an unattainable goal.

COMECON Trade in Perspective

In any appraisal of the economic dimensions of Eastern Europe as a whole, one must take into account the region's aggregate population which totals 336 million. In comparison, the population of both the West European EEC (the Common Market) and EFTA areas amounts to 275 million. But while the share in world trade of the two latter groups of nations exceeds 45 percent, the East European share comes only to 10 percent, of which two-thirds represent intra-Soviet bloc trade. Nevertheless, the COMECON countries turn out about one-third of the world's total industrial goods.

It is estimated that East European per capita annual exports average $55, whereas the industrialized West's average is five times as large. Responsible for this remarkable discrepancy are doubtless several East European administrative factors, such as central planning, bilateralism and foreign trade monopolies as well as—and primarily—the scarcity of exportable, competitive goods.

In 1965, 20.6 percent of East European exports were sold to Western industrialized nations while 21.4 percent of imports were purchased there. Ten years ago, in 1955, the former percentage was only 8.8, the latter 16.3. Because during the intervening decade East Europe's commercial relations with the West kept pace with the expansion of COMECON's overall foreign trade, during the period 1955-60 the region's Western exports rose at the annual rate of 62 percent and its imports at the rate of 77 percent. In the subsequent five years, 1961-65, the growth rates were, respectively, 51 percent and 40 percent. Still, the aggregate foreign trade of the COMECON nations has exceeded only slightly that of West Germany alone, which has but one-fifth of East Europe's population.

Table 1.

Selected Ingredients of East European Economies, 1965

	Population in millions	Imports*	Exports*	Steel Production†	Steel Consumption Per Capita‡	Electric Power Generation#
BG	8.2	1,178	1,179	588	152	10.2
CZ	14.5	2,267	2,689	8,598	524	34.2
EG	17.0	2,546	2,776	3,890	439	53.5
HU	10.2	1,521	1,510	2,520	220	11.2
PL	32.7	2,340	2,228	9,088	271	43.8
RO	19.0	1,077	1,102	3,426	206	17.2
USSR	234.4	8,053	8,166	91,021	376	507.0

*in millions of dollars.
†in thousands of metric tons.
‡in kilograms.
#in billions of kWh.

A Comparison of the East European Economies

Apart from the well-known differences between the land areas of the seven countries, which are, of course, of substantial and undeniable economic importance, the differences chosen here for exposition are contained in Table 1. These as well as the other differentials presented in subsequent tables[1] have prevented the countries under Soviet influence from achieving economic, and to some extent, political consolidation. In fact, they have caused frictions between their national interests, which have, in turn, hampered intra-regional cooperation.

In terms of East European calculations, per capita national incomes of the COMECON countries compared in 1964 as indicated in Table 2. Actual observation confirms that the present economic conditions of East Germany and Czechoslovakia are indeed strikingly superior to those of Bulgaria and Romania.

As is to be expected, these monetary incomes have been reflected in the comparative standards of living and purchasing power of the peoples concerned. Although it is almost impossible to determine and compare the impact exerted on real incomes of these individual command economies by differing government incomes and price policies, the institutionalized "rationing of the purse," the end result of both these nations' productive capabilities and government policies is brought into view in Table 3. This shows the

[1]The statistical information used in this paper is based on the *U.N. Yearbook 1966*, the London *Economist*, East European newspapers, and the Swiss *Neue Zürcher Zeitung*. Additional complementary statistics appear in *Soviet Economic Performance 1966-67*, U.S. Congress, Joint Economic Committee, Washington, D.C.: U.S. Government Printing Office, 1968, esp. pp. 117-123.

Table 2.

Per Capita National Incomes, 1964

	In U.S. Dollars	Index, USSR = 100
BG	469	74
CZ	813	130
EG	844	134
HU	513	81
PL	498	79
RO	423	67
USSR	630	100

Source: *Zahraniční obchod* (Foreign Trade), Prague.

Note: The London *Economist* (May 13, 1967) arrived at the following figures for the 1963 GNP per capita: BG, $690; CZ, $1470; EG, $1400; HU, $1020; PL, $890; RO, $680. The analogous figures for the USA, West Germany and Italy were $3000, $1980 and $1140, respectively.

Table 3.

Ownership of Consumer Durable Goods
(Percent of families)

	CZ	EG	HU	PL
Radios	99	92	87	50
TV Sets	33	38	17	14
Washing Machines	58	18	46	28
Refrigerators	17	16	4	5
Autos	4	n.a.	2	2
Motorcycles	15	n.a.	12	13
Telephones	36	21	10	4
Sewing Machines	70	n.a.	46	19

percentage of Czech, East German, Hungarian and Polish families which own certain consumer durable goods.

These facts, disguising, to be sure, various degrees of repressed consumption, are not revealed in the usually impressive indices of industrial production and economic growth. Table 4 is focused on the former which must, of course, be taken into account in any prospective external economic contacts with the area. In their long-term plans, East European governments have given priority to the engineering and chemical industries.

Table 4.

Industrial Indices for 1965
(1960 = 100)

	Gross Industrial Production	1964-65 Increments	Engineering Industry	Chemical Industry
BG	173	13.7%	228	222
CZ	128	7.9%	135	168
EG	132	6.1%	147	147
HU	147	5.0%	165	221
PL	151	9.1%	195	189
RO	192	13.1%	228	305
USSR	151	8.6%	178	216

Clearly, the productive efforts of the less developed countries in the East European region, e.g. Bulgaria and Romania, which are determined to industrialize and catch up with the more advanced nations, finds expression in the above indices. On the other hand, agricultural outputs have not been able to register comparable achievements and complaints about production lags have been common throughout most of this region.

With regard to a comparison of the industrial origin of the COMECON countries' net material product, the 1964 statistics, shown in Table 5, leave no doubt about the economic contrasts between the industrialized North and the less industrialized South—despite unquestionable strides achieved since World War II by the latter group of nations.

Finally, the exhibited differences in the structure and performance of the East European economies may be also traced to their per capita foreign trade turnovers indicated in Table 6 and given in roubles since the rouble is the unit of account in East European commerical and financial relations.

On the basis on the preceding quantitative evidence it is reasonable to conclude that each of the seven COMECON countries has its economic individuality with some positive and some negative aspects.

Table 6.

Foreign Trade Turnover Per Capita,
1950 and 1965
(In roubles)

	1950	1965
BG	31	229
CZ	103	338
EG	43	312
HU	62	265
PL	47	130
RO	25	103
USSR	16	63

Table 5.

Industrial Origin of Net Material Product

	BG	CZ	EG	HU	PL	RO
Agriculture Fishing and Forestry	34	14	11	21	23	30
Mining & Manufacturing	45	64	72	63	51	48
Construction	7	9	6	10	9	8
Transport & Communications	4	3	6	4.5	6	4
Trade	8	9	14	0.5	10	7
Other	2	1	1	1	2	3
Total	100%	100%	100%	100%	100%	100%
Adjustment for double counting			-10%			

Economic Policies in the Shadow of Liberalization

The inability of the U.S.S.R. to give Eastern Europe the desired economic shape, and the difficulties which the harmonization of those countries' production and trade policies has encountered, have favored and to a degree encouraged reassertion of their national economic interests and sovereignties. East European economic integration (in many ways different from the West European integration schemes) has not succeeded, partly because the southern countries have accused COMECON of slowing down their industrialization. The northern nations have been more ready to accept this organization's original objectives.

Tentative, experimental attempts to liberalize the economic systems through internal market reforms have been made in all East European countries, except Romania.

This economic liberalization has meant giving new importance to market forces on the one hand, and modifying central planning on the other hand. These moderate economic reforms–perhaps more appropriately called administrative reforms–have generally foreseen a relaxation of price regulations, reintroduction of the profit motive, and along with it, recognition of the other factor prices, i.e., interest and rent. In sum, a new system of economic management has been sought, in which incentives to firms are expected to play a new constructive part and cost efficiency is properly valued.

These changes have led Eastern European policy makers to realize that the necessary economic modernization and coveted progress call for the employment, and therefore, importation of sophisticated Western equipment and technology. Thus the East European decision to facilitate and promote commercial relations with West European and other "capitalist" countries has been a rational and purposeful one. So have been the West German, British, Italian and other responses.

Bulgaria, although heavily dependent on the Soviet Union, has introduced a new economic model, and while retaining centrally fixed prices, is about to inaugurate a new price system to include also semi-controlled and free (market) prices. The nation's export drive appears to be successful due to both Western import liberalization and Bulgarian efforts to promote exports of qualitatively superior goods.

Czechoslovakia's reformist policies, inoperative without a new political leadership, have caused not only an internal political crisis, but also an open conflict with the U.S.S.R. Doubtless the Soviets appreciate that a greater degree of independence for the Czechoslovaks spells danger for Communist objectives in the region. Because of the burden of domestic economic and political rigidities, tantamount to developmental bottlenecks, Czechoslovakia's liberalization has not proceeded without interruption; it has, in fact, brought about inflationary pressures. These must be explained by a number of factors among which higher prices, which some industries have been allowed to charge, and obsolescent productive plant loom largest. Disinflationary policies have made it mandatory for the government to revise economic planning, to reduce investment, and to absorb the public's liquid means through a sale of bonds.

Like other Eastern European countries, Czechoslavakia wishes to expand its trade with the West in order to secure both up-to-date industrial equipment, and to earn hard currencies.

East Germany's economic reform has been carried out very slowly and cautiously, as behooves the country's Stalinist leadership. Adoption of new methods of business management and implementation of the latest technological inventions appear to have succeeded in raising East German productivity, especially in the fastest growing electronic and chemical industries. Expanding industrial output made it also possible for the East Germans to increase trade with the other East European nations, and with the Soviet Union in particular. (The entire region accounts for 75 percent, the U.S.S.R., alone, for 40 percent of East German exports.)

Hungary's new economic model resembles Czechoslovakia's and centers on the internal price structure. As a result, new room has been created for the interaction between supply and demand, and government subsidization of industrial enterprises (whose losses it used to underwrite) has been restricted. It is difficult to say whether the latter policy has been satisfactory since there are signs that to some extent, it may have depressed industrial production.

The Hungarians have also liberalized foreign trade but here, too, some obstacles have to be overcome. There are reasons to doubt that Hungary's intensive trade with the U.S.S.R. is a blissful boon because it does not seem to help the country to correct its uncomfortable international trade deficit. The latter is especially responsive to decreases in exports to the West. On the whole, Hungary's weak economy is in need of stronger measures than the latter-day economic reforms.

Poland seems to shy away from liberalizing economic reforms, apparently unwilling to take the political and economic risks which such a policy unavoidably entails. While clinging to central planning, the Poles have successfully promoted their Western trade, especially with the Common Market countries. They have fostered industrial exports, e.g. tools and machinery, but have been unable to reduce the country's balance of trade deficit, in part because of the continued need to import agricultural commodities. Many observers have concluded that the

Polish economy should undergo more radical changes than are those aimed at by the new economic models. Poland's relatively low standard of living is considered to be a multifarious economic hurdle.

Romania has impressed the Western world and some of its East European neighbors by bold international-economic and political moves in which national independence was emphasized. However, in domestic politics and economics the Rumanians continue to adhere to "orthodox" centralism. This has not prevented them from seeking contacts with the West as the promising supplier of advanced technology essential to Romania's economic modernization. West Germany, Italy, the United Kingdom and others have been attracted by Rumanian trade and investment opportunities, and have, in fact, been prepared to compete for them.

Yet the opening of its windows to the West has not interfered with Romania's further solidification of Eastern ties. The country's nationalistic outlook notwithstanding, its cooperation with the Soviets cannot be weakened as the Rumanians depend on the U.S.S.R. for some valuable raw materials, such as iron ore and coke.

In conformity with its determination to pursue policies leading to rapid increases in productivity and output, the *Soviet Union* has also carried out certain economic, or rather administrative, reforms. While rejecting "market socialism," it has heeded Professor Liberman's "new" thesis about the close relationship between profits and efficient production. Interestingly, the provisional 1966-70 long-term economic plan has not become effective as it has been replaced by annual plans.

Raising industrial efficiency is the indisputable objective of Soviet search in the West for new productive methods and new forms of international cooperation. Both are to make it eventually possible for the U.S.S.R. to expand the supply of capital as well as consumer goods. The latter will predictably benefit from the fact that Soviet planners are giving higher priority to improvements in the country's standard of living, in addition to the electronics, engineering and chemical industries.

Quite naturally, this expansionist and modernization policy has been responsible for uninterrupted growth of Soviet imports. Table 7 reveals this as well as U.S.S.R.'s positive trade balance with all major areas, save the industrially developed (Western) countries.

Among the COMECON countries the principal Soviet suppliers and markets are East Germany, Czechoslovakia and Poland; in the West, it is Finland, followed by the United Kingdom, West Germany, Italy and France. In Asia, Japan and India have emerged as U.S.S.R.'s chief trading partners. To the Middle East the Russians have been increasingly attracted not only by their international political interests but also by oil.

Table 7.

Soviet Foreign Trade, 1963 and 1966
(In millions of roubles)

Total:	1963	1966	% increase
Exports	6,545	7,957	21.8
Imports	6,353	7,122	12.2
1. Socialist countries:			
Exports	4,590	5,286	15.1
Imports	4,488	4,738	5.5
of which:			
Members of COMECON			
Exports	3,850	4,365	13.3
Imports	3,779	4,072	7.7
2. Industrially developed capitalist countries:			
Exports	1,135	1,581	39.5
Imports	1,281	1,601	25.0
3. Underdeveloped countries:			
Exports	821	1,091	32.9
Imports	584	784	34.5

Note: In 1966, fuels, lubricants, base metals and wood products made up 59% of Soviet exports to the Industrial West. In comparable imports, machinery and equipment exceeded 32% and wheat totaled almost 25%.

In 1966 "machinery, apparatus and instruments" have accounted for as much as 33 percent of Soviet imports. On the export side, these goods amounted to 20 percent.

COMECON—A Dispensable Agent?

The Council for Mutual Economic Assistance has not fulfilled the expectations of its founders, in fact, its members have all along had a good reason to doubt the organization's ability "to strengthen the economic collaboration of the socialist countries and coordinate their economic development." Yet COMECON's influence on East European economic life, and foreign trade in particular, must not be underestimated. The organization is no longer shrouded in secrecy as it used to be when it served simultaneously, between 1949 and 1956, as an instrument of Moscow's integration and exploitation of the regional economies. Since its revisions in 1956 and 1962, COMECON has played a more positive role in East European economic development.

Its activities have been expanding and comprise (1) coordination of national economic plans (which is COMECON's chief instrument for promotion of regional cooperation); (2) furtherance of member countries' production specialization; (3) encouragement of the construction of important economic projects; (4) sponsorship of scientific and research cooperation; and (5) credit extension.

As COMECON has not been empowered to formulate regional plans, its planning activity is limited to circulation of East European economic plans, which offers these nations an opportunity to examine the plans' compatibility. Having not succeeded in coordinating 5-year plans, COMECON reportedly seeks to participate in 10- or 15- or 20-year regional plans advocated by some. Nevertheless, even without COMECON's direct involvement, the East European nations have harmonized their 1966-70 plans and agreed on production specialization encompassing 2500 engineering products. Still, frequent references to alleged deficiencies in both intra-regional coordination and specialization suggest that because or in spite of COMECON, East European economic harmonization has not made adequate progress to satisfy the nations in question. Notorious over-supply of some engineering goods on an international scale represents failure, not success, of COMECON-induced specialization.

Apart from the 22 standing commissions which implement the Council's integration policies, there are several institutes (e.g., the Institute of Standardization) and multilateral as well as bilateral projects to realize the organization's general objectives. Among the multilateral projects there is the Peace Power Grid, the Friendship Pipeline, the Railroad Freight Car Pool, and the International Bank of Economic Cooperation (IBEC). The bilateral projects include Agromash and Intransmash (established by Hungary and Bulgaria), Haldex (Hungary and Poland) and Iron Gates (Yugoslavia and Romania). The initially trilateral Intermetall (coordinating production and distribution of metallurgical products among Czechoslovakia, Poland and Hungary) has been expanded to include also the U.S.S.R., Bulgaria and East Germany.

Although East European economic integration under the Council's aegis has never become a reality—and is not likely to become so in the future because of the divergent objectives of the integrationists and economic nationalists—COMECON has molded the region's economies and has opened up many areas of common industrial and commercial interest.

But dependence of individual countries on COMECON markets has varied. It appears that Bulgaria is the most dependent nation followed by East Germany, Czechoslovakia, Hungary, Romania, the U.S.S.R. and Poland. As the following graph, reproduced from the *Economist*, demonstrates, East European intra-regional economic relations are predicated on both natural resources, such as coal, oil and iron ore, and manufactures. The graph suggests, clearly enough, why especially Rumanian leaders have felt free to be critical of the organization.

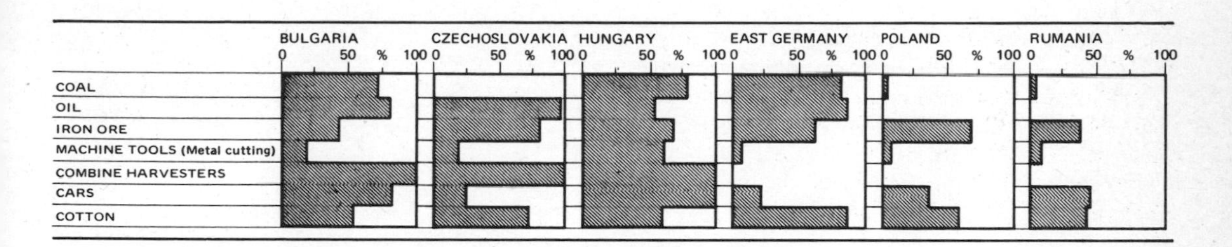

Aggregate trade of the COMECON nations has grown remarkably as indicated by imports, which rose between 1955 and 1965 from $7.3 billion to $19.0 billion, as well as by exports, which increased during that decade from $8 billion to $19.6 billion. However, to a remarkable extent these gains were redistributed in favor of Western industrialized countries, as shown in Table 8.

Table 8.

Geographic Distribution of COMECON Foreign Trade

	1955	1965
Imports		
COMECON countries	65.0%	65.8%
Western industrialized countries	16.3%	21.5%
Exports		
COMECON countries	59.2%	64.7%
Western industrialized countries	8.8%	20.6%

The degree to which individual East European countries participate in intra-regional foreign trade bears a close relationship to their overall economic status as described above and reflected again in the following tabulation of 1965 COMECON trade:

Bulgaria	2.0 billion roubles
Czechoslovakia	4.8 billion roubles
East Germany	5.3 billion roubles
Hungary	2.7 billion roubles
Poland	4.1 billion roubles
Romania	2.0 billion roubles
U.S.S.R.	14.6 billion roubles
Total	35.5 billion roubles

As the corresponding totals for 1961 and 1966 amounted to, respectively, 25.8 billion roubles and 37.7 billion roubles, intra-COMECON trade increased during the 6-year period by 46 per cent. It covered, for instance, 95 per cent of regional demand for coal and oil, 80 per cent of the demand for iron ore and fertilizers, and 75 per cent of the seven nations' machinery requirements.

This latter percentage points up one particularly noteworthy aspect of East Europe's postwar economic development, namely, the dramatic rise in the production and, consequently, exportation of engineering products. Table 9 illustrates the increasing part played by machinery and equipment in the commodity composition of COMECON exports:

Table 9.

Machinery and Equipment as Percent of Total Exports

	1960	1965
Bulgaria	13.6%	25.0%
Czechoslovakia	45.0%	48.0%
East Germany	48.0%	49.0%
Hungary	38.0%	34.0%
Poland	28.0%	34.0%
Romania	17.0%	19.0%

One can appreciate from these figures why Bulgaria and Romania have fostered exports of manufactured goods in order to improve their terms of trade. But this very practice has caused intra-regional frictions and complicated COMECON's task of attuning the East European economies to each other.

The entire COMECON area's export drive in the 1960's manifests itself in the fact that the growth in foreign sales has at times exceeded the growth in industrial output. Table 10 is focused on this comparison.

From among the complaints lodged against COMECON, the most prevalent concerns the unsettled price problem. The East European countries share the view that as determinants of foreign trade, their national price systems are meaningless. The existing prices do not express true economic values of exchangeable commodities and do not provide significant clues for international cost comparisons. Neither do they enable accurate determination of profits and losses. It seems that the northern COMECON countries are prepared, while the southern are not, to overhaul their price structures taking the "capitalist" world prices as guideposts. One also points out frequently that East European "economic reality" is out of line with regional currency relations, i.e., foreign exchange rates.

Table 10.

Increments in Industrial Production and Exports

	Industrial Output	Exports
1956	9.6%	1.6%
1960	10.1%	9.3%
1961	9.2%	11.0%
1962	9.0%	13.7%
1963	6.8%	10.0%
1964	7.5%	7.9%
1965	8.5%	6.0%

Furthermore, there is growing awareness that the implications of implemented economic reforms—which are not, to be sure, internationally coordinated—can hardly avoid placing severe strains on both East European commercial and financial relations and COMECON itself. It is recognized that market reforms are not only incompatible with centralism but also entail new patterns of trade flows not anticipated in the present COMECON arrangements.

Criticisms have been levelled at the Council's continued adherence to bilateralism when multilateral trade channels are generally sought and preferred. Such demands have been directed primarily at the East European International Bank (IBEC) from which multilateralization of its clearing facilities is expected. Unquestionably, expanding East European foreign trade has raised the issue of convertibility of regional currencies, especially of the rouble. (In 1966 the rouble was made transferable).

Although many other pending economic issues are discussed by the East European countries, the problems which originate in and are explainable by their differing levels of economic development, factor endowments, consumption habits, and quality of goods keep recurring. Yet most East Europeans realize that it is trade with the West that can satisfy their growing appetite for more and better consumer goods. Evident is also the COMECON members' endeavor to secure as much freedom of action as their national interests require.

The high degree of production standardization and rationalization, for which the Council is responsible, has given it a *raison d'être*. Nevertheless, its future depends on the compromises of which it is capable in the face of spreading economic nationalism and the new reforms, which have undeniably become a carrier of nationalistic aspirations.

Generally, East European nations seem to be willing to cooperate with COMECON most when their contributions are specified, when the expected gains are apparent, and when their sovereignties remain intact.

Eastern Partners for Western Businessmen

Michael Gamarnikow

Working partnerships between East European governments and Western capital? Industrialists east and west are finding interests in common, as is shown by recent attempts to work out cooperative agreements discussed in the following article.

Last year the governments of two communist countries made a proposal which was unprecedented in the history of East-West relations. Rumania and Yugoslavia publicly invited Western business concerns to come and invest in their industry. They were not, it should be emphasized, asking for long-term credits. Nor were they seeking to purchase Western industrial equipment and installations–a kind of transaction which is quite routine nowadays. They were proposing something different: a working partnership between Western capital and the governments of Rumania and Yugoslavia.

The basic principles of the proposal were perhaps formulated most clearly by Rumania's Deputy Premier Gaston-Marin. Through visiting newspapermen he made the following offer to Western industrial concerns: You are constantly seeking new markets and fresh opportunites for investing capital. You will find a wide scope for profitable investment in our country. We have raw materials and plenty of cheap labor. What we lack is capital, and the knowledge of the more sophisticated modern technological processes. Let us form a partnership. You contribute factory equipment and other capital requirements. You also make available to us your technological know-how. We, in turn, will erect the factory buildings and take responsibility for the supply of raw materials. We will also provide the necessary labor force. (*New York Journal-American*, November 23, 1964.)

What about profits? The Rumanian did not evade this ideologically delicate issue. We understand perfectly well, he said in effect, that no Western concern would ever consider investing capital without getting a return. We are prepared to guarantee profits to our prospective partners. We are also ready to give a firm assurance that the capital they invest will not be nationalized. And finally, we will pay in hard currency.

This is the gist of the Rumanian offer, as outlined by Gheorghe Gaston-Marin. A similar proposal was put forward about the same time by the Yugoslav government, according to the US Department of Commerce. Belgrade invited American industrial concerns and financial corporations to enter into direct economic cooperation with Yugoslav state enterprises. The Yugoslavs would provide the factory buildings, raw material and manpower, while their Western partners were to supply capital, technological experience and marketing facilities. Belgrade also declared its willingness to give Western business concerns the necessary guarantees in the sphere of management prerogatives and joint production decisions, as well as to ensure full convertibility of profits.

Actually, the Yugoslavs are interested in several different kinds of collaboration: Western investment in all branches of industry, with a firm promise of high returns on the capital invested; the use of Western technical expertise in jointly-financed enterprises; and the services of Western sales organizations in marketing the products of such joint ventures, particularly in developing new markets in Asia and Africa. (Both Rumania and Yugoslavia offered to handle the sales of such products in the communist-bloc area.)

Eastern Europe's Capital Shortage

Because of the greater political independence of their countries, Rumanian and Yugoslav spokesmen were able to state publicly what their Polish, Hungarian or Czechoslovak counterparts were saying in private to Western government officials and businessmen. All the communist countries of eastern Europe are desperately short of capital, and large-scale Western investment is their only hope of maintaining their present rate of economic growth while–at the same time–trying to satisfy steadily increasing consumer demand, which in turn requires a more balanced industrial structure. This, at least, was the conclusion of the report submitted by the US Trade Expansion Mission, which toured Yugoslavia in October 1964 and interviewed nearly 300 representatives of Yugoslav state-owned enterprises. According to the mission's report (see *International Commerce,* December 1964), Yugoslavia has now reached a stage in its industrialization in which "further large increments of capital investment are necessary to maintain the momentum developed during the past decade." Yugoslavia must either "consolidate on the industrial base now in existence," which would be "tantamount to turning back the clock," or it must "create a more attractive climate for private foreign investment, or appeal to Western money markets for technical and economic help."

*Reprinted with permission from *East Europe* Vol. 14, No. 9 (September 1965).

There are other reasons, besides their shortage of capital, why the communist countries of eastern Europe are trying so hard to create this more attractive climate for Western investment capital. Some of them, like Poland, have idle manpower resources and are faced with the prospect of millions of new hands entering the labor market in the next decade. Others, like Rumania and Bulgaria, look upon Western investments as the easiest way to speed up their industrialization and to bridge the gap which still divides them even from countries in eastern Europe. Finally—and in many cases, this may be the primary consideration—cooperation with established Western concerns promises easier sales in Western markets of the goods produced by such joint enterprises. This, in turn, would bring increased hard currency earnings to finance essential imports from outside the communist area.

This last reason is the most compelling of all. Long-term credits (admittedly a rather controversial issue so far as the Western governments are concerned) would help overcome the shortage of investment capital. But credits alone do not, as a rule, carry the benefits of technological know-how and expertise, or help to open new markets. Long-term credits, if they can be obtained, are perhaps more palatable from the political and ideological points of view. After all, the Soviet Union borrowed extensively in the late twenties and early thirties, and openly solicits such credits today.

But on purely economic considerations, some form of investment partnership with Western concerns would be much more preferable. This would offer an opportunity to learn Western management techniques and methods of organizing production. With it would come the latest technological know-how and a Western staff to teach this to native workers on a day-to-day basis. And there would be export outlets for the finished products.

This is why all the communist countries of eastern Europe have been making efforts for the last year or so to conclude as many direct economic cooperation contracts with Western firms as possible. Not all of them dared to make such sweeping public offers as Gaston-Marin and his fellow Deputy Premier Gogu Radulescu did in the name of Rumania. Most of them preferred, for obvious reasons, to negotiate quietly, and even in secret, with carefully selected Western concerns. But Polish officials were and still are quite outspoken in soliciting direct cooperation agreements with Western concerns. A large number of such agreements have either been concluded or are still being negotiated.

The effort is by no means one-sided. Many Western businessmen are willing to meet the communist governments more than halfway down the road of co-production. Some Western concerns—of which West Germany's Krupp is perhaps the most outstanding example—have shown considerable initiative in seeking investment opportunities in the communist bloc. The general manager of Krupp, Berthold Beitz, has been negotiating various economic cooperation schemes with Poland, Hungary, Bulgaria, Rumania and Yugoslavia. A contract for a 14-million-dollar synthetic fiber factory, which the Krupp concern will both equip and apparently also manage, was signed in Sofia in March. Negotiations with Budapest are well advanced, and capital goods to the value of six million dollars have been already delivered to Hungary.

Krupp and Poland

Krupp's deal with Poland has attracted the most attention. The status of this agreement is not yet clear. During a press conference in Washington on February 2, Beitz seemed to imply that the negotiations had been successfully completed. "If all goes well, the first joint enterprise will become operational before the end of this year," UPI reported him as saying. "We are in agreement in principle to set up several of such enterprises, and only details now remain to be settled."

But on February 21, less than three weeks after the Beitz press conference, *Trybuna Ludu* in Warsaw published an angry editorial denouncing "exceptionally sensational and ambiguous comments by the press and propaganda centers in the German Federal Republic, the USA and other Western countries. The press suggested that the representatives of Krupp had concluded an agreement that stipulates nothing less than the building in our country of factories that would be the property of West German capital, or a 'joint property' as it is called, of the communist government and Krupp." The party newspaper went on to deny that Poland intended ever to make any "political or institutional concessions" in order to obtain Western capital.

Some observers took the *Trybuna Ludu* editorial to be a direct denial that an "agreement in principle" has been reached as stated by Beitz. Actually it merely implied that the deal had not yet been made final and that Warsaw was not ready to grant political concessions—for which the Krupp negotiators hadn't asked. The outburst was probably prompted by opposition both inside the Polish communist party and from the Ulbricht regime in East Germany. Warsaw clearly resented the world-wide (and often exaggerated) publicity which its dealings with the West German firm evoked. The Poles had obviously wanted to keep the transaction as quiet as possible. But the negotiations in Warsaw were extensively reported in the Western press, often in sensational terms, and even the Italian communist organ *L'Unita* (February 4) indulged in this type of speculation.

In the meantime it has been disclosed in Warsaw that one joint commercial scheme involving Krupp and a Polish state enterprise has been in operation since at least mid-1964. This is an agreement with the Polish trade enterprise, "Cekop," which specializes in the export of complete sugar refineries, to supply industrial equipment for such factories in the developing countries of Africa and Latin America. (*Zycie Warszawy*, February 9, 1965.) It seems probable that after the political dust has settled the agreements on joint industrial production will also go through. While joint *ownership* of the factories equipped by Krupp, or by any other Western concern, seems to be unacceptable to the Polish side (see Premier Cyrankiewicz's statement in Liepzig, as reported by Reuters on March 1), the door has been deliberately left open for all other forms of economic cooperation. In fact, joint ownership of the undertakings was never demanded by Krupp representatives. Berthold Beitz had stated merely that Krupp, as a private investor, would bear considerable risk and expected that appropriate reward for its capital outlay would be guaranteed in the forthcoming agreement with Poland. Apparently Warsaw has no objection to this.

Political and ideological problems apart, there are powerful economic reasons why the proposed joint ventures would serve the interests of both sides. It is no secret that for some time now Poland has been facing a serious economic problem. Like all communist countries, Poland lacks the capital resources necessary to maintain a high rate of economic growth. In Poland's case the dilemma is made more acute by a serious unemployment problem. Because of the very high birth rate in the early postwar years, the economy must provide some 1.5 million new jobs within the next five years. But with the progress of modern technology the creation of each new industrial job becomes increasingly expensive in terms of invested capital. Poland's basic economic problem is thus one of acute disproportion between surplus manpower and scarce investment resources. Warsaw has every incentive to seek Western capital under politically acceptable conditions.

The problem faced by Krupp—and any other huge industrial concern in western Europe for that matter—is the obverse of the Polish one. The Western industrialists have plenty of capital to invest, but their available labor resources are scarce. For many years industrialized western Europe has been importing workers from the relatively less developed areas of southern Italy, Greece, Turkey, Spain and Portugal. Several million foreign workers are now employed in this way—but the manpower shortage persists.

Imported labor is expensive. It not only has to be paid according to the norms of a high-wage area; it must also be provided with housing and special social amenities. Moreover, the present sources of supply are drying up. This makes the labor surpluses of eastern Europe an attractive economic proposition. But for political and prestige reasons communist countries would be embarrassed by a mass migration of surplus manpower. For one thing, this would amount to an open admission that unemployment can persist in a socialized economy. To bring Polish workers to the Krupp factories in West Germany would be simply out of the question for this as well as other reasons. The only realistic alternative is to bring the factories to the workers.

By entering into a co-production agreement with Poland, the Krupp concern would secure for itself new manpower resources. It would also gain new productive capacity without the high building costs which it incurs in Essen. Finally, it would gain a firm foothold in the communist-bloc markets, which for many Western businessmen means investing in the future.

Co-Production Schemes

What is true for Krupp is true for any other large business concern in western Europe. While world attention has been focused on the Polish deal with Krupp, Warsaw has quietly concluded a number of co-production agreements with other west European industrial corporations. The essential feature of most of them is that the Polish enterprise concerned has in fact, become a subsidiary operation of the Western concern, which supplies it with machinery, technical designs, and sometimes even with operating capital such as raw materials and semi-finished components. The Polish state remains the sole owner of this subsidiary enterprise, while the Western concern is paid for its capital investment and technical assistance in the form of the finished product. The Western partner may also have a share in the profits of the subsidiary undertaking, and it retains marketing rights outside the communist-bloc area.

Many Swedish firms have already entered into such joint production agreements with state enterprises in Poland. One can cite the Alfa-Laval concern, which exports fully-equipped slaughter houses in which 30 percent of the equipment is of Polish manufacture. The well-known Swedish Electrolux firm exports refrigerators, the metal or plastic boxes for which have been produced by its subsidiary in Poland. One of Sweden's largest furniture manufacturers, IKEA, ships large supplies of various raw materials to its Polish subsidiary which, using Swedish machinery and designs and working under Swedish technical control, produces semi-finished furniture which is shipped back to Sweden. The Swedish firm finishes it and markets it.

Similar co-production schemes have been set up by other Swedish firms, such as Atvidaberg Furniture Factory, SKF Ballbearing Co., ASEA Engineering

Combine, Ericsson Telephone Company and several smaller firms.*

Poland is seeking to establish similar arrangements in other countries of western Europe. To facilitate them, the Poles have been inserting an industrial cooperation clause in their recent trade agreements. The new trade agreement between Poland and Sweden, signed in Stockholm on March 26, 1965, contains a special article stating that "both governments declare their readiness to facilitate all forms of cooperation between trade and industry in the two countries and on third markets." A similar industrial cooperation clause was included in the recent trade agreement between Poland and Denmark. (*Zycie Warszawy,* June 6-7.)

The Belgians have also shown an interest in various co-production schemes and even in joint production ventures with Polish enterprises. A special mission, composed of key men from eight major Belgian concerns, traveled to Poland early in April to establish contacts with prospective Polish partners. According to information from the Brussels Chamber of Commerce, three Polish enterprises were selected as most suitable for establishing pilot schemes: the Cegielski Combine in Poznan, which specializes in railroad equipment and marine engines; BEFAMA in Bielski (textile machinery); and RAFAMENT in Kuznia Raciborska, a major producer of machine tools. Some Belgian concerns have reportedly made considerable progress in establishing joint Polish-Belgian enterprises along the lines proposed by Krupp.

British firms are not known to have set up such arrangements with Poland. But a public plea for them was made by the Polish side in the course of a high-level Polish-British round-table meeting in Jablonna last March.

Polish Minister of Foreign Trade Witold Trampczynski indicated a readiness to take still another step in this direction by proposing the formation of mixed-capital firms jointly owned by Western industrialists and state-run enterprises. According to the official news agency PAP (July 29), such companies would operate on ten- or twenty-year agreements, and they would, in Trampczynski's words, "be one of the forms which would guarantee the development of our exports."

Italy signed an agreement with Poland on economic, technical and industrial cooperation on July 14. According to press reports, both sides bound themselves to encourage the development of cooperation in all fields of economic life, particularly in electrical engineering, building, agriculture and transportation. The agreement covers co-production arrangements between industrial enterprises similar to those already made by Poland with German and Swedish firms. It applies to the production of finished goods and sub-assemblies, joint exports to third markets, design and construction of industrial plants, exploitation of raw materials and the exchange of information and training. A mixed commission will be set up to supervise the agreement. (*Trybuna Ludu,* July 15.)

None of the joint production arrangements that has been carried out so far is on the scale of the proposed Krupp deal. But the principles are similar. Although Krupp reportedly proposed to provide capital equipment for three factories to be established in Poland, those enterprises were, in effect, to be nothing but subsidiaries of the main Krupp establishment in Essen. They were to produce parts for trucks, road building and mining machinery, which would be shipped to West Germany for final assembly and marketing. From the economic point of view this is the same type of division of labor that is involved in the Polish-Swedish co-production of furniture: cooperation between Western capital and Polish manpower.

Poland is by no means the only communist country that has made such arrangements with Western firms. Hungary's Ministry of Machine Building recently signed a special technical cooperation agreement with Rheinische Stahlwerke, Essen (Rheinstahl). According to its terms, several Hungarian factories are to produce various types of machinery for the Rheinstahl concern. Rheinstahl is to provide technical know-how, and take care of the sales in the West, while the Hungarians are to market the products in the COMECON area. Hungarian enterprises are also producing refrigeration pumps for English Electric Ltd. and air compressors for the French firm Krebs and Hamon. (*Szolnok Megyey Neplap,* January 6.)

Hungary cooperates extensively with various Austrian concerns, especially in overseas construction schemes. The best example, perhaps, is that involving the S.P.G. Electric Company in Vienna and several Hungarian undertakings which are erecting two power plants in India and one in Beirut. Certain turbines and generators for those power plants were produced in Hungary under a subcontract negotiated with the Austrian firm, which is financing the projects.

Recently Hungary took a further step on this path. Professor Imre Vajda, Chairman of the Hungarian Economic Society, suggested in a press conference at the Budapest Trade Fair in May that joint stock companies be set up in Hungary with the participation of Western capital. He said the government would be willing to allow its Western partners up to 49 percent of the stock, but would insist on the controlling interest. Professor Vajda's proposal thus envisages actual co-ownership as an additional security for Western investors. (*Frankfurter Allgemeine Zeitung,* May 22.)

*These and many of the other examples given are taken from the reports of Radio Free Europe correspondents in various Western countries.

A Czechoslovak machine-tool factory recently became a subcontractor for a concern in the US. The Leninovy Zavody enterprise in Plzen (formerly the Skoda Works) is currently producing several machine tools, including vertical and horizontal boring mills, for the Simmons Machine Tool Corporation. The machinery is produced to American specifications and marketed—mainly in the Western hemisphere—by the US company under the trade name "Simmons-Skoda."

Last year the British firm Gallaghan and Sons agreed with the Czechoslovak export company KOVO to cooperate in the introduction of a series of textile machines. These would include a Czechoslovak machine for producing non-woven textiles, supplemented by a Gallaghan machine for the manufacture of semi-finished material. *Rude Pravo* quoted the London *Times* as stating that the series of machines "will eliminate many complicated processes . . . in the traditional method of production and will make it possible to produce substantially cheaper textiles for industrial and domestic use."

One expression of Czechoslovak intentions in this direction was contained in the 1965 trade protocol with Austria. It provided for an increase "particularly in the quotas of those commodities in which it is assumed that trade will be expanded because of the growing cooperation between the production enterprises of both countries." (*Rude Pravo,* December 24, 1964.) However, Deputy Foreign Minister Oto Klicka told the Czechoslovak Radio on May 11 that cooperation between Czechoslovak and Austrian enterprises was still under discussion, including the possibility of cooperating for third markets.

East Germany also has some co-production agreements with Western firms. For instance the Svenska Ugnsbolaget metallurgical works of Sweden has made a deal with the East German concern Stahlmetall concerning siderurgical furnaces. The East Germans have the high-grade clays and silicates required for the lining of such furnaces, produced by Svenska Ugnsbolaget. In return the Swedish firm provides Stahlmetall with the necessary capital equipment and technological knowhow. It is considered quite likely that, apart from its deal with Stahlmetall, the Swedish firm may also set up a fullfledged subsidiary in the GDR in the near future.

Yugoslavia has concluded a co-production agreement with three Western concerns which manufacture rolling stock for electric street railways. The Rade Koncar enterprise in Zagreb will enter into partnership with the ASEA concern of Sweden, Elin-Union of Austria and Secheron A.G. of Switzerland to produce electric traction locomotives. The actual manufacturing will be done in Zagreb, but the Western concerns will supply capital equipment and technical designs. (*Tanyug,* April 14.)

As far as Rumania is concerned, there is no firm evidence so far that any Western industrial enterprise has taken up the offers made by Gaston-Marin and Gogu Radulsecu. But a West German concern, Gutehoffnungshütte of Oberhausen, has reportedly been commissioned to help in the construction of the Galati metallurgical combine. A number of west European firms were interested in the contract, and Krupp reportedly offered to build a rolling mill for Galati on terms similar to those it has offered the Poles. The interest with which the West German capital goods industry views the Rumanian market is evident in the huge West German industrial exhibition which was staged in Bucharest in the second half of May.

On July 26, the Universal Oil Products Corporation (Des Plaines, Ill.) announced that it had concluded an agreement with Rumania's Masini Import to design and construct a $22.5 million petroleum processing plant at the Ploesti oil field. Financing was arranged through the Continental Illinois Bank and Trust Company of Chicago, which provided a $16,242,000 loan payable over seven years at six percent, with 72 percent of the total indebtedness guaranteed by the Export-Import Bank. The Rumanians will pay the balance in cash. (*Wall Street Journal,* July 27. See also Current Developments.)

Forms of Cooperation

This review is by no means complete. It does not cover all of the co-production agreements already in operation or at various stages of negotiation. The sample presented here is both haphazard and fragmentary. This is because communist governments prefer as a rule to keep such deals secret, while their Western partners—with rare exceptions—also avoid publicity. Thus the examples given above are not necessarily the most representative, but they do indicate an unmistakable new trend in East-West economic relations.

New is the operative word. The trend described here did not really begin in earnest until 1964, and is still in its early experimental stages. Neither the communist countries nor the would-be Western investors are sure of their ground, for there are still very powerful obstacles to overcome. While elements on both sides are clearly eager to enter into partnership agreements, there are powerful forces to which the very concept of such direct economic cooperation is anathema. This explains the zigzag course of Krupp's negotiations with Poland. One has simply to accept the fact that the situation is likely to remain somewhat confusing for some time to come.

Nevertheless, one can attempt a preliminary analysis of the new trend. By and large, the cooperation takes three different forms. The first, which does not necessarily involve investment outlays by the Western partner, is primarily a joint venture in a third country. In this type of cooperation, the communist enterprise is essentially a subcontractor supplying certain components for the projects undertaken by its Western associate. The agreements between Hungary and the Austrian SPG company concerning the construction of power plants in India and Lebanon, fall clearly into this category. Here the Western firm provides the communist enterprise only with technical designs and a certain amount of technological know-how, but not with fixed or circulating capital.

Even a subcontracting type of agreement may call for a certain amount of investment outlay by the Western partner. For instance the Swedish Electrolux firm not only purchases refrigerator boxes from its Polish subsidiary, but has also supplied it with some of the equipment necessary for the production of such boxes. The same is true of the agreement concluded between Svenska Ugnsbolaget and the East German Stahlmetall, which is nominally only a contract to provide high-grade clays and silicates for siderurgical furnaces produced by the Swedish firm.

A higher form of economic cooperation involves joint production schemes, like those in operation between certain Polish furniture factories and the Swedish IKEA concern. In this type of co-production the communist factory becomes, in effect, a subsidiary of the Western firm. Here, as a rule, the Western partner has to provide some capital, in one form or another, for its socialized branch factory, unless the enterprise is already adequately equipped for the tasks assigned to it. (This seems to be true of the Hungarian cooperation with British and French firms.)

In this higher type of cooperation, the Western concern not only invests in its subsidiary socialized enterprise, but has to supply technical designs and often technical supervision. It also has to bear the marketing risks. Those expenses and risks, however, must be set off against the lower production costs in the communist subsidiary. On balance, it is evidently a paying proposition.

The highest form of cooperation would be the joint enterprises set up on communist territory along the lines of the Yugoslav and Rumanian proposals, or the tentative Krupp deal with Poland. Apart from marginal projects in the tourist industry, there are as yet no practical examples of such joint enterprises. But enough hard information on the proposed deals is available to give us at least some idea of the basic principles. It is clear that the machinery and installations would be supplied almost entirely by the Western partners, and thus the investment outlay of the capitalist firm would be quite considerable. From the viewpoint of the communist country the influx of capital would be the main advantage of this type of transaction.

Since the communist side is apparently unwilling to tolerate any form of joint *ownership*, the investments made by Western firms in jointly *operated* undertakings would be, in reality, just another method of supplying capital goods on a long-term credit basis. The only difference would be that both the initial outlay and the interest would be repaid not in cash but in kind–*i.e.,* by deliveries of the products manufactured in the joint enterprises. Additional advantages to the communist partners, such as technological know-how, technical assistance, and marketing facilities, would be paid for by profit-sharing arrangements.

Such direct Western investment in the communist bloc would amount to providing capital goods on the basis of a long-term loan, and is bound to provoke the same objections in some quarters as do the highly controversial long-term credits. The risks involved in such joint production schemes are much greater, for there is always a danger that the communist side will infringe the patents by disclosing secret technological processes to a third party. And there is the further risk of expropriation, which in this case would take the form of failure to deliver the finished goods through which the Western investor hopes to recover his capital.

Despite all these hazards, as well as the hundreds of problems inherent in the establishment of such joint ventures,* more and more Western concerns are apparently prepared to enter into co-production agreements with the socialized enterprises of the East.

*Analyzed in detail in an excellent article in West Germany's *Handelsblatt* (Düsseldorf), May 7: "Schwierige Kooperation mit dem Osten."

East-West Trade: How to get in on the Ground Floor Behind the Iron Curtain

The businessman's viewpoint sometimes, if not often, varies from that of the scholar or the federal executive. The editors of Business Abroad *recount some of the impressions they have received from businessmen who are actively engaged in trade with East Europe. They stress the significance of trade fairs and how to deal with the Foreign Trade Organizations. They discredit the oft-supposed credit unworthiness of East-European trading partners.*

In the first 10 months of 1966 Bulgaria, Czechoslovakia, East Germany, Hungary, Poland, Rumania, and Yogoslavia bought $261-million worth of goods from the United States. Since East European imports from the West have risen at a rate of 12% a year since 1958, demand for Western products and know-how should be even higher this year. On Jan. 16 even the self-sufficient Russians bought a two-page ad in *The New York Times* to drum up foreign trade. With U.S. government policy bent on pushing East-West trade, the question for many U.S. companies is no longer whether to do business with the Bloc nations, but how.

"This is a market for sophisticated exporters," according to Gardner H. Pierson, a management consultant whose firm, Amerconsel, Inc., New York, specializes in helping U.S. companies get started in East-West trade. Emphasizing that you can't sell East Europe as you do other areas of the world, Pierson advises Americans to approach the Bloc market with a good supply of patience as well as an active sales plan. He suggests that a three-year program be laid out in advance.

East Europeans know what they want and what is available from Western countries, Pierson told BUSINESS ABROAD. "But the American company with a high quality product and the means to be flexible on methods of payment has a head start in a market that can only grow."

Pierson insists there is no better way to begin than to meet buyers on the spot. "Don't expect to sell widgets through your export manager in Peoria," Amerconsel tells neophytes. "You should make at least one trip to the area to make contacts, measure the market, set terms, and arrange a productive working relationship with government officials in charge of trade with the West."

The Role of FTOs

Since all medium-to-large sized manufacturing and trade enterprises in Eastern Europe are state-owned, Westerners must deal with "Foreign Trade Organizations," or FTOs. Each industry's FTO is autonomous and has the authority to dicker over an import's price, quality, terms of delivery and credit. FTOs are run by "Generalny Direktors"—general directors.

These "busy men who hate to waste time" do most of the buying for factories in their particular industry. But foreigners have noticed recently that individual factories have more and more to say about what should be bought on their behalf. Faced with the necessity to make a profit under the developing communist enterprise system, factories now are apt to enter directly into negotiations in some countries. "It used to be that a foreigner just didn't set foot in an East European factory," one old hand said; but now, outsiders more frequently are allowed to view production facilities.

Basic business must still be done through the FTOs and contact with them is best arranged through each country's Chamber of Commerce. These deliberately accessible organizations resemble Western governments' Boards of Trade. They serve as clearing houses for trade proposals from the West and will direct the foreigner to the appropriate FTO at the proper time. If approval for hard currency payment or sanction for a particular barter arrangement is required, the deal then goes on to the Ministry of Foreign Trade.

Pierson will only deal with the highest official in each of these organizations. "A lesser functionary usually has limited authority and less knowledge about doing business with foreigners," he said. "It's better not to waste his time and yours. Ask to see the man in charge."

Knowing the man in charge is often the key to success in Eastern Europe, and personal contacts are Amerconsel's specialty. Pierson claims the best way to meet "the right people" is to attend at least one of Eastern Europe's major trade fairs: Brno. Czechoslovakia, and Zagreb, Yugoslavia, in the fall; Leipzig, East Germany, and Poznan, Poland, in the spring. The bloc countries usually send full delegations from their state trading corporations. For example, a U.S. exhibitor at the Brno fair could be invited by the Hungarian state delegation to bring his samples by Budapest on the way home.

The Importance of Fairs

The cost of space is relatively low at East Bloc shows (an average $1.50 per sq. ft. versus $2.50 for comparable space in the U.S.), and it is often possible to cancel out the cost of the trip by sales on the spot even if the first firm contract is not negotiated at that time. If necessary, several non-competitive U.S. companies can arrange to pool their resources in one exhibit. If an American firm joins a U.S. Department of Commerce display, the government will pay the freight. Pierson is convinced that exposure at a trade fair is the best way to introduce a new product, to meet potential customers, and to size up the competition.

What is the best way to follow up a successful trade fair exhibit? A foreign company still may not establish a legal office behind the Iron Curtain. Permanent sales representatives work for a number of Italian and other firms in Moscow and Bucharest, but Pierson does not believe it pays for medium-size American companies to engage a permanent sales representative or local agent at first. "Once the doors have been opened, it is much better to make regular trips to the East Bloc from a base in Western Europe," he said. Pierson recommends Vienna where companies like Dow Chemical, General Motors, Honeywell, IBM, Ingersoll-Rand, ITT, NCR, Pfizer, 3M, United Shoe Machinery and Union Carbide have established Eastern European sales offices.

These U.S. giants and their smaller compatriots have found that Eastern Europe wants practically any product that sells competitively in the West. "The emphasis today is on producer goods and will be increasingly on consumer goods," Amerconsel said. Hungary's Chamber of Commerce President Odon Kallos told Pierson: "We want production goods which will enable us to compete with Western Europe in order to earn the hard currency we need so badly."

The main obstacle to more sales in Eastern Europe is the lack of convertible hard currency. Spot cash is only available for high priority goods with tight world markets. But if an American company is imaginative, many profitable alternatives can be worked out. The possibilities for switch, barter, and credit deals are endless, Amerconsel said.

A classic case of how American export imagination won the day under these conditions is Pepsi Cola's saturation of Yugoslavia. "Pepsi is hardly a strategic commodity," Pierson points out, "but the fact remains that its local manufacture does a lot for the Yugoslav economy." Bottles and crown caps are manufactured on the spot and natural mineral water is sufficiently carbonated to use as it comes out of the ground. Pepsi provides bottling know-how, syrup formula, and a prestige name. The Pepsi Cola strategy has been so naturally profitable that Rumania is angling for the right to be the next communist country to join the Pepsi generation.

The Credit 'Problem'

Companies which have worked with Eastern Europeans over the years say "their credit is good and they pay on time." Pierson is convinced that because East Europeans "want to join the world family again" there is minimal danger of piracy on patents, license infringement, etc. "They are willing to pay for patents." License-buying FTOs exist in each country and all details concerning performance, inspection, market limitation, sub-licensing, etc. can be spelled out when a license contract is negotiated. Amerconsel clients who have had recourse to East European courts of arbitration report favorably on their fairness.

If East Europeans are scrupulous, they are also rewardingly loyal, Pierson said. "Someday when currency convertibility is no longer a problem and all other obstacles to East-West trade are removed, everybody will get on the bandwagon." But from his experience, Pierson is sure that where an East European has been dealing with a U.S. company for five years and began when the going was rough, competitors won't stand a chance. "If the American company has built up a good relationship over the years with an East European buyer, loyalty will win out." Now is the time to start building for the future, he said.

The Rise of the Trade Fairs

When doing business in East Europe, the significance of exhibiting at the right trade fair cannot be underemphasized. In the article which follows, some of the more important fairs are cited, along with brief histories and the types of goods that are displayed.

One sphere where the détente in the Cold War has been particularly visible in the past few years has been the international trade fairs in Eastern Europe. Businessmen and trade officials from the West have been increasingly numerous in Brno, Leipzig, Plovdiv, Poznan, Budapest and Zagreb. In the last two years alone Italy's Minister of Trade, France's Ministers of Trade and Communications, Austria's Vice Chancellor Bruno Pittermann, various British officials and the US's former Secretary of Commerce Luther Hodges have made the rounds of most of the East European fairs. In 1964 some 22 nations sent men of cabinet rank to the Brno International Trade Fair in Czechoslovakia alone.

It was not until 1957-1959 that the fairs began to appeal to many exhibitors from outside the Soviet bloc. The French, Austrians, Italians and British were the first to display interest. The West Germans joined in energetically around 1960 and by 1962 had taken the lead in trade with most of the bloc countries. In the past three years the British have increased their efforts to sell to the East, and more recently the French government has been seeking to broaden its commercial ties.

Large Western firms which appear often at the East European trade fairs include Krupp, Telefunken, Rheinstahl, Siemens, Phillips, Standard Oil, Honda, Remington-Rand, ENI, John Deere, and most of the large automobile manufacturers including Fiat, Renault, Mercedes-Benz, Ford, Chrysler, and Triumph.

The communists have encouraged Western exhibitors for reasons both economic and political. Their need for markets in the West and for specific industrial imports which were not always available in the Soviet bloc has increased with the growth of their own industry. In the Cold War era the fair ground was one arena where concrete economic needs could be given their due and where contacts with the West could be encouraged. The fair grounds also offered them a change to try to convince Western businessmen that communist industries did have something to offer on the world market. In the last five years, the fairs have also become a means for making propaganda among the developing nations of the world; visitors from the new nations can talk business (and credits) on an equal footing with men from other countries.

The international trade fairs also provide the East European regimes with a domestic propaganda weapon. Their own citizens are supposed to be impressed at the fairs both by their nation's industrial prowess and by its good relations with other nations. It does not always work out this way, for citizens often come away from the fairs feeling poorer than when they went. The average East European hungers in particular for the automobile, and any exhibit of cars is certain to draw a crowd.

The U.S. pavilions, which stress the common benefits of scientific and technological progress, are also very popular. Along with the usual appliance and fashion displays, these have included a 1964 Brno exhibit on training the blind for industrial employment, a 1961 Plovdiv medical exhibit, a super-drugstore in Pozan in 1964, an automatic laundry in Plovdiv in 1964, and a potato chip maker at several fairs last year. Most of these items have sold well, especially the laundries, the potato chip machine, and supermarkets.

Public Relations

Fair officials have become more and more proficient at public relations. All of the trade fairs sponsor special lectures, symposiums, and seminars on scientific and technical problems relating to specific sectors of the economy or to specific trade problems. These are for experts and are useful points of contact between specialists from East and West. There are also more and more programs oriented toward specialists from the developing countries. Prizes and awards are designed to inspire high aesthetic and technical standards in the displays. Special services are arranged to help out businessmen and trade delegations–like language guides, or the special "Foreigners Club" set up in Budapest by the Hungarian Chamber of Commerce with conference rooms, telephones and telex service.

Other PR gimmicks aim to please the average visitor, from fashion shows and demonstrations to helicopter rides. Recently efforts have been made to sell tourism along with other goods at the fairs by publicizing the attractions of the host city. Some fairs have national days, stressing the music and culture of each participating country.

The greatest fanfare, however, is reserved for the opening day when high government officials and party leaders visit the fair grounds to make the inevitable speeches. Their flavor is generally benign and statesmanlike. Thus Czechoslovak Premier Jozef Lenart observed at the opening of the Brno fair last September that broad trade relations would benefit all nations and

Reprinted with permission from *East Europe*, Vol. 14, No. 3 (March 1965).

contribute to peace, while economic discrimination and embargoes (in official parlance, usually a reference to the trade policies of the Common Market and the United States) are undesirable remnants of the Cold War. At Poznan last summer, the Polish Minister of Foreign Trade Witold Trampczynski touted Poland's export potential to various parts of the world. With regard to the West, he emphasized "mutual advantage and respect for the interests of both partners."

In his keynote speech at the opening of the last Leipzig fair, Deputy Premier Erich Apel of East Germany stressed the competitive side of peaceful coexistence. The Leipzig Fair has always been a meeting place for businessmen from all over the world, he pointed out, and the fact that exhibitors come from different economic systems means that businessmen can compare efficiency and quality on an international level. "Here every country, every enterprise has potential sales if they offer products which meet the highest scientific-economic standards and correspond with the needs of the trading partner as well as with the normal international terms regulating delivery and finance."

A Yugoslav official chose to emphasize the Asia-Africa-Yugoslavia exhibition at the Zagreb fair last year, playing up the links between Yugoslavia and the developing nations of the world. Milos Minic, Vice President of the Federal Executive Council, said that the growing size of the Zagreb International Fair was, in his opinion, a reflection of the "objective necessity of developing world trade."

Although the surge in business conducted at the East European fairs over the last ten years has steadily attracted more exhibitors, it is probable that the importance of the fairs as a marketplace for East-West exchanges reached its peak between 1961 and 1963. As the East European countries relax travel and trade restrictions, the fairs will no longer be so important as a place to make contacts and carry on negotiations. The trend seems to be toward more East-West visits by business and economic experts, toward permanent trade bureaus, flexible trading terms worked out during extended negotiations, long-term credits, and larger, more complicated transactions, *i.e.,* toward more normal business relations between East and West. Thus it is now very difficult to document the amount of business contracted at the fairs, for negotiations are seldom completed at the fairgrounds. As a place to compare and inspect new products, however, the fairs should continue to be an important impetus to foreign trade.

Facts About the Fairs

Hungary. The fair in Budapest is the successor of an international fair established in 1925 and of the Budapest Industrial Fair set up in 1957. It was accredited by the Union of International Fairs in Brussels in 1962, and foreign participation doubled in the next two years. At the last fair in May 1964, there were displays by 1,077 firms from 35 foreign countries and by 833 Hungarian enterprises. Among Western countries, Austria usually supplies the most exhibits, followed by West Germany, France, Britain, Switzerland, Italy and Sweden in that order. Annual attendance from 1959 to 1962 topped one million, but two years ago officials closed the gate some mornings to cut the total by about 100,000.

Space has long been a problem for the Budapest officials, since the fair annually takes over the City Park, to the annoyance of local citizens. A special site along the Danube was set aside in 1958, but landscaping is barely finished and the permanent exhibition halls will probably not be completed until 1969. Meanwhile the agricultural segment of the fair has been made into a separate fall show to alleviate crowding.

Official figures on the value of business contracted in Budapest get sketchier and sketchier. In 1960 it amounted to 146 million foreign currency forints, rising to 800 million by 1963, or roughly from \$6 million to \$34 million at the official exchange rate.* The largest deal reported in 1964 was a 29 million ruble (380 million forints) contract with the Soviet Union for the import and export of various kinds of vehicles.

Czechoslovakia. The volume of business transacted at Czechoslovakia's Brno fair is 20 to 30 times the total in Budapest, and is rivaled only by the Leipzig fair in East Germany. Organized in 1959, the Brno International Trade Fair is an outgrowth of the prewar Prague Sample Fair and the Brno Engineering Fairs of the mid-50s. It is still sometimes referred to as an engineering fair and has been characterized by *Czechoslovak Life* as the "primary specialized supermarket of the socialist countries" (November 1961) and the "world supermarket for machinery" (November 1962).

The First Brno International Trade Fair in 1959 registered sales of over 4 billion korunas, seven-eighths of this with the communist countries. The next year sales reached nearly 6 billion korunas, or one-fifth the value of all foreign trade in 1960. Transactions by the foreign trade enterprises at the Third Fair in 1961 were nearly seven billion korunas (or about \$1 billion at the official exchange rate), 70 percent exports and 30 percent imports. No general figures are available since then, and reports in 1962 stated that trading at the fair had been quiet because of Czechoslovakia's lack of foreign currency.

Last fall, trade with the capitalist countries reportedly doubled the figure for 1963. Nevertheless

*This and other dollar equivalents are given at the official exchange rate. Tourist rates are now much higher, and the value of the dollar on the free market is as much as 2-3 times the official rate in Bulgaria, 5 times in Czechoslovakia, 2.5 times in Hungary, nearly 3 times in East Germany and Poland, and one-third higher in Yugoslavia.

the USSR was still the most important customer with contracts totalling two billion korunas for the import of Czechoslovak goods and 600 million korunas for exports to Czechoslovakia. *In toto*, Czechoslovak enterprises sold vehicles worth 400 million korunas and heavy machinery and metallurgical equipment worth 620 million; they purchased 750 million korunas' worth of machines and equipment in return. To facilitate business in Brno, the Czechoslovak foreign trade enterprises were allowed to sign contracts on the spot, including details on quality, delivery, payment, etc.

Generally speaking, a small number of exhibitors show a great variety of heavy and expensive machinery in Brno. Some 300 firms from 30 countries exhibited at the First Brno International Trade Fair in 1959. After a peak of 635 participants from 45 countries in 1963, the total dropped to 620 exhibitors from 36 countries last year.

The main competition in Brno has recently been between the British and the West Germans, and in 1963 British firms outpaced the West Germans 140 to 92. British exhibitors have emphasized advanced machinery to be used in the engineering, metallurgical, electronic, transportation, and chemical industries. Austria has been a steady third both in exhibits at Brno and in trade between Czechoslovakia and individual Western countries. The number of firms exhibiting from both Italy and Japan dropped off sharply between 1962 and 1963, from 56 and 33 to 32 and 8 respectively.

The Brno International Trade Fair drew crowds of over two million its first year, and over one million the two succeeding seasons. When the general public was restricted to certain hours, the yearly number of visitors declined to about 800,000, including 30,000 foreigners.

Bulgaria. Attendance at the Plovdiv International Fair in Bulgaria is relatively small compared to the others. Visitors have totalled around 700,000 for the last few years, although foreign guests increased from around 7,000 in 1938 to more than 10,000 in 1964.

Biannual since 1958, the fair in Plovdiv is the continuation of a fair founded in the thirties. Since the war the biggest exhibitor at Plovdiv has regularly been the USSR. Participation as a whole has climbed slowly, with firms from 28 foreign countries in 1958 and 36 last year. There were 600 exhibitors in 1964, the same total as six years earlier. By 1956 the Austrians, French, and West Germans were participating strongly, with 90, 80, and 60 representative firms; they still do so, along with more British and more Italian firms.

Among Bulgaria's favorite export items are electric trucks and hoists and industrial lathes: four electric trucks were sold abroad in 1957 and 8,164 electric trucks and 17,170 electric hoists in 1963; the first foreign sale of industrial lathes was in 1955, and the total for 1963 was 1,006. These, and the canned foods and agricultural products for which Bulgaria has long been known, were the main Bulgarian exhibits in Plovdiv last year.

Contracts negotiated at Plovdiv generally represent a substantial proportion of the nation's total imports and exports: the sum of 510 million levas (approximately $75 million at the official rate) registered in 1962 was about 37 percent of the total foreign trade for that year, and the 485 million listed for last year's fair was about one-fifth of the anticipated trade volume for 1964. In contrast to the five-fold increase in transactions from the 18th fair in 1958 (93.6 million leva) to the 20th fair in 1962, the 21st fair in 1964 showed a decline both in absolute and in relative terms.

Poland. Concrete documentation on the Poznan International Fair is leanest of all. Transactions at Poznan in 1960 reportedly accounted for 10 percent of all Poland's exports for that year excluding coal and raw materials, and 68 percent of this was for machinery, plants, and transport equipment. In 1961 the fair's trade turnover was listed at "more than $250 million." Machinery and equipment represented nearly 60 percent of the export contracts signed at the 33rd Poznan Fair last year, and approximately half the total in 1963. In all, the Polish foreign trade organizations signed contracts last year with firms from 62 countries.

Polish machine and industrial equipment industries "should be particularly interested in the possibilities of cooperation with the important producers from the Common Market countries," observed *Zycie Gospodarcze* in summarizing the 33rd fair (June 21, 1964). The West Germans, British, Austrians and Italians all exhibited in large numbers. French firms, however, have decreased their exhibits in the past few years. The Scandinavians have increased displays, but "their markets do not belong to the easier ones [for Poland] because of their high standards of quality." As a whole, the 1964 Poznan fair stressed models of complete industrial plants and specialized heavy industrial machines, with transportation equipment a close second. The article complained that "there was not enough initiative shown in organizing business meetings with foreign exports."

As far as the total number of exhibitors is concerned, the Poznan International Fair is comparable to the Budapest International Fair: 1,216 exhibitors from 56 countries showed in 1960 and 1,577 from 53 countries in 1964. As a public fete the Poznan fair draws fewer crowds than the other trade fairs. Visitors totalled 450,000 in 1964 (9,500 foreigners) and only 320,000 the previous year. Publicity this past year urged visitors to combine a visit to the fair with a tour of the historical sites in the city, and played up the fair's heritage as successor to the annual St. John's Fair founded in 1253.

East Germany. Like Poznan, Leipzig boasts of its medieval precedent. In 1965 the spring and fall fairs will mark the 800th jubilee of the original trade fair, with all the pomp and gala this suggests (as well as three new hotels). Although other sources do not credit the Leipzig Fair with so long a history (West German sources give 1453 as the original date), all agree that it has long been one of Europe's most important commercial events.

The emphasis in Leipzig is less on heavy industrial machinery and more on the highly specialized and complex industrial products turned out by the East German economy. The spring fair is characterized as a "technical and consumer goods fair," the one in the fall as a "consumer goods fair with an offering of technical appliances."

Sales in Leipzig reach impressive totals. Figures are available for the fall fairs only, but the spring fair is generally even larger. In September 1961—in spite of the new Berlin Wall—transactions amounted to 2.9 billion East German marks (about $692 million at the official rate). Exports accounted for roughly 60 percent of this, two-thirds to the communist countries and one-third to the rest of the world. Nearly 90 percent of the imports were from the bloc. At the 1962 fall fair, business rose to 3.3 billion East German marks. The breakdown was virtually identical. In 1963 transactions at the fall "Leipziger Messe" dropped by 200 million marks to 3.15 billion, and most of the decline was in non-bloc trade. Business with the capitalist countries "exceeded the anticipated amount of 700 million East German marks." (*Neues Deutschland* September 9, 1963.)

Since East Germany does not enjoy normal state and economic relations with the rest of Germany, Leipzig has played an important role as a meeting place for German manufacturers. In the mid-fifties, the fair was something of a clearinghouse for German goods: in 1955 out of 7,575 exhibitors at the fall fair, 5,614 were from East Germany, 1,133 from West Germany, and 146 from West Berlin. This left only 69 exhibitors from the other communist countries and 613 from the rest of the world, mostly European.

West German and West Berlin participation dropped sharply in the fall of 1961 because of the wall to only 471 and 23 exhibitors; after the initial shock, however, the West German and West Berliners began to return to Leipzig and their exhibits totalled 587 in 1963. By that year, the East Germans had cut their own exhibits by some 900 and the total had decreased to 6,459. The over-all distribution was quite different from the pattern in the fall of 1955: communist exhibitors had risen to 119 and participants from the rest of the world excluding German firms had increased to 1,038, of which 855 were European.

The pattern in the spring fairs is nearly identical, but the totals are higher. For 1964 there were 8,532 exhibits—5,442 from East Germany, 709 from West Germany, 116 from West Berlin, 294 from the communist bloc, and 1,971 (1,423 European) from other areas. British firms led with 200 displays in 1964.

With the exception of visitors from the Soviet bloc—who came as a demonstration of East European solidarity with the East German regime—attendance also fell off in 1961 after the wall was erected. It too is again on the rise. Over 589,000 persons visited Leipzig for the 1964 spring fair and over 196,000 for the fall fair in 1963, including more than 30,000 foreigners each year. Forecasts for 1965 estimate that 80,000 visitors from abroad will come to the Leipzig Fair.

Yugoslavia. The international trade fair in Zagreb has several points in common with the Leipzig fairs: it has been a sample fair showing more goods from the light and consumer industries than capital goods; it has over 6,000 exhibitors; and it is open for one week in the spring and two in the fall. The Yugoslav government and the Zagreb fair officials go all out to stress the fair's progress and potential as though they were trying to justify its existence and enhance its short history dating from between the wars.

Releases on the Zagreb fair emphasize the variety of exhibitors it attracts. In 1963 goods on display ranged from machine building tools, electrical equipment, automotive products, precision machines, and metallurgical equipment to textiles, leather, footwear, chemicals, wood products, and samples of construction projects and building machines. Over 1,000 domestic and 5,000 foreign exhibitors from 43 countries took part. Visitors that year totalled 1,700,000. In 1964 the proportions of the fair were somewhat larger: 1,202 domestic and 5,013 foreign exhibitors from 53 countries showed; and there were 1,712,000 visitors.

Problems in Conducting East-West Trade: One Company's Experience

George T. French

Just what is it like to do business in East Europe? The Senior Vice-President and Director, Deere and Company, discusses the successes as well as the pitfalls based upon his company's experience.

Deere manufactures a full line of agricultural implements and tractors. In addition, it manufactures industrial machinery of the classes used in home building, in forestry, and in general light construction. It also manufactures lawn and garden equipment, but that is a relatively small part of the operation. Deere is a growth company with an annual volume of sales currently well over $1 billion. Its overseas volume of sales is in excess of $165 million annually.

Specifically, it has pioneered in the design, development, and manufacture of large equipment for large farms. Is there a need for such equipment in Eastern Europe? The answer is "Yes!" With the increasing industrialization of Eastern Europe, agricultural labor is being pulled away from the land, and machinery is needed to replace it. The movement of labor from farms to cities in Bulgaria, for example, is strikingly evident in the last two census counts. In a period of ten years, in spite of an increase in total population of 600,000 persons, the rural population decreased by 300,000 while the population of the cities increased by 900,000.

A sizable part of agriculture in Eastern Europe is composed of large collective farms, and my company's equipment is tailor-made to meet their needs. For example, in Yugoslavia our potential market is growing rapidly because, in their attempt to raise productivity, the big state farms are seeking larger farm machines than are produced in Eastern Europe or, for that matter, in Western Europe.

Eastern Europe wants to increase its trade with the West. This is evident from recent visits of trade missions from various Eastern European countries to the United States, as well as from the fact that Poland has just become a full member of GATT, along with Czechoslovakia and Yugoslavia, while Hungary, Rumania, and Bulgaria enjoy "observer" status in GATT. The desire as well as the need to trade is there.

Am I saying that our success in the Eastern European markets is a sure thing? Not at all! There is a need throughout that area for the products Deere and its competitors produce. There is a desire to obtain these products to mechanize agriculture. But desire by itself is not equivalent to demand; the purchaser must also have the funds or the ability to obtain funds in order to convert his desire into effective demand.

East-West trade has more than doubled in the last decade, a faster growth than that enjoyed by trade within Eastern Europe or among the Western countries by themselves. But East-West trade has been, and is, only a very small part of total world trade. In 1965, total world trade amounted to $184 billion, while East-West trade amounted to $12 billion, or only 7 percent of the total.

I suppose that everyone might not agree as to what countries are included in the Eastern European group. In my approach to the subject, I include the Comecon countries, including the Soviet Union, of course, and I also include Yugoslavia.

Comecon includes within its perimeter over 330 million people—almost 60 million more than the countries of the EEC and EFTA combined. The arable land within Comecon is four times that of the EEC and EFTA combined, and is considerably greater than that of the United States and Canada combined.

My company has sold its products in Eastern Europe since 1912, but sales have been minimal, with the exception of substantial quantities sold to the Soviet Union between 1929 and 1931, and to Yugoslavia during the past few years. Indeed, such sales as have occurred outside of these two general exceptions have been mainly for test purposes. To give you an idea of the volume of business involved, our exports to Yugoslavia totaled $1.5 million in 1966, which represented 10 percent of Yugoslavia's total imports of such goods. This $1.5 million figure is 1 percent of the total of all classes of U.S. exports to Eastern Europe.

Many companies have been relying mainly upon the same methods of doing business as they use in the West, but the point has now been reached where if sales to Eastern Europe are to be increased, solutions must be found to certain major problems which exist in our relationships with that part of the world. Three major problems need resolution:

1. The existence of vastly different systems of marketing and merchandising.

Reprinted by permission of the publisher from AMA Management Bulletin 119, *Financing East-West Business Transactions.*

2. The fact that United States exporters to Eastern Europe face greater restrictions than their Western European counterparts.

3. The problems of finance and credit.

The first major problem area relates to marketing techniques. North American businessmen know how to set up regional marketing units for their products, and generally speaking, we know how to go about finding independent businessmen to become dealers or distributors for our products. However, in most Eastern European countries, goods generally are not distributed by independent businessmen, but rather through state-owned enterprises; and the importation of goods is tightly controlled by government authorities. The profit motive on the part of the marketing organizations is absent in some Eastern European countries, and in others profit margins are controlled too tightly to allow for adequate service facilities and for the support of adequate inventories, replacement parts, and so on.

In most of these countries, the decisions to import and to sell Western-produced goods are made by government agencies. In order to move from the Western profit-oriented system of business procedures to the Eastern methods of commerce, a new concept of marketing relationships must be developed. For example, the procedure of sending product specifications or Western-style advertising literature to an appropriate government agency is not sufficient. Personal contacts are a necessity, and these contacts, to be effective, must be with the levels of government people who have the authority and the power to influence and to make purchasing decisions. Therefore, competent, high-level people must represent us in making these personal contacts. We are represented by a Yugoslav who looks after our interests in Hungary, Rumania, and Bulgaria, by a very competent German territory manager, and by a division manager with a record of success in Eastern European affairs. Frequent visits and contacts by the top men in our European headquarters and by corporate officers and directors from our U.S. company have proved effective in establishing long-range programs.

This is not the only marketing problem. In North America we make great use of the techniques of advertising on radio and TV and in newspapers and magazines. In addition, some of us have been successful in using direct mail advertising. However, in Eastern European countries the chief promotional technique is through exhibitions at trade fairs. Deere has participated in such fairs in Yugoslavia and Czechoslovakia and plans to do so in Bulgaria this year. Typically, we use exhibits in pavilions set up by the United States Government displaying the types of machines we think are needed. It is important that these exhibits should be manned by people who are effective communicators and who know the products well. These presentations lead to actual demonstrations of products in the field, which we believe is of vital importance.

The U.S. Department of Commerce has been doing a fine job of promoting goods produced in this country via trade fair exhibits in Eastern European countries. If a company is serious about establishing markets in those countries, it should participate in these numerous trade fairs. The U.S. Department of Commerce would be pleased to provide dates and other pertinent details.

Another marketing problem is in the area of after-sale service. Companies which produce such products as processed foods or clothing do not have this problem to the same degree as do companies manufacturing complex mechanical equipment. In our own case, because we manufacture tractors, combines, and other complicated mechanical devices, we need to ensure the existence of good customer service. A user of our goods would be dissatisfied with our product if he were unable to obtain the necessary repair parts or if qualified servicemen were not available to make those repairs which require special mechanical know-how or special tools to accomplish the job.

Picture, if you will, the problems of establishing a competent service organization and of training a competent service organization and of training its members in a country which severely limits the right of foreigners to enter. And picture the problems of establishing adequate supply depots for repair parts in a country which exercises a high level of government control over the purchase and importation of materials and components. In addition, there are difficulties of securing ideal or even adequate locations for such facilities.

I have not mentioned all of the many technical matters that can be significant barriers. Others include the preparation and printing of operators' manuals and service publications in the language or languages of the host country. And—another example—many times importation of replacement parts is not allowed because a similar type of item is locally produced; but in actuality, the differing engineering and manufacturing standards result in locally produced parts which are not compatible with our machines. In this connection, we actively support the work of such organizations as the United States of America Standards Institute and the International Standards Organization, to which most Eastern European countries belong.

Each Eastern European country has its own personality, its own customs, its own concepts of doing business, and its own degree of government control. To illustrate this point, of all the Eastern European countries, doing business in Yugoslavia is more nearly like doing business in Western Europe. The Yugoslav Government has provided a significant degree of decision-making authority for its business enterprises. It is our judgment that if a Yugoslav enterprise can make adequate arrangements for convertible currency or for credit, it is relatively free to import anything it chooses. Furthermore, in Yugoslavia, there are distributors who have about the same concepts of business relations and marketing as we have in the West.

At the other extreme is the Soviet Union, with its very high level of central government control. Although various government-owned enterprises are being given more prerogatives by the government, and although we often read of the new profit motive concept that is being instilled in some of the state factories, farms, and trading enterprises, the fact remains that, for any significant importation, central government approval is still required.

The other Eastern European countries have their own distinct places between these two extremes. Sometimes the government control is indirect. In Czechoslovakia, for example, import control is achieved by establishing different currency exchange rates for different specific products. However, interesting changes are taking place in the economic policies of all Eastern European nations, reflecting deliberate interest in placing business and production on a more market-responsive basis, and today's ranking of liberalization may not be the same tomorrow.

With these illustrations we have indicated the seriousness of this first major problem area—that is, the sharply different concepts of marketing and merchandising between East and West.

The second major problem area applies to the United States as distinct from other Western countries. Our trade with Eastern Europe faces greater limitations than other East-West trade. Partly as the result of these limitations, in 1966 only $375 million of U.S. trade, or less than 1 percent of our foreign commerce, was with Eastern Europe. In contrast, West German trade with Eastern Europe exceeded $2 billion. The comparable figure for the United Kingdom was about $1 billion.

While export controls of the U.S. Department of Commerce have been and are continuing to be liberalized, still today U.S. exporters to Eastern Europe and subject to greater restrictions than the exporters of other Western countries. We recognize the need for export controls on "strategic goods" and comply with the controls "to the letter." I only wish to point out that the U.S. "strategic goods" list is longer than that of any other Western nation, and thus United States-Eastern Europe trade is not on an equal footing with other East-West trade.

Another point, in the case of the Soviet Union and East Germany, is that there appears to be a policy of not purchasing from U.S. firms if the product is available elsewhere.

United States-Eastern Europe trade is also on unequal footing in the important field of government credits and the insurance of commercial credits, and in the farm machinery business, where credit is essential at both the wholesale and retail levels of trade. However, I want to point out that progress has been made. In July 1964, the U.S. Export-Import Bank was authorized to provide normal commercial credit guarantees on industrial export transactions with Rumania. In October 1966, the President of the United States extended the authorization to include Poland, Czechoslovakia, Hungary, and Bulgaria.

However, before granting guarantees, the Export-Import Bank demands greater assurances than those required by its Western European counterparts, for example, Hermes in West Germany and COFACE in France. Hermes accepts the guarantee on Yugoslav promissory notes of as many as 16 different trading banks, but our Export-Import Bank will only accept the guarantee of the Yugoslav Central Bank, which unfortunately is no longer available.

Even though Deere is an American company, we enjoy substantial advantages as a result of our Western European presence. We have several major factories in Germany, France, and Spain, sales branches in the larger Western European countries, and a headquarters in Heidelberg. Our European-manufactured goods can be shipped to the Wastern European countries with the benefit of the more liberal credit insurance facilities available for European-produced goods.

This is not the only advantage in the field of East-West trade derived from having Western European operations. Others are:

- The geographic proximity to the Eastern markets, which facilitates travel, communications, and thus sales and service to the area.
- Multilingual personnel.
- A combined European-American corporate image.

I shall now touch upon the third area, the financial problems facing Deere and almost any Western firm attempting to sell in the potentially vast Eastern European market.

At the top of the list of financial problems is the limited amount of "convertible" foreign exchange abailable to the Eastern Europeans for their purchases of Western-made agricultural machinery. Their "convertible" foreign exchange reserves are considered to be at a minimum "consistent with maneuverability in foreign trade." Their access to suppliers' and other credits, such as those available from the Soviet-controlled banks in London and Paris and credits available from Western banks, are limited, and their gold production and gold holdings are also limited. For these countries to be able to increase significantly their purchases abroad, they must be able to sell abroad. Trade is still a two-way street.

In certain countries, there are particular obstacles that restrict East-West trade. For example, in Czechoslovakia, each enterprise must earn its own foreign exchange through sales of its goods abroad before it may import. When the director of the Export-Import Agency of Czechoslovakia called on us in Moline last summer, he was accompanied by the commercial director of the Czechoslovakian company which manufactures tractors and implements. They were traveling together in an effort to sell their products in exchange for the importation of ours.

Eastern Europe has increased its exports to the West in the last few years. A large part of the credit for this must go to the able Eastern European operators, since some Eastern European countries are allowing greater contacts between state firms and foreign businessmen, thus bypassing the central planners who are often unaware of the possibilities of the Western market or unable to cope with its "mysteries." A very recent example: Since January 1, 1968, and subject to certain conditions, Hungarian enterprises which have applied for and received permission from the Council of Ministers on a case-by-case basis are allowed independently to handle export and import contracts without the intervention of any state organization concerned with foreign trade.

Most of the products that Eastern Europe exports—raw materials, various food products, and relatively simple manufactures—while of considerable interest to Western Europe, face limited prospects in the United States. Thus Eastern Europe will continue to have difficulty in financing the purchase of U.S. goods unless and until it moves to multilateral trading and free, convertible exchange. Unfortunately, this may be a long way off, but one can hope that we will help shorten the time.

Western businessmen are developing ingenious ways of getting around the shortage of convertible foreign exchange. Two of these methods are switch-trading and barter. Deere has not yet used switch-trading techniques; however, we are actually starting to use bartered Eastern European raw materials in our Western European manufacturing operations.

Local assembly and/or partial manufacture are possible ways to reduce foreign exchange requirements. Deere has not yet used these techniques, but we have some proposals under consideration.

Another way for a company to make it possible for Eastern European countries to buy its products is for the company to buy Eastern European goods which complement its own product line and to sell them in its regular territories through its own established sales organization, thus eliminating the need for the Eastern European producer to learn the marketing methods of the West or to build marketing and service organizations abroad. Deere has not agreed as yet to do this, but it is currently considering one or two such proposals. It is probably no accident that the one Western country—West Germany—that is best able and willing to do this is also the one that does the most business with Eastern Europe.

As I indicated earlier, credit is essential in our industry at wholesale and retail levels of trade. Farm machinery companies typically accept purchasers' notes and discount them at their commercial banks. Commonly two to five years' financing is demanded by Eastern European governments as well as by end-users. The exporter has the opportunity to secure, through the buying agency in most countries, a guarantee from a bank which is placed on the draft or the promissory note to the exporter. Government export insurance organizations in Germany, France, Italy, and the United Kingdom accept these guarantees from trade banks in Yugoslavia and from central banks elsewhere. In this way these notes are conveniently discounted by Western European banks on goods manufactured in their countries.

However, a new problem has appeared recently in Yugloslavia. Now in order to secure a bank guarantee, the purchaser must make a deposit of 50 percent of the value of the purchase in his bank in local currency and leave it there for the duration of the credit. This, plus the down payment we require, becomes excessive for the buyer—and leaves us with a choice between accepting notes with only the guarantees of our distributor and of the state farms, which guarantees we must hold in our own portfolio, or of passing up the business transaction entirely.

Pressures of Growth on the Polish Marketing System

Dr. J. Hart Walters

Marketing in Eastern Europe is a confusing and complex experience to anyone unfamiliar with how the system operates. Western businessmen cannot hope to be successful unless they understand existing market structures and how to adapt to them. Professor Walters, Chairman of the Marketing Department at Temple University, is an authority on the Polish marketing system. While the Polish system is not synonymous with other East European systems, he points out that there are significant common elements that are of value when doing business anywhere within the bloc.

The most significant force influencing the functioning of the marketing apparatus in Poland has been the rapid growth of her economy. This growth has generated considerable pressure on the marketing system and on the consumers' goods sector as a whole. Some of the phenomena to be discussed might exist in any economy that has been rapidly growing from a peasant to an industrialized status; others are distinctly outgrowths of the economic planning characterizing contemporary socialist states.

Demand Pressure: Type I

From the standpoint of the marketing system, as from that of any industry serving consumers, an important source of pressure (and also of opportunity) is population. At the end of the War, Poland had suffered a considerable population decline. This was due to territorial and population transfers to the U.S.S.R., repatriation of "Volksdeutsche" to Germany, destruction by the Nazis of virtually its entire Jewish population, as well as the loss of substantial numbers of other Poles in the War, resistance movement, and extermination camps. In 1946, Poland's population was somewhat less than 24 million, compared with a prewar figure of approximately 34 million.[1] By 1966, the population had increased to almost 32 million, a gain of about one third.[2] In addition, a substantial shift of population from rural to urban locations occurred during the postwar period. In 1946, less than 32 per cent of the population was living in cities and towns; by 1966, urban dwellers represented 50 per cent of the populace.[3]

For the marketing apparatus and consumers' goods sector, these changes meant the bringing of an expanded and entirely new group of the population into a greater degree of reliance on retail facilities for the meeting of their subsistence needs. Traditionally, the rural population had produced a significant share of its own consumption. Between 1946 and 1966, over 8 million "new" consumers were shifted from partial to total reliance on the marketing system.[4] This same phenomenon is illustrated by changes in the chief means of support in the population. Approximately 40 per cent of the prewar population was listed as "nonfarm;" by 1966, this was over 66 per cent.[5]

Pressure on the trade system is implied by the fact that, not only was there a high rate of population growth in general, but that there were important *structural* changes. *More* increase occurred in urban growth than in total population growth, due to a slight decline in the rural population. During the period, 1946-66, the urban population doubled.[6] The urban trade market would therefore have doubled, even assuring no changes in per capita consumption.

Besides the growth of population, consumption also increased considerably. Between 1950 and 1966, total real consumption in Poland increased 176 per cent.[7] *Per capita* real consumption increased by 116 per cent during the same period.[8] Thus, while the *rural* population declined slightly, its consumption increased in the neighborhood of 100 per cent. If the doubling of the *urban* population is then taken into account, total real consumption in the cities and town increased by over 200 per cent.

As would be expected, the increase in consumption is reflected in retail sales data. On the basis of 1961 constant *złoty* prices, retail turnover as a whole increased more than 200 per cent during the 1950-66 period.[9] The increase was slightly less in the countryside, but greater in urban areas. In short, three times as many goods passed through the retail apparatus in 1966 than in 1950. The pressures of more goods moving through the (expanded) retail system are also indicated by the increases in sales per establishment in the socialized sector.

The pressures of increased retail volume described above can only partly be attributed to the institutions of Polish, socialist planning. The basic rate of growth of population operates somewhat inde-

[1] *Rocznik Statystyczny: 1961* (Warsaw: Główny Urzad Statystyczny, 1961), p. 13.
[2] *Rocznik Statystyczny, 1967* (Warsaw: GU5, 1967), p. 22.
[3] *Ibid.*, p. 33.

[4] *Rocznik Statystyczny, op. cit.*, p. 32.
[5] *Ibid.*, p. 43.
[6] *Ibid.*, p. 32.
[7] *Ibid.*, p. 83. Increases in constant, 1961 prices.
[8] *Ibid.*, In constant, 1961 prices.
[9] *Ibid.*, p. 332.

pendently of the prevailing social institutions; similar rates can be observed elsewhere. The shift from a predominantly rural to a more urban population is also a general characteristic of an economy in the process of industrializing. The unusually rapid *tempo* of that shift and the particular direction of that shift is a function of the pace of industrial development, which is at least a partial consequence of socialist planning and direction of the economy.

Demand Pressure: Type II

While the marketing system has had to face the pressure of greatly expanded volume arising from population and consumption increases, another pressure of an equally fundamental sort has been operating. National income (and therefore total production) has been increasing at a more rapid rate than consumption (and therefore the production of goods intended for personal consumption). Consumption has been increasing very rapidly, but it has declined as a percentage of the national income. In 1949, for example, "consumption of material goods from personal incomes" was 77.8 per cent of national income; by 1966 it had declined to 63.9 per cent.[10] By the same token, production of consumption goods increased about 324 per cent during the 1950-66 period, while that of producers' goods rose about 563 per cent.[11] Gross money wages payments increased 537 per cent during the same period.[12] Expressed somewhat differently, average wage and salary payments *per capita* rose 250 per cent during the 1950-66 period,[13] while *per capita* production of "objects of consumption" increased about 200 per cent.[14]

The meaning of these disparities can be expressed in the simple terms of a considerable and continued pressure of demand on the entire sector responsible for supplying consumers' goods to the population. Such relationships are reflected as shortages of goods relative to demand ("sellers' market"). They are reflected equally in the relationship between the demand for and supply of marketing services.

Pressure on Marketing Services: Type I

The problem of a shortage of trade services is more difficult to express quantitatively. The number of persons of population per retail selling point has declined, from 245 in 1950, to 172 in 1966, indicating some improvement in terms of the number of people that have to move through any one retail establishment.[15] At the same time, constant *złoty* retail sales per person of population have increased 141 per cent during the sixteen-year period.[16] Calculating from these data and from data on sales *per establishment*, i.e. real, *per capita* sales per establishment, it is found that the *average purchase made by any "one" person at any "one" retail selling point* had increased by about one-half during the sixteen-year period.[17]

The simple meaning of the latter calculation is that the average customer of a retail establishment in 1966 was purchasing approximately half again as many goods as he would have purchased in such an establishment in 1950. When it is realized, further, that food sales have declined as a percentage of total sales, the pressure of increase clientele with increased purchases would be relatively greater in non-food establishments.

It could thus be hypothesized: while fewer people have to "move" through each retail establishment than in 1950, since each person purchases more goods therein, he will therefore spend more time in the establishment. *The phenomena of crowding and queues, so frequently alluded to in the Western press as a symptom of shortage and poverty is thus, paradoxically, at least partly a function of increased affluence and, even more paradoxically, of a more efficient operating scale in retail units.* While real shortages of goods, both short-term and chronic, *in relation to demand*, do and in fact must exist because of the disparities referred to earlier, the journalists' picture of bare shelves is simply incorrect.

Demand pressure, type II, as well as the pressures on trade services just indicated can properly be characterized as a result of Poland's version of socialist planning. Demand pressure, type II, results from the conscious decision to achieve the maximum possible rate of accumulation, i.e. investment out of income, with a consequent relative curtailment of consumption. Given the added factors of (1) a level of personal consumption that was in the prewar and early postwar years exceedingly low by Western standards, (2) socially and politically necessary wage increases without corresponding price increases, (3) greater-than-expected increases in farmers' incomes, the continued relative curtailment of production in the consumers' goods sector as well as the rigidity of the retail pricing system can only increase such pressures.

---

[10] *Rocznik Statystyczny, 1967, op. cit.*, p. 87.

[11] *Ibid.*, p. 119.

[12] *Ibid.*, p. 546.

[13] *Ibid.*

[14] *Rocznik Statystyczny: 1967, op. cit.*, p. 119 and calculations.

[15] *Ibid.*, p. 340. Hodoly and Jastrzębowski show that the prewar number of persons per *all* trading establishments was about 70, but that the number of persons per establishment of the *shop* type was about 263 persons. Present statistics break the trade network, but not sales, into shop and non-shop categories, so a comparison of present with prewar data is not valid. A. Hodoly and W. Jastrzębowdki, *Handel Wiejski w Polsce Międzywojennej*, (Warsaw: PWG, 1957), p. 15.

[16] *Ibid.*, p. 332, 258.

[17] Calculated from *ibid.*

Pressures on Trade Services, Type II

The pressures on trade services discussed hereabove are essentially the result of disparities in economic forces that, not being resolvable by a market, are a function of the basic direction and emphasis of Polish planning. Other kinds of pressures, reflecting the particular concepts of organization used, produce certain results in the sphere of services.

The principal organizational feature that creates a pressure on services is the high degree of assortment-specialization typical of Polish retailing. While Polish retailing is "broken down" into branches that to some degree reflect broad, consumption-associated groups of goods, the breakdown itself is (a) traditional, and (b) tends to reflect grouping in terms of production characteristics rather than consumption associations.[18] Manufacturer-ordered assortments are not, however, peculiarly Polish, but characterize retailing in much of Western Europe, as well. The tendency towards manufacturer-ordered assortment in Poland reflects the fact that a considerable number of retail trade establishments are "factory stores" operated by a given manufacturing enterprise or industry.

Numerous examples of this specialization can be cited from observation. A "Chemia" plastics-chemical-synthetics shop will contain an assortment of, among other things, synthetic fabric yard goods (but not necessarily the other materials required to make a suit), phonograph records (but not phonographs, and maybe not even needles), molded plastic toilet seats (but not the metal mounting hardware). A paint store may have paints ranging from household enamel to automotive lacquer, but not always paint brushes.

The State retail trade enterprises, as distinct from factory branch outlets, do tend to organize shops into assortments more clearly identified with consumption characteristics. However, similar patterns of assortment can be observed even in department stores. For example, a common household funnel can be located separately in the plastics, enamelware, and metalware departments, each grouped with other items manufactured from like materials rather than with each other.

Food stores are also specialized. Except for some of the larger self-service stores and the few really large supermarkets which offer some selection of prepackaged meats and fresh produce, food stores are broken down into general (mostly dry) groceries, meat, fish, produce, bakery, and dairy stores.[19]

The inevitable result of this kind of specialization is to generate considerable pressure on the time and effort required by consumers to meet their needs. Food store specialization has meant that daily food shopping requires visits to several different establishments. This is complicated further by the fact that there is not even necessarily a consistency of assortment among shops of the same type. General grocery store "A" may characteristically carry item "X," but general grocery store "B," not.

For requirements not in the typical course of daily shopping, the pressure on the consumer's time and energy is often greater. Not infrequently the consumer must undergo a rather considerable "searching" effort to find an article he thinks of as suitable. The less frequent the purchase, the more difficult the problem, for the precise nature of assortment at a given establishment may have changed since the consumer's most recent exposure to it. The change may be due to that establishment having exhausted its stock, although another establishment might have received a fresh shipment, unknown to the consumer. Not having an automobile, the drain on the consumer's time to go to other establishments can be considerable.

A further factor exacerbating this apparent mismatching of supply with demand is the general lack of information calling the consumer's attention to such specific changes in the supply situation. It is left primarily to him to seek out this kind of information, although such facilities as information booths are available in the larger cities. Information on the availability of scarce and strongly-demanded items, particularly imports, is as a rule disseminated widely through the daily press. Media advertising by specific retail establishments of the existence of particular items of merchandise is almost totally absent on any kind of regular basis.

Reason for the Pressures

The general inadequacy of trade services is explained in Poland as being part of the general phenomenon of the "sellers' market." The latter is defined in the traditional terms of a pressure of demand on relatively short supplies at existing price levels. It is pointed out that "in capitalism the

conditions of a sellers' market leads to increases of price, which ordinarily denote a tendency towards re-establishment of the balance of demand with supply, or towards liquidation of the sellers' market. In socialism because of the rigid price system, these same market forces foster a service phenomenon . . . which I would be inclined to call minimization of services."[20]

---

[18]See Z. Misiaszek, *Zasady Ustalania Asortymentów dla Sieci Detalicznej* [Bases of Establishing Assortments for the Retail Network] (Warsaw: Biblioteka Instytutu Handlu Wewnętrznego, 1960) for a thorough and critical discussion of the assortment problem.

[19]For a more detailed classification, see Misiaszek, *op. cit.*, pp. 26-27.

[20]W. Jastrzębowski, "Rynek nabywcy," *op. cit.*, p. 4. Jastrzębowski uses the term, *minimalizacja swiadczeń.* The Polish noun, swiadczenia (pl.) literally means "benefits" or "services" with the connotation of something that is *due* or *obligatory*. By using this term rather than the *usługi*—"services," Jastrzębowski strongly implies that these are services that *should* be rendered to the public.

And further: ". . . the phenomenon of minimization of services can be

understood as a tendency of human functioning which, in the case of buyer-seller transactions is expressed as a tendency for the seller to give to the buyer only what he must give, and not what he can give."[21]

Expressed differently, since there is a "sellers' market" in contemporary Poland and a generally short supply of consumers' goods in relation to demand for them, it is not a matter of any great difficulty for a retail establishment to dispose of its stock. Since (1) the retail establishment is prohibited from changing the price of any item in its stock to mirror demand conditions more accurately; (2) since its own profitability depends solely on its ability to achieve maximum turnover of those items that are already in demand; and (3) since "those items that are already in demand" can, by definition, be sold at existing price levels, there is literally no material incentive for the establishment to offer a high level of services.

The lack of incentive to offer a high level of services can be expressed in several ways. At the level of the individual *sales clerk*, there is no *direct* incentive to offer anything but the dispensing of the goods that are available. The clerk has an indirect interest in the turnover of the establishment being as high as possible, because wages are related to the level of sales. But this interest is undifferentiated as far as specific goods are concerned.

At the level of the *establishment*, since nothing can be done to stimulate movement of slow items, it is interested only in turning over fast-moving items that are already in strong demand. Because the items are already in strong demand, it need do nothing other than have them available, and its primary effort would be oriented towards maintaining adequate stocks. When the demand items are out of stock, there is not even a particular incentive for the establishment to be open. If its management so decides, it can close down for "inventory" or for "reception of goods," in truth for any reason it desires.[22]

The establishment and the enterprise which controls it *are* interested in goods that carry the higher margins, but unless that article happens to be in strong demand at the prevailing price, there is little the management can do to expand demand. It can not lower price, and the gross margin is so low that the establishment or enterprise simply could not stand the expense of either promotional or service-improving costs that might increase sales.

By the same token, there is therefore neither incentive nor possibility for the enterprise to make important alterations in one of the most basic elements of service, that of assortment. The enrichment of assortment at individual retail points is also inhibited by institutional barriers, in addition to the economic barriers previously alluded to. To expand in any important sense the assortment carried by its establishments, an enterprise would either have to consolidate with other enterprises or obtain goods that traditionally "belong" to other branches. Any such consolidation would, at the minimum, require approval of the controlling local or regional Peoples' Council, and might, in addition, require a substantial revamping of distribution channels with possibly drastic investment implications.

In theory, an enterprise or establishment can vary its assortment. In practice it has no mechanism to "bid" for short-supply goods that are destined for those enterprises defined as their major distributors.

Another Service Pressure: Suitability of Goods

There are two basic elements in the suitability of goods for consumers. The first of these is the quality of the goods themselves, in terms of an item being designed as the consumer needs it and being made well. The second of these is the suitability and adjustment of the structure of assortments to consumers' preferences.[24]

While "the source of low quality of goods moved into distribution occurs in production,"[24] the suitability, i.e., the correspondence of design of goods to consumers' needs and preferences is to a considerable degree a function of the ability of the marketing apparatus to act as a "transmission belt" in communicating preferences to the production sector. The success of this transmission depends first on the responsiveness and sensitivity of trade organizations to consumers' preferences, and secondly, upon the responsiveness of "industry" both to preferences expressed to it by the trade apparatus, as well as directly by consumers.

The problem of intrinsic quality, i.e., that a product is technically well-designed and made to operate as it is supposed to, is correctly perceived as being a function of the technological development of the industry and the skill of its workers. Given the rapid pace of industrialization, requiring in effect the transformation of an essentially peasant population into an industrial labor force, it is inevitable that there will be a "large flow of unqualified laborers into industry."[25]

---

[21]W. Jastrzębowski, "Rynek nabywcy," *op. cit.*

[22]"Zamknięte–remanent," Closed for Inventory, *Handel Wewnętrzny*, No. 4 (1959), p. 103.

[23]See E. Wiszniewski, *Handel Uspołeczniony w Warunkach Szybkiego Wzrostu Gospodarki Socjalistyzcnej* [Socialized Trade in Conditions of Rapid Growth of a Socialist Economy] (Warsaw: Państwowe Wydawnictwo Ekonomiczne, 1962), p. 9.

[24]Wisniewski, *op. cit.*, p. 10.

[25]Wiszmewski, *op. cit.*

Over the postwar years, complaints of the poor quality of much of the output of socialized industry in Poland have been legion. In recent years, this situation has improved vastly as a result of (1) better industrial design by the growing cadre of graduate engineers, (2) upgrading of the skill of the labor force through on-the-job training and after-hours education, (3) establishment of more precise technical norms, product specifications, and a grading system, (4) adoption of more rigorous procedures of quality control, and (5) institution of factory guarantees to consumers for virtually all manufactured goods. The problem of intrinsic quality is by no means fully solved to the satisfaction of either consumers or planners and administrators. But it can safely be regarded as improving and as largely solvable within the present institutional framework.

The problem of *suitability*, i.e., the matching of (a) the assortment and (b) the design of goods to consumers' preferences is another question, however, in which the present institutional framework plays the determining role.

From the standpoint of planning in general, and even more specifically from an operational standpoint, "trade" is regarded as a "profession" or "division of the national economy, which as a result of the social division of labor is specialized in carrying out buyer-seller transactions and other trading functions, and hence in realizing the distribution of goods."[26] And further: ". . . it is said of trade, that it is occupied with the purchase of goods with the objective of their resale, neither producing them nor consuming them."[27]

While, in the article referred to, trade is also treated, functionally, as an activity in which producers and consumers are engaged, it is nonetheless true that economic specialization in Poland has tended to draw a sharp line between marketing and manufacturing. A part of this line relates to economic incentives; and part of it is more strictly organizational.

Just as the marketing enterprise operates within an environment of fixed supply and resale prices, so, in effect does the manufacturing enterprise. In general, a factory has the incentive to achieve the largest possible total volume of production in terms, not of a "pile" of specific goods, but in aggregate value. The precise nature and balance of assortment to be produced is, as a rule, its own prerogative. Since the prices for each article the factory produces may bear little direct relationship to its cost, the margins for different articles in the productive assortment of a given factory can vary considerably. The factory management will thus have a tendency to emphasize production of those items, the margin for which is highest. It would be largely a matter of chance whether such an assortment would correspond directly to consumers' preferences. Indirectly, the broader limits of consumers' preference, or really consumers' tolerance would have some effect, for the accumulation of inventories would eventually call for changes.

However, the fact of the "sellers' market" to a considerable degree inhibits such adaptation. A factory producing, say, shoes may structure its assortment for its own "convenience." The consumer might be dissatisfied, but he needs shoes enough to accept the factory's offering rather than go without.

The degree to which consumers' preference could then be satisfied depends largely on the availability of suitable, alternative choices. In an economic sense, this choice has been limited by the general conditions of the "sellers' market": if there aren't enough goods to go around, demand is not satisfied, and so, by definition, neither can preferences be met.

The availability of alternative choices depends, moreover, on the institutional framework especially the relative absence or presence of monopoly. The general statement that "the State" is a monopoly is only partly true, insofar as monopoly would be defined in terms of confrontation of the consumer with a single enterprise that is the sole producer or seller of a given class of goods meeting a given area of his needs. Socialized enterprise in Poland, firstly, is simply not that monolithic in its organization. Secondly, economic specialization itself often requires that the production of given articles be organized into several, rather than one factory. Thirdly, the post-1956 decentralization has meant that different factories producing the same line of goods are often organized as separate enterprises. Fourthly, there are a substantial number of cooperative, as well as handicraft establishments producing consumers' goods at varying scales of operation.

There is thus the nucleus of some competition in production; and there are directly competing products with different trademarks and brands on the market, which may or may not bear differences in price. With competing *food* products, two different brands of, say, canned tomato juice of a given grade would most likely have the same price fixed. Depending on the simultaneous availability of the two, the consumer can exercise preference (and does, let it be added).[28]

This competition between producers is often reflected only weakly at the retail level. If "Brand A" is locally available, probabilities are that "Brand B" is not, because the enterprise controlling a given number

[26] W. Jastrzębowski, "Handel i pojęcia pokrewne" [Trade & Related Conceptions], *Handel Wewnętrzny*, No. 5 (1960), p. 12 (reprint).

[27] W. Jastrzębowski, *op. cit.*

[28] Author's observation. Competition also exists between Polish and foreign products. A substantial proportion of canned foods, for example, is imported from the other Socialist nations.

of establishments received a shipment from the manufacturer of "Brand A" and has distributed it among the different selling points under its control. When there is *retail competition* at the local level it is possible that "Brand A" might be available in State, and "Brand B" in cooperative outlets.

As a general rule, a *single retail selling point* will not simultaneously carry the two brands. If the consumer wants to exercise a brand preference he has first to obtain the information as to where his preference can be satisfied, and secondly to make the necessary trip. Given the fact that the great majority of consumers must either shop on foot or rely on public transportation, the climate is hardly conducive to the efficient exercise of preference.[29]

There is little evidence to indicate that retailing enterprises are as yet sufficiently sensitive to the phenomena of brand preferences to take this into account in their ordering and inventory policies. In part, this lack of sensitivity reflects operational problems, one of which is the shortage of display and storage space in the physically-small units of Polish retailing. In addition, inventory management is vastly simplified by avoiding the carrying of directly competing brands. At the same time, there seems to be at least an implied attitude that the retailer's function has been adequately fulfilled as long as he provides a given article of a given grade. In part, this flows from a mechanistic interpretation of socialist criticism of product differentiation, brands, and the practices of brand competition in capitalist economies.[30]

With manufactured, *non-food* items, the picture is somewhat more complicated, and it is more difficult to make generalizations. For some product lines, there is only one Polish brand, which may (or may not) be supplemented by a partial or complete competing line from another socialist country (e.g., Polish "Foton" photographic films and East German "Orwo" films). In other lines, there are competing Polish producers. Competing products with either or both design and price differences can appear on the market.

For manufactured goods, there appear to be more examples of direct competition at the retail level (i.e., appearance of competing goods in the same shop), than is the case with food items. This is partly illusory, because the relatively higher prices of manufactured, non-food goods often militate towards slower turnover. Since the retailer has no ability to lower price to clear the market, "Brand A" may linger on the shelves long after the arrival of "Brand B."

[29] This section of the discussion is based on the author's observations, and upon discussions with Polish specialists in the field.

[30] The inference is the author's. Any fear of abuse of brands seems unwarranted in view of the universality of grade labeling in accordance with defined, objective product standards, as well as price control.

Conclusions and Mechanism for Change

In evaluating the various pressures discussed in the preceeding pages, it is important to attempt a separation of those arising from purely demographic and non-institutional economic forces, and those that are a function of Poland's socialist institutions. In a basic sense, it is impossible to make such a sharp separation, for neither set of forces (to the extent that they can even be identified separately) can properly be categorized as independent variables.

It might thus be hypothesized that the marketing system simply has "more to do" as a result purely of population growth, rapid "urbanization" of the population, increased income, wider distribution of purchasing power, and more production of consumers' goods that have to "move" through that system. Even if the above movements could be isolated from the phenomenon of socialist planning, the tempo of growth of the marketing system itself and its method of adaptation to the above mentioned changes are very distinctly a function of socialist institutions.

The over-riding condition of the marketing system's adaptation to change has been that of the "sellers' market" in consumers' goods and marketing services. The relative shortage of consumers' goods in relation to demand is itself a function of the conscious decision of planners to accumulate at the relative expense of present consumption. The rigidity of consumers' (and other) prices is an institutional expression of planning which prevents the "automatic" liquidation of the sellers' market, which in turn leads to "minimization of services," since sellers need make no special effort to dispose of their wares. The structure of material incentives for individuals and organizations at different levels is also a reflection of planner-defined relationships that tend to produce the results spoken of.

It is a legitimate question to ask if the difficulties, which have been freely and sharply acknowledged by Polish authors, are an inevitable consequence of socialist planning of growth in a weakly-developed economy. The answer to this question depends largely on the objectives of that planning and adherence to them in the process of their execution. If the basic objective of planning is to mobilize scarce resources and direct their use towards (1) rapid industrialization, and if that rapid industrialization emphasizes (2) the rapid development of basic industrial capacity, i.e., heavy industry, a direct technological requirement of that planning is (3) an emphasis on the accumulation of producers' goods at as fast a rate as possible. As a direct *economic* consequence, it is therefore largely inevitable that present consumption, and the development of the entire consumers' goods sector of the society *must, in a relative sense* be curtailed. The "sellers' market" in consumers' goods and marketing services with *its* particular consequences is therefore almost inevitable, given these objectives and any substantial degree of adherence to them.

Inevitable or otherwise, these have been the basic facts of Polish development of the consumers' goods sector under her particular version of socialist planning. It is thus more relevant to ask: What is the potential for change, and wherein lies the *dynamic* for change, given (1) Poland's current level of economic development; (2) her projected plans; and (3) her institutional framework, including projected changes in that framework?

The basic condition for elimination or substantial amelioration of the pressures and difficulties referred to is *liquidation of the sellers' market*. Can the sellers' market then be liquidated within the present framework of Polish social and economic institutions? The answer would be a qualified "yes" as far as the basic *goods aspect* of the sellers' market is concerned; because:

1) Consumers' goods production will increase (continuing an already rapid rate of expansion).
2) While the rate of capital accumulation will continue to be high, consumers' goods production is scheduled to increase at an increasing rate.
3) The assortment of consumers' goods will be broadened.
4) The numbers of different establishments producing given lines of consumers' goods will increase, further expanding the nucleus of competitive production.

Assuming that the basic goals set forth in the perspective, current, and next long-term plans can be met, (and there is no reason to believe that in broad terms they cannot), the "sellers' market" can be thought of as being liquidable in the aggregate sense. The specific time period for its liquidation can not, of course, be predicted.

From the standpoint of consumers' services, several elements of planning goals appear promising:

1) The number of marketing establishments will continue to increase.
2) Emphasis is to be on more modern forms, including self-service, preselection, and broader lines of assortment in convenience-goods outlets.
3) A much more rapid rate of expansion of the labor force in marketing than has heretofore been the case is planned.

Other problems, however, remain unsolved:

1) The mechanism of adaptation to specific elements of consumers' preference: In this connection, the quality of information should improve because of intensified market research efforts; but no guarantees for correct use of the information are yet provided because:
2) Conflicts in the structure of incentives between maximization for the producing firm and optimum assortment in response to consumers' preference have not been resolved, nor has a framework that assures their resolution yet been established, although the incentive problem is under continuous discussion.
3) Organization of marketing enterprises horizontally, rather than as large-scale, broader-assortment, vertically-integrated concerns: The basic organizational separation between production and trade, and the unlikeliness of "backwards integration" by marketing organizations is an inhibiting factor for this development.
4) Rigidity of the pricing system still prevents effective balancing of supply and demand in terms, especially, of rapid adjustment to change. Fundamental alteration of the pricing system can not be predicted.

The point of the immediately preceding discussion is to hypothesize: the basic goods aspect of the sellers' market can be liquidated under present methods of planning and administration, but the very presence of relative "plenty" in such an environment will produce new problems. Essentially, and in the broadest possible terms, it will be a problem of the existence of plenty under a set of institutional conditions that have been designed fundamentally for administering a situation of scarcity.

Trading with the Soviet Union

The Editors of Business International

There is an unmistakable trend among Eastern European countries toward independence from the Soviet Union. However, attitudes and policies are and will continue to be influenced by the USSR. The editors of Business International offer insights into just how a state-controlled trading company works and touch upon many of the less formal and less well known aspects of negotiating a sale . . . information which may be crucial to the businessman.

The Soviet foreign trade system differs markedly from that with which Western traders are familiar. Soviet foreign trade has been a state monopoly since 1918. The State itself conducts foreign trade, through the organs specially set up for that purpose, and determines which organizations shall directly engage in foreign trade operations, what sort of goods shall be traded, and in what volume.

The Ministry of Foreign Trade of the USSR, the central administrative organ in this field, is headed by a Minister who is appointed by the Presidium of the Supreme Soviet after presentation by the USSR Council of Ministers. He is assisted by several deputies directing various aspects of the Ministry's work, and by a collegium including these deputies plus certain chiefs of administration, which deals in an advisory capacity with problems of practical management, progress in the implementation of trade agreements and foreign trade plans, and preparation of the most importnat directives and instructions.

The Ministry is divided into a number of specialized administrations and sections with supervisory, advisory and liaison functions. Regulation and control of imports is handled by two administrations, one dealing with machinery and equipment and the other with raw materials and other manufactured goods. A second pair of administrations deals with exports, with a similar commodity breakdown. There are also five trade administrations with geographic responsibilities, covering trade with the European communist countries, Asian communist countries, non-communist countries of Southeast Asia and the Near East, African countries, and other Western countries. Other administrations deal with currency, financial, planning, economic, customs, legal and treaty, and transportation questions, market analysis and quality inspection of export goods.

Local representatives of the Ministry throughout the country ensure control over the filling of orders placed with manufacturing enterprises for export goods and take the necessary steps to effect delivery. Either alone or in cooperation with local representatives of the State Inspection Commission (Gosinpektsiya), they verify the quality of export goods, exercising general control over packaging, marking and preparation of technical and shipping documents by the producing enterprise.

Those representatives whose territory includes ports and border railroad stations are responsible for seeing to the prompt supply of transportation funds for import and export commodities and the proper storage of freight at transshipment points.

Local representatives of the Ministry of Foreign Trade also supervise the work of the Foreign Trade Organizations (FTOS) in their territory, and may issue orders to correct defects in the work of these organizations. FTOs must keep the representative informed of orders placed with enterprises in his territory.

How the Soviet Union Buys and Sells

The actual purchase of foreign goods and sale of Soviet products abroad is the responsibility of the 32 All-Union Foreign Trade Organizations, juridically independent agencies under the general control of the Ministry of Foreign Trade. A list of these organizations is given in Appendix VI. Each FTO is exclusively entitled to trade with other countries in its particular field of activities, selling the USSR's entire export production and buying all its import requirements in that field.

Each Foreign Trade Organization is headed by a Chairman, with several deputies who are in charge of operational offices handling different parts of the list of commodities or equipment for which the FTO is responsible. Some FTOs are divided first into export and import departments, which in turn are subdivided along the lines of the commodities list assigned to the FTO.

The staff of an operational office consists of a director, his deputies, senior engineers or marketing specialists, foreign correspondence specialists, and an economist. In addition, each FTO has a planning-economic section, an accounting department, a market analysis section, personnel section, transportation sec-

Reprinted with special permission from Chapter V, "Trading with the Soviet Union," *Selling the Soviet Market*, published by Business International Corporation, pp. 20-27. (Editor's note: *Selling the Soviet Market* is one of the most complete analyses on doing business in the USSR, including data on sales and purchasing contracts, advertising costs, Foreign Trade Organizations and tariff schedules.)

tion, technical bureau with the catalog library, legal group and general group.

Each FTO has its own rules determining its legal status and specifying the sphere of its activities, functions, rights, amount of capital, etc. An FTO carries out business deals and other legal activities in its own name and may lodge complaints with, or answer before, courts and arbitration agencies.

The Foreign Trade Organizations conduct export and import operations within the framework of the state foreign trade plan, which is part of the overall national economic plan of the USSR. The plan reflects the import needs and export possibilities of the Soviet economy for a definite period. It is prepared by the Ministry of Foreign Trade, which reviews the short-term plans of the FTOs and the Gosbank and determines priorities, and then submits its overall plan to the State Committee for Planning (Gosplan). There is a certain degree of flexibility in implementation of the final trade plan, permitting modifications to take account of changing needs and possibilities of the national economy, as well as alterations of trade-policy conditions in particular foreign markets.

The Ministry does not give instructions to the FTOs for the conclusion (or non-conclusion) of any particular transaction, but guides and supervises their activities in line with the overall trade plan and with short-term commercial plans drawn up by the individual FTOs in cooperation with the Ministry, which define the quantity and value of each FTO's turnover, the amount of "credits" needed from the State, the expected net income from commissions, and the estimated amount of "taxes" due to the State.

The FTOs' short-term import plans are based on orders received from factories and distribution organizations in the 47 economic regions of the country, after screening by the Regional Economic Council that heads up each region. They take into account planned and existing bilateral agreements, the national production, the investment and consumption plans, prices, and the conditions of purchase and sale and the balance of payments with particular foreign currency areas. Usually the FTOs have more requests than their allocated funds will cover. But the Gosplan can approve additional "credits" for excess requests.

For exports the FTOs' responsibilities are, in order of priority, to fulfill their obligations under existing bilateral agreements, to export goods under barter arrangements, and to export goods to earn foreign exchange for financing imports. The FTOs put their requests for exportable goods to the various Regional Economic Councils. In case of dispute as to whether the goods requested for export are needed for domestic consumption, the Gosplan decides who has priority.

The export side of the Ministry's foreign trade plan is based on two factors: estimates of resources available for export, and estimates of possible sales in foreign markets. Like the import section, it covers a seven-year period and is broken down into annual plans of greater detail. As has already been mentioned, Soviet industry is not geared to supply world markets, but primarily to meet home demand. Exports are regarded only as an instrument for obtaining needed foreign goods. However, there are indications that in the near future the Soviet Union may direct some of its manufacturing facilities increasingly toward the export market.

The FTOs implement their import plans essentially as agents for their "clients" within the framework established by law, receiving a commission for carrying out the customer's instructions. The Soviet organization acting as a client, having received authorization to import commodities or equipment, gives an FTO an import requisition showing the commodities to be bought in a specific quantity or value, in accordance with the foreign trade plan. While the FTOs, therefore, do not actively promote the sale of foreign goods in the USSR, they can and do make recommendations to their clients.

Western businessmen–unable to sell directly to the real buyer (the FTO's client)–must make their approach through, and conclude their transactions with, these monopoly trading organizations. Contacts with the FTOs can be made in various ways: through Amtorg in New York, Soviet foreign trade missions and commercial consulates, the USSR Chamber of Commerce, FTO foreign distributors and by direct mail or advertising.

1) *Amtorg Trading Corp*, a New York corporation (355 Lexington Avenue., tel. MU 2-7404), handles more than half the total dollar value of US-USSR trade. In the absence of a trade agreement with the US, the USSR established Amtorg as a US corporation to carry out trading functions in place of a trade mission. (Amtorg's stock is believed to be held by the Soviet Ministry of Foreign Trade, the Gosbank and the Bank of Foreign Trade.) It acts as an agent of the FTOs in the US, collecting commissions from them for the goods it handles.

The main advantage of Amtorg is that it is a US company with which US manufacturers can deal on a cash basis and with a minimum of paper work. (US manufacturers should be aware, however, that Amtorg is required to file all transactions with the US Department of Justice under the Foreign Agents Registration Act of 1938; such transactions then become public information.) Amtorg may also have greater knowledge of FTO requirements than an intermediary export house because of its direct relationship. And a US firm can maintain closer communications with Amtorg than with the distant FTOs.

Some US firms, however, have reported that Amtorg's inability to make primary decisions has caused difficulties and that Amtorg is not well equipped to handle negotiations involving complex equipment. Companies frequently use Amtorg initially in order to explore commercial relations with the USSR, later establish direct contact with the FTO concerned as negotiations advance.

2) *Soviet foreign trade missions* are located in practically every major country except the US. Their functions are to promote the development of Soviet trade with the host country, to represent the interests of the USSR in all matters pertaining to foreign trade, and to take all necessary steps in the name of the USSR with respect to trade operations with the host country.

The legal status of a trade mission is defined by trade treaties and special agreements on trade agencies concluded between the USSR and foreign states. Since the trade mission is an integral part of the Soviet embassy in the country, the chief of mission and his assistants enjoy all rights and privileges accorded to members of diplomatic missions, and the buildings occupied by the trade mission enjoy diplomatic immunity. Unlike the FTOs, foreign trade missions cannot be sued.

A trade mission comprises operational sections which handle preparation (and, where necessary, conclusion) of foreign trade contracts; a financial accounting unit; economic, transportation and legal groups; and a secretariat. The operational sections are staffed by officials of the various FTOs.

When contracts with foreign firms and organizations are prepared and concluded in the USSR, the FTO must send copies of all documents to the trade mission concerned. In those cases where the contracts are drawn up in foreign countries, they are signed in the FTO's name on the basis of a power of attorney granted by it and certified by the Foreign Trade Ministry.

The foreign trade mission also supervises the work of Soviet foreign trade inspectors. When inspection of manufacture and witnessing the testing of products in foreign countries are provided for in the contract, these inspectors, appointed by the organizations originating the orders, are sent out from the USSR.

3) *Soviet commercial counselors.* In countries with which the USSR has diplomatic relations but where there is no Soviet trade mission, the USSR's diplomatic representation includes either commercial counselors or attachés. These officials can furnish general information about trade with the USSR and assistance in preparing a trip to Moscow. Except in the US, the commercial counselors can also advise or assist Western manufacturers in neogtiating contracts with the FTOs.

4) *The All-Union Chamber of Commerce* (6 Ulitsa Kuibysheva, Moscow K-3; M. V. Nesterov, President), representing different organizations interested in promotion of foreign trade, has a staff relationship with the various FTOs. Its main functions are: establishing contacts with foreign business organizations such as chambers of commerce and export institutes; organizing Soviet participation in international trade fairs, and helping to organize foreign trade and industrial exhibitions in the USSR; receiving foreign trade and industrial delegations, and sending similar delegations abroad; issuing certificates of origin and of quality for exported goods; processing patent and trademark applications and claims within the USSR; and arbitrating trade and maritime disputes through the arbitration commissions under its jurisdiction.

5) *FTO foreign distributors.* Many of the FTOs have local distributors representing them in foreign countries. Prospective Western buyers can obtain a list of these by writing to the FTO in whose product line they are interested.

6) *Direct mail.* In writing directly to an FTO, a would-be foreign supplier should supply as much product and price information as possible (and compatible with his government's restrictions on export of unpublished data).

7) *Advertising* in foreign or Soviet publications is an indirect method of reaching the FTOs. The USSR now permits foreigners to advertise in any of its publications.

Selling to the USSR

A firm may play either an active or a passive role in attempting to win a share of the Soviet Union's import orders from the West, now running at close to $2 billion annually. The passive approach is simply to inform the FTO that handles its products and the Soviet trade mission or other trading organization in its country of the firm's existence, of the nature, quality and prices of its goods, and of the extent of its after-sales servicing. The firm supplies by mail as much product detail as possible–including price lists, catalogs and anything else available in printed form–and usually backs this up with personal contact. If a sufficient impression is made, the firm will be contacted when an FTO has an order for its products.

In contrast with European-USSR trade, a fairly sizable portion of US exports to the Soviet Union in the past was handled by export brokers (e.g. Primary International, Intertex, M. Golodetz, Greg-Gary, all of New York). The manufacturers were completely insulated from the USSR buyers, and all the sales promotion was handled by the brokers. However, this practice is lessening in importance, largely because the FTOs prefer dealing directly with manufacturers.

In assessing the potential Soviet market for his products, a manufacturer should study carefully foreign trade statistics, as well as the various USSR foreign trade agreements, which give clues to the volume and variety of potential merchandise exchanges. He should also study the seven-year plan, to determine the long- and short-range requirements of the USSR.

More active firms will supplement these basic steps with visits to Moscow and with efforts to reach those who originate the orders—i.e. the managers of producing enterprises, distributing organizations, and national and provincial research institutes inside the USSR. In other words, as in Western markets, they will attempt to create demand for their products. But since factory visits are quasi-impossible unless a deal is already in the works, Western firms have two principal ways of reaching these audiences—through advertising and trade fairs.

Another method of promoting exports to the USSR is to use the services of an agent with some form of so-called "permanent establishment" in the country. At present, Novasider SpA of Torino, Italy, is the outstanding example of the very few European firms specializing in this field. Novasider handles, for a commission, the promotion and negotiation of sales to the USSR and products of a number of large Italian companies including Edison, Fiat, Ansaldo and Pirelli, as well as the European plants of the US' Carborundum Co. Since early 1961, Novasider has maintained a *de facto* (though not officially recognized) branch in Moscow, in the form of a four-man team operating from three rented rooms in the Sovietskaia Hotel. The team has recently been permitted to install a telex and direct phone line (without having to go through the hotel desk operator). In 1962, Novasider organized at its own expense a trade fair in Moscow, with major Italian firms—Pirelli, Montecatini, Snia Viscosa, Finmeccanica—exhibiting a variety of their products and equipment. Novasider has also been handling on behalf of Fiat the negotiations, started some two years ago, for setting up a tractor plant in the USSR.

New Opportunities for Advertising

The USSR now permits—and even encourages—foreigners to advertise in any of its ad-carrying publications. This permission, formerly confined to a few technical and scientific periodicals, was extended in 1963 to some 150 such monthlies (with circulation ranging from 3,000 to 480,000 copies) as well as some big daily newspapers, economic and scientific dailies. The rates, which are uniform for all periodicals irrespective of circulation, are extremely low.

Many Western companies still argue that it would be a waste of money to make use of this new opportunity, since the Foreign Trade Ministry and the FTOs have the final word on what should be imported. However, USSR officials maintain that the system is changing—a claim supported by Western experts and observers. More and more, the end-users determine what is to be imported. Under the present trend of decentralization in economic planning, the right of decision on purchases of industrial equipment is increasingly being shifted to the factory managers and chief engineers, and import lists are set up according to their requirements. If a manager can prove that a certain type of foreign machinery or equipment could improve the productivity of his plant, he now has a good chance of getting it.

Experienced Western firms feel that advertising in the USSR gets their products known not only by the end-users but also by the many people who can influence the decision to order: officials in the FTOs, the Ministry of Trade and the production ministries, the State Bank, the chambers of commerce and the regional economic councils, all of whom may influence the allocation of exchange and decisions on specific orders. (For the same reasons, it may be worthwhile to mail descriptive literature directly to some of these bodies.)

Western companies that have utilized advertising in the Soviet Union feel that they received a greater return than on their advertising in Western countries, not only because ad rates are low, but also because the ads are read very attentively as a source of information on products available in the West. However, they warn that one should not expect immediate results.

So far, German, French, British, and Japanese firms have made the greatest use of the extended advertising possibilities in the USSR. More than 100 German companies already use USSR news media—including such well-known firms as Mannesmann, Krupp, Degussa, Salzgitter and Siemens, but also smaller ones like Pfaff (sewing machines), Jagenberg-Werke (paper machinery), Benz & Hilgers (butter-packing machinery) and Lindemann (machinery). Advertising of Western consumer goods in the Soviet Union is still very rare.

All Western advertising in the USSR must go through the All-Union Agency Vneshtorgreclama (for its address, prices and other details. Vneshtorgreclama, which also places ads for USSR products in Western media, recently launched a campaign to attract more Western companies to advertise in the USSR ("If you plan to sell in Russia, don't forget advertising."). It is also sponsoring a new Russian-language periodical carrying advertising and articles about foreign products, to be circulated mainly among FTO officials.

Manufacturers can also advertise in the Russian-language monthly "British Industry & Engineering" (Britanskaya Promyshlennost i Tekhnika), which circulates among factory managers and buying agents in the USSR. (For details, contact British Industrial Publicity Overseas Ltd, Walter House, Bedford Street, London W.C. 2.)

Trade Fairs: an Important Meeting Ground

Western firms can also promote their products, and meet Soviet officials who make or influence buying decisions, through trade fairs and exhibitions in the USSR and other East-Bloc countries. A number of companies have actually made on-the-spot sales at these. The most important fairs:

The Poznan International Trade Fair (Poland) covers a wide range of consumer and industrial goods. With 106,000 sq.m. of exhibit space (57,900 reserved for foreigners), Poznan in 1963 attracted over 450,000 visitors, and exhibitors from 78 countries (including 167 from the US alone). Since Poland has been able to maintain friendly trade relations with virtually all nations, both East and West consider Poznan a primary target point for mutual exchange of wares.

The International Brno Trade Fair (Czechoslovakia) has developed into a specialized show for the engineering and metallurgical industries, with some consumer goods from the engineering industry. With 65,000 sq.m. of covered and 60,000 of open-air exhibit space, Brno in 1963 had 851,000 visitors and 632 foreign exhibitors from 45 countries with 16,000 engineering exhibits. Since the US Government discourages US participation at the Leipzig Fair, Brno has become an important show window for major US firms wishing to trade with the East.

The Zagreb International Autumn Fair (Yugoslavia) covers both industrial and consumer goods. Over a million visitors came in 1963 to see the wares of 4,953 exhibitors from 54 Western countries. The Zagreb Fair has one of the largest fair grounds in the world (five million sq.ft. of exhibit space); its efficient installations and general organization are reflected in growing number of Yugoslav and foreign exhibitors. There is also a smaller Spring Fair at Zagreb.

The International Trade Fair of Budapest (Hungary) has 260,000 sq.m. of exhibit space for industrial and consumer goods. In 1963 it drew a million visitors and 2,000 exhibitors, including 716 foreign exhibitors from 27 countries. The 1963 fair witnessed an increase in business activity over previous years, with total transactions of about $68 million.

The Leipzig Spring Fair (German Democratic Republic) celebrated its (approximately) 800th anniversary in 1964 with exhibits from 8,600 firms from 64 countries occupying 3.5 million sq.ft. of covered and open space. The fair drew visitors from 91 countries, come to examine and compare products ranging from machines, tools and transport equipment to electronic goods, cameras, textiles and clothing. Though the immediate commercial benefit from Leipzig Fair participation is considered small, more than 200 UK firms (the largest group from any foreign country) found it important enough to warrant sending exhibits—and five were awarded gold medals, lending prestige to their firms' names in Eastern European business circles. The Federal Republic of Germany, France, the Netherlands, Belgium, Italy, Austria and Sweden were also strongly represented by their private manufacturers. The US Government discourages participation by US companies.

The International Trade Fair of Plovdiv (Bulgaria) is fast growing in importance for Western manufacturers of capital and consumer goods. Business transacted at the fair soared from $12 million in 1960 to $344 million in 1962, when there were exhibits from some 20 Western countries. The fair grounds cover an area of 510,000 sq.m., with 65,000 sq.m. of roofed pavilions. The US Government and a number of US firms participated in the 1964 20th Julilee Fair in Plovdiv.

In addition to these regular annual or semi-annual fairs, various countries have staged shows in Moscow. For instance, the UK and France held a two-week show of agricultural machinery and products in May 1964. An international fair for construction machinery and equipment was held in Moscow in September 1964.

A manufacturer could also stage a private show in Moscow to display its total product line. The USSR Chamber of Commerce must be contacted to make the arrangements.

Visits to Moscow

Active firms usually dispatch executives to Moscow to improve communications with the FTO officials (e.g. Kaiser Industries, Union Carbide, Pfizer, National Steel, Westinghouse, General Electric, Blaw Knox). US firms often choose to send representatives from their European subsidiaries or branches. Some firms have sent executives to Moscow for an extended stay of one to three months (Imperial Chemical Industries, Montecatini, Dalmine, Asahi). Others have set up a quasi-permanent office in a Moscow Hotel (Krupp, Ataka), while others use the services of an established agent such as Intertex or Novasider.

While a personal visit to Moscow is recommended, Western manufacturers should be forewarned that, unless thoroughly prepared and carefully planned, such visits can be frustrating and disappointing. The visitor should set up appointments by advance correspondence with the various FTOs, because he may not be able to do so after arriving in Moscow. Many who neglected this step have hung about hotel lobbies for weeks, trying to contact Soviet officials.

It is best to undertake the trip only after invitation from an FTO, which will then take care of appointments with various Soviet officials and all other arrangements.

For his travel arrangements and to obtain a visa to enter the USSR, the company representative can contact a European office of Intourist,* or American Express, which represents Intourist in the US. The

*Intourist, the Soviet tourist agency, has offices in all large hotels in the USSR, and in major Western Capitals.

local Soviet trade mission, or Amtorg in New York, can also be very helpful to a manufacturer preparing a visit to the USSR.

Negotiating the Sale

The most demanding stage of the sales process is the actual negotiation. USSR buyers insist on discussing the sale slowly and thoroughly and are wary of such open-end clauses as references to "usual commercial practice," etc., which indeed are dangerously vague terminology where transactions between private firms and Soviet state agencies are involved. It is not uncommon either for FTO buyers to play off several companies against each other, keeping them all guessing. Another frequent hazard is the matching of a single foreign executive against a team of skilled Soviet negotiators.

While some businessmen complain that negotiations are unduly protracted and costly, others point out (with some exaggeration) that "once a sale is made, the whole market is sold." Therefore, they feel that their overall sales costs in the USSR are the lowest in the world.

Many companies have spent years just "talking" with FTO officials in Moscow or with trade missions or Amtorg in the West. Although some of these firms have sold nothing as yet, they continue to maintain contacts. But several US firms have ended up getting an inside track on prospective USSR purchases, only to have the US Department of Commerce delay the grant of an export license until someone else got the order.

The negotiation and drafting of a sales contract with an FTO normally require the assistance of specialized legal counsel because of the detailed–and, to Western firms, sometimes unfamiliar–clauses on which FTO negotiators will insist at the start. Whether a Western firm can argue its way out of terms and conditions it considers particularly undesirable will of course depend on how badly the goods are wanted by the USSR and on the existence of alternate suppliers.

The experience of recent years shows that, once a contract has been signed, the FTO may be expected to adhere closely to all provisions and to make sure that its foreign trade partner does likewise. On numerous occasions, foreign firms have felt that this letter-of-the-law attitude was carried to an extreme.

The laws of the USSR contain a number of regulations, binding on Soviet trade agencies, on the form and procedure for signing contracts regardless of the nationality of the contractor and regardless of where the contract is concluded. For a contract to be valid in the USSR, several basic conditions must be met: the parties must possess legal capacity; the contract must be concluded in the proper written legal form; its contents must not conflict with the law; and the object of the contract must be specific or susceptible of being specified.

A foreign purchase or sales contract must be signed by two FTO officials including, if the contract is concluded in Moscow, the President of the FTO (or his deputy) and another authorized person, or if the transaction is concluded outside Moscow two persons authorized by the FTO President. All financial documents must bear the signature of the FTO President as well as that of the chief accountant.

FTOs place orders with foreign firms only in written form, stipulating (as in a contract) their terms and conditions and the deadline for acceptance by the seller. A contract for an order issued by a buyer is considered to have been concluded if the seller confirms in writing, within the deadline, his acceptance of all the conditions set forth in the order. If the seller accepts the order conditional upon different terms, he is considered as having rejected the order, and his counterproposal is considered a new offer.

Because of the pecularities of Soviet laws, it is particularly important for foreign firms to be careful as to where their contracts are concluded, under which country's law they are to be executed and what provisions are made for arbitration. As an illustration, the statute of limitations in USSR contract law is three years, but if a contract with an FTO is concluded outside the USSR the statute of limitation of the country in which the contract is concluded applies.

Financing and Insuring the Sale

Business transactions between Western countries and European communist countries are financed in one or more of the following ways: 1) cash payment in convertible currencies, 2) debiting and crediting bilateral clearing accounts, 3) barter, without foreign exchange transaction, or 4) credit.

Exchange risks have not been a problem in trade transactions with the USSR, since all financial arrangements have been made in hard currencies. The Soviets prefer simple financial terms. They are noted for prompt payment and adherence to contract terms.

A leading role in the field of short-term (30-180 day) credits for trade between the UK and the USSR is played by the Moscow Narodny Bank Ltd in London. Narodny, a wholly USSR-owned bank operating in the orthodox City tradition, specializes in financing Commonwealth countries' trade with the East. With a capital of only £4.5 million and very small (less than £5 million) ordinary deposits, Narodny can nevertheless finance transactions running into hundreds of millions of pounds. Its correspondents' deposits reach £158 million, of which the bulk is contributed by the USSR State Bank (Gosbank) and Foreign Trade Bank (Vneshtorgbank), and it can discount paper on the UK market.

Now that the credit-worthiness of Soviet state import organizations is regarded as satisfactory, UK exporters generally sell on sight credits rather than the payment-against-documents terms customary in the past. Besides sharing this business with other London banks, Narodny also makes advances against guarantees from the importing country's State Bank; such guarantees of payment after a fixed period, say six months, are now very popular with Eastern European countries. Narodny also extends credit to the relatively small UK importers of USSR consumer goods such as watches and cameras. In October 1963 Narodny opened a branch in Beirut.

In Paris, the local counterpart of London's Narodny Bank is the Banque Commerciale pour l'Europe du Nord ("Eurobank"). Wholly owned by USSR state banks, Eurobank is for the most part managed and staffed by French nationals. It was incorporated in France in 1925 and has a capital of *Fr*50 million; its correspondents' deposits of more than *Fr*2.5 billion rank it among the 10 largest French banks. Eurobank does a substantial part of its business in short-term financing of commodity exports (principally from South American and other areas) to East European countries other than the USSR. It has also been financing sizable French imports of USSR commodities.

Because the 1934 Johnson Act prohibits the extension of private "loans" to foreign countries in default on their debts to the US Government, most business transactions between the US and the USSR have so far been conducted on the basis of cash payments against shipping documents or within 30 days of shipment, or by opening a letter of credit on a US or other Western bank. However, under the current interpretation of the Johnson Act, US manufacturers and private US banks may extend "normal commercial credit" to USSR state purchasers (i.e. up to six months, or up to five years for capital goods normally sold on such terms). But the Export-Import Bank of Washington is prohibited under another recent statute from either financing directly or guaranteeing credits for exports of manufactured goods to the USSR.

In the absence of long-term US credits, and the absence of guarantees to help them obtain permissible short- and medium-term financing, some US firms have used a foreign intermediary—trading company or broker—who is sometimes able to get financing from his own sources, or have switched to supplying from plants located in countries that do extend credit to the USSR. One US company, to win a Soviet order amounting to several million dollars, solved the long-term credit problem by having one of its foreign subsidiaries act as the contracting party and manufacture the goods.

Most other West European countries do not impose such restrictions, and in some cases sales are made with long-term financing covered by government export credit insurance. But, of course, these government credits and guarantees are available only to exporters of locally manufactured goods.

Thus, the UK's Export Credits Guarantee Department will insure credits relating to shipments of UK goods under the Anglo-Soviet trade agreements. ECGD's services are fully available to support trade with European communist countries on the same basis as for trade with other parts of the world. Its premium rates vary from country to country; those for the Soviet Union are low, reflecting that country's high credit rating in ECGD's eyes. Only short- and medium-term export credit policies were written for East-West trade until June 1964, when the first 12-year credit arrangement—covered by a financial guarantee of the ECGD—was signed in connection with the export of a fertilizer plant to Czechoslovakia. This was followed in September by an ECGD financial guarantee for a £24 million, 15-year loan extended to the USSR's Vneshtorgbank by the UK's Midland Bank and Insurance Export Finance Corp (formed by UK insurance companies for long-term export financing), covering a Soviet order for a polyester plant (using ICI knowhow) to be built in Siberia by a UK consortium. Such financial credits are not subject to the five-year ceiling imposed on insurance of supplier credits under the Berne Union agreement.

The French Government, as of December 1964, stands poised to follow the UK's lead in authorizing extension of long-term credits to cover sales of industrial (particularly petrochemical) equipment to the USSR. A consortium of four French banks has already agreed to provide such credits to the emount of some *Fr*2 billion for 10 years' term (including three years of prefinancing), subject to the issuing of a guarantee by the French state-controlled COFACE export credit insurance agency. COFACE—which already insures short- and medium-term credits to French exporters on sales to the East Bloc, with terms and conditions adjusted on a country-by-country basis—has gotten the green light to cover credits exceeding five years under the new French-USSR trade agreement.

The German Federal Government, on the other hand, is not inclined at present to encourage transactions involving extension of long-term credit to Eastern Europe. The government-sponsored Hermes export credit insurance institution will, however, guarantee short- and medium-term credits within the five-year ceiling set by the Berne Union.

The USSR itself is solving part of the problem of inadequate guarantees and insurance. The state foreign insurance monopoly, Ingosstrakh—under the jurisdiction of the Ministry of Finance—has subsidiaries and representatives outside the territory of the Soviet Union that are able to insure foreign exporters' manufacturing risks (including political risks) and risks of default or protracted payment, and, importantly, to insure either the importer or exporter—depending on conditions of sale—against damages in transport, transshipment, warehousing and/or erection and trial runs in the case of machinery. This new and growing activity of Ingosstrakh is important, a few private Western insurance companies are willing to insure shipments to the USSR.

Garant AG, a wholly owned subsidiary of Ingosstrakh (incorporated under Austrian law and with headquarters in Vienna) has, since its creation in 1958, been cashing in on increased East-West trade. Garant can insure East-West transactions in either direction, as well as trade between communist countries, and is reportedly even going into the West-to-West export insurance business.

In practice, it is unusual for a Western exporter to take a Garant policy if he can obtain guarantees from his national export credit insurance agency. But Garant is useful when the national agency will not insure a particular transaction because of the nature of the goods, or the terms under which they are sold (longer than normal credit), or the country of destination. For instance, while France's COFACE does not usually agree to cover credits to Indonesia or Egypt, a French exporter can turn to Garant to insure sales to those countries.

At present, Garant does about 50% of its business with West Germany and the rest with other European countries. It generally adjusts its rates to those prevailing in the country of the exporter. Cost of a combined nonpayment-nontransfer risk policy averages 2%. Today, most European banks that are active in the field of export financing will grant credits on normal terms on the basis of a Garant policy. Garant has by now become well known in European trade circles and maintains close business relations with insurance companies, banks and private enterprises in more than 40 countries.

The principal business of Garant is insuring against default and protracted payment. If, for one reason or another—red tape, failure to obtain hard currency in time, etc.—an Eastern European importing agency fails to make payment within 60 days from the date due, Garant immediately remits the amount to the insured.

Garant manufacturing-risk insurance covers risks of cancellation of an order, non-acceptance of delivered goods, and also the risk that goods cannot be delivered because of a sudden import ban, break-off of diplomatic and economic relations, civil strife, confiscation or other "political" event or measure.

In addition, Ingosstrakh and Garant offer shipping insurance (including damage or losses due to war, civil strife, confiscation, strike, and presumptive loss of goods during transport), warehouse insurance, and insurance against breakage and malfunction of machinery up until after trial runs.

In practice, however, Western manufacturers sell most often on an f.o.b. basis, leaving freight and insurance costs to be borne by the East European customer, which can make its own arrangements with Ingosstrakh or Garant. This is particularly true of US exporters for, although there is no law or regulation—US or USSR—prohibiting direct ship traffic between the two countries, direct runs are very rare because of the low volume of trade (and because of US longshoremen's common refusal to load or unload Soviet vessels). Shipping arrangements usually call for offloading at Antwerp. Rotterdam, or some other European port for transshipment to the Soviet Union. The USSR generally requests a c.i.f. quotation to one of the above ports—largely for information purposes—but the final sale is almost always consummated on an f.o.b. basis.

Ingosstrakh has two other foreign subsidiaries, Blacksea & Baltic, in London, and Schwarzmeer & Ostsee, in Hamburg. But these two do a much smaller volume of business than Garant.

East-West Trade Arbitration

It is generally agreed by both sides that it is essential to include in contracts dealing with East-West trade matters a clause providing for arbitration of disputes arising from such contracts, and to stipulate clearly the place and method of arbitration—whether by a permanent arbitral body or through *ad hoc* arbitration.

FTOs usually include in their original conditions arbitration by the Foreign Trade Arbitration Commission of the All-Union Chamber of Commerce in Moscow. There are a number of reasons why foreign private firms often dislike the idea of arbitration in Moscow—in particular, the fact that the Chamber of Commerce is a quasi-governmental body, that all 15 men on the panel of arbitrators are of course Soviet nationals, and that arbitration fees (0.5% to 1% of the amount claimed, or of the award if the claimant wins his case) are stiff if large sums are involved. On the other hand, the Moscow Arbitration Commission has achieved a good record of impartiality and decided many cases in favor of non-USSR parties. (The outstanding subject by the Western legal community was the 1958 decision against Jordan Investment Ltd. In that case the Commission rejected Jordan Investment's $2 million claim for damages arising from Sojusnefteexport's failure to deliver Soviet oil to Israel as per contract, on the ground that the denial of an export license by the Ministry of Foreign Trade to Sojusnefteexport constituted *force majeure*—since FTOs are independent entities not liable for actions of the Government. The USSR Government had had all oil deliveries to Israel suddenly stopped in 1956 because of the Israeli-Arab conflict. The oil sale contract involved made no reference to the export-license contingency.)

The Arbitration Commission applies either Soviet or foreign law, as required in the contract. Western firms should be aware that, if the contract does not specify what country's law is to govern disputes, that of the place where the contract is signed (usually Moscow) will automatically apply.

The Chamber of Commerce also has a 25-member Maritime Arbitration Commission, covering disputes related to remuneration for salvage and assistance rendered by one vessel to another, collisions between vessels or damage to port installations caused by ships, chartering and marine insurance agreements, etc.

In practice, FTOs' requests for arbitration in Moscow have often been resisted successfully by Western suppliers, as for that matter the FTOs have also systematically turned down counter-offers to have arbitration before the International Chamber of Commerce. In such cases the parties have settled upon arbitration at the domicile of the respondent, in a third country such as Sweden or (less commonly) Switzerland, or in London for maritime cases.

When agreeing to neutral arbitration, Western firms find it desirable also to provide for inspection by neutral agents. For if there is trouble with a plant and the Western party is not allowed to take photographs nor to have a neutral agent inspect the premises, it is impossible to produce valid evidence to the arbitrators.

A notable development that will hopefully facilitate East-West arbitration procedures is that the USSR was one of the first countries to ratify the European Arbitration Convention, which will afford equal and equitable protection irrespective of the parties' nationality or economic system. The Convention foresees a wide range of possibilities for settling disputes both by permanent national arbitration bodies and *ad hoc* arbitration bodies. It also provides that the parties concerned cannot arrive at an agreement on the mode of arbitration.

Financial Aspects of United States Trade With the Socialist World

Paul Gekker*

Financial institutions play a major role in the expansion of international commerce. Any consideration of financing trade in Eastern Europe must accord a respectful position to the role of banks and questions of currency convertibility. Paul Gekker, a leading authority on the Soviet Banking System and East European Affairs and an economist with the Federal Reserve System, notes that the Soviet State Bank is playing an increasingly central role in the expansion of East-West trade. He concludes that the recently expressed view that Socialist countries may raise long term capital in the Euro-Bond market may not be entirely visionary.

In studies of what we have come to call Soviet-type countries, we have usually proceeded in a fairly straightforward and rather simple way. Typically, we have reasoned that the centrally planned economic systems in these countries result from a particular form of political rule by Communist parties, which is a perfectly serviceable way of looking at the matter. In this exercise we have usually taken the Soviet Union as the standard model, for the natural reason that this is the Communist country in which a planned system, designed to implement politico-economic tasks laid down by the central political authorities, has been in operation for the longest continuous time. No doubt we have been conditioned to this somewhat simplified view by a necessary preoccupation with various aspects of our confrontation with the USSR. This made it difficult to imagine that the Soviet Union might in some ways occupy a rather unique position as one member of an interestingly disputatious family of Communist states.

It is essential to recognize, however, that from a point of view that is crucial to our present concern with foreign trade and finance, the Soviet economy is very much something of a special case. This is not simply a matter of acknowledging that the economic systems in the smaller countries in Eastern Europe are not now carbon copies of the Soviet blueprint, if indeed they ever were. What it does mean is that important economic consequences follow from the sheer size of the Soviet continental land mass just because this geographic expanse carries with it an abundant and varied endowment in natural resources. How and why such resources are used are separate questions, although we should be aware that the particular priorities given in the Soviet growth model—pattern might be a preferable word if "model" tempts readers to think in excessively formal terms—will have a great deal to do with determining the level and direction of Soviet foreign trade.[1] It will also have implications for the way in which this trade is financed.

The task of spelling out the distinction between the Soviet Union and the Eastern European countries would be far simpler if it were possible to abstract from the implications of the Soviet Union's super-power position, to ignore the economic aspects of the geopolitical role which this nation state—either as Russia or as the Union of Soviet Socialist Republics—seems destined to fill. These implications can only be hinted at. The essential point is that the existence of significant and varied natural resources creates something like a natural condition for economic self-sufficiency. Because of its size and resource endowment, the Soviet Union is in a position to obtain many of the benefits of the division of labor and the specialization of economic activity by its unaided effort—without the bother, so to speak, of foreign economic entanglements. Stated differently, self-sufficiency attributable to the existence of a rich endowment in natural resources implies the possibility of pursuing domestic policies which, within fairly wide limits, can ignore the economic constraints of living in a world in interdependent national states.[2]

*The author is Senior Economist in the Division of International Finance, Board of Governors of the Federal Reserve System. The views expressed in this article do not necessarily represent the opinions of the Federal Reserve Board.

[1]The author has had the benefit of advance reading of several of the papers included in a volume edited by Alan A. Brown and Egon Neuberger, *International Trade and Central Planning*, published by the University of California Press. Subtitled "An Analysis of Economic Interactions," this collection of contributions by leading specialists breaks new ground in the theoretical study of foreign trade in the planned economies. The book is a pioneering effort; as it becomes better known, the Brown-Neuberger volume will surely occupy an important place in the literature which the international trade theorist is presumed to be familiar.

[2]This overstates the case, of course, though simplification ought to be a permissible device provided one is aware of the dangers of carrying it to unacceptable lengths. Anyone who imagines that there is some easily ascertainable relationship between national size and any broad measure of economic progress ought to consult the volume edited by E.A.G. Robinson, *Economic Consequences of the Size of Nations* (New York: St. Martin's Press, 1960), which abundantly reveals the lack of any acceptable general explanation. On the other hand, we are concerned in trying to say something about the consequences of size—about the importance of scale, basically—in the context of a rather specific universe, the "Socialist camp."

None of this holds true, in remotely the same degree, for any country in Eastern Europe. The ratios of foreign trade to national income in the Eastern European countries are no doubt lower than they would be under alternative economic policies but they are all higher by far than in the Soviet Union. According to one study, ratios of imports to gross national product in Eastern Europe in 1964 ranged from a low of 10 per cent for Poland to a high of 24 per cent in the case of Bulgaria.[3] Numerous studies show much lower trade ratios for the Soviet Union; as measured by exports, the ratio to GNP was under 3 per cent in 1964.[4]

This relatively high degree of "openness" in the Eastern European countries has an important bearing on the degree of flexibility that can be followed in the conduct of external economic affairs. In this quick survey we cannot do more than hint at the connection between foreign trade and growth in the planned economies, a vast subject by itself.[5] But the examples of some smaller, highly industrialized countries in Western Europe which are not rich in natural resources demonstrate that foreign trade is "an effective escape from the penalties of smallness."[6] Given the fact that sizable efficiencies of scale exist in most manufacturing industries, a small country must stagnate unless it mass produces a narrow range of goods, relying on foreign trade to provide markets for its few outputs as well as sources for a big proportion of its consumption requirements. The textbook illustration in the area we are concerned with here seems to be Czechoslovakia.

The interesting discussions of economic reform now going on in the planned economies furnish unmistakably clear evidence in support of this reasoning. It is possible to go through a mass of published material dealing with the problems of improving the operating efficiency of the Soviet planned system in the Russian press and specialized periodicals–to say nothing of whole books–without meeting up with so much as a whisper about external economic relations. In Eastern Europe, it seems fair to say, economic reform is virtually synonymous with the search for greater rationality in foreign trading activities.[7]

II

The peculiarities of financial dealings with Communist countries stem directly from the special way in which foreign trade is conducted in these centrally planned economies. In the Soviet case, the underlying conditions were established very soon after the Bolshevik assumption of power, and these foreign trading arrangements have not been modified in any significant respect in the half century since then. The general outlines are quite familiar. The Soviet economy is governed by a national economic plan, and a part of that plan has to do with foreign trade. Foreign trade is a state monopoly, organized chiefly in order to insulate the domestic economy for external influences so as to permit fulfillment of the planned tasks.

The connection in the planned system between the domestic economy and the determination of the level and direction of foreign trade is generally explained on the following reasoning. The national economic plan indicates a need–generates a demand, let us say–for imports; the demand for imports creates, in turn, a need for exports–means of payment.[8]

As we know, the monopoly of foreign trade and the monopoly of foreign exchange go hand in hand. The insulation of the domestic economy requires that the structure of internal prices and costs be divorced from prices and costs in the world outside. This divorce is symbolized in the exchange rate, which is only a formal, definitional link between these separate price/cost structures, domestic and external. Generally speaking, foreign trade is conducted on the basis of

[3]Maurice Ernst, "Postwar Economic Growth in Eastern Europe" in *New Directions in the Soviet Economy* (Washington: U.S. Government Printing Office, 1966). Not surprisingly, these import ratios are generally lower than for market-oriented economies in Western Europe, of roughly comparable size, population, etc.

[4]Herbert S. Levine, in an extension of earlier data worked out by Franklyn D. Holzman, cited in Brown and Neuberger, *op. cit.*, page 255, fn.

[5]In his study of Eastern Europe, Ernst has some highly suggestive analytical conclusions, necessarily greatly condensed, on the relationship of imports to domestic growth. See Ernst, *op cit.*, pp. 898-905. For the USSR, consult the careful study by Franklyn D. Holzman, "Foreign Trade," in *Economic Trends in the Soviet Union*, edited by Abram Bergson and Simon Kuznets (Cambridge: Harvard University Press, 1963).

[6]The phrase is from *Economic Consequences of the Size of Nations*; see Professor Robinson's introductory essay, pp. XV-XIX.

[7]Strictly speaking, of course, only in those countries in which there is any talk at all of economic reform. We would not want to suggest economic reform in Eastern Europe is unconcerned with matters besides foreign trade, or that foreign trade is not of interest to Soviet reformers; but the contrast is nothing short of startling. In any event, there is a spectrum here, and a subtle shifting of what Wiles terms "the rate of decay of these varying orthodoxies." Peter J. D. Wiles, "Foreign Trade of Eastern Europe: A Summary Appraisal," in Brown and Neuberger, *op. cit.*, p. 167.

[8]In much of the literature on Soviet-type economies this fairly unobjectionable though rather simplified explanation has been equated with the notion that the central planners (and the political leadership) in these countries are motivated by a drive to achieve autarky. One of the merits of the volume edited by Brown and Neuberger is that it contains a long overdue correction of this misleading view. See their introductory essay (pp. 9-13 especially) and the paper by Wiles, who gives Brown credit for launching the attack on "autarkic" explanations of foreign trade behavior in the centrally planned economies.

world market prices.[9] The exchange rate functions merely as an accounting device, used to convert foreign currency values of imports and exports into domestic equivalents for internal planning purposes. In a word, the Soviet ruble is inconvertible, as are the currencies of the Eastern European countries.

This raises the question of how Soviet trade is financed. We have to distinguish between trade of the Soviet Union with other Communist countries–trade within the family, that is, which accounts for about two-thirds of total Soviet trade–and Soviet trade with the rest of the world. The distinction is important because trade among Communist countries need not require international means of payment. This is, in fact, the situation with respect to trade within the group of Communist countries at the present time. Trade is directed almost entirely in bilateral channels; the limited financial dealings are entirely mechanical, and of no interest. The trading partners normally aim at achieving a balanced level of trade (plus services) over some specified period; and provision is made for temporary imbalances, to take care of seasonal needs and other more or less self-reversible movements. The trading rules, formalized by treaty or agreement, typically provide that persistent imbalances by liquidated in prescribed ways, and also within specified periods, usually by the deficit partner working off the debt by shipments of goods.

The necessity for these arrangements illustrates that the great defect of bilaterialism, which tends to restrict commodity trade to levels determined by the country with the more limited export capabilities.[10] The obstacle to any general expansion of trade in the Communist group just because trade is organized along bilateral lines led to the establishment in late 1963 of the International Bank for Economic Cooperation (IBEC), which began operations in 1964. The Bank's chief function is to provide machinery for multilateral clearing in transferable rubles among its COMECON member countries.

The multilateral clearing system operated by the IBEC marks an advance over bilateral arrangements because it makes it possible for a member country to try to balance trade with all other COMECON nations combined rather than separately with each trading partner. The resulting level of trade within the group will be higher than the sum of commodity exchanges by all countries, on a bilaterally balanced basis. But the potential increase in COMECON trade has not been realized, basically for two reasons. First, the COMECON countries still plan and try to implement their mutual trade along bilateral lines, starting with trade talks between pairs of countries. When they have reached agreement on bilateral trade, negotiation proceeds on an attempt to match bilateral surpluses and deficits with imbalances incurred by the bilateral trading partners elsewhere in the COMECON system.[11]

The second obstacle to an expansion of trade is created by the inconvertibility of the transferable ruble. Some Eastern European countries have earned surpluses in trade with the COMECON group as a whole and have argued that these surpluses ought to be partially convertible into gold or convertible currencies. Conversely, deficit countries within the group would settle in gold or convertible exchange, at least in part. This general position is apparently shared by the Eastern European countries but the attitude of the Soviet authorities is not really known.[12]

These comments on the conduct of trade without the use of international means of payment apply to some extent to Soviet trade with the lesser developed countries, which represented 11 per cent of total Soviet foreign trade in 1967.[13] This trade is also

[9] Among Communist countries, would market prices are averaged over five-year periods, the idea being to eliminate the effects of fluctuations due to cyclical or other "disturbances." Or so it is said. The effect is simply to add an extra ingredient of inflexibility to the built-in irrationality of trading among Communist countries. The measure of this inflexibility is that in the interim between revisions of the five-year world market base price arrangements, changes in the commodity terms of trade in world markets will work capricious effects on individual countries in the group. This can become a political issue. See the interesting comments by Peter Wiles, in Brown and Neuberger, *op. cit.*, pp. 170-173.

[10] We do not really need the example of Communist country foreign trade as evidence of the tremendous disadvantages of bilateral trading. Anyone who remembers the conditions under which trade in Western Europe had to be conducted in the early postwar years recognizes the problem. Similarly, switching trading is not something newly invested for East-West trading purposes; it also has antecedents in the bilateral world of early postwar Europe. See "How Switch Trading Works," *The Economist* (London), January 14, 1967, where this technically complicated market and its practices are very well described. But switch trading is not quite the novelty that the article makes it out to be.

[11] There are eight COMECON countries–Bulgaria, Czechoslovakia, East Germany, Hungary, Mongolia, Poland, Romania and the USSR. If we remember that the trade negotiators are really trying to match deficits and surpluses of physical commodities, we get some notion of the complexity of the task of coordination involved in arranging this mutual offset, which requires 28 different bilateral agreements.

[12] It is useful to be reminded–as Holzman tells us–that on the evidence of their limited trade in the prewar period, the present-day Communist countries do not constitute a "natural" trading area. See Franklyn D. Holzman, "Soviet Central Planning and Its Impact on Foreign Trade Behavior and Adjustment Mechanisms," in Brown and Neuberger, *op. cit.*, page 282.

It is also interesting that the countries identified with arguments for partial convertibility of the transferable ruble–Poland, Romania and Hungary–depend on other Communist countries for somewhat lower shares of their total trade than as the other COMECON nations.

[13] Statistics on shares of trade, cited here and elsewhere, have been taken from the most recent Congressional study of Soviet developments prepared for the Joint Economic Committee: *Soviet Economic Performance, 1966-67* (Washington: U.S. Government Printing Office, 1968).

organized along bilateral lines, and arrangements for repayment of loan aid extended by the Soviet Union generally provide for payment in goods, wholly or in part. All of these bilateral devices have the effect of making a virtue of shortages of convertible exchange on both sides: in the case of the LDC's, a shortage stemming from limited marketing opportunities in convertible currency markets and, on the Soviet side, insufficient exchange with which to purchase the products of the lesser developed countries.[14]

The case with respect to Soviet trade with convertible currency countries is distinctly of a different order, in the sense that internationally acceptable means of payment have to be found. Here too, if trade with all convertible currency countries combined were exactly balanced, there would be no need for convertible currencies, or only for such amounts as would be required to tide over seasonal and other short-term swings in the accounts. But this condition is not likely to be realized, in part because an exact equivalence between receipts and payments cannot possibly be planned. The principal reason why exact balance has not worked out, however, is the observable fact that the Soviet Union appears to require imports from convertible currency countries to a total value exceeding its earnings from sales of Soviet products in those markets. The resulting deficit requires payment in some internationally acceptable form. In this connection, one needs to bear in mind that the Soviet Union holds gold and foreign exchange reserves (which are perhaps substantial) and that this condition, along with others already mentioned, sets the Soviet Union in a class apart from the Socialist nations in Eastern Europe.

The size of Soviet gold (and foreign exchange) holdings is a closely held secret; no information of any reliable sort has been available for very many years. From the only direct evidence we have, the Soviet sales of gold in Western markets, one might deduce a reluctance on the part of the Soviet authorities to dip into gold stocks except for emergency needs. But the evidence is not conclusive by any means. Even before its large sales, averaging just over $500 million in 1963-65 in connection with massive wheat purchases made necessary by poor harvests, the Soviet Union regularly disposed of amounts averaging $250 million annually in the preceding six years (1957-62). The published estimates of the Bank for International Settlements and the International Monetary Fund, from which these data are taken, show no gold sales in 1966 or 1967; and there are no market reports of Soviet gold sales so far in 1968.

Whatever the size of Soviet gold holdings–the most recent private estimate, noted in *The Economist* in March of this year, suggested that a figure of $3 billion might not be unrealistic–the adequacy of the Soviet gold stock should be judged in the light of two considerations. In the first place it is open to the Soviet Union to adapt to unforeseen developments affecting its balance of payments by direct means. In this paper we cannot properly investigate the interesting theoretical questions regarding the nature of the balance of payments adjustment process in the planned economies but we can note some basic points. In his studies, Holzman has shown that the burden of adjustment to external disturbances falls for the most part on the foreign trade sector directly rather than via price or income effects.[15] Oleg Hoeffding, in a careful study of Soviet reaction to balance of payments problems posed by the need for massive grain imports in 1963-65, has demonstrated Soviet ability to take decisive direct action combining an expansion (and re-direction) of exports and a restriction of imports.[16] Needless to say, this ability to maneuver in the foreign trade sector is greater in the case of the Soviet Union than for the other COMECON countries, not simply because of the Soviet Union's superior bargaining power–not an inconsiderable factor, to be sure–but because the USSR is relatively less dependent on foreign trade.

The second consideration bearing on any judgment concerning the adequacy of Soviet gold and foreign exchange reserves involves a less complicated idea. It used to be fairly common to measure the adequacy of a country's gold reserves by calculating the number of months of imports which the reserves would purchase. This sort of calculation was bound to be exceedingly rough. It was made on a gross basis (no account being taken of export earnings) and it was no doubt misleading for other reasons, but there seems little harm in resurrecting this old rule-of-thumb for purposes of broad illustration. A given country's

[14]It is customary to think of the Soviet economy as beset by shortages of goods in general, in which consumer-oriented productive activities are in addition secondary priorities in the central planners' scheme of things so that, it is argued, the Soviet Union is in a position to make good use of almost any products it can obtain from the LDC's in payment for its loan aid. This is of course exaggerated, as was shown by the example of Soviet re-exports of Egyptian cotton some years ago. But it is still true that the Soviet Union does take some "unessential" imports in order to exploit what it views as targets of opportunity in the lesser developed world. It is therefore reasonable to assume that trade with the LDC's is, in contrast to much of the Soviet Union's traditional commodity trade with industrialized countries, politically rather than economically motivated. See the author's "Die sowjetische Hilfe für Entwicklungslander," *Handbuch der Finanzwissenschaft* (Tübingen, 1965) Vierter Band.

[15]In two papers: "Foreign Trade Behavior of Centrally Planned Economies," Henry Rosovsky, editor. *Industrialization in Two Systems: Essays in Honor of Alexander Gerschenkron* (New York: John Wiley & Sons, 1966); and the article cited in footnote 12, above.

[16]Oleg Heoffding, "Recent Structural Changes and Balance-of-Payments Adjustments in Soviet Foreign Trade," in Brown and Neuberger, *op. cit.*, pp. 312-337.

reserves were of course measured in terms of imports from all sources, in keeping with the condition of currency convertibility that prevailed almost everywhere when this method of measurement was in vogue. We have seen, however, that the Soviet Union's requirement for international means of payment is determined almost exclusively by the need to settle its payments deficit with convertible currency countries.[17] That being the case, we should measure the Soviet gold stock against only a share–roughly one-third–of total Soviet imports. From the data on Soviet "hard currency" imports in 1966 and 1967 we can derive an average monthly import value of $142 million over this two-year period.[18] If we accept the latest private estimate of a gold stock amounting to $3 billion, the Soviet reserve would be sufficient to finance imports from hard currency areas for a period of 21 months. This is a rather high ratio of reserves to imports.

This line of speculation is no doubt amusing but does not lead us very far. We might instead revert to the subject of Soviet reserve management, as revealed in sales of gold. In the period prior to the last two years, the appearance of Soviet gold on Western markets could lead one to something like a view of a "normal" level of annual gold sales, for the purpose of settling the Soviet hard currency deficit, with additional amounts to take care of emergency requirements in some years. The notion of emergency sales assumes, of course, that the Soviet authorities might at the same time be undergoing a balance of payments "adjustment" by direct means, as shown in Hoeffding's study. The absence of sales during the past two and one-half years does not fit the pattern, to be sure, but may be explainable on other grounds.

The accompanying table tries to match the Soviet Union's hard currency deficit with known sales of Soviet gold over a period of nine years. Obviously, the table is an approximation. For one thing, the trade deficit shown understates the current account deficit by some unknown margin. The statistics exclude net hard currency payments for trade-related services (freight, insurance, etc.), on which statistics are not available. We also have no data on other services but to judge by occasional information on the flow of travelers, the Soviet Union unquestionable earns net hard currency receipts from tourism.

The data shown in the table on gold sales are presumably accurate though the numbers have probably been rounded, perhaps to the nearest five million.

USSR: Hard Currency Trade and Finance, 1959-67

(Millions of U.S. dollars)

Year	Soviet Exports	Soviet Imports	Trade Deficit	Gold Sales
1959	565	590	- 25	300
1960	745	1,015	-270	200
1961	865	1,060	-195	300
1962	915	1,180	-265	230
1963	960	1,280	-320	550
1964	1,010	1,545	-535	450
1965	1,325	1,545	-220	550
1966	1,480	1,745	-265	—
1967	1,640	1,670	- 30	—

Sources: Trade statistics from *Soviet Economic Performance: 1966-67*, p. 98; data on gold sales from Bank for International Settlements, Annual Reports.

There is of course no necessary correspondence year by year between the trade deficit and gold sales; in view of what is known of the approximate nature of the deficit shown in the table, any close correspondence in any single years would in fact be automatically suspect. For the sake of illustration, if we run totals for the nine years we derive a trade deficit of $2,125 million and gold sales of $2,580 million. The larger total for gold sales–$455 million–should measure the difference between the deficits on current account and on trade. This works out to an average net deficit on all non-trade accounts (but including freight and insurance, since the trade data are on an f.o.b. basis) of about $50 million per year.

What is to be made of the absence of gold sales for the last two years? In this period one would suppose that the Soviet authorities had intensified their efforts to cut down on hard currency payments and increase hard currency receipts; and the measure of their success is the very significant reduction in the trade deficit from 1966 to 1967. Possibly, they have also been able to turn the services account around; they have, for example, acted vigorously to promote tourism. In addition, however, the most recent period has witnessed a considerable expansion of credit by the industrialized exporting nations, in connection with Soviet purchases of industrial machinery and equipment, and this Western lending activity has undoubtedly made it possible for the Soviet authorities to conserve their gold.[19]

Unfortunately, we cannot adequately document this lending activity, at least for the very recent past, but some statistics assembled in 1967 by the European Economic Commission illustrate the dimensions of what is familiarly termed the credit race. The data

[17] The qualification is necessary because the Soviet Union has made some gold and convertible currency loans to other countries. Besides, the transferable ruble now in use by the COMECON group could be given some form of partial convertibility, involving an additional (perhaps only contingent) claim on the Soviet reserves.

[18] Calculated from data in *Soviet Economic Performance: 1966-67*, page 98.

[19] In his study of the Soviet balance of payments adjustment expereince of 1963-65, Hoeffding makes the interesting argument that Soviet reserve management policies should be understood as including the utilization of commodity reserves. See Hoeffding, *op. citt.*, pp. 335-337.

cover long-term lending (over five years' duration) by the six Common Market countries and seven other nations that are members of the Berne Union–Austria, Denmark, Japan, Spain, Sweden, Switzerland and the United Kingdom–for the preceding three years. (1964-66).[20] In this period total long-term lending by these countries amounted to $4,477 million, on which $857 million (or 19.1 per cent) was for the Eastern European area. Of this share, $435 million–fully 10 per cent of the grand total–went to the USSR, and an additional sizeable sum, $197 million, went to Romania. These two countries combined accounted for almost three-fourths of long-term credit extended by the industrialized nations to the Socialist group in these three years.

III

We now turn for a closer look at some of the mechanics of financing Soviet and East European trade, which we limit to trade with convertible currency countries, along the lines of the distinction made earlier. It follows from the inconvertible status of the ruble that other currencies must be used in trade with countries outside the Socialist group of nations. Until a few years ago, the isolated position of the Soviet currency also meant that Western financial institutions played a major role in providing many banking services connected with foreign trade finance.

In trade between any countries whose currencies are freely convertible–between Italy and the Netherlands, for example–the question of whose institutions provide the financing is largely a matter of indifference. It might be convenient to assume that Italian banks finance sales to Holland and that Dutch exports are financed by banks in the Netherlands, but anyone even slightly acquainted with the working world of foreign trade knows that this is not even a useful simplification. In reality, the question of which institutions do the financing may be a matter of established trading practices or banking connections, or perhaps of specialization by individual banks in certain types of financing. Then again, the locus of the financing may shift with changes in the monetary climate, with differences at any time in the relative degrees of credit ease or tightness prevailing in national money markets. Furthermore, the financing need not be limited to banks in the two trading countries, so that an Italian export might be financed by a Swedish bank while a French bank might stand behind the sale of Dutch goods. What is more, the financing may involve not only lire and gilders; some vehicle currency–sterling or the dollar–could very well be at the center of the arrangements. Finally, the rise and rapid development of the Euro-currency markets has created entirely new credit links, which may entitle us to say that for a very wide range of banking operations connected with foreign trade the nationality of the banking institution is quite irrelevant.[21]

The two Soviet financial institutions engaged in dealings with the outside world–the State Bank of the USSR (*Gosbank*) and the Bank for Foreign Trade (*Vneshtorgbank*) have built up extensive correspondent relationships with leading banks in all Western countries, including the United States.[22] Starting from a situation characterized by the existence of deep and widespread mistrust on the part of financial interests in virtually the entire outside world, the Soviet banks have over the years worked steadily and successfully to cultivate a first-rate commercial credit standing in Western financial centers by prompt and painstaking observance of the strictest discipline in their external financial dealings.[23]

In accordance with normal practice, the Soviet banks maintain working balances on deposit in Western banks with which they have found it convenient to establish mutual relations. Over the years, one would suppose the Soviet institutions to have experimented with techniques for maintaining these funds at minimum levels consistent with the volume of payments they were intended to cover. It is certain, however, that the Soviet authorities have made every effort to hold no more than absolute minimum funds on deposit in banks in the United States for the reason that they

[20] The E.E.C. study is summarized by Philippe Lemaitre in *Le Monde* (Paris), August 13-14, 1967.

[21] This is not to say, obviously, that Euro-currency operations by banks of a particular country are not of interest to its monetary authorities. We cannot deal with this wider question here.

[22] In former years, it was almost exclusively the State Bank (the Soviet central bank) that engaged in these dealings, but beginning in 1961 the Bank for Foreign Trade was reorganized and given increased operating responsibilities for foreign trade financing. See the author's "The Banking System of the U.S.S.R.," *The Journal of the Institute of Bankers* (London), June, 1963; reprinted in Morris Bornstein and Daniel R. Fusfeld (eds.); *The Soviet Economy: A Book of Readings,* Revised edition (Richard D. Irwin, Inc., 1966).

The pattern of separating the foreign departments of central banks and reconstituting them as specialized foreign trade banks has been copied throughout Eastern Europe. See George Garvy, *Money, Banking, and Credit in Eastern Europe* (Federal Reserve Bank of New York, September 1966), pp. 41, 96-98. Garvy's book is an invaluable source, and the only comprehensive one, on banking organization and operations in this area. The newest Foreign Trade Bank, which was still part of the central bank when Garvy wrote, was established in Romania in June 1968.

[23] For some of the evidence on credit worthiness see *Government Guarantees of Credit to Communist Countries.* Hearings before the Committee on Banking and Currency . . . on S. 2310, November 20-22, 1963, pp. 170-171, 195; *East-West Trade.* Hearings before the Committee on Foreign Relations . . . Part I, March-April 1964, *passim; East-West Trade, A Compilation of Views . . .,* Committee on Foreign Relations, U.S. Senate, November 1964, pp. 187-210.

probably fear these funds might be restricted in some way. At the present time, however, this is probably no longer a practical consideration. In any event, the volume of funds needed to cover regular transactions to be effected in the United States cannot ever have been large, given the quite limited volume of our direct foreign trade. Besides, surplus working balances that were available in earlier years, and which the Soviet banking authorities did not choose to keep in this country, were instead placed in European financial centers. Considering that these funds largely provided the initial impetus to the development of the Euro-dollar market, these Communist balances have had a remarkably wide impact in the international financial world.

The general expansion of Soviet foreign trade is a development of the post-Stalin period, although the development did not gain momentum for some years after the Soviet dictator's death in 1953. The rapid increase in trade in the past decade has involved a corresponding expansion in the volume of financial transactions; and the Soviet authorities have no doubt found it convenient as well as highly practical from the standpoint of economy, to attend to an increasing share of the necessary financial details themselves. Their dependence on important banking institutions in other countries will undoubtedly continue in very large measure. Nevertheless, they have become influential financial operators in their own right by promoting the rapid development of their two banks in the West–the Moscow Narodny Bank in London, and the *Banque Commerciale pour l'Europe du Nord* in Paris. These banks, formerly rather small and inconspicuous, have since 1950–but expecially in the last few years–emerged as important institutions, enjoying widespread correspondent relations with banks throughout the world.[24]

As noted earlier, these Soviet financial dealings also involve United States banks, whose services are required for transactions connected with Soviet foreign trade. The scale of operations conducted with or on behalf of the Soviet banks is probably more extensive than one might suppose from the very little publicity which such activities ordinarily receive, but the fact that United States trade with the Soviet Union has lagged significantly behind the general expansion of East-West trade in recent years means that American banks are not so intimately involved in Soviet financial dealings as are their counterparts in most other countries.

The rather modest dimensions of United States trade with the Soviet Union reflect a general position toward such exchanges which differs quite fundamentally from the attitude prevailing in the other, highly export-oriented industrial countries, whose share of Soviet trade–about one-fifth in 1967–seems to be steadily rising, though by slow degrees. The negative U.S. attitude toward this trade has also been formalized in the adoption of barriers, in the form of discriminatory tariffs (chiefly the denial of most-favored-nation treatment) and credit restrictions. In this latter category we have the prohibition under the Johnson Act against the extension of credit on other than normal short-term commercial terms, prohibitions against the sale on credit of surplus agricultural commodities under Public Law 480, and the prohibition against Export-Import Bank financing for any sales except of agricultural products.

These restrictions serve to limit Soviet purchases of United States goods and they place serious obstacles in the way of any Soviet effort to increase sales in this market, but whether the basic position would be much affected if these restrictions were removed is not at all certain. The obstacle to any steady expansion of United States trade with the Soviet Union is not the existence of financial and other restrictions but the difficulty in finding Soviet goods that would be acceptable in this market.[25] If one accepts the common assumption that there exists a Soviet demand for technologically advanced industrial machinery and equipment, it is difficult to see how this demand could be satisfied without a change in the prevailing attitude–official and private–toward the extension of intermediate and long-term credit which are the normal conditions for financing sales of capital goods.

The prospects for some such development of the United States side are not encouraging, but the trend elsewhere toward the provision of longer credit terms by other industrial nations is not easy to ignore. That development could continue–for the Eastern markets are no longer to be thought of as cyclical safety valves for occasional export ventures–and perhaps in new directions. The recently expressed view of the Assistant General Manager of the Soviet-owned Moscow Narodny Bank, suggesting that the Socialist countries might raise long-term capital in the Euro-bond markets–besides being an intriguing idea–may not be entirely visionary.[26]

---

[24]Garvy, *op. cit.*, pp. 107-108. Some of the detail on the history and development of these two Soviet banks is given in the author's "The Soviet Bank for Foreign Trade and Soviet Banks Abroad: A Note," in *Economics of Planning* (Oslo), Vol. 7, No. 3 (1967), pp. 183-197.

[25]As things stand, United States-Soviet trade is very near to balance, the only exception in recent years having been a U.S. export surplus in 1964 when large sales of wheat took place.

[26]M. Madden, "Lifeblood of East-West trade," *The Times* (London), June 21, 1968, *The Soviet Union, A Special Report* (Supplement), page vii.

Foreign Trade and the New System of Management

Jan Pleva

The impact of foreign trade upon a national economy has been the subject of considerable discussion by Western Economists. In the following article, a noted Czechoslovakian writer has projected the role that foreign trade will play under the new system of management adopted in his country. Although written in 1964, this article is of particular significance in view of current reforms underway throughout Eastern Europe.

To make clear the role foreign trade is to play in the new system of planned management, its relation to the whole national economy, we must give at least a brief summary of the present situation.

I believe that some negative factors in the field of foreign trade were caused primarily by: (1) the system of management by armchair administrators, who issued directives on a nation-wide scale, and (2) insufficient comprehension of the tasks of a state monopoly in foreign trade.

Administrative management, by issuing directives according to indices set down to the last detail in the plan, was a pheomenon which appeared in other branches of the national economy as well. In the first place, there was a gradual reduction of the independent powers of enterprises, particularly in those of the trade groups. The bureaucratic way of working had a great talent for worsening results by issuing more and more directives, when the first did not lead to anything. And, on the other hand, its resistance to self-improvement seemed to harden. The worse the results, the heavier the hand of "correction." Besides the unhealthy growth in the administrative apparatus at the expense of operational bodies, this system of management forced an ever greater shift upward of detailed decisions.

In consequence, there was a constant "improvement" of planning methods and directive indices, making them "more precise" and creating a more cumbersome apparatus. It is also worthy of note that the directive was seldom projected into reality; indeed, the contrary was true, it was farther and farther removed from reality and there arose what one might call "permanent planning": more and more frequent adjustments to adapt the plan to the real situation, instead of the reverse. This adjustment was even carried out in many instances as an afterthought, to provide for "material interest" or the payment of premiums.

The role of monopoly in foreign trade was usually regarded in the past as a way of protecting it from the influence of the capitalist economy, from the economic "cold war." But other functions were more or less neglected: (1) as a link with the world economy in general and the socialist system in particular; (2) as a valuable index of development of world technique and technology; (3) as an instrument of world division of labor–a criterion of development in this sphere of our own economy and an element of healthy competition as a counterbalance to the unfavorable results of production monopolies on the domestic market.

I believe we may say that this aspect led to a certain shortcoming in the differentiation of forms of monopoly in foreign trade. I have in mind the fact that essentially similar organizational forms and cooperation with production enterprises were used for such different products as artificial flowers, electric current, shoes and power plants. From this point of view, foreign trade then became the object of numerous criticisms by the production enterprises.

The work performed by the Ministry itself–like that of other central offices–reminded one rather of the practice of a general directorship of foreign trade, where the operative work and detailed planning of the work squeezed out the function of supervision, that of drawing up the concepts and long-term perspectives. The tendency to "push" the power to decide, up to the highest positions, led to an insufficient use of the trade possibilities possessed by our enterprises of foreign trade because of their size and importance, as compared with the private enterprises of capitalism. Instead of carrying out the tasks of an executive body of a foreign trade monopoly as a connection and a yardstick between internal and world economies, the foreign trade enterprises had to restrict their activities to the role of accountants, balancing foreign trade, often literally "at any price."

These circumstances, together with the economic aspect (to which we shall return later) led not only to a cumbersome administration within this sector, but also to a worsening of the realtionships with those in production. The production enterprises felt this keenly and began to set up their own "export" departments; and, as if in revenge, the foreign trade enterprises established their own technical departments that carried out some of the functions which had been performed inadequately by the production enterprises. Much unnecessary duplication resulted.

Reprinted with permission from *Eastern European Economics*, Vol. III, No. 4, 1964, published by International Arts and Sciences Press.

A one-sided understanding of the role of monopoly in foreign trade gave rise to a theory and practice that ran somewhat as follows:

Production units have wholesale prices set for deliveries to foreign trade. These prices are theoretically fixed as stable prices, but in practice have tended to rise. Production is "protected," that is, separated from the influences of world prices. Therefore any material interest whatever disappeared in studying world prices or in improving technique and technology for further development. On the contrary, with the existing method of planning and judging economic results, it could be easier to carry out tasks by neglecting technology and the quality of the product—and this has often happened.

In like manner a situation was created in the foreign trade enterprises similar to that in production enterprises. Since the costs for carrying on foreign trade were covered from the state budget, as well as any possible difference in internal and foreign prices, and finally, since the direct trade costs (transportation, etc.) invoices were made out simply *tel-quel* ["as is"], direct interest in efficiency of operation disappeared from the social criteria. The workers and the sector as a whole were judged exclusively according to the fulfillment of the balanced accounting items in value terms, without regard to the actual goods produced or the economic results. Good workers with initiative are driven to passivity by such a system. It is of more benefit to an enterprise to sell one large item at a loss than to sell laboriously a larger number with high efficiency and greater return.

Differences thus gradually arise between production enterprises and those in foreign trade, and furthermore between the enterprises and society as a whole. Since there have been attempts to reduce costs in foreign trade, this has resulted in a one-sided and mechanical reduction in number of workers, without sufficient analysis of the actual needs, and sometimes with a concomitant worsening of quality. Of course, not every reduction in manpower is a saving, either. This trend was projected into commercial practice in a neglect of certain territories or of smaller size goods that may bring a higher return. Reducing the number of employees abroad had, furthermore, a negative effect of higher costs in the accounts of representatives abroad.

The Role of Price of the World Market

When we speak of world prices we must note that there are no precisely fixed world prices as such. Instead there are price levels and trends in world markets. This price level is, of course, the most concentrated synthesis of all production and economic influences under which the goods are produced and sold, and is a criterion of international exchange values and world technical advance.

But the present system has been deprived of this criterion. Movements in world prices, showing, among other things, the world progress in technical development, were not reflected here. The price level of internal prices gradually diverged from the world price level, and—what is worse—in this process there occurred far-reaching deformations of price relationships. From the standpoint of foreign trade, some products became advantageous and others disadvantageous and still others sold at deficit prices. Of course, this was true for the economy as a whole, not for the particular production enterprise, because there was no repercussion there—it formed its wholesale price without regard to efficiency.

One may say that, on the contrary, the existing deformation of price relations in imports caused enterprises to have an interest in importing the most costly raw materials, which were processed in a primitive manner and reexported. This was the logical result of the method of measuring productivity of labor and planning wage funds. Importing cheaper raw materials and processing them by means of more advanced technology, perhaps with more labor for the same quality, but cheaper, production, means that the enterprise is economically penalized and does not fulfill the plan. Similarly foreign trade administrators then get into difficulties, also, with the balancing of their planned imports and exports.

Furthermore, circumstances compel frequent changes in these balances, and this contributes to further loss of perspective.

It is natural that when prices are separated from reality and there is no accord between internal, export and import prices, it becomes practically impossible to measure the efficiency of foreign trade, both in regard to an appraisal of labor expended and in regard to an evaluation of the use of raw materials bought for foreign currency. Political consciousness and the great efforts of many good workers cannot surmount these difficulties, because the economic interests of the enterprise and their own frequently lead elsewhere. Besides, it is often impossible to express concretely the interest of society as a whole.

This situation is not improved in the least by the system which forbids imports unless the domestic producer of the same commodity signs a statement that it is unable to meet the domestic demand. This becomes another means of monopolization: from the production aspect, this is a means of clocking technique, of preventing entry of products that are new in form or advanced in other ways, goods which could introduce an element of competition and force the producer to improve quality and take other measures.

The deformation of prices in relation to the world level has still further consequences. Since price is the deciding factor in net return, there occurs a similar deformation in the branch structure of production. It is impossible to find out which of the products are advantageous to produce, with a view to world parameters, and which are not. Furthermore, no one is interested in finding this out under the existing conditions. The efficiency of the investments that have been made cannot be judged and, without this as a corrective and without any long-term outlook, there is no proper guide for investment policy.

A gross underestimation of the capabilities and initiative of the workers and a rigid centralization of decision inevitably cut down on the workers' urge to create and their interest in the results of their work. They begin to wait for "higher wisdom" to express itself. It was shocking to find, when we were discussing the principles of the new system of management, that some workers were afraid to propose the elimination of some targets that had been set by directive, even though they knew these harmed production.

Since the opinion exists that corrective measures which it is necessary to take in foreign trade are related more or less to contacts with the capitalist systems alone, we should pause to consider this idea. According to this, value indices and therefore prices play no special role in contacts with socialist countries, because here it is a case of mutual fixed obligations (either trade agreements or agreements on division of production programs and cooperation) that must be carried out and that cannot be affected by value indices. And, since over 70 per cent of foreign trade is with socialist countries, this whole matter is not considered so important. And on top of this, recommendations are made even today to create special prices for the socialist world market.

In the first place I should like to state the fact that from the very beginning of the development of economic relations within the camp of socialism, world prices have been and still are used, for no one has been able to find a better objective measure of value equivalents. Besides, it is quite natural that this should be so, since the trade with socialist countries is in goods and therefore value must enter into the game. To achieve a certain stability, prices were agreed on within the framework of the Council of Mutual Economic Assistance, constructed on the basis of world prices, but with the elimination, as much as possible, of temporary market fluctuations, and by means of other correctives that were to have constant validity. But even these prices did not achieve complete stability and were subject to change. Therefore it was necessary to carry out adjustments in those cases where they diverged too far from the world level. And, of course, there could be only one world level, for, if we are to measure the ability to compete, and the progress made in the two camps, this cannot be done with two different yardsticks.

The concept of stability of prices cannot be explained dogmatically as a concept of unchangeability. Every economy must be protected, including the common market of socialist states, against speculations that are economically unjustified, against crisis and boom, against the economic "cold war." Of course, world prices are at the same time a synthetic expression of technical progress and when the latter changes, prices will change, as is necessary and proper. A price system cannot have the purpose of protecting against such objective circumstances.

So if we should eliminate the effect of value relationships on the economic relations among socialist countries, we should have the same difficulties as are felt within the country, but extended to an international scale. The equivalence of the exchange of goods would be disturbed, which would have an immediate and unfavorable effect on the coordination of production, which should be the chief form of economic cooperation within the socialist world system. The exchange of goods would cease to develop on the basis of mutual advantage and the injured partner would sooner or later try to avoid carrying out his obligations.

I believe that the economies of the socialist countries will be strengthened by long-term plans based on the economic interests of all participants. Not only this, but all economic relationships must be constantly examined and adjusted from the standpoint of the development of all the other markets, the growth and development of technical progress throughout the world.

Moreover, it is necessary to base the long-range as well as the annual operational plans on a combination of all the valid obligations between countries. Agreements on division of production programs and cooperation must be based on long-term contracts between the enterprises that are carrying them out. Without this linking of the social interests of both parties with the interests of the enterprises and a concrete form of assuring that the contract is fulfilled, there will logically be a failure to carry them out, as there has been in the past. Without this economic assurance, the separate interests would prevail over the interests of society as a whole.

So I am of the opinion that, as a prerequisite for success in introducing the new system of management, not only in foreign trade, but also in the whole economy, it is necessary to take the following steps in the sphere of foreign trade: (1) change the method of setting up the plan; (2) project into the production sphere the influence of world prices; and (3) link the material interest of the enterprise with that of the individual in seeing that economic results are as good as possible.

Setting Up the Plan

The fundamental contribution that foreign trade could make toward the further development of the entire national economy should be primarily long-term planning of the best type of goods to produce, from the standpoint of efficiency. This could be done through territorial division and commodity distribution of output for ten to fifteen years to assure the long-range development of the chief sectors of production. Of course this would require a further improvement and extension of market analysis, price trends, etc. But the production sphere would have the data for reliably correcting its plans for capital investments according to world trade.

In the most important sectors, the long-range plans would be based on this territorial and commodity division of production, thus providing conditions for establishing the most efficient distribution of production tasks among the different sectors. Therefore from the standpoint of external contacts, i.e., the extension of cooperation within the framework of the Council of Mutual Economic Assistance, the level, the trends and proportions of world technical development would influence the plan for extending or restricting production capacities.

It is recommended that the indices that are set by directive be limited to volume in terms of value, expressed in foreign prices and divided among the different payment sectors. In this way there would immediately appear extensive possibilities for changing the whole commodity structure, making it more efficient. These changes would be restricted mainly by the existing structure of production and its elasticity, where the changes would again be reflected.

Furthermore, a scheduling of volume of imports and exports of a relatively small number of especially important items would be necessary.

At the same time, however, it would be necessary to abolish the system of affidavits from the production enterprises stating they are unable to cover needs for the particular product imported. On the contrary it will be necessary consistently to make it possible to import foreign products having the most progressive elements, which would have the effect of enriching the domestic market and of stimulating better production by comparison with world products.

The obligations established among countries in the socialist camp could be itemized, if necessary, in commodity, physical terms and in value terms in the plans of the responsible enterprises.

We must also realize that the above-mentioned indices would be projected in the plans of both production and foreign-trade enterprises.

Finally, the setting up of joint indices for planning results of production and of foreign trade, and their evaluation, would need to be promoted by projecting the effect of foreign trade into the gross income of the enterprises, those engaged in production and those in foreign trade, through the working of world prices. This would mean a coordination of the interests of production enterprises and those in foreign trade, the replacement of administrative measures and directives by the relationships of an economic system of management, and it would be possible to replace the global system of "anonymous" control that cannot be checked on by a system of norms for financing price differences, costs of circulation, and management.

The plan of production and foreign trade would include export and import targets in foreign prices and price relations. Thus there would come about a concept of mobile prices of foreign trade that would express the system of mutual price relations that is often considerably different from the internal price relations. These prices should be expressed in Czechoslovak crowns by means of conversion coefficients of the so-called sector differential indices. These coefficients would arise as completely objective indices by comparing the total volume of foreign trade operations over a given period of time (the best would be the preceding year) and in a given sector of the economy (either the economy as a whole, or a branch of production, a range of goods, a group of types of goods, or one type of goods, whichever is most suitable) in standard wholesale prices and in actual sales prices. The same could be done for a certain territory or in a currency sphere without regard to type of goods. Theoretically it would be desirable to utilize one conversion coefficient, but this is impossible at the present time.

By using sector differential indices and projecting foreign prices into domestic production, we should accomplish the following:

1) In the first place, the prices that prevail abroad will begin to affect the gross income of the production enterprises and thereby of the foreign trade enterprises; the effectiveness of foreign trade will be immediately visible and measurable for the individual enterprises, and will be an essential concern of the enterprises.

2) Where the foreign trade operations are in the same structure as in the previous period, the economic results of production will be the same. But at once some products will become advantageous to produce, others disadvantageous. There will automatically be an endeavor to take appropriate steps in regard to disadvantageous products, or to transfer exports to those products that we are able to produce well (as judged by world prices).

3) In connection with the measures taken in the spheres of planning, wage policy, etc., there will probably be a change in views on the advantages of importing certain raw materials and their use in production for export.

4) The production sector and foreign trade will begin to assign one another price limits and a necessary and constructive discussion will ensue. The end solution must be the projection of these differences

directly in production and in a definite way foreign trade must share in economic results.

At the same time, enterprises in foreign trade must be interested not only in the volume of foreign currency, but also in the economic result of their trade. Here the following measures might be recommended:

1) Establish, first of all for enterprises in foreign trade, a trade margin of a certain per cent of the price, and perhaps in the case of imports, a fixed sum per unit from which they would be obliged to cover all costs, management and wages. A differentiated margin could be set on the basis of past experience.

2) To arouse an interest in economizing in direct trade costs, all prices should be set freight prepaid at the Czechoslovak border and direct foreign costs should be based on the carrier's quotation. This will bring about an interest in reducing these costs, which does not exist today.

3) Set aside a certain share of the return, even if small, to go to the foreign trade enterprises as a reward for selling at a good price. Since the share going to production and to foreign trade cannot be set objectively, this must be done by agreement.

The material interest of the production enterprises should, however, be increased in the following ways: (1) offer a share of the foreign currency for exceeding the export targets, to be used as the enterprise needs (machinery, spare parts, technical literature, etc.); (2) offer a share of savings in foreign currency spent on imports, e.g., cheaper raw materials that are processed by better technology to produce goods of the same quality, etc. Here the economic desirability of the savings should be strictly judged, so that quality would not be sacrificed; (3) after sufficient reserves are created, other forms of bonuses in foreign currency could be considered, e.g., for introducing a new, desirable product on the foreign market or some great improvement in packaging, etc.

Material interest of individuals could be expressed in production by improving the relation between free prices in foreign trade and production costs in the case of exports. Other ways of earning bonuses could be by exceeding the export targets, savings in imports and in the foreign currency that is used in processing.

In foreign trade the chief indicators will be net return, volume of receipts, improvement of the relationship between production costs and the price received on the foreign market, the level of the absolute difference between the price limit and the price actually received, etc. Here a system would need to be drawn up, differentiated according to enterprise and workplace in individual cases.

Relation to Domestic Trade

Relations of foreign trade to internal trade should not differ to any considerable degree from the relations to production. When the affidavit need no longer be signed by the domestic producer that he is unable to cover the need for a certain product before it can be imported, it would be necessary for internal trade to negotiate contracts with foreign firms and become an equal partner in assuring the import of goods for the domestic market. Furthermore, especially as far as industrial goods are concerned, it would be necessary to extend the range of commodities and at the same time arouse competition among the enterprises that are backward in range, quality, and so forth. And we must also eliminate certain unfavorable results of production monopolies as they affect our consumers.

The question of retail prices would be resolved, under the new price system, in the sector of internal trade. I believe that questions of the form of tax, and so on, would not need to be solved in the sector of foreign trade.

Organizational Questions

I am of the opinion that introducing principles of economic management, of a new concept of the guiding function of central governmental bodies, connected with a centralization of long-range plans and investment activity and the decentralization of the power to carry out the planned provisions, should necessarily be projected into the sphere of foreign trade. After all, the reduction of operation activity by the ministry will bring a new organization of operational powers within the enterprises. The ministry will no longer do detailed short-term planning, but there will be an enormous increase in importance of planning long-term price trend activity and control.

Foreign trade is a very sensitive organism, especially in regard to the stability of relations that have been built up and the mutual confidence of the partners. This is also true in relations among nations of the two world systems. Every measure must be well considered and it is necessary to proceed in different ways according to different sectors and branches. Furthermore, the following principles must be observed:

There must be an increase in independence and operational flexibility of the foreign trade enterprise as a whole and within this same framework, of the individual trade groups, so that the director can really trade with full rights and responsibility. At the same time it is necessary to consider coordination of the range of goods to harmonize the sectoral organization with the demands for a commercial line of goods.

Organizational requirements must be drawn up for the enterprises from the standpoint of optimum size and method of trading—as a marketing group or as an independent trader.

There must be a full use of all organizational measures that would bring the production enterprises and the foreign trade bodies closer together.

In practice, carrying out the last point would run up against great differences in opinion and, actually, is the main bone of contention. Production enterprises uphold the view that they are willing to take over greater responsibility for foreign trade, but they also demand greater rights in carrying this out, going so far as to propose the distribution of enterprises of foreign trade among the economic units of the sectors, trusts, etc.

Some foreign trade officials see in this a violation of their monopoly position and almost seem to fear the liquidation of foreign trade enterprises. This is very dangerous because it gives people an unfounded fear of losing their jobs.

In the first place, I believe that there never was a question, and never will be, of liquidating the foreign trade enterprises as independent legal entities.

Taking the foreign trade activity out of the direct production sphere to independent trade organizations is a worldwide trend that no one intends to reverse. It is otherwise, of course, in the question of subordinating one governmental body to another and in handling some special problems. I should like to express my opinion on some possible forms of organization:

1) The simplest and most practical improvement for combining the two sectors would be to set up joint bodies for production and foreign trade. If no other title is found, I should call them steering committees. These committees would be made up of representatives from both spheres with enough power to act (thus differing from advisory councils, which have not proved effective) to make decisions in the following matters:

a) to adopt long-term projects for development and investment in foreign trade;

b) to adopt long-term plans and annual schedules for foreign trade;

c) to evaluate the cooperation, make proposals for taking joint measures for solution of common questions of material interest, etc.

2) Another form of very desirable cooperation could arise where production and foreign trade overlap, where duplication occurs. It would be advantageous to combine the commercial and technical services of both parties in a unified joint organization working at the disposal of the directors of both types of enterprise. This solution is for example proposed by the Ministry of Health between the foreign trade enterprise Chemapol and the similar unit in its ministry. A like proposal could come under consideration for the Ministry of Food Industries. I believe this is a very valuable initiative that could be extended to include joint sample rooms, offices abroad, etc.

3) In some cases there is need to distribute part of the activity of some foreign trade enterprise to a production enterprise, because it is not actually a foreign trade activity. In practice, this is the sale of power which results from power-distribution or it could be the question of solid fuels or any other special problem. I believe that it would be proper in these cases to empower the organizations in questions to carry out the entire operation, because they do it in practice, anyway.

4) In the interest of carrying out economic experiments, it has already been decided that enterprises which sell costume jewelry in foreign trade, as well as those dealing in metal-working machines, should become an integral part of production. It would be a question of including these or some other enterprise in an economic unit for the sector. Naturally they would remain independent legal entities and operational bodies of state monopoly, that is, the exclusive exporters or importers within the units to which they have been attached.

The experiments must be judged by the results and then we must proceed to further proposals for joining governmental bodies. In judging the proposals we must very carefully examine the advantages from the aspect of organization, range of goods, necessity for linking imports and exports of the same type of goods in one trade group, etc. In no case would it be possible to allow any atomization of foreign trade activity. On the other hand, I do not consider proper the view that any carrying out of foreign trade beyond the bound of the Ministry of Foreign Trade is a violation of state monopoly. State monopoly in foreign trade does not consist of a certain ministry or enterprise carrying it out, but in the fact that the organization is empowered exclusively by the state. The necessity for certain changes in the organization of foreign trade and its linking with production is not specifically Czechoslovak. In Hungary and Poland they are carrying out a number of experiments. In the GDR they have begun recently to set up sister societies in foreign trade for the production enterprises. There is no reason to try to avoid changes that must be carried out to make the entire economy more healthy and raise it to a higher level.

I consider very important the question of the stage of transition to the new system of planned management. The conceptions and methods of the old and new system are so different that the new cannot mechanically follow on the previous situation. Nor can the whole system of management and of indicators change from one day to the next. The transitional period requires a very well thought-out procedure, where some directive indices will need to be retained, even though in the final solution they will be eliminated. The question of the impact of foreign prices and of price comparisons is theoretically very simple. But in practice there are a number of difficulties. The necessary measures will not always be popular among the workers, for they complicate their lives.

Hungary's NEM: Reorganization or Basic Reform?

Joseph Szabados

In order to be successful in the foreign market, the businessman must understand how the economy of the country functions. For the firm contemplating trade or some form of business venture in Hungary, the following article will be of particular interest as it focuses upon the manner in which the price system must be transformed in order to be in line with industrial reforms.

One of the knottiest problems in connection with Hungary's New Economic Mechanism (NEM) is how to transform the price system so that it jibes with industrial reform. The aim is not a free-market economy. To allow prices to find their own level would obviously lead to inflationary chaos, so the NEM is based on the gradual loosening of controls.

The problem is made more intractable by the rigidity of the price control system inherited from the old mechanism. Under it, wholesale and retail prices were separately fixed by the state without regard to costs. In addition, the enterprises were insulated against the effect of foreign market prices. It was not until 1959 that price-fixing for industrial goods was slightly relaxed and only in 1967 that production costs began to be reflected in consumer prices.

When the NEM went into effect at the beginning of this year, about ten percent of goods and services reached the consumer at a price that bore some relation to real production costs. Thirty percent were sold at prices inflated by turnover taxes, and the remaining 60 percent were priced below cost.

In an attempt to rationalize the price structure, the NEM incorporated fundamental price reforms that will be introduced gradually over a period of ten to 15 years. Some 10,000 persons were employed throughout 1967 to make the calculations on which the price guidelines of January 1968 were based. The aim of the reforms was summed up in a Central Committee resolution adopted in May 1966. Prices, it stipulated, were to correspond to supply and demand within the framework of state priorities. A small group of prices was to be fixed centrally, but subject to regular adjustment at more frequent intervals than in the past. The sharp difference between consumer and manufacturers' prices was to be eliminated, and world market prices were eventually to prevail.

The step-by-step introduction of the new structure was to start by relating consumer prices to production costs. Price fluctuation in response to the market would at first affect only a small number of products, and foreign trade was to remain under state control at least for the next few years.

Fixing Production Costs

Under the NEM, the prices charged by an enterprise must take into account taxes and such normal cost factors as salaries, raw materials, repairs and maintenance. But the distinctive characteristic of the new "producer price system" is that production costs now include the 5-percent levy on fixed and working capital, the equivalent of capital interest, and are much less rigid than under the old "fixed-price system." Another important change is that the centrally determined profit margin, which is built into prices, will in the future be directly proportional to the value of the fixed and working capital involved in production.

Under the old fixed-price system, profit was calculated as a specific, percentage of costs, fixed for each branch of industry. The enterprises could thus raise their profits by manufacturing costlier articles out of more expensive raw materials or semimanufactured products. The new system, on the other hand, sets profits at a specific percentage of fixed and working capital, so that, to increase their profits, the enterprises must work economically, that is to say, they must use their capacities to the full by achieving maximum production with a minimum labor force, making the most efficient use of their capital, keeping their unsold stock as low as possible, and selling at the highest feasible prices.

Profit margins are set by the National Material and Price Office in such a manner that the more uneconomical enterprises will earn minimum profit (2 percent) and those with greater growth potential, particularly those engaged in foreign trade, will earn profits that may even exceed the general 6-percent rate. The only products that are excepted from these criteria are luxury items that may be priced in direct response to market fluctuations.

Where Prices Are Fixed

With those exceptions, the National Material and Price Office sets all prices for domestic raw materials, semifinished products and capital goods. Transactions among enterprises will therefore continue to be based

Reprinted with permission from *East Europe*, Vol. 17, No. 6, (June-1968).

on centrally determined prices. While freer than before, consumer prices until 1970 will be subject to two criteria: inflationary tendencies must be curbed and no decline in living standards must be permitted for any major segment of society.

The consumer prices introduced at the beginning of the year fall into four groups:

- Fixed prices set by the state. These apply to most foodstuffs, basic services and medicines, and cover 20 percent of domestic trade.
- Ceiling prices, for which the state sets a maximum that may not be exceeded. These apply to inessential foods, essential clothing, household utensils and paper products. They account for 30 percent of domestic trade.
- Guideline prices that may not vary more than 5 percent above or below the state's limits. These apply to canned foods, inessential clothing, mass-produced housewares and sugar products, accounting for 27 percent of domestic trade.
- Free prices, which apply to imported textiles, articles of haute couture, jewelry, handicrafts and certain agricultural commodities. They make up 23 percent of the domestic market. (Under the old system, only 15 percent of domestic trade was free of price controls.)

Amount and Significance of Price Changes

The effect of the new system was two-pronged. With the partial elimination of subsidies, the general level of industrial prices went up 7 percent; consumer prices, on the other hand, declined one percent when the rates and variety of turnover taxes were reduced. The consumer price level, however, was still higher than wholesale prices not only by the fixed profit margin but also by an additional three percent. The rise in manufacturers' prices was justified on the ground that the state had to continue supporting agriculture and public services out of the revenue from the turnover taxes on industrial products, particularly textiles.

Most food prices, which are still controlled under the NEM, continue to be lower than production costs would warrant and have to be subsidized. For obvious social and political reasons the government wishes to avoid an increase in food prices, at least during the transitional period while the NEM is gathering momentum. This also explains why one of the main changes of the new system, the inclusion of production costs in prices, is not being applied to the agricultural sector.

Nevertheless, wholesale agricultural prices have risen. The level of the prices that the state pays to the collectives will go up 8 percent this year—enough, according to Rezso Nyers, the architect of the NEM, to guarantee the profitability of agricultural enterprises in all but exceptional circumstances. Had the producer price system been applied to agriculture, farm prices would have risen by 13 to 14 percent.

For the time being, therefore, the state will continue to support the collectives. They will be able to obtain essential industrial products at reduced prices, and those that run into the red will receive direct state subsidies. There is likely to be a shift in the incomes of the collectives. Those that particularly benefit from reduced prices will lose some, or even all, of their price supports, which will be plowed into the marginal farms. There will, however, be no diversion of part of the national gross agricultural income into other sectors of the economy (such as the development of industry at the expense of agriculture), as there was under the old system.

Easing into Consumer Price Reform

The new consumer price system—or at least the first phase of it that was introduced in 1968—is more cautious about abolishing fixed prices than the first drafts of the reform indicated. In May 1966, Nyers stated that fixed and ceiling prices would be set for only 40 percent of products and that free prices would be permitted for 30 percent of the commodities on the domestic market; other products would vary within state guidelines. But fear of inflation and the carry-over of old habits led the authorities to enlarge the list of goods subject to price controls. Nevertheless, the new consumer price level is more elastic than the old and hence more sensitive to inflation. For this reason the government wants to keep price increases in 1968 down to 2 to 3 percent. Much will depend on how price changes affect everyday life. The government is committed to maintaining relative price stability.

In some measure the new price system still distorts the Hungarian economy. Industrial production is favored; agriculture is underestimated; services are neglected—a situation that encourages economic imbalance. Correction would involve a radical change in the price structure: speedy evolution toward a market-oriented price system and, above all, inclusion of the impact of world prices in the reform. The new price structure, the decentralization of enterprises, the emphasis on profit as the yardstick of economic success—these can bring meaningful results only if the same principles are applied to the most important sector of the Hungarian economy: foreign trade.

The New Economic Mechanism and Foreign Trade

Hungary's foreign trade comes to 37 billion foreign-exchange forints (about $3 billion) a year and accounts for 40 percent of national income. In Europe, only Belgium, the Netherlands and Norway have a greater dependence on foreign trade. The tremendous significance of foreign trade can be seen in the fact that, on the basis of the 1961-1965 figures, a one-percent increase in national income required a 1.5 percent increase in imports. The same data show that the ratio of imports and exports to national income will reach 45 to 46 percent by 1975. About 70 percent of Hungary's foreign trade is presently done with the members of Comecon (36 percent with the Soviet Union). By the end of the third five-year plan in 1970, this proportion is due to rise to 72 percent (40 to 42 percent with the Soviet Union). Hungary imports between 80 and 100 percent of its most important raw materials (crude oil, iron ore, pig iron, petroleum products and timber) from the Soviet Union; it exports to it a quarter of the output of its entire machine-building industry.

Comecon's preponderant role in Hungarian foreign trade and the country's chronic foreign-trade deficit with the West are the fundamental reasons why, despite NEM and industrial decentralization, foreign trade remains overwhelmingly under central control. Under the NEM, foreign trade can be freed only to the extent that it does not disturb Comecon's trading and monetary practices and does not entail a tremendous rise in imports from the West.

Central direction insures that it will not go beyond these limits. Within them, the goal of NEM was to put an end to the practice of regarding domestic prices as unconnected with the price level of similar products produced abroad (in the case of exports) and with the prices the enterprises must pay abroad (in the case of imports).

The NEM establishes a contact between the foreign market and the enterprises, but it is indirect. It is not based on "the wild play of world-market forces," but on a system of centrally built-in economic incentives and on the influence of political preferences. In addition, during the initial years of transition, foreign trade will continue to be subject to central administrative direction: exports and imports will require licensing by the Ministry of Foreign Trade.

The Enterprise's Foreign-Trade Activities

Under the old setup, foreign trade and its financing were, with few exceptions, the exclusive responsibility of the state-run foreign-trade agencies. These agencies purchased the enterprises' products at the fixed domestic price, and whatever profit or loss was made in the sale abroad was chalked up to the foreign-trade agencies. The same agencies also sold imported goods to the enterprises at fixed domestic prices, regardless of purchase price.

The NEM abolishes this rigid separation of prices. Thirty-eight industrial and commercial enterprises have been granted the right to import and export independently without having to go through the foreign-trade agencies. This right was given only to enterprises manufacturing products that do not compete with each other, and whose production and sales operations form a single unit. They are not, however, allowed to use their foreign-exchange earnings as they wish. Furthermore, certain enterprises that are the sole users of some foreign products are allowed to import directly.

Aside from those exceptional cases, exports and imports remain largely in the hands of the country's 29 specialized foreign-trade agencies. Under the NEM, however, the enterprises are no longer tied to fixed domestic prices, but will receive the actual value in forints of their exports or will pay the actual value of their imports. The new role of the foreign-trade agencies is thus that of middlemen between the domestic and foreign enterprises; in some cases they will act as agents on the domestic producers' behalf. Unlike past practice, it will also be possible for the domestic enterprises to choose the foreign-trade agency they wish to deal with, to sharpen competition among the state-owned agencies.

The new arrangement thus establishes a direct link between the enterprises' income and expenditure and the results of their foreign-trading efforts. The government, however, will step in when an enterprise's own interest conflicts with that of the national economy—for instance, when an enterprise finds it more profitable to trade with the West than to do business with the members of Comecon as prescribed by bilateral trade agreements. The government will see to it that the "interest of the national economy prevails," by economic means if possible, by direct intervention if necessary. Since the Ministry of Foreign Trade issues all import and export licenses, the government has the opportunity to regulate all foreign trade. It will thus continue to insure that bilateral trading agreements are fulfilled. In this respect, the only change is that the enterprises involved will have some say in drafting new agreements.

The Foreign-Trade 'Incentives'

Apart from directives, the state's foreign-trade preferences are realized by its foreign-trade pricing policy. The policy has two aims: increasing exports to the West, and expanding over-all trade with the members of Comecon.

The state has preserved its monopoly on foreign exchange: all currency earned from exports has to be turned over to the National Bank, which will finance imports by those enterprises that are authorized to buy abroad. The forint equivalents of foreign currencies are calculated by the authroities with the aid of "foreign-currency multipliers." The general use of these multipliers is the NEM's most important incentive to foreign trade.

The multipliers, which set the exchange rates between the forint and other currencies, were in effect by the beginning of 1968 and represent a de facto devaluation of the forint. The degree of devaluation varies: it is greater with respect to the convertible Western currencies than it is to the eastern European monies (except the Yugoslav dinar). The multipliers show what forint inputs is needed to produce a commodity designed to realize one unit of foreign currency on a foreign market.

The multipliers are based on the ruble and the dollar; the forint equivalents of convertible currencies are calculated according to their dollar parity. The exact exchange rates have not been published, but from Western press reports and Hungarian references to them it can be calculated that the multipliers set the US dollar equivalent to 60 forints and the ruble to 40 forints. Vis-à-vis the dollar and convertible currencies, therefore, the devaluation of the forint is fivefold; vis-à-vis the ruble it is threefold. The practical use of the multipliers, however, is only in domestic accounts between the National Bank and the enterprises. The noncommercial exchange rate (for tourists and foreign remittances, for instance) was also changed with respect to convertible currencies, but less radically. At this rate, the National Bank now pays 25 percent more than before, that is, one dollar is set at 30 forints.

Getting to the Western Market

The main purpose of the devaluation is to promote exports, particularly to the West. Through the use of the multipliers, the enterprises earn more for their exports than they did in the past and more than they would by selling on the home market. At the same time, the cost of imports has gone up, especially from the West. In the case of enterprises that still run at a loss even with the multipliers, the state will aid them with direct subsidies if necessary.

Four other incentives are included in the NEM during the transitional period. They are aimed at curbing imports from the West and stimulating those from Comecon countries.

- A new commercial tariff penalizes imports from those countries (chiefly Western) that do not accord Hungary most-favored-nation treatment and favors imports from Comecon members. The customers are payable in forints calculated with the foreign-currency multipliers, which increase the costs of imports from the West.
- To import consumer articles, domestic trading enterprises may obtain unlimited amounts of rubles and other eastern European currencies from the National Bank. The amount of exchange that may be obtained for imports from the West, however, is set by the state in its yearly plan.
- The deposit system stipulates that an enterprise that imports from the West must bank for two years a forint amount several times greater than the value of the imports. It is not required to do so to import from the East.
- The banks offer various credit and financial arrangements to facilitate imports of machinery from the Comecon countries.

In sum, in foreign trade the NEM preserves central control, though it is applied by economic measures rather than by directive. Simultaneously, it goes to greater pains than formerly to stimulate the export drive. It is obvious, however, that economic and political forces have a greater impact on this sector of the Hungarian economy than elsewhere. When they are coupled with Hungary's persistent foreign-trade problems, they preclude free foreign trade and hobble the enterprises' ability to pursue a rational foreign-trade policy.

Arguing for a Change in Policy

Several of Hungary's leading economists have been disturbed by this tendency and have argued that the nation's economic woes cannot be cured by a one-sided foreign-trade policy. Bela Sulyok, First Deputy Finance Minister, took a stand for freeing foreign trade at a Comecon conference on prices in Budapest. It was not good economics, he said, to try to "exchange the autocracy that existed within individual Comecon countries for socialist-camp autocracy." Going one step further, Dr. Imre Vajda, professor of foreign trade at Budapest University, wrote in the first issue of the new economic monthly *Gazdasag* that economic cooperation was necessary between "socialist and capitalist Europe." As a first step he recommended establishment of a clearing union between East and West, similar to the former European Payments Union.

Hungary's present foreign-trade situation undoubtedly favors those who, for political reasons, oppose increased economic orientation toward the West. Their influence can be detected in the NEM foreign-trade regulations. Yet, if foreign trade does not show some improvement in relation to the West, it is possible that instead of greater economic liberalization there will be retrenchment. Economists in Hungary have argued for a more liberal Western credit policy, joint production ventures with Hungary and lifting of embargoes and tariff restrictions on Hungarian commodities.

Where Does the NEM Go from Here?

In its present form, the NEM is a temporary compromise that can move in either of two directions. A return to a capitalist type of free-market economy is virtually out of the question. So is a return to the old type of rigid, centralized control. What is more likely is that the NEM will either evolve into a patched-up remodeling of the old system or into a reform that puts economic (and to some extent, political) power into the hands of the managers and economists.

The NEM contains the roots of a dual system: the "old order" in which the party retains some of its privileges, and the "new order" in which the managers, along with specialist, intelligentsia and civil servants, have the education, ability and experience to mount a serious challenge to the party's monopoly of power. Educationally, the party is at a great disadvantage. While the majority of the managerial class is drawn from university graduates, only 7 percent of the party's 600,000 members have any kind of university training.

And there is no relief visible in the future. In 1963 at Budapest's five universities, only 2.5 percent of the students were party members; that percentage is now down to 1.1.

Trying to Ward Off Change

Party opponents of the NEM, though they cloak their objections in ideological arguments, fear that the reforms will rob them of their power. Their concern was embodied in a May 9, 1967, resolution of the party Political Committee, which deplored that "in filling state and economic positions in a one-sided way, skill is the determining factor and political requirements are neglected.... State and economic leaders, exaggerating the demands of training, do not like to admit party members to their domain.... In some cases recently, experts who were not politically acceptable have been placed in leading positions."

It is noteworthy that the charge is leveled as much against the leaders of the administration as against the economists, implying that the party and state apparatus are at odds. The aim of the resolution and similar statements was to restore the balance between the "new order" and the "old." Yet nine months later in a report on the execution of the resolution the committee again complained of cases of promotion where "the party unit concerned had a diametrically opposite opinion to that of the state of economic officials."

The NEM also looks to the emergence of a third force: the trade unions. There have been indications that the reforms' "material incentives" have caused bitterness among some workers. Such envy gives the feeble party units in the enterprises a chance to work with the trade unions to intimidate the managers. but if it should also prompt the trade unions to start defending the workers' interests, it could lead to a healthy development in Hungarian life.

What the outcome of this incipient test of strength may be depends in very large measure on the managers themselves, and their skill and courage in exploiting the opportunities offered by the NEM. The vigor and imagination that they bring to bear may not only enhance their role and prestige but may also help to overcome the protectionist shortcomings of the NEM—its price policy, its restrictions on the distribution of the enterprises' profits, its insulation from foreign trade. For in the short run the success of the NEM depends on the number and caliber of its managers. In the long run it will depend on the enterprises' ability to compete with foreign manufacturers. How these two elements are combined will determine whether the NEM is simply an industrial reorganization or a basic reform.

Chapter 5

THE FUTURE OF EAST-WEST TRADE

To Russia with Trade

Sidney Scheuer

Reasons why the United States should adopt a more liberal policy towards trade with East Europe are candidly pointed out in the following article. While continental businessmen vault a "rusty iron curtain" seeking contracts, U.S. executives sit by, immobilized by archaic national policies they themselves deplore.

A bill providing for East-West trade liberalization has been submitted to Congress. The Administration supports it. The United States Chamber of Commerce, the Committee for Economic Development, and various trade associations have also considered this subject and published their views. Each in large measure approximates the conclusions reached by the others. None feels the existing trade situation is satisfactory. All favor change. Yet no hearings have been held on the bill and almost no one is advocating that it receive the consideration it deserves.

Worldwide East-West trade in 1961 was $9.4 billion; in 1965, it was $14 billion; and in 1966, $15.1 billion. The figures include trade with Red China but exclude trade with Cuba and Yugoslavia. Of the 1965 and 1966 trade, the world's biggest trader, the United States, did only $280 million and $380 million worth. And those amounts were just about evenly divided in exports and imports. Are we selling them only the equivalent worth of what we buy—restricting our sales to limit of our purchases? All U.S. trade with the East is subject to government license, as it has been since trade restrictions were imposed in connection with the cold war. But the world has changed since the cold war!

While the rest of the free world plunges into East-West trade and supports it with long-term credits and government guarantees, the United States maintains disciminatory tariffs, formidable licensing procedures and credit restrictions that effectively ward off almost all business opportunities with the East. The effect is a loss to U.S. exporters of their share of the $15 billion of trade because the U.S. government refuses to liberalize the "cold war" trade restrictions. Quite a cost! Particularly when the U.S. government is urging exporters to redouble efforts to bring in new business.

This rigidity in trade posture yields undeserved political dividends to France and to Russia. These countries' declared objective is to reduce U.S. influence in Europe. The longer the U.S. turns away from trade contacts with the East, the easier it will be to implement this objective.

Hence, two purposes urgently argue for a liberalization of U.S. restrictions: (1) to allow our exporters to pick up some of the $15 billion worth of business and (2) to jump in and participate in the growing rapprochement of Eastern and Western Europe. Trade bonds are tangible and long-lived. Trade is the lifeblood of nations. No diplomatic maneuvering can be as effective as trade in determining a country's orientation. Unless we compete in East-West trade, future historians may conclude the United States stood by and helped "freeze itself out" of an increasingly united Europe.

Trade expansion is the cornerstone of American policy. This posture becomes us. We have nothing to gain from curtailing trade. After many years of close observation, frequent visits, and discussions with officials in the Kremlin, Ministers and Vice Ministers of many agencies in Russia and other East European countries, I am convinced that, on balance, East-West trade is both economically and politically more advantageous to us than to the East. It generates employment here, contributes to our balance-of-payments objectives, and aids in maximizing the operation of our productive facilities. No more than anyone else can we afford to ignore the important trend that it is developing. The political and economic cost of having abstained from East-West trade is already considerable and will become more so. The advantages which such trade could have yielded have been lost sight of in the phenomenal prosperity of the U.S. during the 1960's. Had we participated as other nations have, our share of the trade would by now be a welcome addition to current order obligations.

Are these views unrepresentative of the business community in the U.S.? The answer is an emphatic "no." The Foreign Relations Committee of the Senate in its examination of East-West trade published in November, 1964, included "A Compilation of Views of Businessmen." On the question of whether or not this trade should be expanded, it received 128 replies: 105 favored trade; nine did not; eleven refrained from comment; and three indicated an unsatisfactory experience. The prevailing view of those few who were opposed was that Russia is and always will be our enemy. In this writer's view this position invites permanent conflict, perhaps ultimate catastrophe. The adamancy of the position effectively precludes the possibility of peaceful evolution. I suggest that instead of adamancy we substitute an affirmative, self-confident posture. Fear ill accords with our country's abilities and its enormous resources. Laws proscribing business with the East express a lack of confidence in our effectiveness and the potential of our influence. They are negative and isolationist.

Remember that the United States conceived and implemented Lend-Lease, the Marshall Plan, AID, spearheaded the International Monetary Fund and the World Bank, advocated the "open door" policy toward China, and pioneered many other equally creative acts of statesmanship. Changing times now demand equally creative initiatives in the area of East-West trade.

Comes the Thaw! Will Business Be Ready?

Once this is recognized, and the official obstacles to East-West trade are cleared away, it will be up to the businessman to take advantage of the opportunities. This won't always be easy. Doing business with the East involves an entirely new set of operating considerations. It is not possible to generalize because each country follows somewhat different practices and procedures. Moreover, major changes are occurring continuously. Obviously, one does not deal with a Russian the same as with a Pole or a Rumanian or a Czech. However, all have in common the fact that they operate as agents of a corporate state.

Organization Chart, Soviet Style

The state dominates all business dealings. In Russia each major branch of industry is administered by an All-Union (Central Government) Ministry in Moscow which is responsible for all developments and all factories in that particular branch of industry. There are 21 of these All-Union ministries. An All-Union Council of Ministers coordinates the 21 All-Union ministries. Gosplan (the Central Planning Committee) is the administering arm of the All-Union Council of Ministers. There is a local Gosplan in each Republic which is the administering arm of each Republic's Council of Ministers. The national Gosplan also acts as the link between the State Committee for Material Supplies and the State Committee for Science and Technology.

The State Committee for Material Supplies is a new organization whose responsibilities cover everything dug out of or grown on the ground, or manufactured therefrom within the Soviet Union as well as products of the same kind obtained abroad. The State Committee for Science and Technology is responsible for major industries not under the responsibility of the 21 All-Union ministries, and for those mixed endeavors such as, for example, oceanographic research. It is a body of great importance. American businessmen who are interested in exporting technology to Russia would be well advised to work closely with it. This Committee undertakes joint cooperation on research and development with comparable organizations in the West. It also is the link between the All-Union Council of Ministers and the Republic (local) Council of Ministers in the USSR's 15 component republics. The Republic Council of Ministers supervises local ministries which direct the operations of local enterprises in each industry sector. The Republic ministries of each industry are responsible to the All-Union Ministry of each industry.

The Ministry of Foreign Trade controls all foreign trade activities. The Soviet's foreign trading corporations operate under this ministry's authority. These corporations administer all importing and exporting of commodities, plants, processes, products, licenses and know-how. They are the business arm of the Soviet State. Each corporation handles the trade in the line of business assigned to it. U.S. businessmen may find opportunities for cooperation with them in third markets: for example, joint ventures when two or more countries participate in supplying the components of one order. Barter trades, and variations thereof, are particularly interesting to this Ministry.

That Special Touch

Western businessmen may not adequately appreciate that a special approach is needed when negotiating with officials of Soviet trading corporations. These officials have huge responsibilities. To negotiate effectively with them, western businessmen must have relatively high executive seniority in their business. Also, an immense amount of costly and time-consuming personal attention to detail is essential.

If one does business in Russia frequent visits to Moscow are usually preferable to maintaining permanent representation. The cost of stationing one man in Moscow for a United States company is between $50,000 and $60,000 yearly. This includes all costs—salary, hotels, transportation and communications. The cost of periodic visits is far less and probably more effective. Communications from Russia to the home office are not easy. Periodic visits allow the businessman to bring his problems personally to headquarters for detailed discussions, a freshening of viewpoint, and devising of bottleneck-breaking formulas. Moreover, it is difficult to find executives who are adequately self-sufficient to endure the pressures and strains involved in the lonesome assignment of the foreign businessman in Russia.

In doing business in Russia one must expect to experience a society that is long on theory and short on applied technology and the kind of topflight managerial and operating talent capable of undertaking major responsibilities in competitive societies. This is not to disparge Russia's enormous economic accomplishments. Similar executive shortages exist throughout the world. Nonetheless, this demands a more-than-normal patience, endurance and effort on the part of the supplier in the performance of contracts with Russia.

European suppliers have usually grouped into consortia to handle major transactions in the East. The typical consortium is an organization independently set up which submits proposals, negotiates and acts as prime contractor on behalf of a group of subcontractors. The consortium supplies the products and supervises their installation and activation. The consortium has full contractual responsibility. Japanese trading houses operating abroad perform similar services: they negotiate and coordinate the sale of industrial plants and know-how, and frequently also market a wide range of Japanese products. In consortium transactions, Japanese machinery manufacturers are subcontractors of the trading house.

In trading with the East, United States companies would do well to establish themselves with other companies in consortium arrangements. Purchasers everywhere, as in Russia, will choose to deal with one large contractor rather than many small contractors. Buying corporations in Russia have huge and diversified responsibilities. The work loads of their officials are extremely heavy and, consequently, whenever possible, these officials prefer to deal with one contractor on complicated projects.

Experience Helps

I speak from extensive experience, as our own organization has performed such services: it has negotiated for and established integrated projects that require machinery and know-how from many sources. And it has taken responsibility for financing, shipping, installation, supervision, and activation of plants. In other words, it has concerned itself with all contract requirements. Communist countries have established a long record of scrupulous contract fulfillment and payment as buyers and sellers. Serious concern in this regard is not necessary.

Businessmen of today must perform services far beyond the limitations of operating successful industrial enterprises. They are indispensable instruments of domestic and international policy. If their activities are conducted with statesmanship and integrity, enormous political dividends can accrue. They can and do contribute to breaking down and counteracting false propaganda which otherwise may go unchallenged. It has been demonstrated that when United States operating personnel function in relations with their opposites in the USSR, the result is most favorable: many questions are raised and new evaluations developed. Without such opportunities these valuable interchanges would not take place. An interesting incident, one of many that illustrate this point, occurred on the occasion of President Kennedy's assassination. On that day representatives of our company, who were supervising and coordinating a plant installation in Russia, were visited in their hotel by a delegation from the plant who came with flowers to express their sympathy. All of which goes to reinforce an ancient adage: it is far easier for people than governments to communicate and empathize.

To conclude, I would like to quote the following principles enunciated by the late Wroe Alderson in an earlier issue [Vol. I, No. 1, Winter 1966] of this *Journal*:

"1. Communication between world powers is always safer than noncommunication.

"2. Marketing messages provide the framework for international order while insistence on ideologies always presents hazards.

"3. Communication can pass from friendly messages to unfriendly messages but seldom can the reverse occur—at least not abruptly.

"4. The first step in restoring good will is to move from unfriendly messages to objective and factual communication about goods, equipment transactions, and payments. If this ground is well laid. friendly intercourse once more becomes possible."

Prospects for Profits - East Europe --- the Next Two Years

The statistics in this article present all the evidence that is needed to reveal just how amazingly fast the six markets of Eastern Europe–Bulgaria, Czechoslovakia, East Germany, Hungary, Poland, and Rumania–are growing as purchasers of goods made in the non-communist industrialized countries. While each market is opening up at different rates and the rate of expansion of each varies from year to yaar, there is little to indicate that the rate at which this market is growing will slow in future years.

Streamlining and modernization of their economies is the basic problem faced by all six of the East European countries. They have reached a stage of economic development at which they must now make a basic shift in their goals: from brute quantity to better quality. It is this need for quality–better goods in and of themselves, but perhaps more important a more efficient use of resources and better technology–that has spawned the much-discussed economic reforms. This development, and the problems that it raises for highly centralized economies seeking to loosen up at least somewhat, will preoccupy planners and managers in East Europe until the end of the decade and beyond.

The degree of reform, however, differs considerably from country to country. Hungary and Czechoslovakia are pushing reform the furthest and fastest (apart, of course, from Yugoslavia). Poland and East Germany form a second category of more moderate or cautious interest in reform, and Rumania and Bulgaria are moving the slowest.

The reform involves reduction of the number of centrally fixed targets; greater freedom for managers to determine their product-mixes and their inputs, greater discretion on investment, and greater emphasis on net return–i.e., profits–rather than gross output. Profitability, of course, is directly related to prices and costs–full costs, including a charge on fixed capital–a striking innovation for East Europe.

Two elements of the reforms have particular significance for western businessmen: first, the new costing method's underlying purpose is to enforce discipline in using scarce resources. This gives each manager a specific and concrete interest in obtaining the best techniques and the latest technology as well as the cheapest sources of supply. The keen interest of East Europe for know-how as well as goods per se will continue to mount.

The second element is the possibility that East European manufacturing enterprises will be buying directly from western suppliers rather than through their import monopolies, the foreign trade organizations. Hungary will allow 23 enterprises to conduct their own foreign trade in 1968 and 19 more in 1969.

The Opportunities

In overall terms, the communist countries of Eastern Europe offer the fastest growing regional market in the world. It looks as if they will continue to increase imports rapidly. The market for the 11 most important industrialized countries expanded by a sizzling 28% last year, and by 16% in the eight years through last year. Planned trade figures for 1970 in most countries indicate the intention to continue to import at this annual rate. Hungary's foreign trade, for example, is to reach *F*26 billion (tourist exchange rate is *F*23.48:US$1) in each direction, compared to 1966 exports of *F*18.71 billion and imports of *F*17.38, a 49.6% increase in imports in four years.

In terms of types of goods that eastern countries are particularly interested in, there are considerable specific differences from market to market. But Western executives can gear their sales strategies to fit the basic framework of East European economic goals for 1970. These indicate three broad areas:

1) Goods and know-how that contribute to the modernization and rationalization of industrial production. This can include a wide variety of items. Well-known is Czechoslovakia's avid interest in buying computers. What is more, recognizing its need to expand and up-date its industrial know-how, in 1966 it signed more licensing agreements with foreign firms than in the five previous years combined. Hundreds of agreements have been concluded with East Europe for industrial machinery and equipment of all sorts, for sophisticated automated machines and plants and for the accompanying know-how.

2) The need to improve agricultural output is urgent, and–in contrast to the '50s–a number of countries (Rumania in particular) are now beginning to invest considerable sums in farming. Fertilizer plants, agricultural machinery of all sorts, and processing plants are among items in demand. On the more specialized side, the UK's Taylor Woodrow constructed a chicken farm for Hungary, including controlled-environment buildings and equipment, 18,000 chicks (one-day old), and technical assistance in running the farm (including a guarantee of the equipment–and the performance of the checks).

How East Europen Imports . . . Have Been On The Increase In The Past Eight Years

(in $ million)

Exporting Country	Bulgaria			Czechoslovakia			East Germany			Hungary			Poland			Rumania			Total			Percentage Increase	
	1958	1965	1966	1958	1965	1966	1958	1965	1966	1958	1965	1966	1958	1965	1966	1958	1965	1966	1958	1965	1966	1966/65	1966/58
Austria	4.3	25.3	24.9	18.7	37.2	44.0	15.3	28.4	30.4	19.6	42.4	38.9	31.3	31.9	35.5	4.5	21.9	26.0	93.7	187.1	199.7	6.7	113
Belgium	2.2	4.6	8.4	11.3	22.8	22.0	9.0	11.9	23.6	5.2	11.0	11.3	15.8	13.8	15.2	1.0	6.2	7.4	44.5	70.3	87.9	25.0	98
France	4.7	23.7	42.6	17.5	35.4	63.2	6.6	69.1	62.3	10.7	20.7	25.2	16.1	35.6	67.3	14.1	43.8	50.1	69.7	228.3	310.7	36.1	346
Germany	13.8	55.2	108.1	61.3	100.6	125.7	190.6	297.8	404.8	28.8	76.8	92.7	78.8	91.5	93.8	22.4	115.6	139.4	395.7	737.5	964.5	30.8	144
Italy	3.8	32.6	36.4	11.4	41.9	49.4	4.4	16.1	20.6	9.3	37.2	37.3	19.1	50.2	63.8	8.0	47.1	45.1	56.0	225.1	252.6	12.2	351
Japan	*	10.9	24.5	.3	8.7	4.3	3.7	1.1	2.5	*	2.3	2.8	.8	5.4	3.0	*	15.2	21.9	4.8	43.6	59.0	35.3	1,129
Netherlands	1.3	11.8	19.6	7.9	15.4	19.4	14.3	19.8	21.5	4.0	10.3	11.0	11.7	13.0	13.3	1.7	4.3	6.0	40.9	75.1	90.8	20.9	122
Sweden	.3	5.9	10.8	7.6	18.9	22.3	16.8	32.1	35.2	3.6	9.5	11.6	23.8	30.9	30.6	.2	7.3	13.8	52.3	104.6	124.3	18.8	138
Switzerland	1.5	6.9	9.9	14.8	19.0	21.5	5.4	8.3	12.1	6.5	11.3	14.2	10.8	14.7	17.6	2.6	8.2	13.6	41.6	68.4	88.9	30.0	114
United Kingdom	1.5	10.8	20.7	13.2	40.6	49.5	7.4	23.2	44.5	8.9	21.5	28.3	32.9	70.6	98.3	4.4	27.1	28.8	68.3	193.9	270.1	39.3	295
United States	.1	3.6	3.6	1.5	27.7	37.3	.4	12.6	24.9	1.7	9.3	10.1	105.2	35.4	53.0	.9	6.4	27.2	109.8	95.0	156.1	64.3	42
TOTAL	33.5	191.3	309.5	165.5	368.2	458.6	273.9	520.4	682.4	98.3	252.9	283.4	346.3	393.0	491.4	59.8	303.1	379.3	977.3	2,028.9	2,604.6	28.4	167

*Less than $100,000. Source: U.S. Dept. of Commerce export statistics.

3) Consumer goods are now generally receiving a much higher priority. Automobile companies—Fiat, Renault, Volkswagen, Simca, among others—have been racking up agreements with East Europe, but soft goods and speciality items are also being bought. At the 1967 Poznan Fair, for example, Prouvost sold Poland about *Ffr*300,000 worth of sweaters. American Machine and Foundry Company sold a 12-ally bowling center to Rumania.

Those companies willing and flexible enough to embrace new and somewhat unorthodox business arrangements can find special kinds of opportunities in Eastern Europe associated with what are called cooperation agreements. These dealings are certainly not without special headaches, often including principally the problem of payment, but East Europeans are particularly keen to buy when they can also sell, or at least see opportunities for future sales. This can mean an arrangement to sell in third markets, some type of barter, or the western firm taking part of the output for its own internal use or for marketing in the west. It is doubtful whether any of the six countries will follow Yugoslavia during the next few years in taking tentative steps toward welcoming foreign direct investment.

The Pitfalls

The costs of bargaining with East Europeans are not likely to decrease. The very fact that trade is growing means that there is more competition, and a company can spend a lot of money before seeing any return. Further, the relationship between these costs and probable return is by no means as easy to estimate as in a free-market economy. No company-particularly a newcomer—might risk having an executive team spend six months or a year or more with no results.

Fluctuations in the rate of growth of a country's economy, particularly if substantial amounts of hard foreign exchange have to be diverted to the purchase of food, can disrupt planned foreign trade. Companies have found, for example, that talks that had been progressing well suddenly stalled. Often the reason turns out to be that planned foreign exchange simply was not available.

A particularly large question mark is the outcome of the reforms. If they do not work out as well as planned, considerable economic chaos could result, not the least of which might be that nobody—enterprise managers, foreign trade officials, central planners—would really know who had the authority to do what.

Views East-West Trade Effect of Reforms, Controls

J. Mishell George

The U.S. Department of Commerce is directly concerned with all aspects of East-West trade. In this article, the special assistant to the Director, Bureau of International Commerce, discusses the effects of economic reforms in Eastern Europe and the impact that these reforms will have on Western businessmen.

During the past few years, most of the countries of Eastern Europe have been engaged in a series of economic reforms. These reforms have engendered much discussion, both in the countries themselves and in the Free World. In many cases, the extent and details of the reforms are still being worked out. It is thus rather difficult to determine the overall effect these reforms might have.

It is possible, however, to sketch a general picture of what is going on in the area and to obtain an impression of what the future has in store.

These reforms do not signify a rejection of their fundamental ideology, or adoption of "capitalist" beliefs and practices, but reflect some modifications within the existing system. The reforms indicate a response to a need for change within the system, not a change of the system itself.

In spite of the differing economic conditions in the various countries, the ultimate objectives of the reforms display clearly common features. All of them seek an economic mechanism which will treat day-to-day operations with more efficiency and less central regulation, and which will simultaneously furnish rational economic criteria for long-term decision-making.

Key facets of the complex reform process are price reforms, decentralized decision-making and responsibility, profit orientation (or profitability), and improvement of planning.

Most East European countries are currently revising their pricing systems in an attempt to bring outdated, administratively determined prices closer to current cost considerations. It should be noted, however, that the new prices do not accurately reflect what are usually considered "normal market factors," i.e., capital charges, rent, marginal cost criteria, etc.

The current stress on profitability, which is prevalent in the current East European reforms, has two main objectives.

First, it seeks to eliminate waste such as that caused by tied-up inventory, idle machines, and inefficient manpower utilization. The reforms attack this problem by measuring the success of an enterprise in terms of profits as a percentage of capital invested.

Second, it seeks to have producing enterprises pay closer attention to the needs of the consumer. Prior to the reforms, enterprises were considered successful if they fulfilled or overfulfilled the Plan target in terms of volume of output. Questions of quality, durability or attractiveness of product were more or less immaterial. Enterprises worried only about the quantitative aspect of production. With the advent of the reforms, however, the enterprises receive rewards only if and when the goods they produce are sold. If the product does not sell, the enterprise suffers. This situation forces the producer to pay more attention to the wishes of the end-user.

The emphasis of the reforms on decentralized decision-making and responsibility varies depending on the country in question. In several cases, the decentralization process only added another bureaucratic layer or two to an already cumbersome bureaucracy. Whatever the extent of decentralization, however, it should not be taken to mean that enterprises will have full freedom of choice to buy, sell, produce, or invest.

Current indications are that the economic reforms will inevitably have some impact on the foreign trade of Eastern Europe, in terms of volume, composition, and relative importance, and will also facilitate improving trading relations with Free World countries.

In general, the current stress on greater satisfaction of consumer needs will mean an increase in East European imports of such consumption items as automotive vehicles, clothing, and furniture, as well as the plant, equipment, and materials needed to produce these items domestically in the future.

A system of priorities will continue to be used in determining the composition of East European imports. Likewise, the utilization of State Trading Agencies will continue. In fact, the U.S.S.R. has expanded the number of its State Trading Agencies, Enterprises, will, however, be granted greater flexibility in determining and satisfying their own import needs.

In many cases, a portion of the total amount of foreign exchange earned by an enterprise through exports will be made available for the use of that enterprise in fulfilling its import needs. Several of the

Reprinted from *International Commerce*, December 11, 1967.

reforms also indicate that an enterprise will be permitted to obtain foreign exchange in order to import machinery and equipment, provided that the use of the imported material will eventually result in greater export earnings.

As far as the geographic distribution of Eastern Europe's foreign trade is concerned, current indications are that trade between the East European countries will still account for about 70% of their total international trade, at least for the next five years.

With their own wry sense of humor, some Eastern Europeans describe their socialism—in Western terminology, their communism—as the longest road *from* capitalism *to* capitalism. The changes in Eastern Europe that have been described are still a far cry from capitalism as it is generally known, but they do represent movement toward accommodating some of the growing needs of the people and the economies of Eastern Europe in a broader set of international relationships. And each country is developing its own set of responses to this situation.

Thus, Eastern Europe can no longer be viewed as a monolithic bloc, but as a number of individual countries whose primary interest is increasingly the promotion of their own national growth and development rather than the advancement of international Communism.

Moreover, these changes are viewed as important contributions to the lessening of East-West tensions and the development of mutual understanding and appreciation of each other's problems and aspirations. They justify a more hopeful outlook in U.S. relations with Eastern Europe, and support the President's policy of exploiting "ideas, education, culture, trade, technical cooperation, and mutual understanding through world peace and prosperity" in his effort to create better understanding between East and West.

Of course, improvement of U.S. trade relations is not a panacea for easing East-West tension, but increased trade contacts can contribute importantly to achieving that objective. As President Johnson has said, "the intimate engagement in peaceful trade, over a period of time, can influence Eastern European societies to move along paths that are favorable to world peace."

If we are to achieve our objectives in the economic and trade fields—as well as in other areas noted—it is important that there be a wide appreciation within the U.S. of the problems involved and of our efforts to resolve them.

What are the principal obstacles to improved economic and trade relations between the United States and Eastern Europe?

On the U.S. side:

➤ Low level of interest on the part of most U.S. firms in East-West trade and limited exposure to the trading practices of Eastern European trading organizations, and the little knowledge they possess of the import needs and the export products of Eastern European countries.

➤ Limited credit or credit guarantee availability in contrast to that available from other countries.

➤ Lesser public acceptance of export or import trade with Eastern Europe.

➤ U.S. withholding of non-discriminatory tariff treatment for their products.

➤ Legislative and administrative restrictions on export-import trade.

On the Eastern European side:

➤ Tight governmental control of international trade, including implicit export and import control programs.

➤ Limited gold production and gold reserves.

➤ Non-convertibility of own currencies in world money market and limited availability of freely usable foreign currencies.

➤ Lack of public exposure or availability of advanced technological developments of interest to U.S. industry.

➤ Lack of orientation of design and production of goods meeting needs of U.S. market.

➤ Unfamiliarity with U.S. market and marketing techniques.

➤ Limited ready availability for U.S. businessmen of meaningful information on their market and limited access to likely users and consumers.

➤ Extensive use of closely-managed bilateral trade agreements.

➤ Unsettled financial debts to the U.S.

Trade Controls

Comment is pertinent here on the controls that exist over trade between the United States and Eastern Europe. Too frequently, an unduly significant role is attributed to trade controls on the East-West scene. (See article "East-West Trade Reviewed" in *International Commerce* Jan. 9, 1967.)

It is important to note that both the United States and Eastern European countries exert trade controls. Eastern Europe's controls, while not explicitly directed to trade with the United States, cover the broad spectrum of their export-import trade, but are not always apparent because they are an implicit part of their entire structure for the conduct of foreign trade. But their controls are much broader than those of the U.S., and are likely to remain so even under the changes they are now instituting. The impact of their controls is difficult to gauge.

U.S. trade controls, on the other hand, are the subject of published law and regulations. While we have a number of import controls, relatively few are of significant trade importance to Eastern Europe. The most important is probably the embargo which has been in effect since 1951 on the import of seven types of furs from the U.S.S.R.

However, there is a substantial export control program operated primarily by the Department of Commerce under the Export Control Act of 1949. These controls toward Eastern Europe are based primarily upon national security considerations and began in early 1948. They have, however, changed substantially in the intervening years.

Although some years ago it could have been justly claimed that U.S. export controls were an important deterrent to increased trade with Eastern Europe, this is no longer true. The current impact of U.S. export controls on the level of U.S. exports to Eastern Europe is quite modest. The principal effect is to prevent certain specific transactions and the funds which may have been scheduled for such purchase can, of course, be used for other purchases from the United States.

A substantial share of recent U.S. exports to these destinations occurs under general license, i.e., the exporters do not even have to submit an export license application to the Department of Commerce. In addition, export licenses are issued for signficantly more exports to Eastern Europe than are shipped under such licenses.

Lastly, the number of export license approvals has been increasing, and most applications are approved. In 1966, 5,300 cases were received for commodity exports and about 1,550 for technical data exports, representing a total of almost 7,000 applications or a 21% increase over the number received in 1965. During 1966 about 5,500 applications were approved, as compared with about 4,300 in 1965. In 1966, 110 applications were rejected, in comparison with 161 in 1965.

This analysis should not be taken to mean that there may not have been potential applications which, if submitted, would also have been denied. The trade community is aware that for certain goods and technology our policy for Eastern European destinations is denial, and, therefore, firms may not submit export applications. There may also have been possible additional sales to Eastern Europe for which export licenses would have been approved had application been made for export licenses.

It is worth noting that a decade ago the export of most basic industrial items to Eastern Europe would have been denied. Today most such items are likely to be approved.

For example, of the more than $4 billion of goods exported by Western Europe to Eastern Europe in 1966, the overwhelming bulk, both in value and in kinds of goods, consisted of items that the United States either allows to be exported to Eastern Europe under general license or is willing to license very liberally to that area. They included large amounts of foods, beverages and tobacco; crude materials (such as hides and skins, textile fibers, and fertilizers); fats and oils; medicines, dyes, and plastics and other industrial chemicals; machinery, transport equipment and miscellaneous manufactured goods.

To date, however, U.S. exporters have been unable to sell these items to Eastern Europe or to sell only in small amounts. The basic causes are not to be found in our export control restraints, but rather in some of the other factors already noted. Thus, as a result of the continuous streamlining of U.S. export controls and updating of our licensing policies, these controls operate now as an effective trade restraint toward Eastern Europe on only the relatively narrow strategic sector of goods and technology and have little effects on the total level of trade.

A U.S. export control program that protects the national security and welfare interests of the United States is still maintained. But increased trade in peaceful items and technology with the countries of Eastern Europe is welcomed.

For the first nine months of this year total two-way trade with Eastern Europe amounted to over $292 million–$153.5 million in U.S. exports and $138.5 million in imports. This trade was at an annual rate of just under $400 million.

The United States total takes on added perspective, however, with consideration of two additional factors.

First, United States trade figures do not include exports by the overseas subsidiaries or licensees of U.S. firms. Rather, these are reflected in the trade statistics of host nations. Although solid figures are not available, such trade between European-based U.S. subsidiaries and licensees and the U.S.S.R. and Eastern Europe appears to be growing rapidly.

Second, trade statistics are limited to commodities. Not included is the sales price or other monetary value of technical data or services. Yet such trade constitutes an increasingly important share of exports eastward by U.S. industrial and engineering firms. An increasing number of such transactions have been licensed under the Export Control Act.

Thus, it seems clear that U.S. two-way trade with the U.S.S.R. and Eastern Europe is showing reasonable growth and would appear to have a significant potential for future expansion across a diverse range of peaceful products. To what extent and how quickly that trade potential will be realized by both sides depends in part on an improvement in our general relationships and in part on the removal of the specific obstacles to trade which have already been cited. Considerable effort and patience will be required on both sides to achieve a continuing increase in the flow of commerce.

Doing Business With and In East Europe: The Present and a Look Toward the Future

Phillip D. Grub

The author, who headed the first official U.S. seminar team in marketing and management to Eastern Europe, observes the changes which are evident in these countries today. He concludes that the key question for the future is whether these countries will continue to grow economically and industrially at the same pace as they have in the last decade.

Eastern Europe has become a significant and viable export market in the past decade. Indications are that this market will continue to grow in importance for the products of multinational firms as these countries attempt to not only regain their pre-war trade position but to forge ahead in their plans for growth and development. Countries that lost much of their individual identity for the past two decades are now beginning to take new form as nationalism, which was suppressed for many years, becomes a part of the liberal ferment that is developing in East Europe.

A major part of this nationalistic surge is geared toward the economic reforms which are evident in such countries as Czechoslovakia, Hungary, and Rumania. The need for modernization and economic reform has long been a major problem in these countries. While Yugoslavia has encouraged private enterprise in the past, it has only been recently that this has begun to be evident in Czechoslovakia, Hungary, and Poland.

Leaders in all of these countries are looking to the West for modern management and marketing methods that can be quickly adapted into the socialist system of enterprise. As a result, decentralization of management, establishment of profit centers, and increased pressure upon plant managers for updating methods of production and maximizing efficiency have caused sweeping reforms and created need for modern equipment and technology.

In keeping with this changing atmosphere in East Europe, the potential markets for United States products are indeed significant. Yet, in spite of the growth of the market potential in these countries, there appears a lack of aggressiveness on the part of United States business to tap these expanding markets. Other countries, principally in West Europe and Japan, are moving rapidly to fill orders and gain important inroads as the Eastern European countries liberalize their trade policies.

The changing situation in Eastern Europe is of particular interest in view of the United States balance of payments problem. The markets which American firms are losing to their Western allies could help substantially to narrow the balance of payments gap. Furthermore, for many products, if initial market entry is not gained now, these markets will be lost for the future because the firms that gain the initial inroads will then become the major suppliers of parts and equipment.

Present Trade Position

Total United States trade with Eastern Europe is quite insignificant. According to recent United States Department of Commerce figures, American trade with East Europe is about .6 percent of total United States trade for 1967. Although the United States share of total world exports is approximately 16 percent, East Europe accounts for only approximately .3 percent. The following table show the erratic pattern of United States trade with East Europe from 1963 to 1967.

U.S. Trade with East Europe, 1963-67

(millions of dollars)

Year	Exports to East Europe	Imports from East Europe
1963	166.8	85.1
1964	339.9	102.3
1965	140.0	141.6
1966	197.8	182.2
1967	195.1	179.8

Area includes Albania, Bulgaria, Czechoslovakia, East Germany, Hungary, Poland, Romania, and the USSR.

Source: U.S. Department of Commerce data.

While United States trade with East Europe was a mere $375 million, total 1967 Eastern European trade with Western countries was estimated at $15.3 billion. Japan and Western Europe, on the other hand, accounted for about $9 billion of this trade.

World trade has been increasing, according to United States Department of Commerce and United Nations data, at about 8 percent a year. During this same period, East-West trade has risen approximately 12 percent annually.

In testimony before the Senate International Finance Subcommittee, Ambassador to the United

East European Trade, 1963-67
(millions of dollars)

Year	Global Trade		Trade with Free World		Intra East Europe Trade	
	Exports	Imports	Exports	Imports	Exports	Imports
1963	17,184	16,798	5,255	4,786	11,929	12,012
1964	18,652	18,620	5,824	5,732	12,828	12,888
1965	20,009	19,743	6,538	6,296	13,371	13,447
1966	21,221	20,703	7,166	6,967	14,055	13,736
1967	23,232	22,237	7,700*	7,600*	15,532*	14,637*

Area includes Albania, Bulgaria, Czechoslovakia, East Germany, Hungary, Poland, Romania, and the USSR.
*Estimated
Source: International Financial Statistics, International Monetary Fund, Volume XXI, No. 7, July 1968, p. 35.

Nations, George Ball, testified that American restrictions on trade with East Europe serve only one purpose: that is, to prevent American businessmen from aggressively seeking markets there. Such restrictions, he testified, present no handicaps to East Europe.

In addition to the growing market for export goods, there are increasing instances of licensing agreements as well as some joint ventures within the various Eastern European countries. American business investments overseas are important sources of income for United States firms as well as being significant contributors to the prosperity and development of the countries in which they are located. This direct investment overseas by United States firms is an important factor in "bridge building" because it puts American management in contact with their East European counterparts. In so doing, the American executives are instrumental in transmitting American technology, and methods of doing business, to their East European counterparts.

Official United States policy since 1964 has increasingly placed restrictions on the flow of private capital for investment purposes overseas. With the easing of East-West tension, investment in these countries could be opportune for both the United States government as well as the firms concerned. Furthermore, present export controls are based on policy derived when the United States was almost the sole supplier of advanced technological and capital equipment. This is no longer the situation as is evidenced by the rapid progress made in these fields by leading Western European countries and Japan.

Not all barriers to expanded East-West trade are due to political unwillingness to make the exchange. For example, it is clearly evident that while many United States manufacturers are more than willing to sell their wares in East Europe, there is often little production, especially in the Soviet Union, that United States importers are willing to buy. The principal difficulty, therefore, is to find areas where trade is mutually advantageous.

Organizing for East Europe

The problem of how to organize for trade in East Europe is of concern to many firms. During my recent visit to East Europe, which included Bulgaria, Czechoslovakia, Hungary, and Poland, as well as visiting headquarters of many firms doing business in East Europe in Vienna, Paris, Brussels, and London, no consistent pattern or approach to East-West trade was found. Few firms had established permanent sales representatives in any of the countries visited. The most common pattern was to have a regional sales office either based in Geneva or Vienna, that would handle sales to the Eastern European markets.

The most important contact with the East European markets was through the various trade fairs where American companies of their European representatives would have an exhibit. Active follow-up on the leads derived at the trade fairs would be made by the sales representatives if firm contracts were not made during the fair. Many of the sales were placed through American subsidiaries in Europe rather than the parent company because of problems of obtaining necessary financing or because of lack of hard currency.

The majority of representatives for American firms at the Poznan and Budapest trade fairs reported directly to their companies' European headquarters. For the most part, they were representatives of a European-based subsidiary rather than the parent company located in the United States. Depending on the individual company, sales representatives would either report to a regional director or the head of a sales division. A major United States pharmaceutical firm, whose European headquarters is in London, directs all of its Eastern European sales activities through their West German office. Another American firm, which is a primary producer of kitchen utensils, has special sales representatives for the various Eastern European countries which operate out of their Amsterdam headquarters. Other United States companies, on the other hand, have created a special department for sales to various East European countries with the personnel reporting directly to the head of international operations in the United States headquarters.

The size of the department and its position within a company will, of course, depend upon the magnitude of operations. An English machine tool executive confided that they were adding a special division just to market in East Europe because of growing sales potential. A Dutch electronics manufacturer, on the other hand, stated that his firm would not actively solicit any additional business this year, although they would participate in several trade fairs, because of their backlog of orders. Such a demand for their products, he stated, would be greatly diminished if United States firms were actively engaged in selling to the East European countries.

When queried as to the reason for the selection of a regional headquarters for trading with East Europe, most firms say that they chose a city because of either its proximity to the market or because a particular city was considered to be politically neutral. In the first category, Vienna appeared to be the preferred base. The Viennese bankers are accustomed to trading with the various Eastern European countries and their proximity lends easy access to the markets and the East European capitols where most business is transacted. Furthermore, overhead costs are relatively low and there is an abundance of multi-lingual personnel to assist in translations and conducting business.

Geneva is particularly popular because it is the headquarters for so many international firms. Furthermore, Geneva is considered to be a politically neutral city. The same argument could be made for any other city in Switzerland. Swiss bankers have an undisputed reputation for their expertise in international finance and can offer advice and assistance to the businessman engaged in trade with the Eastern European countries. This is especially helpful when the lack of foreign exchange requires trade to be on a barter basis or the businessman to become involved in a switch deal or some other less formal means of transacting business.

While the foreign trade organization has been the principal means of selling to the Eastern European countries, there is increasing evidence that this is fast becoming passe. Due to the increased decentralization of operations among East European firms, contracts can be negotiated directly by the enterprise director in many of the countries. Most notable of all is Czechoslovakia, although this is also true to a limited extent in Rumania and Bulgaria. Most business is, however, still transacted at the annual trade fairs as has been true for centuries.

The Role of Credit

For the most countries of East Europe, there are no credit-granting institutions other than banks. To a very limited extent, banks have been used to finance fixed investment, but the main role of credit has been to provide the bulk of financing of inventories for production and distribution. As such, consumer credit and the financing of cooperative and individual home building have become important only in recent years.

In Poland and Czechoslovakia, both private and cooperative dwellings may be financed through the state banks. Length and the amount of credit available for the financing of housing varies as to whether the dwelling will be individually or cooperatively owned. While credit to farmers has been the practice for many years, loans to developed private industry and housing have only begun to be made recently.

In none of the countries visited was there evidence of credit being made available to foreign firms wishing to establish a joint venture within the country. For domestic enterprises, priorities are granted according to the importance of the operation to the annual plan.

Expanding Markets

Perhaps an insight into the marketing conditions in several countries would be beneficial at this point. In Hungary, for example, keen interest was displayed in United States industry, their products, and how firms are managed. The climate for export opportunities, licensing agreements and joint ventures is certainly limited; however, receptivity toward opening the Hungarian market to United States firms was evidenced. This was particularly true in the computer and electronics industry areas. Interest was displayed in possible joint ventures with American firms in which they could jointly reach third country markets.

The Hungarian economy appears to be making rapid strides as is indicated by the building of new structures, restoration of older buildings and the expansion of plant and equipment. The regard for American products is high and they are preferred to those of most of the European competitors. This is especially true in computer equipment, building materials, and construction equipment.

The Hungarians are definitely interested in consumer products, especially style merchandise. People on the street are fashionably dressed, particularly the women. Dresses worn at the opera, for the most part, would be as appropriate for Paris, Vienna, Rome or San Francisco where high-fashion is the order of the day. Mini skirts worn by the young moderns were prevalent on the streets. Younger men preferred the highly tailored suits that connoted Italian and French design.

As part of its economic reform, Hungary has introduced a new tariff schedule. This is a move on the part of the Hungarian government to encourage exports and transform Hungary's administrative price system into one that is more in keeping with world marketing conditions.

The three-column customs tariff comprises preferential duties, MFN duties and maximum duties. Preferential duties apply to products from developing countries and are based on international agreements. MFN treatment will be accorded all countries granting the same treatment to Hungarian imports. Under present arrangements, duties may be significantly reduced or eliminated, according to contractual arrangements. The maximum rate of duty is applied to countries discriminating against Hungarian imports and/or applying their own maximum duties to Hungarian products. Special consideration has been given to consumer goods under this new system.

Further signs of liberalization in Hungary were reported in April of 1968. Private artisans were given the right to carry out work for state enterprises and certain manufacturers were allowed to sell their products on the open market on an individual basis. The result of this move is to facilitate the operation of small scale private industry and bolster the supply sector.

To promote the sale of foreign countries' products in the Hungarian market, organizations such as Produktinform have been developed. Produktinform (Institute of Technical and Scientific Information of the Ministry of Metallurgy and Machine Industry) provides the technical publicity and information through periodicals and other media to reach prospective customers in Hungary.

Produktinform does not provide direct commercial functions as yet; however, it offers its services to parties desiring to trade in Hungary. Its major contribution is that it serves as a storer of information on trade needs and prospective clients.

Czechoslovakia

Czechoslovakian firms are anxious to import more United States goods, especially building materials and equipment as well as elevators, machinery, and computer ware. As one executive stated: "Why should we purchase European technology that may be five or more years old when we can get the latest from the United States? However, to buy we need the hard currency and that is only attainable if the United States market is open to us through MFN treatment." Other items of interest in United States goods focused upon water pollution plants, contact lenses, machine tools, textile machinery and equipment, and laundry equipment.

In many of these areas Czech businessmen were interested in possible licensing agreements with United States firms or their subsidiaries. In the past, all licensing agreements have been purchased outright; however, recent agreements have been on a per-unit produced profit-sharing basis.

Sixteen foreign firms are now doing business in Czechoslovakia. Equity participation has been the exception in the past, but now each business opportunity is considered in light of its own merits. Firms interested in doing business in Czechoslovakia should begin discussions on an unofficial basis with appropriate industry or trade organization representatives and then officially when details have been thoroughly explored. The Czech Chamber of Commerce will assist in arranging informal discussions with appropriate businessmen, according to the Chamber president, Dr. Otakar Koutsky.

The Czechs are most interested in receiving MFN status with the United States. Such action would, they feel, give a significant economic boost to their economy by putting them on par with their chief competitors: West Germany, Poland, Italy, and Japan.

Just how would MFN treatment effect specific companies? Jewelry exports to the United States would probably double, according to Jablonex executives, from $3 to 6 million in sales per year. The reason for this increase is that the high discriminatory duties on finished goods would be eliminated. Currently, Czech glass stones are exported to third countries where they are made into costume jewelry and then transhipped to the United States. With MFN treatment, the total process would be completed at the Czech factory where excess capacity currently exists and savings in transhipment and middlemen's profits would reduce the price of the Czech goods to United States buyers. Jablonex executives also feel that greater quality control in costume jewelry production would result if they were able to assemble their products locally with their own skilled craftsmen.

In turn, MFN consideration would increase almost fourfold the volume of men's jewelry imported by Czechoslovakia from the United States. Demand for American jewelry production equipment would also rise because the Czechs feel that United States equipment is the finest obtainable in the world and the increased production would require major purchases of new equipment.

A further area of potential business for United States firms may be found in laundry and drycleaning equipment. Much of the work at present is done by hand and it takes several days to get laundry and drycleaning finished. Because of the inefficient methods presently being used in Czechoslovakia, persons who are able take their goods to Germany to be drycleaned due to the superior methods employed there.

A question might be raised as to the impact of the Soviet invasion of Czechoslovakia on the future of trade and trade relations. It is apparent that there has been a definite disruption of trade, however, Western businessmen report that trade relations are beginning to resume pre-August conditions. What is noticible at this point is that there has been a slow down in Czech plans for industrial expansion . . . but that officials are still moving toward a revitalization of industry throughout the country.

Poland

Poland provides an interesting contrast to Hungary and Czechoslovakia. Rather than being on the move, Poland appears to either be sliding along or going backward. Professors of marketing and management appear to be well informed as to the latest technology and techniques used in the United States; however, there is little evidence that this is being practiced by Polish industry. Organizations are caught up in a web of bureaucracy that is second to none.

While stores in Warsaw showed an apparent lack of merchandise, the shops in Poznan were very well-stocked. This, no doubt, was an attempt to provide a showcase for visitors to the Poznan fair. In consumer oriented stores, long lines are often formed to buy goods and 20 to 25 minute waits to get in to be waited on are not at all unusual.

Selection of goods is only part of the retail sales effort to frustrate the consumer. After merchandise has been selected, one has to then get in a second line to pay the bill. After completing that feat, one must go to a third line to pick up a purchase. If you have not given up by then, you are ready to exit. One thing to remember–do not change your mind at any point as it really causes havoc and disrupts the total system.

The potential market for American goods appears to be quite dim in Poland. Poland, like other East European countries, has a significant shortage of hard currencies thus handicapping it in its sales transactions with Western countries. However, many United States firms are actively engaged in licensing arrangements in Poland, especially to produce goods that can be marketed in other East European countries that would otherwise be excluded due to currency restrictions or import priorities.

Future Prospects for United States-East European Trade

In spite of the many handicaps toward trade expansion, there is every indication that the markets in the various Eastern European countries will continue to grow in the future. The extent of that growth, however, depends on several variables.

For example, even if United States restrictions on trade with Eastern European countries were eased, it is highly doubtful that the extent of trade would be increased significantly in the near future. First, there is the desire for these countries to be somewhat independent and not have to rely on outside markets. Secondly, there is a lack of financing necessary for the purchase of United States goods.

If long-term financing were granted to the Eastern European countries, it is highly dubious that this would expand trade either. The reason for this belief is that these countries must have something to sell in order to get the necessary exchange to meet credit payments when they come due. At the present time, there is little in the way of merchandise that American firms wish to buy in East Europe.

What officials in these countries fail to realize is the influence of customer demand in Western markets. They are not accustomed to selling in a competitive situation where choice and quality are major forces in determining consumer preferences.

Another problem that these countries would have to overcome is the lack of goods available for export that are currently desired in the United States market. For example, Herend China, manufactured in Hungary, is very popular in the United States. Artex, the export organization which handles overseas sales of this china, indicated that the plant was operating at full capacity and total output was being sold at the present time.

In Czechoslovakia, the same situation was found true at Glass Export. Czechoslovakian crystal, among the finest in the world, is in great demand in Western markets. However, Glass Export officials indicated that they were able to sell all of the existing production and that current orders were exceeding capacity to produce. This would indicate that countries would have to channel some of their initial investment into segments of the industry that would net them immediate returns in terms of hard currency.

Further, distance is another major factor. There is a lack of awareness of products that are available from the United States, as well as what would sell and where. Again, even if the demand for United States goods was there–and it certainly is in the consumer goods industry–the lack of necessary foreign currency handicaps the sale of goods within the East European market.

Aside from the lack of hard currencies that negate East Europe as a prospective market, there are other indications that place these countries in a more favorable light. First, all of the Eastern European countries are implementing new economic reforms and applying techniques that will improve the quality of their products, efficiency and expertise of management, and the profitability of enterprise. Further, the nationalistic trends have created a degree of competitiveness among the various Eastern European countries, and it is evident that the leaders in each nation are desirous of their own country being placed in positions of market leadership.

It must be recognized that the realities of world industrial production changed significantly since the United States instituted the present export controls which have been the basis for United States-East European trade policy. Fifteen years ago the United States was the sole world supplier of most industrial and advanced technological equipment; today numerous countries compete effectively with the United States in the world market for capital goods. Present United States restrictions on trade with East Europe do not hurt these countries at all; they only are instrumental in preventing American businessmen from aggressively seeking markets there.

A key question for the future is whether the Eastern European countries will continue to grow economically and industrially at the same pace as they have during the last decade. If they do, prospects for expansion of American-East European trade are excellent if East-West trade policy is liberalized by both parties concerned.

Supplementary Bibliography

Books and Brochures

American Management Association, International Management Division, *Financing East-West Business Transactions,* American Management Association, No. 119, 1968.

Balinsky, A.; Bergson, A.; Hazard, J.N.; and Wiles, P., *Planning and the Market in the U.S.S.R.: the 1960's.* New Brunswick, N.J.: Rutgers University Press, 1967.

Berg, Michael von, *Die strategische Bedeutung des Ost-West Handels im Rahmen der weltpolitischen Auseinandersetzung,* Leiden: A.W. Sijthoff, 1966.

Brzezinski, Zbigniev, *Alternatives to Partition for a Broader Conception of America's Role in Europe,* New York: McGraw-Hill, 1965.

Bromke, Adam and Uren, Philip E., editors, *The Communist States and the West,* New York: Praeger, 1967.

Campbell, John C., *American Policy toward Communist Eastern Europe,* Minneapolis: University of Minnesota Press, 1965.

Carleton, William G., *The Revolution in American Foreign Policy.* New York: Random House, 1963.

Collier, David S. and Glasser, Kurt, eds. *Western Integration and the Future of Eastern Europe,* Chicago: Regnery, 1964.

Committee for Economic Development, *East-West Trade–A Common Policy for the West.* A statement on national policy by the Research and Policy Committee of the Committee for Economic Development. New York: CED, 1965.

East-West Commercial Relations, Brussels: European League for Economic Co-operation, 1965.

J. L. Felker, *Soviet Economic Controversies–the emerging marketing concept and changes in planning 1960-1965.* Cambridge, Mass. and London: M.I.T. Press, 1966.

de Gara, J.P., *Trade Relations between the Common Market and the Eastern Bloc.* Brussels: College of Europe, De Tempet, 1964.

M. L. Harvey, *East-West Trade and U.S. Policy,* New York, National Association of Manufacturers, 1966.

Krengel, Rolf, *Die Bedeutung des Ost-West Handels für die Ost-West Beziehungen,* Gottingen: Vandenhoeck & Ruprecht, 1967.

Schaffer, H.G. ed., *The Soviet System in Theory and Practice–Selected Western and Soviet Views.* New York: Appleton-Crofts, 1965.

Schmithoff, C.M., ed. *The Sources of the Law if International Trade–with Special Reference to East-West Trade.* New York: Praeger, 1964.

Thomas, John R., *"U.S. East European Relations: Strategic Aspects,"* Research Analysis Corporation, 1968.

Ward, B., *The Interplay of East and West–Points of Conflict and Cooperation.* With a new epilogue. The Sir Edward Beatty Memorial lectures. New York: W.W. Norton, 1962.

Wirtschaftsplanung im Ostblock. Beginneiner Liberalisierung? (Im Autrag der Deutschen Gesellschaft fur Osteuropakunde), Stuttgart: Kohlhammer /1966/.

Zebot, Cyril A., *The Economics of Competitive Coexistence,* New York: Praeger, 1964.

Government Documents

A Background Study on East-West Trade. Committee on Foreign Relations, U.S. Senate. April 1965.

Background Documents on East-West Trade. Committee on Foreign Relations, U.S. Senate. February 1965.

Compendium of Papers on Legislative Oversight, Review of U.S. Trade Policies, U.S. Senate, Committee on Finance, 90th Congress, 2nd session, February 7, 1968, Washington: U.S. Government Printing Office, 1968.

Consular Convention with the Soviet Union. Hearings before the Committee on Foreign Relations, U.S. Senate. . .On Executive D, 88th Congress, 2nd Session, January 23, February 3 and 17, 1967.

"Controversy over Proposed Expansion of East-West Trade," *Congressional Digest,* June-July 1967, pp. 162-192.

East-West Trade. Hearings before the Committee on Foreign Relations, U.S. Senate. Part II, February 24, 25, 26, 1965. (A continuation of the Hearings in March-April 1964, listed above as Part I, which constitutes the complete record of hearings on this subject in the 88th Congress, 2nd Session.)

East-West Trade. A Compilation of Views of Businessmen, Bankers, and Academic Experts. Committee on Foreign Relations, U.S. Senate. November 1964. (A supplement to the March-April *Hearings.*)

East-West Trade. Hearings before the Committee on Foreign Relations, U.S. Senate. Part I, March-April 1964

East-West Trade. Hearings before the Subcommittee on International Finance of the Committee on Banking and Currency. U.S. Senate. Ninetieth Congress, Second Session, June-July 1969, Parts I, II and III.

Export Controls. Hearings before the Subcommittee on International Trade, Committee on Banking and Currency, House of Representatives, June 5, 1963.

Export of Strategic Materials to the U.S.S.R. and other Soviet Bloc Countries. Hearings before the Internal Security Subcommittee, Committee on the Judiciary, U.S. Senate, Parts 1-4. October 1961. (Material on U.S. export control procedures is printed in Part 2, pages 182-209.)

The Fiat-Soviet Auto Plant and Communist Economic Reforms. Report pursuant to House Resolution 1043, 89th Congress, 2nd Session, for the Subcommittee on International Trade, House of Representatives (Subcommittee print). March 1, 1967.

Foreign Commerce Study (Trade with the Sino-Soviet Bloc). Hearings before the Committee on Interstate and Foreign Commerce, U.S. Senate. May 5 and 6, 1960.

The Future of U.S. Foreign Trade Policy, Volume I, Hearings before the Subcommittee on Foreign Economic Policy. . .Joint Economic Committee. July 11, 20, 1967.

The Future of U.S. Foreign Trade Policy, Volume II: Submitted statements. Hearings before the subcommittee on Foreign Policy. . .Joint Economic Committee, 1967.

Government Guarantees of Credit to Communist Countries. Hearings before the Committee on Banking and Currency, U.S. Senate. . .on S. 2310 (the "Mundt" amendment,) November 20-22, 1963.

Herman, Leon M., "East-West Trade: An Overview of Legislation, Policy Trends, and Issues Involved." Library of Congress, Legislative Reference Service. Washington, D.C. June 17, 1968.

Herman, Leon M., *A Background Study of East-West Trade; prepared for the Senate Committee on Foreign Relations.* 89th Congress, 1st session. Washington: U.S. Government Printing Office, 1965.

Issues and Objectives of U.S. Foreign Trade Policy, A Compendium of Statements Submitted to the Subcommittee on Foreign Economic Policy, Joint Economic Committee, September 22, 1967.

Kohler, Foy D., "Constructive Initiatives in East-West Relations," *Department of State Bulletin* Vol. 56, No. 1446 (March 13, 1967), pp. 406-413.

Mainland China in the World Economy, Hearings, and Report, Joint Economic Committee, 1967.

A New Look at Trade Policy Toward the Communist Bloc, by Samuel Pisar. Subcommittee on Foreign Economic Policy, Joint Economic Committee. November 10, 1961.

The Political Stakes in East-West Trade. A report. . . submitted to the Subcommittee on Foreign Economic Policy. . .Joint Economic Committee . . .by Senator Jacob K. Javits. February 2, 1962.

"The Question of U.S. Trade with the Communist Bloc—Pro & Con," *Congressional Digest,* February 1964, pp. 37-64.

Recent Developments in East-West Relations. Hearings before the Subcommittee on Europe, Committee of Foreign Affairs, House of Representatives. October 18, 1966.

Recent Developments in the Soviet Bloc. Hearings before the Subcommittee on Europe of the Committee on Foreign Affairs, House of Representatives. Part I, January 27-30, 1964; Part II, February 18, 19, 25, and March 4, 10, 1964.

Report of Special Study Mission to Europe, 1964. Committee on Foreign Affairs, House of Representatives (House Report No. 15). February 3, 1965.

Shipping Restrictions on Grain Sales to Eastern Europe. Hearing before the Committee of Foreign Relations, U.S. Senate. September 17 and 27, 1965.

Solomon, Anthony M., "East-West Trade," *The Department of State Bulletin*, Vol. 53, No. 1376 (November 8, 1965) pp. 739-746.

The Soviet Economic Offensive in Western Europe. Report of the Special Study Mission to Europe . . .of the Committee on Foreign Affairs, House of Representatives (House Report No. 32). February 7, 1963.

To Amend the Export-Import Bank Act of 1945. Hearings before the Committee on Banking and Currency (House). April 11, 12, and 28, 1967.

Trade Restraints in the Western Community With Tariff Comparisons and Selected Statistical Tables Pertinent to Foreign Economic Policy. Subcommittee on Foreign Economic Policy of the Joint Economic Committee Congress of the U.S. 8th Congress, 1st Session. Washington: U.S. Government Printing Office, 1961.

The United States and World Trade. Challenges and Opportunities. Committee on Foreign and Interstate Commerce, U.S. Senate. March 14, 1961. (Chapter 4, "The Challenge of Sino-Soviet Trade.")

U.S. Congress, Senate Subcommittee on International Finance, Banking and Currency Committee. Hearing on SJ Res. 169 East-West Trade, June 4, 13, 27, July, 17, 24, 25.

U.S. Congress, Soviet Economic Performance: 1966-67, Subcommittee on Foreign Economic Policy. . .Joint Economic Committee, 90th Congress, 1st Session. 1968.

U.S.-U.S.S.R. Trade Relations. Committee on Foreign Relations, U.S. Senate. June 24, 1959.

Articles and Periodicals

Adamovic, Ljubisa, "Increased Exchange of Goods between East and West," *Review of International Affairs* (Belgrade), Vol. 11, No. 256 (December 5, 1960), pp. 13-15.

"American Management Seminar Finds East European Officials Alert to U.S. Trends and Trade Prospects," *International Commerce*, Vol. 74, No. 30, (July 22, 1968), pp. 2-4.

Anderson, Earl V., "East-West Trade," *Chemical and Engineering News*, Vol. 45, (July 10, 1967), pp. 76-90.

Arsic, Draginja, "East-West Trade in International Relations," *Review of International Affairs* (Belgrade) Vol. 15, No. 334 (March 5, 1964), pp. 10-11.

Bailey, Norman A., "The Long-term Credit Strings Attached to Trade with the Soviet Union," *The Magazine of Wall Street*, (December 12, 1964), pp. 301-303.

Barnet, R. J., "Coexistence and Cooperation in International Law," *World Politics*, Vol. 18, No. 1 (October, 1965), pp. 82-91.

Berman, Harold J. and Garson, John R., "Probable Effects of the Proposed East-West Trade Relations Act Upon U.S. Import, Export, and Credit Controls," *Vanderbuilt Law Review*, Vol. 20, pp. 279-302.

Berman, Harold J. and Garson, John R., "United States Export Controls–Past, Present, and Future," *Columbia Law Review*, Vol. 67, No. 5 (May 1967), pp. 791-890.

Brass, H. and Schulmeister, D., "Input-output Analysis as an Instrument for Coordinating Production and Foreign Trade," *The American Review of Soviet and Eastern European Foreign Trade*, Vol. 2, No. 3 (May-June, 1966), pp. 25, 49.

Burck, Gilbert, "Challenging East European Market," *Fortune*, Vol. 76 (July, 1967), pp. 122-124.

"Businessmen Appraise East-West Trade, (Russia and Her Satellite Nations)," *Harvard Business Review*, Vol. 44 (January, 1966), pp. 6-8.

"Canada is Booming East-West Trade; It's Both Boom and Headache for U.S. Firms," *Business Abroad*, Vol. 91 (September 19, 1966), pp. 24-26.

"Canada's Trade Relations with Eastern Europe," *Foreign Trade* (Canada), Vol. 129 (1968) No. 2, pp. 3-41.

Clesner, Herschel F., "Foreign Investment and Technical Agreements in Yugoslavia–1967," Spring Issue of the Patent, Trademark, and Copyright Research Institute's publication, *IDEA*, pp. 21-36.

"Der Einfluss der UdSSR und des sozialistischen Weltsystems auf die internationalen Wirtschaftzbeziehungen," Aussenhandel, Vol. 17, (1967), No. 11, pp. 7-14.

Deutscher, Issac, "Russian Problems and U.S. Politics, *The Nation*, Vol. 199, No. 3 (August 10, 1964), pp. 43-45.

"Do Problems of Expanding Trade with the Communist Bloc Outweigh Potential?" *Magazine Wall Street*, Vol. 117 (December 25, 1965), pp. 345-70.

Dondey, K.H., "Economic Cooperation between the Two Systems in Europe (I)," *Review of International Affairs*, (Belgrade) Vol. 17, No. 383 (March 20, 1966), pp. 10-12.

"Dumping and Central Planning," *Journal of Politics and Economics*, Vol. 74, (June 1966), pp. 250-64.

"Eastern Europe Breaks Out of its Bonds," *Business Week*, (November 20, 1965).

East-West Trade, Newsletter on Business and Economic Affairs, distributed by Economic News and Research-FNS, Inc., 280 Madison Avenue, New York, New York.

"Economic Content of Soviet Trade with the West," *Law and Contemporary Problems*, Vol. 29 (Autumn 1964), p. 971.

Faude, E. and Maier, W., "The New Economic System of Planning and Managing the Economy and Foreign Trade Profitability," *The American Review of Soviet and Eastern European Foreign Trade*, Vol. 2, No. 2 (March-April 1966), pp. 27-68.

Gross, H., "Trading with the East," *East Europe*, Vol. 14, No. 6 (June 1965), pp. 6-9.

Gross, Hermann, "Kennedy-Runde und Ost-West Handel," *Der Donauraum*, Vol. 12, (1967), No. 3 pp. 121-133.

Grote, G., "Problems of Realizing the New Economic System of Planning and Managing the Economy in the Area of Foreign Trade," *The American Review of Soviet and Eastern European Foreign Trade*, Vol. 2, No. 2 (March-April 1966), pp. 3-26.

Gyorgy, Andrew, "Diversity in Eastern Europe: Cohesion and Disunity," *Canadian Slavic Studies*, Vol. 1, No. 1, (Spring 1967), pp. 1-22.

Holbik, Karel, "Comecon and East European Economic Nationalism," *Zeitschrift fur die gesamte*

Staatswissenschaft, Vol. 122 No. 4 (October 1966), pp. 721-740.

Jurasz, Witold, "Polish-American Economic Relations," *The American Review of East-West Trade*, Vol. 1, No. 10 (October, 1968), pp. 7-13.

Karlsson, Gunnar Adler, "Problems of East-West Trade–A General Survey," *Economics of Planning*, Vol. 7 (1967) No. 2, pp. 119-182.

Kohlmey, G., "Economic Growth and Foreign Trade," *The American Review of Soviet and Eastern European Foreign Trade*, Vol. 2, No. 3 (May-June 1966), pp. 3-24.

"Lawyers Look at East-West Trade Thaw," *Business Lawyer*, Vol. 20 (April 1965), pp. 525.

Mosely, Philip E., "The United States and East-West Detent: The Range of Choice," *Journal of International Affairs*, Vol. 22 (1968) No. 1, pp. 5-15.

Narpati, Ballash, "Le Commerce Est-Ouest," Reflets et perspectives de la view economique, Vol. 6, No. 5 (September 1967), pp. 347-356.

Notel, R., "The Role of the United Nations in the Sphere of East-West Trade," *Economia Internazionale*, Vol. 18 No. 4 (November 1965), pp. 643-662.

Otto, G., "Problems of Linear Optimization in Foreign Trade Practice," *The American Review of Soviet and Eastern European Trade*, Vol. 2, No. 3 (May-June 1966), pp. 50-64.

"Private Boycotts vs. the National Interests," *Department of State Bulletin*, Vol. 55 (September 26, 1966), pp. 446-452.

Prybyla, Jan S., "The Convergence of Western and Communist Economic Systems: A Critical Estimate," *The Russian Review* Vol. 23 (January 1964), pp. 3-17.

"Red Traders Seek More Western Suppliers," *Business Abroad*, Vol. 91 (October 17, 1966), pp. 17-18.

"Sale of $50.00 Mill in U.S. Machine Tools for Red Auto Plant Wins Congressional OK," *Automotive Industry*, Vol. 136 (April 1967), p. 110.

Shulman, Marshall D., "Some Implications of Changes in Soviet Policy Toward the West, 1949-1952," *Slavic Review*, Vol. 22, No. 4 (December 1961), pp. 630-640.

"Soviet Bloc Markets: Weighing the Pros and the Cons," *Business Abroad*, Vol. 90 (December 13, 1965), pp. 11-14.

"The Soviet Union & Trade in Patents and Licenses," *International Affairs* (Moscow), (September, 1966), pp. 127-129.

Staller, G.J., "Patterns of Stability in Foreign Trade: OECD and COMECON 1950-1963," *American Economic Review*, Vol. 57 No. 4 (September 1967), pp. 879-888.

Stanovnik, J., "The Moscow Agreement and World Trade," *Review of International Affairs* Vol. 14, (Belgrade) No. 325 (October 20, 1965), pp. 12-14.

Stanovnik, J., "Integration–On A Regional or World Basis?" *Review of International Affairs*, (Belgrade) Vol. 14, No. 309 (February 20, 1963), pp. 8-10.

Stanovnik, J., "International Trade without the Cold War," Review of International Affairs (Belgrade), Vol. 14, No. 324 (October 5, 1963), pp. 7-8.

Stolte, Stefan C., "Economic Developments in the Soviet Bloc," *Bulletin, Institute for the Study of the USSR*, October 1967, pp. 29-35.

"Trade Mission From Minneapolis Reports on Talks with Soviets, Other East European Buyers," *International Commerce*, (November 27, 1967), pp. 1-3.

"Trade with Russia? Both ayes and nays," *Business Week*, October 5, 1963, pp. 29-30.

Thomas, John R., "U.S.-East European Relations: Strategic Aspects." Paper RAC–P–37, April 1968. Research Analysis Corporation, McLean, Virginia.

"Treasury Regulations Affecting Trade With the Sino-Soviet Bloc and Cuba," *Business Lawyer*, Vol. 19, pp. 845-846, (July 1964).

Tucker, Robert C., "Russia, the West, and World Order," *World Politics*, Vol. 12, No. 1 (October 1959), pp. 1-23.

"U.S. to Give Russia Machine Tools for Auto Plant," *Iron Age*, Vol. 199 (March 9, 1967), p. 15.

Vaganov, Boris, "Monopoly over Foreign Trade in the Soviet Union," *The American Review of East-West Trade*, Vol. 1, No. 10, (October, 1968).

Velebit, Vladimir, "Prospects of International Economic Co-operation following Abatement of Tension," *Review of International Affairs* (Belgrade) Vol. 11, No. 234 (January 1, 1960), pp. 14-19.

"Why Russia Wants Long Term Trade Policy with the U.S.," Steel, Vol. 160 (March 13, 1967), p. 52.

Wilczynski, J., "Dumping in Trade between Market and Centrally Planned Economies," *Economics of Planning*, Vol. 6, (1966), No. 3, pp. 211-227.

Wiles, P.J.D., "Fifty Years After: What Future for Communism?" *Lloyds Bank Review*, No. 86, October 1967, pp. 36-48.

Wooldridge, Jonathan, "The Full Story of Russia's Organizational Setup and Technique for 'Trade and Raid'," *Magazine of Wall Street*, Vol. 110, No. 13 (September 8, 1962), pp. 598.

Wyczalkowski, M.R., "Communist Economics and Currency Convertibility," *International Monetary Fund Staff Papers*, Vol. 13, No. 2, (July, 1966).

Zhelev, G. "On Using a Proper Base of Price Formation on the International Socialist Market," *American Review of Soviet and Eastern European Foreign Trade*, Vol. II, No. 4, (July-August, 1966).

Zyzniewski, Stanley J., "Soviet Foreign Economic Policy," *Political Science Quarterly*, Vol. 73, No. 2 (June, 1958), pp. 206-233.